Pictures of Music Education

COUNTERPOINTS: MUSIC AND EDUCATION
Estelle R. Jorgensen, editor

PICTURES
OF MUSIC
EDUCATION

ESTELLE R. JORGENSEN

INDIANA UNIVERSITY PRESS
Bloomington and Indianapolis

This book is a publication of

Indiana University Press
601 North Morton Street
Bloomington, Indiana 47404-3797 USA

www.iupress.indiana.edu

Telephone orders   800-842-6796
Fax orders   812-855-7931
Orders by e-mail   iuporder@indiana.edu

♾ The paper used in this publication meets the minimum
requirements of the American National Standard for Information
Sciences—Permanence of Paper for Printed Library Materials, ANSI
Z39.48-1992.

Manufactured in the United States of America

Library of Congress Cataloging-in-Publication Data

Jorgensen, Estelle Ruth.
   Pictures of music education / Estelle R. Jorgensen.
      p. cm. — (Counterpoints. Music and education)
   Includes bibliographical references and index.
   ISBN 978-0-253-35612-3 (cloth : alk. paper) — ISBN 978-0-253-
22298-5 (pbk. : alk. paper) 1. Music—Instruction and study. I. Title.
   MT1.J677 2011
   780.71—dc22

                                                         2010042647

1 2 3 4 5 16 15 14 13 12 11

To my fellow students,

whose imagination can ignite music education

CONTENTS

PREFACE

Should music education be construed in metaphorical terms? Can one metaphor suffice as a basis for music education? If not, how should one adjudicate the claims of possible metaphors? If metaphors have limited usefulness, might models also constitute useful means of conceptualizing music education? If no metaphor or model suffices as the sole basis of or means of conceptualizing music education, could a comparative strategy drawing upon both metaphors and models be useful? What would such an analysis look like? How could the various metaphors and models be evaluated critically as well as constructively for music education? What would be the usefulness of this analysis for the practice of music education?

My search for answers to these questions was galvanized by a presentation by Virginia Richardson on the metaphor of stewardship as a basis for doctoral programs in music education.[1] Rather than critically evaluating its limits or place in conjunction with other educational metaphors, Richardson teased out aspects of the metaphor of stewardship for education. I worried about whether this metaphor could account solely for doctoral programs in music education, let alone all of the phenomena that count as music education around the world. Now my attempt to answer these questions began in earnest.

Writing *The Art of Teaching Music,* I planned to include a chapter on metaphors and music education to assist teachers in thinking figuratively about their work. In an incomplete essay written years before, I had explored aspects of the grounds and limits of metaphors and models and their possibilities for music education,

and I returned to this essay as a basis for the chapter I now intended to write. I suspect that this chapter outgrew its bounds and became the kernel of the present book because these questions were with me all along but I had not systematically addressed them. Now, they presented with greater urgency.

In the way of writing books, I was helped greatly by friends and colleagues. I first acknowledge my intellectual debt to Iris Yob, whose pursuit of figurative meaning-making in her dissertation and subsequent research, especially as it relates to religious and artistic education, prompted me to consider music education from a figurative as well as literal perspective.[2] This book leans partly on her groundbreaking work in religious education. Her philosophical writing alerted me not only to the important contributions that metaphors can make to our understanding of music education but to the pitfalls inherent in over-literalizing them and causing them to lose their evocative character by "freezing" them in time and space.

Among the host of others who helped me were those who prodded me to think more carefully, critically, and constructively, and who were never satisfied with either my questions or my answers. Invitations to speak on several of the emerging pictures gave me opportunities to think through important aspects of the analysis in public settings, and provided critical insights into my work.[3] Natalie Kreutzer inquired about whether there would be any pictures to accompany the text. The more I thought about the reasons she proffered in bringing together art and philosophy, the more convinced I became that she was right.

Upon hearing of my interest in myth and music education in earlier writing,

Cathy Benedict suggested that I needed to read Philip Pullman's trilogy, *His Dark Materials,* and promptly sent me a boxed set of books that I read avidly.[4] As was true for the others I had explored, opening up Pullman's fantasy world turned out to be an immensely rich and evocative exercise. Still, when we are taught, we often learn unexpected things. I was fascinated by the little drawings at the beginning of each chapter, each enclosed in a box, and opening up a world visually as well as through Pullman's excellent prose. These drawings seemed exactly the sort of thing that might be helpful in this writing—but how to find the artist to draw them?

I am fortunate in having met Millicent Hodson, choreographer, dance historian, and artist on the occasion of her visit to Indiana University Bloomington.[5] Based in London and in the midst of a busy international career as a choreographer mounting historically informed performances with leading ballet companies, she and her husband, art historian Kenneth Archer, are in demand around the world. Hodson's drawings conveyed a vitality, sweep, and evocative character that I found captivating. I was delighted when she agreed to my commission to do the pictures for this book. Happily, she was familiar with the Pullman drawings and eager to collaborate on a project where she was free to respond only to word-clues. It is rare for a philosopher to be able to join with an artist who is also a scholar in her own right. I did not seek illustrations where an artist draws on the program of a text. Rather, I hoped for independently constructed drawings, unfettered by my text but related to the particular words chosen for each chapter heading. Hodson produced just that; her pictures are based on her own conceptions of what the words I have used as names for these pictures evoked for her. I am reluctant to analyze the correspondences and dissonances suggested by the combination of drawing and text in each chapter. Rather, I prefer to resist analysis and simply let them be, in the hope that this marriage of picture and text can accomplish something that neither taken alone could do.

Following a conference presentation of one of the metaphor and model pairs, Randall Everett Allsup asked me why I had chosen to combine metaphor and model as I have.[6] This question stayed with me to trouble anew the waters of my approach in this book. Why could I not rest entirely in the metaphors, and why the need to systematize things in the accompanying models they evoke? As I now perceive things, I could not let go of either the metaphor or model for what each offers for music education. I wish to allow the metaphors' wings to fly and prompt word pictures by telling the reader enough to grasp them imaginatively (and what I may have failed to do, Hodson has certainly accomplished by artistic means), and then save my systematic analysis for the accompanying model where it is required. In so doing, I am working in the ground between metaphor and model—either as metaphoric model or as modular metaphor, depending on how one regards the resulting combination of the two.

Although I am concerned with the practice of music education, and this was a particular interest in *The Art of Teaching Music,* I return to crucial theoretical questions that relate to its philosophical foundations. My present purpose is to chart another way whereby music education can be conceptualized and researched. The pictures in this book are interesting for the array of practical possibilities they evoke and for their implications for music educational research. Beyond invoking psychological, sociological, anthropological, historical, or other philosophical perspectives, one can examine music education systematically in ways that are particularly music educational. Other foundational disciplines are important to the work of music education, but they ought not crowd out ways of thinking about music education that are grounded in the nature and work of music education itself. This is one approach to thinking about music education: music educationally.

The organization of this book is very simple. In chapter 1, I distinguish metaphor and model, show how they intersect, and describe and defend the approach taken in succeeding chapters. In chapters 2 through 13, I systematically present paired pictures of metaphor and related model in turn, by briefly describing each metaphor, systematically sketching dimensions of the derivative model, and critically examining it. These chapters can be read more or less independently and in differing order. Chapter 14 concludes with a meta-analysis of the pictures and their implications for music educational thought and practice. I plough new ground by suggesting an approach whereby other metaphors and their associated models might be elaborated systematically and delineating the lines of more robust theoretical frames for comparative approaches to music education.

This analysis opens important questions, and these remain at book's end. As becomes clear in these pages, there needs to be a correspondence between the imaginative ways in which musics are made and taken and traditions are transmitted and transformed around the world, and the means whereby they are thought about conceptually and studied empirically. Music educators are challenged to find these ways and means and apply them to their particular lived situations. Other philosophical questions also emerge. Among them, matters of value are important considerations in comparing and adjudicating these pictures. This process evokes an array of sometimes intractable problems concerning those values to which music educators should be committed and that have yet to be more fully addressed, and it remains for another writing to develop a careful and systematic approach to these issues. Nevertheless, this book takes us some way in addressing them, and it is an invitation to examine this gallery of pictures and see its possibilities for music education.

ACKNOWLEDGMENTS

I am indebted particularly to Iris Yob, Patricia Shehan Campbell, and Randall Everett Allsup, who read this manuscript in its entirety, to Linda Bucklin whose secretarial assistance was invaluable in preparing the manuscript, to the editorial staff at Indiana University Press, particularly Jane Behnken and Candace McNulty, for their editorial assistance in clarifying my ideas and my language, and to the production staff at the Press for transforming the manuscript into a published book. To all those who have nudged me in the directions this book has taken, my profound thanks.

Pictures of Music Education

1
METAPHOR AND MODEL

Regarding music education broadly, transformatively, and artfully invites us to think imaginatively about the ways in which its work is and ought to be carried on. In this book, I juxtapose metaphors and models and see a rich array of pictures that illumine the nature of music education. Although this study applies specifically to music education, it could also be understood to illuminate general education. It is possible that the pictures I paint of music education may also apply at various levels of instruction, from elementary to advanced, across the entire life-cycle, and reveal its work in sometimes surprising ways. So, while my purpose is a modest one of picturing music education, an imaginative reader may see, here, a view that might be more broadly useful to the work of music and education.

Combining figurative and literal aspects of music education in the pictures to follow contrasts with a long-standing preoccupation by music teachers with modeling aspects of their work. Models have been used because of the complexity of music and education and the pedagogical task of systematizing and simplifying difficult ideas in terms that can be readily grasped, studied, and tested. They are also regarded as important scientific tools of investigation in the field. And today's educational public demands that ideas be rigorously tested and quantified in ways that demonstrate accountability to policy makers and public alike.

Still, music education can be pictured through metaphor as well as model. Each has strengths and limitations. Rather than discrete entities, they overlap in a manner reminiscent of the intersections between art and craft, listening, performance, composition, and improvisation, and teaching and learning. This "ground between" models and metaphors is a place of irony, paradox, and dialectic, yet it is the principal stuff of education and music. I see metaphor and model imaginatively and evocatively, as entry points or beginnings rather than final conclusions or endings, and the pictures painted need to be read both figuratively and literally. Keeping metaphor and model continually in mind requires pictures that are open to multiple understandings and that are also systematically described with regard to how the various facets of music education are addressed. My choice of the word pictures in this book emphasizes the generative ideas associated with metaphors and their associated models for music educational practice.

Music teachers use metaphors constantly, and much of our talk about how to play and sing and the various characteristics of music is metaphoric.[1] In teaching singing, for example, rather than telling the young singer to "inspan the nasal pharynx," a teacher might say, "Imagine a deep yawn while producing the tone."[2] In this way, the teacher cuts through ideas that might otherwise be very technical and not necessarily helpful to enable the student to intuitively grasp how to sing. Musical terms are also shot through with metaphors. Musicians speak of "bright" and "dark" sounds, "pure" and "dirty" timbres, "masculine" and "feminine" registrations and themes, "straight" and "bent" tones, "thick" and "thin" textures; and conducting gestures express certain musical pitches, dynamics, articulations, and other interpretative nuances.

Why not push further the idea that much pedagogical talk and practice in music is metaphoric, to think metaphorically about music education itself, so that the approaches used to explore how people come to know music are consistent with the nature of the musical experience itself? The arts are "understood" experientially as aesthetic or artistic ways of knowing through the free play of imagination.[3] Reason, intuition, feeling, and sensory perception are driving forces of understanding music imaginatively.[4] Music is comprehended literally in terms of sonic elements or particular practices associated with these sounds and figuratively in terms of what these sounds stand for, and it seems reasonable to view it metaphorically, as some have done.[5] That music's "vital import" is grasped imaginatively also suggests that music education can likewise be seen metaphorically as an array of images that are grasped imaginatively.[6] Such a position would align music education with music as an imaginative enterprise, evidence consistency between the thing studied and the manner of its study, and potentially illumine the work of music education.

Regarding music education metaphorically has the potential to subvert the preeminence of scientific, objective, and rational ways of thinking and doing. Whereas models are often tested according to the canons of science, metaphors rely on imaginative and subjective understandings that are more amenable to philosophical reflection and qualitative description. Thinking of music education metaphorically might be worrisome to those who want only to regard the field scientifically, logically, rationally, and literally; it may seem too artistic, fanciful, and likely to generate different interpretations of music education, along with divergent, inconsistent, and even conflicting ideas and practices.

This is a knotty issue. On first glance, it may seem that by emphasizing metaphors rather than models, I seem to accentuate the artistic over the scientific ways of thinking about the work of music education. Since there is so much modeling in music education, focusing on metaphors seems an unusual way to go. Before leaping to conclusions too quickly, let us try on the idea. The fact that metaphoric thinking about music education may lead us in different directions than modular thinking need not concern us, since this is the nature of the search for new knowledge; we may discover new insights when we make uncommon choices. Whether or not there is a quarrel between metaphors and models also depends on how we define these terms. If metaphors and models are closer than may appear at first glance, the apparent gap between art and science may be bridged, and navigating between metaphor and model may yield various ways in which they might be brought together.

These matters are very consequential for how we think about the work of music education. In the past, philosophers of music education have sought to develop models that constitute grand narratives or all-encompassing views of music education. Among the grand narratives forwarded recently, Frede Nielsen would have us regard music teaching systematically in the context of what he calls *musikdidaktik* or *music didactology*.[7] His conceptual model is intended to be universal in its compass of artistic and scientific elements. In a different vein, David Elliott and Thomas Regelski criticize what they characterize as the grand narrative of *music education as aesthetic education* (MEAE), proposed by Bennett Reimer, for its failure to account sufficiently for the practices of musicians and music teachers and learners and the social and cultural contexts for these practices.[8] They propose, instead, a *praxial* view of music education, a grand narrative of a different sort, regarding music education as a host of socially grounded, multifaceted, divergent, and sometimes incommensurate musical practices.

Nielsen's didactic theory is especially interesting because it proposes a conceptual model that purports to systematically explain everything in music education around the world; presumably, it can be applied to all the particular situations in which teachers work. Once teachers identify the properties of situations to which a particular theory might be appropriately applied, they imaginatively and intuitively decide which particular theories or approaches are needed to inform their work. In so doing, they exercise *tact* (from the Latin *taktus,* taking its cue historically from the "touch" or the musical beat given by the conductor) and employ an intuitive "touch" in determining how theories are called on or applied in these circumstances.[9] Although Nielsen acknowledges the artfulness of music teaching, he also emphasizes the scientific information that grounds it and the need for conceptual frameworks that explain music education systematically. Assuming that human beings share many commonalities wherever they are around the world, Nielsen's theory should presumably apply everywhere.

Metaphors lead us in a very different direction. Instead of tending toward the one right or best way, the one all-encompassing grand narrative, no matter what it be, thinking about music education metaphorically opens up many possibilities of seeing the work of education in ways that defy reduction to a single universal principle or set of principles.[10] By embracing "the many" as opposed to "the one," thinking metaphorically subverts the search for the "grand narrative," the "one true or best way," or "high road" to music education that has characterized the field in contemporary times.

In the face of these two potentially conflicting possibilities, it might be tempting to think in terms of either/or so as to plump for one while repudiating the other.[11] If we resist this temptation in order to embrace them both, the one *and* the many, how shall we navigate theoretically and practically between these two very different conceptual and practical positions? In responding to this question, my first step is to distinguish metaphor and model and show how they might be brought together. My second step is to show how this approach can be accomplished, practically speaking, in music education.

DISTINGUISHING METAPHOR AND MODEL

A metaphor is a type of symbol; that is, one thing stands for something else. Nelson Goodman describes a metaphor colorfully as "teaching an old word new tricks" or "an affair between a predicate with a past and an object that yields while protesting."[12] Two or more sets of images that do not belong in the same family are brought together in reference to one or the other in ways that startle or surprise.[13] For Goodman, these shifts in reference are not a "mere distribution of family goods" but "an expedition abroad. A whole set of alternative labels, a whole apparatus of organization, takes over new territory." In this way, "a metaphor might be regarded as a calculated category mistake—or rather as a happy and revitalizing, even if bigamous, second marriage." Here, there is a sense of "conflict" and "attraction as well as resistance—indeed, an attraction that overcomes resistance."[14]

Max Black suggests that metaphors are more than comparisons of one thing with another. Associations that relate to one image are brought into conjunction with those that relate to another, resulting in an enriched meaning of the thing referred to as well as that to which it is referred—a so-called "interaction view" of metaphor. He points to the "principal" and "subsidiary" subjects of the metaphor and notes that "metaphor works by applying to the principal subject a system of 'associated implications' characteristic of the subsidiary subject." The metaphor thus "selects, emphasizes, suppresses, and organizes features of the principal subject by implying statements about it that normally apply to the subsidiary subject." In this way, one is "forced to 'connect' the two ideas."[15]

How are models different from metaphors? At first, it is important to notice that models function similarly to metaphors. Black observes that "to speak of 'models' in connection with a scientific theory already smacks of the metaphorical." Both necessitate grasping an array of ways in which one field informs the other. They also "reveal new relationships; both are attempts to pour new content into old bottles."[16] The difference, for Black, lies in the fact that "a metaphor operates largely with *commonplace* implications" that require "only proverbial knowledge" for the metaphor to be understood, whereas a model requires "control of a well-knit scientific theory" and its "[s]ystematic complexity and capacity for analogical development."[17] Time also takes its toll; what once might have been metaphorical, fresh, and tantalizing may become literal, bland, and ordinary.[18] For Black, information-processing models of teaching that were metaphorical when they first emerged gradually came to be taken quite literally and no longer surprise. So, the distinction between metaphors and models partly reduces to a matter of historical perspective.

Metaphors enable us to relate together things that might be thought to be dissimilar or even radically different. Presenting a conjunction of images and related associations, they enrich our understanding of these things. Still, they can only be pressed so far. They are mainly grasped figuratively rather than literally, subjectively rather than objectively, and given the tension between the two sets of images implicit in a metaphor, the correspondence between the things related together cannot be 100 percent. Consequently, literal interpretations of a metaphor result in its breakdown, as a metaphor is wrung out excessively and becomes pedantic.[19] A metaphor evokes various images based on individual experiences or what we might call "assumptive frames of reference" that are understood subjectively.[20] Also, it cannot be refuted by individual instances in which correspondence is not found but rather by reference to the fitness of the whole. As such, it may best be studied non-scientifically, for example, phenomenologically.[21]

Iris Yob suggests that the distinction between metaphors and models may best be drawn in terms of their exemplification: while "many models function metaphorically," "not all models do." For her, "Metaphoric models, like metaphors, can be distinguished from the literal only by examining how they function in a particular context." Nor is it the case that models are known only cognitively while metaphors are known only emotionally, since cognition is not emotion-free and emotion is not cognition-free; both are understood cognitively and emotionally.[22] Yob gives us an intersecting view of metaphors and models, suggesting that, by and large, metaphors function figuratively and models are taken literally, although at least one class of models, namely metaphoric models, also functions figuratively.[23] We might also think of modular metaphors, those metaphors that may also function somewhat literally as models but may be closer to metaphor than model.

I like this comparative and functional view of metaphors and models because it allows us to think of their borders as being somewhat fuzzy as one melds into the other. Although they may be distinguished conceptually, there are important intersections and correspondences between them. Metaphors enable us to relate music teaching to things that might be thought to be dissimilar or even radically different. Such a disjunction of images and related associations enriches our understanding of music teaching, but also of these other things and their associations. Once we begin to think systematically about the implications of these metaphors, press them into service, and generate a more systematic understanding of music teaching, we slip into models that require a systematic understanding of the ideas and practices beyond common places. Metaphors may still ground them, but they are also models that may be worked out, tested, and applied to specific situations. Figurative and subjective interpretations associated with metaphors are now accompanied by literal and objective understandings required by models. This juxtaposition of metaphor and model produces tensions, paradoxes, and a rich array of figurative and literal possibilities and conversations between them. In the ground between metaphor and model, as metaphors are elaborated into fullblown models, modular metaphors and metaphoric models, respectively, spark the figurative and subjective associations with things dissimilar from music teaching and between the abstract models and the phenomenal situations with which they may be associated.

Since it is possible to freeze a metaphor or, alternatively, to squeeze the life out of it by excessive literalism, metaphoric models need to be thought of rhapsodically and systematically, subjectively and objectively, figuratively and literally, and they need to be described qualitatively and quantitatively. It is also important to carefully distinguish ideas and practices, since it is possible to mistakenly interpret theories and practices and lose the driving force behind them. For example, when Zoltán Kodály writes that it is possible to implant in the "child's soul" the "chief basic phenomena of music" through "fifty-four well-chosen songs," does he mean to be taken literally or figuratively?[24] Are his ideas necessarily bound by the specific circumstances for which he devised them, or can they be recast for very different circumstances? Although his ideas were implemented in a communist educational system in Hungary at the time, are they anti-democratic, or are those who promote Kodály's ideas as part of democratic education nearer the mark?[25] Let us muddy the waters even further. Even if we are able to determine definitively Kodály's intentions, should we care, since once he has floated ideas out into the world, they take on a life of their own and it is up to others to make what they want of them? And, to go further, is there an advantage to these various interpretations of Kodály when they prompt an even richer grasp of the ends and methods of teaching sight singing? The ambiguity arising from different understandings of Kodály's ideas and practices may evoke various responses to these questions, and it may be impossible and even undesirable to arrive at, or agree on, a single definitive response to them.

Still, I want to go further than just settling for ambiguity. Although philosophers wish to clarify things as much as possible, Israel Scheffler notices that ambiguity is a feature of our ordinary use of language.[26] The fact that we use metaphors so often in our teaching also suggests that, intuitively, we recognize their appropriateness to our work. We see them prompting diverse thought and action and focusing that thought and action in quite specific ways. As experienced teachers, we may find some metaphors so useful in evoking certain behaviors that we use them repeatedly and pass them on to our students. As teachers, we seem to be after those metaphors that are most generally effective, even though we expect different responses from students. The widespread use of a particular metaphor suggests that teachers have found it generally effective in helping students develop musical skills. Imagination feeds on ambiguity, and we need to keep alive metaphoric thinking if we are to spark imaginative thought and action. Embracing ambiguity allows us to sort through ideas and come to different conclusions about them. Sifting through these ambiguities also enables us to better understand each other's views and practices, and it prompts other ways of thinking and doing than those we might presently know and endorse.

The tensions between model and metaphor can be seen as a *pas de deux* as the dancers sometimes come together and other times move apart. Alike, as dancers, they nevertheless take on their own personae. Contemplating Millicent Hodson's drawing of the Chosen One and the Ancestor in her reconstruction of a ballet for Stravinsky's *Le Sacre du printemps,* I see the Ancestor crouching, a bearded male cloaked in an animal skin, facing an ecstatic Chosen One, leaping forward, arching upward, head back, arms extended, and hair flying.[27] They are alike in their intensity but different in their posture and demeanor. This picture serves as a model of the dancers' costumes, stance, and movement. It is also a metaphor for the dynamic interaction between the dancers and the relationship between metaphor and model.[28]

SOME METHODOLOGICAL ISSUES

Some might regard my approach as exemplifying one that has gained ground in the field of comparative religion: namely, what Edward Slingerland has described as "conceptual metaphor theory," drawing on the work of George Lakoff and his colleagues.[29] Although conceptual metaphor theory is relevant to my own work, it is not the driving force behind it, nor does my own approach parallel it in all respects. Slingerland's work is of interest in his grappling with questions of how to examine religions comparatively and in its similarity to the sorts of questions I ask, notably: "If music education cannot be described solely with reference to one metaphor, conceptual schema, or practical manifestation, how can these different approaches to music education be understood comparatively?" In the way of interesting correspondences, although I came upon Slingerland and Lakoff after my own project was well under way, our interests lie in comparing the many ways in which musics and religions are manifest around the world.

Although my present task resonates with conceptual metaphor theory, it also differs from it in important ways. Conceptual metaphor theory aims to map what is evidenced in the phenomenal world onto ideas and conceptions of that reality. For example, notions of journey, traveler, destinations, and itinerary are seen as implying abstract notions of purposeful life, the person living the life, life goals, and life plans. "[S]uch abstract subjects as the world, ourselves, our place in the world, and our normative relationships to others" are grasped through metaphors. The proponents of this approach argue that metaphors are so basic that rather than focus on data in the phenomenal world, it is important to attend to the underlying metaphors.[30] I am critical of this reading of conceptual metaphor theory because of its somewhat simplistic focus on metaphor to the exclusion of model, and on the figurative to the exclusion of the literal. My own approach is a more ambiguous, comparative one allowing for the prospect of both metaphor and model. At very least, I would want a broader construal of conceptual metaphor theory that would encompass metaphor and model, theory and practice. It is only in the sense that my analysis ploughs ground between metaphor and model that conceptual metaphor theory should be read to apply to my present project.

Similarities between the kinds of comparative questions addressed by writers in religious studies such as Slingerland and those in music and music education that are my present focus are not surprising. Susanne Langer observed that the arts, myths, religions, and rituals share ways of symbolization and knowing that go beyond discursive and propositional discourse.[31] The consonance between Slingerland's comparative study of religious metaphors and my own comparative investigation into the role of metaphors and their ancillary models is rooted in similarities in the sorts of symbolic understandings in the religions and arts.

Juxtaposing metaphor and model means that the analysis falls in the territory between metaphor and model—what we might call "modular metaphor" or "metaphoric model." On the one hand, I do not want to literalize the metaphor but leave it wings to fly. On the other, it is important to systematically outline how a related model derives from the metaphor and is more or less consistent with it (although, the model may be less ambiguous, multifaceted, and evocative than the metaphor). In this way, each model is not equivalent to its corresponding metaphor but a systematic portrait that might derive from the metaphor. The ambiguity of the metaphor also suggests the possibility of several different models, of which the one I present is an instance.

In suggesting that music education is both metaphor and model, I face two tasks. The first requires each metaphor to be construed in ways that are evocative of, yet apart from, the work of music education, since the metaphor has one foot in a realm that is distinct from and even foreign to the world of music education. The second mandates that the various aspects of each metaphor are systematically teased out into a full-blown model that derives from the metaphor. In this case, each metaphor can be expected to play out in all of the aspects of music education: music, teaching, learning, instruction, curriculum, and administration. And one way to preserve the tension between each metaphor and model is to create a paired list of metaphors and associated models.

My purpose in these pages is primarily conceptual, namely, to sketch metaphors and models that others may later embellish and upon which they may hang specific empirical evidence. Since I cast these metaphors and models at a high level of generality, they potentially open up a nest of others construed more specifically. Each of us also brings the backgrounds of our personal experience and knowledge of empirical research to our assessments of these metaphor–model pairings, and unpacking them is primarily a philosophical enterprise. Accordingly, throughout this book, I mainly cite philosophical writing and historical evidence of these pictures—especially in music education. It remains for later researchers to test them conceptually and empirically.

Some of these metaphors and models have been tried out in the past and there is nothing particularly new in them. If they are not new, why write about them? Given the ancient roots of music education, it is intriguing to see the possibilities of metaphors and models that may have fallen into disuse. Scholarship is the process not only of discovering things that have not been observed or understood before but of recovering things that may have become lost or forgotten, reviving them so that they may live again, and presenting them in fresh ways. To borrow Black's metaphor with a twist, scholarship is also a matter of pouring "new wine into old bottles."

As theoretical types, each of which might be described systematically by a profile of characteristics, these pictures are viewed comparatively. Although they are conceptually distinct, practically speaking, we notice overlaps between them. Their boundaries are fuzzy and messy as one melds into another. Notwithstanding the seepage from one metaphor–model pair to another, we are justified in examining each separately in order to grasp its conceptual focus and limits. As we do this, it becomes apparent that all have advantages or contributions and are limited or flawed in one way or another. When taken alone, none suffices.

How are we to systematically consider the work of music education? Here, I draw on an earlier essay in which I propose a conceptual model of the various facets of music education.[32] These elements are illustrative rather than exhaustive, delimiting and focusing attention on the aspects of music education that are discussed in this book. As theoretical types, they are construed as mutually exclusive and conceptually distinct one from another even though, in the phenomenal world, their borders may be fuzzy as one melds into another. They include the following: the *field of study or practice,* in this case, the nature of music and musical experience; *teaching,* or the way in which wisdom is passed from one person to another; *learning,* the manner in which an individual acquires or develops knowledge, understanding, skills, and wisdom; *instruction,* the pedagogical interaction of teachers and students; *curriculum,* the means whereby teachers and students encounter the field of study or practice; and *administration,* the organization of instruction. Thinking about music education in terms of these elements allows us to see how the various pictures of music education translate into particular aspects of our work. Given their crucial role in the succeeding chapters, it is important to briefly describe them before going on to examine the pictures themselves.

Music refers to the means and ends whereby what counts as music is made and taken—in particular, the beliefs and practices that accompany certain sonic phenomena. An admittedly Western viewpoint, this is only one of the important images of music that we might investigate. People around the world may not call what they do music; what we think of as music may serve an ancillary although integral role in other events that comprise dance, art, poetry, ritual, and myth. Still, people around the world play with audible sounds of various sorts, and we are justified in thinking about music sonically as well as in other ways. Thinking of music as beliefs and practices that identify and are identified with groups as well as individuals also suggests that it is reasonable to think of music sonically and socially, and to suggest that music is what people say it is.[33]

Teaching describes the means and ends whereby the one-knowing passes on knowledge or wisdom to the one-who-does-not-yet-know. In this view, which privileges one among several models of teaching, whoever serves as the teacher has the greater experience and expertise than the student, the one with less experience and expertise in this particular respect. Sometimes a student, bringing some particular knowledge exceeding that of the person who normally serves in the role of teacher or of other students in a group instructional setting, may assume a teaching role. Thus, despite the general assignment of teaching to one assigned the role of teacher, it may be accomplished by students and teacher alike or by people working in informal circumstances where instruction is not the primary purpose.

Learning is the means and ends whereby one comes to know and transform the subject matter—in this case, music—and other things. Again, this view is just one of the approaches to learning. We typically think of the student as the learner, as the one with less knowledge and experience, and this is often the case. Still, these traditional roles may be exchanged and altered as teachers become learners along with students. A student also comes to know other things besides the intended subject matter, since much learning is incidental, informal, and about matters having little to do with the subject of instruction, music. Consequently, learning is both focused and diffused, both to the point of and quite apart from the intended instructional objective(s).

Instruction is the means and ends of interactive engagement of teacher and student in a pedagogical setting. This social and psychological interaction between those involved may be formal and informal. Within an array of different settings, it may be designed as a way of cultivating teaching and learning, or it can occur unexpectedly and serendipitously, sometimes in contexts that are not intentionally or overtly pedagogical. This interactive conception of instruction is somewhat different from other views of instruction—for example, those that focus on what teachers say and do to prompt student learning (a concept much more akin to my notion of teaching).[34] Still, rich possibilities lie within this concept of an interpersonal interaction and engagement of people involved in passing on and receiving wisdom, beliefs, attitudes, and skills from one to another.

Curriculum refers to the means and ends whereby learners engage with the subject matter. Definitions of curriculum typically vary from notions of the subject matter or program of study undertaken by students to more recent critical notions of the power structures underlying the engagement of students with the subject of study. All of these conceptions of curriculum involve some engagement of teachers and learners with subject matter. My own experiential focus highlights learners' sense of becoming and the ways whereby their initially intuitive grasp of a field of study or practice gradually approaches the systematic understandings of its exponents (even if they eventually reject these understandings). This engagement, unlike that in instruction, has primarily to do with the intersection of people and the field of study or practice.

Administration refers to the means and ends of organizing the context in which instruction transpires. All instruction takes place in some sort of institutional and organizational framework that shapes and delimits the nature, operation, and expectations of other aspects of music education.[35] It constitutes an important means whereby the other elements are coordinated. Although important, this present focus on organizational context is only one of the approaches that might be taken to organizational and administrative matters.

These descriptions of the various aspects of music education, and the descriptions and analyses of pictures to follow, represent a few of many possibilities. Metaphors are syntactically dense in that they feature infinite gradations, semantically dense in that their meaning is inherently ambiguous and diverse, and replete in that all that is needed is there. As such, they are known artistically, and people see them differently. Not only is my own experience and understanding of each metaphor circumscribed but the particular perspectives and elements of music education on which I focus are also partial and finite. Rather than being dismayed by the fallibility and incompleteness of the pictures to follow, I see these qualities as strengths. These pictures express instances of the ways in which music education can and should work; they present examples of the strengths and limitations of metaphoric and modular approaches to music education. Beyond the grand narratives of the past or the either/or concepts that have too often characterized music educational thinking, they have a more modest purpose of opening other fruitful avenues for understanding the ways in which people come to know music. In the evident complexities and tensions one with another, they illustrate the contributions of dialectical, dialogical, and dynamic ways of thinking about, being in, and doing music education. They also suggest means whereby music teachers and others interested in their work can bring together disparate things that, even should these disjunctions create stress and conflict, may prompt fresh insights and understandings.

PICTURES OF MUSIC EDUCATION

The gallery of pictures of music education can be thought of as verbs and nouns, dynamic and static, processes and products, means and ends. Although we might observe them developing over time, it is also possible to take a snapshot of how they appear at a particular time. They are not presented in order of importance but comprise a multifaceted and diverse world of music education that is multilayered in meaning. Given an embarrassment of riches in the metaphors and models that might be included, it is more problematic to omit a picture than to notice possibilities. Just as soon as I think of making an end to the list, other interesting pictures emerge. Some are omitted from this writing for reasons of space and because I have written on them elsewhere.[36] The pictures in this book reflect my own experience, and I have tried to capture those that relate not only to one aspect of music education but broadly to all of its elements. I hope that they can prompt other new, different, and interesting pictures in the future.

Among the characteristics of the metaphor–model pairs, they refer to persons, places, and processes. Some may be more familiar to us than others because we may have encountered them elsewhere in the musical and educational literature. Rooted in different times, some have ancient provenance, while others are of more recent origin. Although they are described as independent entities, they combine and intersect in various ways and are likely to be found in conjunction with others. Various beliefs, attitudes, values, and practices shape each metaphor and its related model. And some appear to be more important than others, depending on our vantage points and life experiences.

My task in forwarding these particular pictures of music education is akin to a curator who assembles and interprets an art collection. On a visit to the Metropolitan Museum of Art in New York City, a section titled "The Eye of a Curator" attracted my attention. It represented the work of the Museum's previous curator, who had found these pieces that caught his eye and interest. In the same way, these particular pictures of music education have caught my imagination. As with the curator's collection, I have assembled them over a working lifetime, and they represent my own "take" on the images of music and education.

Since music education is conducted with an eye to the public good, I have also chosen the pictures with this in mind. For example, there is a redemptive quality in the activist who challenges the status quo and transgresses norms and laws in order to undermine and even overthrow forces of evil.[37] Sinister aspects also lurk in pictures that may appear superficially to point toward the good. Although we hope that guides are people of integrity, this is not always the case; some may mislead or abuse travelers who are dependent on them. It becomes abundantly clear that all of these pictures of music education have bright and dark sides, strengths and limitations; while sometimes pointing toward the good, they nevertheless can be seen to imply evil. The pictures have an ethical valence predicated on certain beliefs, attitudes, values, and practices, and it is impossible to escape judgments about their ethical or aesthetic worth. Education is an ethical undertaking; even though I attempt to assess each picture evenhandedly, my account is necessarily personal, reflecting my experience and ethical commitments.

I sometimes find myself in deep disagreement with aspects of the pictures that follow. It was occasionally difficult to write about them dispassionately and even-handedly, so as to leave readers with the space to interpret them imaginatively and freely. This difficulty is natural, since we all live by particular interests, commitments, beliefs, attitudes, and values. Some may fault me when my prejudices creep in; others may claim that my perspectives ought to be even more evident, since they help frame my own commitments. I cannot see how to avoid these problems, and it seems impossible, practically speaking, to elucidate and richly describe these pictures without drawing criticism on both counts. I also want to respect the beliefs, values, and practices associated with these metaphor–model pairs—to complicate what might otherwise constitute too facile and stereotypical a por-trait—in order to observe their features, nuances, ambiguities, and discontinuities. They are artful and, as such, ambiguous and imaginatively grasped, subjectively and objectively known. Through treating these pictures dispassionately, I hope to prompt others to bring different perspectives to bear on them, interpret them vari-ously, and develop other compelling pictures of music education.

In painting these pictures, it would be easy to slip into a descriptive mode and address only literal situations in schools or empirical realities in the phenome-nal world.[38] There is nothing wrong with describing things literally so long as the descriptions are accurate and widely shared. I have noticed, however, that when teachers hear situations described that they believe do not apply to them, they are inclined to dismiss the entire argument. Music teaching is very place- and person-specific. The difficulty of using literal examples is that they are taken literally rather than figuratively.

I am more intrigued by the possibilities of "what might be" rather than "what is." Although it is necessary to confront the often dark side of music education and the reality that things are not as we wish they were, I am hopeful for the future; were I not, I could not be a teacher.[39] Whatever the challenges we face as teachers, we hope to improve the way things are. When as teachers, we lose hope, we lose the spark that ignites our desire to help our students come to know music; when as students, we lose hope, we lose the heart to overcome the challenges in our way and persevere toward achieving our goals. It is crucial, then, to see these pictures from the perspective of hope for what might otherwise be and for how we might be able to improve our present situations. Accordingly, my focus is upon the possi-bilities of these pictures for music education and what they have to teach us about the ways we come to know music.

All of the pictures rely on eye rather than ear, constituting visual metaphors for musical and music educational phenomena. This is a deliberate move, because juxtaposing eye and ear requires us to think of one sensory modality in terms of another. To use other sonic phenomena as metaphors for music and music education might be tempting, since we might think of music education as we think of particular musical events—for example, an improvisation or a rhapsody. Still, doing so would narrow what can be said about music; our thinking would be restricted to one musical or sonic phenomenon serving as a figure for different musical and music educational phenomena. The juxtaposition of these sensory modalities may be startling and surprising, and this is an important function of metaphor. In describing visual metaphors for music and music education, I underscore differences in these sensory modalities and imply that music as it is understood in the West is thought of primarily in aural terms. Although limited, this musical image is resilient historically in the Western classical tradition that is my own heritage, and it merits exploration to see where it leads.[40]

As a way of intriguing the imagination and drawing the reader into the word pictures painted throughout this book, the small drawings by Millicent Hodson at the head of each chapter juxtapose art and philosophy, the figurative and the literal, lightness and darkness. I asked Hodson to create these drawings without the benefit of my text in order to introduce ambiguity between our interpretations of the metaphors and their related models. Her drawings need to be understood as providing a different point of entry into the text; the attendant tensions and discontinuities between her drawings and my text illumine metaphor and model alike. And these similarities and differences open spaces for other people to do their own thinking about what these pictures mean for music education.

My description of the pictures of music education is systematic in the following sense: I describe the metaphor and its related model in light of the aspects of music education identified above—field of study and practice (music), teaching, learning, instruction, curriculum, and administration. Each chapter is organized accordingly. Combining and preserving the tension between metaphor and model in the various pictures of music education is a delicate balance. My strategy in accomplishing this tension is to let each metaphor stand unhindered by possibilities for music and education and to describe it quite apart from the related model, without any necessary reference to music education. I then tease out implications of each metaphor in a model respecting those identified aspects of music education. We may then make imaginative leaps between the metaphor and the accompanying model, and between the model and our own situations. My examples are general and evocative in order to avoid unnecessarily limiting the ways in which these pictures can be understood, and to allow freedom in applying the analysis to different particular situations. The claims of space also have required that references to the work of other scholars and more detailed examples are included in notes at the end of this book. Since it is important to think about each picture as a whole and step back from being preoccupied with the detail, I assess each picture's contributions and limitations to music education. In the last chapter, I step back even further in order to examine what can be learned from the entire gallery of pictures and to notice the wider implications for music education.

In sum, I have suggested reasons why combining metaphors and models of music education in pictures opens a fruitful direction for music educational thought and practice. I have distinguished metaphors and models and preserved an analytical tension between them, observed their commonalities and differences, discussed important methodological issues that undergird the analysis, and differentiated the various aspects of music education identified above. And I have provided an overview of the pictures of music education to be discussed in subsequent chapters and their implications for thought and practice. We now begin our visit to the gallery to see what we can see. Since we may also encounter sounds as well, we also listen for what we may hear.

2
BOUTIQUE AND CONSUMPTION

I begin with a widespread and powerful pair, the boutique metaphor and its related consumption model of music education. As one of the principal metaphors
for education in our time, evoked in music education in particular, it offers a reasonable place to begin. Its roots may be in the distant past, but it has grown in
prominence especially since the Industrial Revolution and the rise of capitalism as
a central ideology of Western society. The boutique, from the French "small shop,"
often associated with the sale of women's fashionable clothes and jewelry, and even
still further back from the Greek *apotheke* meaning a "storehouse," provides a rich
picture for our contemplation.[1] As we think systematically of ways in which the
boutique impacts music educational thought and practice, we slip into a consumption model of music education that does not necessarily have a one-to-one correspondence with the metaphor. Rather than tease out literal interpretations of
the boutique for music education, I prefer to think more evocatively about music
education with the metaphor in mind. This analysis prompts a critique of the consumption view of music education, and we see there a very mixed bag.

THE BOUTIQUE

Anyone who has visited the United States will be familiar with the shopping mall, an icon of late modernity, dependent upon the automobile for its existence, surrounded by acres of parking spaces that permit people to leave their cars and walk into spaces apart from the rest of lived life. Shoppers—once inside, free from the vagaries of temperature and the natural elements—find nothing to hinder them, or their shopping. Replicated all around the world, anchored by great magnet stores, driven by the forces of capitalism and the profit motive, the shopping mall exists solely for the purpose of consumption. Its intention is to please and prompt the shopper to purchase goods and services. Choice abounds, and customers must select among all these enticements. We picture the high dome of the foyer or central meeting area, a cascading waterfall or other prominent water feature, luxuriant plants, arcades lined with small shops, each beckoning the customer. Friends and family gather to pass the time, eat, drink, shop, and browse. Music, lighting, arrangement of goods for sale, and all of the mall's accoutrements are calculated to entice shoppers to linger in this place and spend their money here. We may imagine the mall as a temple to capitalism and the boutique as its inner sanctum.

Those familiar with old European and Asian cities may conjure up a quite different image of the boutique. I think, for example, of Oxford Street in London, or High Street in Edinburgh, lined as they are by boutiques of all sorts and thronged by shoppers and passersby. Now, multinational corporations make inroads into buildings that once housed boutiques owned by private individuals, erasing their individuality and even eccentricity by applying the same formula globally in the interest of standardization and economies of scale. In Asia, the boutique may be a small alcove in a bazaar in which people haggle over goods and prices in the midst of a teeming marketplace. All of this buying and selling happens in a dynamic and changing general context; each small shop is impacted by its location. The shop may be closer to the rest of lived existence if located elsewhere than in a shopping mall, but civic planning has often determined where particular boutiques can be located. For example, in New York City, where laws have protected and encouraged small boutiques, there are significant differences in particular areas and the stores that are located in them. We might go to Greenwich Village for one thing, to Harlem for another, to Times Square for still another, and beyond Manhattan, to other boroughs. In the kaleidoscope of different places, the boutiques express their specific localities.

We stop and gaze at a shop window decorated with objects designed to tempt us to enter. Something may catch our eye. We go into the shop to look at it more closely and consider whether we would like to purchase it. Because the merchant knows that the more the time we spend in the store, the more prone we may be to buy, we may wander some distance into the store before finding the items that attracted us in the first place. Sales staff may greet us, anxious to help us find something to buy. They also know that if we are offered other things besides what we initially came for, we may purchase more than we originally intended. Choices may be heaped upon us as we examine the merchandise and decide what we want to purchase. The lack of money may be a hindrance, especially if we would like to buy more than we can afford or the prices in this particular store are higher than we would like to pay. Ultimately, we base our decision whether to buy partly on the nature of the things on offer and partly on our ability and willingness to purchase them.

The shop's ambience affects us. Its choices of color, furnishings, pumped-in perfumes, and sound tracks help to brand it and strengthen its impact upon us. We hear the conversations of other shoppers or sales staff and gaze about the store taking in its atmosphere, lighting, placement of goods, the music, the merchandise, and the attitudes of shoppers and sales staff. The boutique's atmosphere may appeal or repel; if repelled, we may leave abruptly; if we feel comfortable, we may linger longer. We make these decisions intuitively, often without articulating our reasons, and perceptively, as we see, hear, smell, and touch. Our intuitions, perceptions, and feelings play an important role in determining whether or not we linger (and buy) in this boutique. We may reflect later on the experience and determine why we felt as we did about this shop if we are planning another expedition.

As we grow older and more experienced, we may make quick and often unconscious judgments about which boutiques we are willing to enter. For example, if a store window features mannequins in clothing without price tags, we may step inside the boutique to see what things look like or at the price tags on merchandise nearest the door. A quick glance may determine whether we decide to stay. Entering the store does not necessarily mean we will make a purchase. We may notice that this boutique features merchandise we like, but we decide to go to another shop with lower priced goods to find something more affordable. And we call on past experience and our knowledge of our personal circumstances in making these decisions.

The boutique highlights stylistic, differentiated, and specialized products. Style depends on a social assessment that carries an aesthetic valence deemed positive and above common or ordinary levels of taste. More than merely a descriptor of what is, style connotes how things ought to be. We say of people outfitted in a particular way that they have style, a certain grace and quality that is exemplary and normative and that others seek to emulate.[2] As a phenomenon of social taste, fashion is often fickle and fleeting. The built-in obsolescence of things on offer in the boutique is intentional; the merchant wants customers to keep on buying, and what is in the shop is transitory so that customers will dispose of or add to what they buy this year by buying something next year. If the price of an item is high, sales staff want a customer to believe that it represents a good long-term "investment"; that is, high price is justified by classic or stylistic qualities likely to catch others' eyes or remain fashionable for a long time. Even here, the sales staff wish the customer to return and make another high-priced "investment" in the near future.

Given the indefinable quality of style and the peculiar properties of the boutique's merchandise, comparisons with less exclusive or even discount stores are sometimes difficult; consequently, merchants may charge a premium on what they offer. Some who frequent New York's Fifth Avenue boutiques can afford these highly priced goods; others just "window shop" and find cheaper versions in Chinatown in downtown Manhattan. Merchants regularly decide what the market will bear and who will bear it as they differentiate their boutiques and price the things they sell.

The boutique's intimate size and personal service are refreshing at a time when many large stores promise low prices but service is poor, or we must interact electronically with computer-generated voices or salespeople half a world away who cannot deviate from their scripts. Here, we may meet personally with the sales staff, receive assistance in making our purchases, and enjoy special services, for example, a cup of coffee as we search for an article of clothing or a book to read. Excellent sales staff want us to leave the boutique pleased with our purchases, so that we will return. As shoppers, we experience pleasure or frustration as we talk with sales staff, search for the things we want to buy, and are or are not successful in finding them.

Although its etymological roots conjure up stores selling such things as clothing and jewelry designed to attract women shoppers, the word *boutique* has come to have a broader meaning, referring to firms offering goods and services for men as well. In business, for example, "boutique" refers to a small, specialized, often privately owned firm offering advice and plans for investment portfolios, accounting services, business management, architectural and interior design, and the like. So a word that is associated, at least in the French, with feminine interests and desires broadens to include masculine concerns and yearnings. As the boutique is co-opted to serve masculine interests it also recaptures the ancient and pervasively masculine notion of a storehouse generally operated by men. Notwithstanding a broadening in its meaning, its diminutive size still retains something of its feminine association.

The independently owned store is fragile in our present world, where large may be seen as more desirable and powerful than small. Despite the boutique's fashionableness, elitism, and exclusivity, its smallness leaves it vulnerable to large national chains with the muscle, marketing reach, and pricing power to exploit those unable to resist its lure and force. Merchants may dream of uniting their boutiques into a chain in the hope of increasing the scale of operation, pricing power over suppliers, and profits. The seductiveness and lure of increasing size and bigger returns on investment may cause merchants to destroy the one-of-a-kind boutique they set about to create in the first place by replicating it. As stores grow and multiply the pressure to standardize the merchandise increases, and providing the level of personal and skilled service and uniqueness of goods for sale becomes more challenging. That which begins as intimate and unexpected may become public and predictable, and that which begins as feminine may become masculine in outlook and practice.

Experiencing the boutique is a social experience, whether one finds it on the streets, thoroughfares, roads, or malls, advertised with catchy signs and billboards, or tucked away where only those "in the know" may find it. In the e-boutiques emerging on the electronic highways, the experience of encounter may be virtual. Still, customers would not place orders unless merchants displayed pictures, made available samples of goods and services, and promised return of them if they are not to customers' satisfaction. There may also be telephone calls, and we may meet a parcel delivery person at our door rather than sales staff in a shop.

CONSUMPTION

The boutique metaphor is enshrined in Arthur Powell, Eleanor Farrar, and David Cohen's *The Shopping Mall School,* a descriptive account of an American high school.[3] Music is seen as one of the boutiques from which students make their selections. A product of late capitalism, the modern American high school is a place governed by the self-same capitalistic values as the shopping mall, with its reliance on customers and the importance of choice of things to buy and sell. The school's values are those of marketing, product orientation, financial cost-benefit analysis, and quantification. Marketing involves bringing teachers and subject matter to the attention of students, advertising their benefits, "selling" their value, and packaging subject matter in formats desired by policy makers and participants in music education. Product orientation refers to the emphasis on prepackaged and easily used curricular products, with student performance as an instructional outcome. Financial cost-benefit analysis means assessing fiscally the resources required to generate results, such as instructional objectives, programs, and methods. Quantification is the process of turning all aspects of the education process into numerical values. These values are embodied in data-driven decision-making as educators seek to demonstrate accountability to educational stakeholders with a corporate mind-set. In music education, these wider educational realities are reflected in the current emphasis on national standards, instructional objectives, accountability measures, and choice-based approaches to instruction. Critics of standardization and corporate intrusion into music education, such as Julia Eklund Koza, are a minority of voices.[4]

Here, I sketch elements of a consumption model of music education as if music education were based exclusively on consumption. Although somewhat unrealistic practically speaking, this assumption allows me to clarify elements of this model conceptually. It is possible to see the receptive and acquisitive elements of music education; that is, how it is received by the people it is intended to benefit and the ways in which people seek to possess it.[5] Focusing on aspects of choice also avoids ideological associations of consumption with words such as capitalism and allows a more dispassionate examination of the model in terms of its benefits and problems.

Music. When I refer to music being "consumed," I mean that it is thought of and used as a commodity. "Culture consumers" can be thought of as those listeners who buy recordings and listen to music as they might purchase or possess goods or services. Listeners "own" recordings, possessing them as valuable markers of personal identity or social status.[6] As music becomes a commodity, it is devalued and demeaned. Its past stature as a thing of spiritual power that possessed humans has been inverted, so that the people now possess the music and assign value to it as they would any other of their chattels, be they treasured antiques, pieces of furniture, or paintings.

Music can be seen as a complex and international web of transnational corporations, each with distribution systems, licensing agreements, copyright protections, and marketing systems. On the fringes of these mass production, distribution, and marketing systems are the small independent niche operators who service specialized markets and compete to sell their products. This web of corporate connections also encompasses other cultural and political entities and aspects of culture. Consumption focuses on how these products are taken by those who buy and use them. Consumers have many opportunities to access music electronically via the internet, in discount stores, and in boutiques focused on particular musics. This complex world of music business exists for the purpose of profit-making through creating and catering to consumers' musical interests.

Viewing music as a corporate enterprise rests importantly on the marketing of music to consumers. Marketing is a form of "taste-making"; it familiarizes consumers with music, hypes it so that they want to possess and make it their own, and through these means helps shape the public's musical taste and preference.[7] Marketing is also differentiated to appeal to specific target audiences characterized by qualities such as age-group, style preference, gender, and ethnicity. It not only reflects differences among consumers but also helps create and sustain them, producing fragmented musical publics with differing specific musical interests. Music produced in order to be consumed is also a matter of fashion.[8] Marketers driven by a profit motive and desirous of creating and meeting the needs, interests, and wishes of consumers have contributed to a fragmented musical marketplace. New means have been developed to differentiate musical products and artists and bring music onstream in order to satisfy the demands of consumers for the newest and latest musical fads.

Teaching. The consumption model of music teaching vests teachers with the responsibility of enticing students to spend their time with music and of providing attractive and satisfying learning experiences that prompt students to return for more. Rather than taking the long view and regarding the possibilities for students' future growth and development,[9] teachers focus on what their students want in the present moment and deliver preplanned knowledge to them in the hope of transforming present impulses further down the road.[10] In serving the present interests of students and other participants in music education (their clients and customers) and giving them what they want, popularity wins over esoteric ends and what is wanted in the present moment trumps what may be needed for long term musical development.[11] This proposition rests on the assumption that pleasure derives principally from immediate success, and that it may be diminished by activities that require surmounting significant challenges and spending prolonged time to develop the requisite understandings and skills. Carl Orff's answer to this need for immediate reward and instant gratification is grounded in his belief in *primitivism,* the idea that the young trace the history of civilization in their life cycles, and in *musical rationalism,* the notion that music has evolved into more complex forms over time, culminating in the Western classical tradition.[12] For Orff, and his colleague Gunild Keetman, the instruments of the Instrumentarium can be played simply and do not require students to possess sophisticated instrumental skills.[13]

Choice constitutes an important mechanism whereby music teaching operates, and more choice is preferable to less because strictures on choice prevent the free operation of the forces of supply and demand.[14] From antiquity and throughout the world, much music education has been and remains a matter of choice. Where choice of teacher and student is mutual (a situation that I have called Type I instruction), there is likely to be a better "match" of interests, personalities, teaching and learning styles, and values that may make it possible for teachers to work more effectively and achieve better results than they can in situations where they have no choice (Types III and IV instruction).[15] Following this reasoning, the greater the choice, the greater the likelihood that teachers may experience a heightened sense of self-determination in their work and happiness and satisfaction in working with students. Although teachers are obligated to transcend their natural inclinations, the presence of choice may be an important factor in their satisfaction (and longevity) as teachers. Teachers also vary in their appeal to students, and those whom students choose most often are most likely to succeed in this environment.

Learning. A consumption model of learning focuses on the recipient of the teacher's instruction. As educational clients, students (and their guardians, who we hope act in their best interests) expect to receive musical instruction of a particular quality that meets their desires. Learning is arbitrated by the immediate pleasure it brings the student and its benefits for student performance. Where education is conceived as a matter of providing client-driven services, student learning becomes the principal marker of teacher effectiveness, and student hedonistic desires are crucial in shaping what is learned. In focusing on the present as opposed to some distant and imagined future, learning in this model is consumed with the short-term aspects of learning and focuses on immediate and demonstrable musical learning for its own sake and as an end in itself rather than a means to other and future ends.

The learner is the recipient of musical instruction that comes from the teacher.[16] Knowledge is quantified as a source of power and offered to the student as a product of worth. One might think of this product in terms of a "stock" of cultural knowledge that is transmitted from one generation to the next.[17] Still, rather than a vision of cultural wealth that presumes a two-way conversation between teacher and student, this is a one-way transmission of the stock of knowledge from teacher to student. The learner assumes a passive and receptive role and is effectively disempowered and dependent upon the teacher, who often provides knowledge for a fee or through taxation. Knowledge is not constructed by the learner but passed on as a more-or-less static inventory by the teacher, and it may become "inert" or not a living thing for the learner.[18] Treating knowledge as a commodity also devalues it from something of inestimable and spiritual value to a possession or a chattel.

Choice is also a basic principle of learning. Students' choices of their teachers, among other things, enable them to opt for those instructional situations that optimize the likelihood of their success. In Type I instructional situations, where student and teacher both have choice, students can opt for instructional situations that best meet their desires and impulses and choose teachers who work at their desired levels of engagement, skill, and interest.[19] The self-selectivity of students for instructors may result in the most congenial circumstances for student learning; teacher and student are most likely to get along well, and this congeniality may result in the greatest learning. Again, there is an underlying assumption that students will respond to teachers positively if the conditions are right. Where choice is not present, students may be more likely to subvert the learning process and reduce their effort and time commitments to learning when it is not to their liking. If things deteriorate beyond their zones of tolerance, they will, if at all possible, opt out of the instructional situation. Philosophical assumptions regarding the benefits of student choice for learning are predicated on the proposition that emotional response and sensory appeal directly affect cognitive functioning and the learning process.[20] These interconnections between mind and body suggest that the presentation of material is important, and that students are more likely to learn it easily if it is attractively presented.

Instruction. Interactions between teacher and student fall into at least four theoretical or logical types.[21] At one end of the polarity is a situation that I call "reciprocal empathy"—the mutual attraction of teacher and student; at the other extreme is "reciprocal antipathy"—the mutual repulsion of teacher and student. In between reciprocal empathy (++) and reciprocal antipathy (--) are Aristotelian logical possibilities of (+-) and (-+) where teacher or student has choice and the other does not. Labeling these four logical possibilities Types I (++), II (+-), III (-+), and IV (--), we see stark theoretical contrasts between situations where teachers and students have choice and those in which they do not. Modeling these alternatives suggests that teachers and students are more likely to encounter difficult and unproductive instructional situations in Type IV than in Type I instruction. In most institutional settings, the reality is somewhere between these theoretical extremes; and although teachers are trained to reach out to students to whom they might not normally be attracted or wish to work, these underlying social-psychological realities impact music instruction. A perception of choice is potentially more productive of enhanced student learning than the sense of being trapped in an unhappy situation.

The interaction between teacher and student is mainly a one-way transmission of knowledge from teacher to student. As the inferior and passive partner, the student interacts with the teacher in ways that evidence this inequality, and the social distance between student and teacher is greater than where teacher and students are mutual learners or partners in a conversation in which knowledge is constructed by each learner. Although teachers and students operate on the basis of incomplete information, the approach is imaginative in the attractive ways in which material is presented. Teachers also have faith that they can interpret others' signals and signs correctly and catch their students' interests.

Curriculum. An array of attractive musical offerings is organized in order to entice as many different students as possible. More is better than less, since this allows the music enterprise's profits and influence to increase. As a product rather than process, and created for students rather than by and with them, curriculum is driven largely by commercial interests and policy makers. It is student-centered only in the respect that it is marketed to students who consume it, and it takes student interests into account only as a means of shaping the curriculum for the broadest array of students to consume and the largest market possible.[22] It is important to underscore that profits, per se, are not necessarily a bad thing, since they provide a stream of financial resources for the improvement of the product. There is also a growing market in for-profit education in which music plays a role. In the universe of educational and musical literature, music education is at a disadvantage since its market is relatively small and specialized. Curricular materials typically drive instruction in the consumption model, and music education's modest size leaves it at the mercy of large corporations. Authors must often write to the mass market rather than for more specialized audiences.[23] Intellectual and esoteric things in music education may be downplayed when music educational texts are pitched to a general audience of music teachers.[24] In the present circumstances, publishers of research book series, journals, and websites in music education are challenged to ensure the integrity and continuity of their publications.

The music curriculum is designed to create positive student responses and measurable achievements and to win the support of administrators and other powerful policy makers, who determine how resources will be spent and the nature of music programs in their jurisdictions. The emphasis is on "best practices" or those that can be demonstrated to show the greatest student interest and achievement. Rather than build curricula around music teacher capacities, standardized materials are often "teacher-proofed," using formulae that enable the curricula to be taught in spite of teachers rather than because of them. Those who produce instructional materials do this in order to demonstrate accountability for the success of these products and to ensure insofar as possible that those who use them can be effective. Educational policy makers want to know which curricula work best in practical situations, and the curriculum is assessment-driven so as to demonstrate student achievement in each aspect of the subject matter presented. The provision in music textbooks of such features and ready-made assessment material as questions for further study, highlighted concepts that are illustrated in the surrounding narrative, and test and quiz sheets limit and direct the particular aspects to be assessed. Textbook manufacturers and other licensing agencies also foster constant changes in the curriculum (and the materials needed to deliver it). Published materials typically feature the latest gadgetry, gimmickry, and packaging designed to appeal to educational clients and customers. Changing student interests and built-in obsolescence contribute to corporate profits.[25]

Popularity inevitably wins over esoteric ends because it creates wide public appeal for the music curriculum. Today, music educational textbooks are mainly published by corporations with a wide array of interests in culture and information; large multinational corporations are often more interested in what sells well than in serving specialized and more limited markets. In today's highly competitive world, even the boutique music publishers are interested in wide sales in order to remain in existence. Since large corporations control the principal distribution networks, smaller publishers must often undertake niche marketing and compete with larger publishing houses by differentiating their products. Although technological advances have also facilitated new electronic publishing, marketing, and licensing arrangements, the smaller and more specialized publishers must think fiscally about the wide appeal of textbook materials. In this environment, materials that are of more limited appeal are inevitably sidelined.

Administration. Choice also plays a central role in the organization of music education. Many music courses, especially at the secondary and tertiary level and into adulthood, are offered as electives rather than as required subjects. If students are not attracted to particular teachers or course offerings, policy makers may discontinue them and the teachers may be released. This is so because the cost of each unit in relation to the benefit of each unit of expenditure is the final arbiter for the success of music education. In an environment in which schools are under economic pressure, it is not surprising for policy makers to discontinue music courses or charge fees for musical instruction so that they can focus on those things they deem most central to the school's academic mission. Rather than pay a musician to teach full-time at a school, it may be more cost-effective to hire part-time or adjunct teachers for the hours they teach. And this trend toward part-time and adjunct labor is increasingly common.

Administrators with this mind-set are prone to be utilitarian, to emphasize what works and is perceived to be necessary and practical. Music is often regarded as less essential than other subjects, and non-visible aspects of musical study are seen by the public as less useful than visible aspects (especially in fostering a school's public relations and prestige). In these circumstances, musical study or its most invisible aspects may be marginalized in the interest of those things that are perceived to be more useful and visible. Much hangs on the effectiveness of musicians and educators in remaining in the public eye (and ear) through means of musical performances, mounting campaigns to retain musical study, and demonstrating its utilitarian value. In this model, justifications for music on the basis of its social uses may be more convincing than claims for music's value for its own sake.[26]

Administrators are preoccupied with issues of accountability, particularly fiscal stewardship, because those to whom they answer approach education from a corporate mind-set. Things must be counted carefully with a view to producing the most results for the least expenditure of resources, as well as demonstrating the greatest transparency in reporting the use of resources and the results obtained. Education in our time is increasingly expensive, and fiscal considerations are particularly important since administrators are often under financial pressure. Quantifying resources and costs may appear seductively objective; the development and application of formulae may make an administrator's task appear straightforward and technical. Although such data are often incomplete and it is difficult to observe and quantify important aspects of music education, administrators base their decisions on what is observable, quantified, and objective. In so doing, they are more likely to be in step with other educational policy makers. The claims of accountability inevitably generate bureaucracies to handle the increasing flow of data and process the information gathered, and burden teachers with generating data upon which decisions can be made at higher levels. Creating educational hierarchies is likewise affected by pressures toward increasing scales of operation and requirements to demonstrate accountability.

CRITIQUE

Consumption appeals to the capitalist spirit. Situating music education within a pervasively corporate mind-set helps make it more transparent and accountable to policy makers and public alike in an environment driven especially by corporate values. Its universalist stance spreads the benefits of musical education as widely as possible and enables as many as possible to participate musically as full members of society. This widespread access to culture can enable as many as possible to participate musically as full members of society.

On the other hand, it may be worrisome to those who are leery of capitalism, less persuaded that choice is the right mechanism for music education and that hedonistic behavior is the best basis for a public undertaking where the interests of the many as well as the few need to be preserved. If unbridled capitalism prevails, choice may founder as a means of ensuring that none are disadvantaged. Some do not know how to choose well; others believe that they have no choice, and the interests of these people also need to be safeguarded. Since those who make the choices often do so from disadvantaged positions of relative ignorance or power-lessness, this model cannot be relied upon as a sole basis for music education. The business reality of the "survival of the fittest" in a harsh environment where no quarter is given to those who fall ill or fail to do well runs counter to the spirit of music education that most teachers with whom I am acquainted seek to cultivate.

Among the advantages of consumption, music's connections with the rest of life and the role of popular music as an expression of society are important aspects that help establish the relevance and importance of musical study to contemporary culture. Given today's mediated musical world, taking advantage of students' present musical impulses provides ways to bridge popular and other more esoteric musics further removed in space and time. Emphasizing performance also affords ways to enhance a school's public relations, a utilitarian approach to music that is readily grasped by policy makers and participants in music education. The results of a product-centered approach to education are also especially valued when they can be seen and heard. Distributing music internationally through the media enables people to access music previously unavailable to them, broadening the possibilities for musical acculturation. Such acculturation has long been a feature of musical life. The consumption model acknowledges the close ties between music and economic, political, and religious power that have existed since time immemorial and respects classical and vernacular musics, especially when they are desired in the cultural marketplace.

Among this model's shortcomings, music's devaluation as a commodity to be bought and sold subordinates artistic and musical interests to commercial powers that be that must thrive or die within a cutthroat economic environment. The loss of an inestimable spirituality in the face of a pervasive musical commodification amounts to a potential loss of a sense of wonder and awe in the face of mystery. A holistic world view of interrelated arts performed often within rituals and associated with myths is replaced by an atomistic view in which music and the other arts are treated as specialized products. This approach contributes to and enhances materialism rather than acts as its critic or corrective. Recorded music featuring flawless and artificially constructed performances undermines live music making, which is naturally flawed, vulnerable, and often spontaneous. Considering music statically rather than dynamically, as product rather than process, emphasizes performance and other visible elements of musical study to the detriment of other aspects of musical experience. The model's emphasis on popularity also diminishes the spaces and times in which more esoteric and remote musics can be heard and replaces a live human endeavor with a canned musical culture in which stars, rather than collaborative and anonymous music making, prevail. Its "winner-take-all" competitive environment diminishes the role of the greater proportion of music makers, who live and work in relative anonymity. When it does this, it dehumanizes the many losers as well as the few winners of the competitions.

Teaching's reliance on the gaze, on the teacher's close observation of students and appraisal of their impulses and desires, can be appealing; assessments are likely to be subjective and idiosyncratic and to result, collectively, in a multiplicity of teaching strategies that meet the differing interests of students. The music teacher's personality is acknowledged as an important aspect of the teaching process and the model suggests means whereby the best teachers may attract the most students and be rewarded within the educational system. Examining teacher results also moves the assessment of effective teaching from impressionistic judgments to rational decision-making, whereby evidence supports the judgments made.

Nevertheless, seeing teaching from the perspective of consumption renders music teachers powerless in comparison to more powerful others in the educational system. The model's feminization and music's limited importance puts it at a disadvantage compared to other subjects, such as numeracy and literacy, that may secure better educational deals and a more central place in general education. Ultimately, those representing economic, political, religious, and other interests decide who will be hired to teach music in publicly supported schools, what space and time will be allocated to music instruction, and who and what will be taught and learned. This context may delimit what music teachers can accomplish musically. When teachers are the purveyors of prepackaged and pretested music programs, their professionalism is undermined as their work is reduced to that of technicians who apply materials designed by others. Choice may also be illusory, since teaching strategies touted as varied and adapted to the needs of students may become standardized and difficult to accommodate to the particular impulses of students in a given situation. Mechanisms of choice and free market forces of supply and demand also privilege those teachers who take popular positions and whose teaching is most related to what students want to learn, rather than esoteric and less accessible things they may need to learn for the purposes of their long-term development. Evaluating teaching in quantitative terms of numbers of students and positive student evaluations may reward popularity over other desirable teaching qualities and privilege attributes that are more amenable to quantification over those that are not. When students resist learning difficult and esoteric material, teachers in search of high evaluation scores may pander to the present interests and impulses of students and deny them the musical development that should be their right.[27]

Among the potential contributions of applying consumption to learning, the appeal to hedonistic desire, instant reward, and popular interest and impulse is clear. This approach relates learning to the rest of lived existence and the contextualization of learning and relevance to students' personal experience motivates them to build upon their initial impulses and contributes potentially to their musical and personal growth. Regarding students as consumers cultivates a strong interest in their personal development and makes pleasure a vital part of educational learning. Learning is thereby potentially more diverse and idiosyncratic, as students focus on those things that are of most interest to them. Where students may choose their teachers, congenial instructional situations in which to learn are possible—situations that take individual personalities into account. For those learners who desire a strongly teacher-directed learning process, there is the comfort of teacher-directed instruction and packaged materials that students can absorb. The immediacy of success contributes positively to student motivation and experience of success all along the way.

Still, there are other disadvantages. Students and their guardians do not always know what they need to learn or how to choose wisely, and some may have more choice than others. Passive and receptive learning also render students powerless, dependent upon the teacher, and oppressed as they cannot name their worlds and do not possess the freedom to construct their own realities. Since learning is seen as the prerogative mainly of the student and is largely receptive and even passive, students may become disinterested in and bored with musical study. It is not surprising that students will encounter difficulties in learning. Focusing only on materials and strategies that are immediately accessible deprives them of opportunities to learn patience and persistence as they move from the simple to the complex, from the accessible to the difficult, and from activities that bring immediate rewards to those producing long-term results. Such patience and persistence might stand them in good stead as they negotiate later life. Failing to learn these life lessons not only sets students up to miss opportunities that music affords but, worse, underscores their expectations that music and life should and will always be easy. When this turns out not to be the case, a student may be frustrated or resort to cheating in order to find an easy way through difficulties. The model's emphasis on learning products rather than the learning process captures only a slice of the array of possible learning outcomes, and learners naturally concentrate on demonstrating the desired outcomes (just as their teachers assist them by teaching to the tests). Shifting to behaviorally oriented instructional objectives atomizes knowledge into small testable chunks and degrades those less demonstrable ends of music education that elude ready measurement. Where quantitative measures of learning are unavailable, qualitative rubrics may likewise contribute to an atomistic approach to music learning by breaking down content into small pieces.

Among the benefits of the consumption model is the interaction between teacher and student, preferably under conditions of choice, that forms the basis for instruction. This allows for natural dispositions and individual preferences to play a role in instructional arrangements. Since teachers are viewed as the primary providers of knowledge, the model takes advantage of their wider knowledge and experience while also recognizing the individual personalities and dispositions of teachers and students. Its largely one-way flow of information values efficiency in terms of time-effectiveness and cost-effectiveness. And its focus on products renders instructional results transparent, and accountability evident, to music education policy makers and participants. Instruction is also fraught with potential problems. Consumption's reliance on free market forces of supply and demand initially results in competition between teachers and students who seek the best possible situations. Ultimately, though, economies of scale come into play as organizations seek more power and profit and act to reduce this competition. Without external controls, competition leads inexorably to monopoly as corporations strive to reduce their competition and gain power in the market place. This "survival of the fittest" trope overlooks education's obligation to the poor, the weak, and those who are least able to choose wisely or fend for themselves. Standardization also makes it more difficult for teachers and students to respond to each other and the subject matter in ways that maximize the possibilities for variety and individualization of instruction. Large educational organizations inevitably reduces opportunities for Type I instruction, in which both teacher and student have choice. Type I instruction may be more expensive and less cost-effective than Type IV instruction, as it is more difficult to arrange for teacher and student choice than to standardize decision-making. Student passivity and receptiveness are likely to render instruction less effective in prompting conversations between teachers and students. It may be more difficult to remedy those situations in which the instruction does not meet the needs and interests of students or take advantage of its rhapsodic developments. Should teachers misread their students' signals and signs, the prepackaged and unresponsive nature of instruction provides limited opportunity to rectify the difficulty and reshape the nature of instruction, at least in the present moment. Students readily grasp when questions are not real or important and teachers wish lessons to go in particular directions, and as they acquiesce to teachers' wishes, their apathy and disinterest may grow. Disinterest in the subject matter can then easily transfer to disinterest in the teacher associated with this material and make it more difficult to create situations in which teachers and students are mutually attracted to each other. The very corrective mechanisms that teacher and student choice might seem to afford are less available as instruction becomes more standardized.

To its credit, since curriculum in the consumption model benefits from careful packaging and material receives attractive presentation, subject matter may be more interesting and tempting for students to learn than if it is left to individual teachers with limited resources to find and assemble. This curriculum begins where students are, reflecting their interest in the present world and focusing on their present impulses and desires, and, in optimal circumstances, widens their musical understanding. Its orientation toward popularity makes it potentially relevant to the rest of students' lived lives. Prepackaged materials also give teachers access to a much wider pool of expertise on which to draw in framing their curricula, reducing the time and effort teachers must take to design their own programs and materials and leaving them freer to focus on other aspects of curriculum.

Among its drawbacks, building the curriculum principally upon music of wide appeal to students overlooks the fact that popular music is a means whereby the young break away from the authority of the older generation and establish their own identities. Sometimes young people might prefer teachers (or other authority figures) not to co-opt their music in the classroom but to respect its separateness from adult culture. At present, popular musics go in and out of fashion quickly; by the time a teacher engages a new trend, it may already be out of fashion, supplanted by something else. Since appearances can deceive, this focus on the decorative aspects of curriculum can obscure an absence of intensity, solidity, and depth in the subject matter.[28] Students may be short-changed, learning far less than might otherwise be expected of them. When financial and musical considerations collide in designing and arbitrating the curriculum, financial considerations may be paramount. Subjects that are esoteric, less accessible to the general public, or less financially viable in their appeal to limited markets may be downplayed or dismissed. The pressure to standardize and quantify the curriculum may undermine the variety and individualization that consumption first promises.

Administration evidences several advantages with this model. Its hierarchical, specialized, and segmented arrangement of music education illustrates the same top-down leadership style, focused on accomplishing specified objectives, as that in corporate and military organizations. Since each level and aspect of the system is specialized, this model provides a way of focusing the talents of those involved in the enterprise. Marketers, curriculum experts and developers, and teachers focus their energies on a narrow array of specific objectives. The model's focus on accountability also makes its operation transparent to all who share its financial burden and renders its costs and benefits in fiscal terms. This reality makes decision-making more technical and the array of considerations more limited. Since decision-making is data-driven, it is rational rather than intuitive, perceptive, or feelingful, and this rationality is appealing to those with corporate and scientific mind-sets. There is also something evocative and personally empowering about the boutique management's independence and grasp of all of the elements of the enterprise. Administrators are able to shape their musical organizations independently of others.

As the organization grows, hierarchical, top-down decision-making may focus so intently on results that it fails to take sufficient account of bottom-up decision-making. The larger the organization grows, and the more removed administration is from the individual teacher able to make decisions about the particular students in her or his care, the less power the teacher has to influence decision-making at the highest levels. Administrators can be isolated from the music teacher's day-to-day work and enact policies with insufficient regard to how these impact teachers and learners. Whether all of this counting actually improves the quality of work performed is very much in doubt, yet it takes time away from other important and productive activities and can easily deflect the attention of administrators and policy makers from the larger tasks of music and general education. Viewing things so mechanistically, atomistically, and quantitatively and making decisions on the basis of a narrow range of considerations may be unrealistic and oppressive for music teachers. Teachers may find such an atmosphere stifling, and some of the very best walk away from teaching because they cannot tolerate their powerlessness. When this occurs, something of the independence of the boutique has been lost. The longing of music teachers for empowerment that allows them more opportunities to shape their teaching situations and make decisions independently of others reveals how readily other interests and institutions co-opt music education.

SUMMARY

These pictures of the boutique and consumption are evocative of music education in ways that are bright and dark, particular and widespread, figurative and literal, idealistic and pragmatic. We see them differently depending on our vantage points and our individual and collective backgrounds. Opportunities and advantages for the work of music education, when looked at differently, may constitute challenges and disadvantages. These ambiguities, ironies, tensions, and paradoxes raise theoretical and practical challenges for music education. Among the possibilities of these pictures for good and evil, teachers may be empowered and oppressed. Just as the manager of a boutique may resist the lure of a chain or conglomerate, the darker side of market forces make such resistance difficult if not impossible. Finding ways to take advantage of consumption's best features and avoid its pitfalls requires negotiating the specific situations in which we live and work. Our choices are central to the work of music education, and these pictures open ways of thinking specifically about the nature of decision-making on the part of teachers, students, policy makers, and the public.

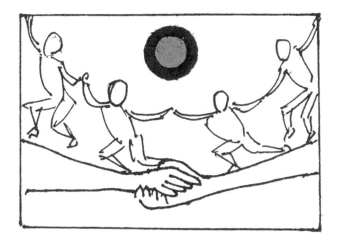

3
VILLAGE AND COMMUNITY

The importance of pictures of music education as *village* and *community* can be traced to several causes. The village resonates with the myth and memory of simpler times and rural places apart from the whirl and pace of the modern metropolis. Its psychological appeal arises from nostalgia for a more uncomplicated and unhurried life and desire for mutuality especially when families are small, fragmentary, and disconnected. Social humanistic world views in which education serves as a political agent of democracy also shape these pictures and express the hopes of ordinary people who seek to determine their own governance untrammeled by powerful others. In education, they are glimpsed in the writings of John Dewey, Maria Montessori, Maxine Greene, Jane Roland Martin, Nel Noddings, Parker Palmer, Raymond Gaita, and Paul Woodford.[1] Beyond the village are the various aspects of the community model: music, teaching, learning, instruction, curriculum, and administration, and the model's contributions and hindrances to music education.

VILLAGE

One of the villages on Cape Cod has its roots in the early seventeenth century. Within sight of the sea, this village is strung out as a ribbon settlement along an old highway. We pass the various buildings that comprise its core—church, shops, tavern or inn, meeting house, town square, village green or park, post office, general store, restaurant, and garage—with cottages and large homes clustered in adjacent streets and scattered into the countryside. Traffic is often heavy and villagers bustle about their business, run errands, and converse with others. At a neighborhood pub of a Sunday afternoon, villagers gossip as they watch a football game on television, and we hear the hum of people packed into a small space, laughter, heated conversations, sometimes raised voices, and the clanking of glasses and tableware evocative of village pubs in other places. Since these people share this place, live in close proximity, and attend some of the same religious, athletic, artistic, and social events, they have much in common.

In memory's eye, I think of suburbs that have a similar "village-like" quality about them. My old neighborhood in Matlock Heights, Bloomington, Indiana, was once a farm. Now it is comprised of cottages built in the 1950s, quintessential Indiana stone ranches set in park-like lots, where most of the neighbors know and watch out for each other. On its borders are two churches and several businesses. Although very different from the Cape Cod village, it functions much as a village might. Walking through the neighborhood, neighbors stop and talk to each other; an association of neighbors gathers several times a year to picnic and discuss local issues. Diminutive size and boundedness give the neighborhood a quality of distinctiveness and separateness similar to that the Cape Cod village enjoys. Neighbors include single people, couples, and married people with children; come from different cultures; comprise university students, retired people, professionals, and tradespeople, with ages ranging from babies to seniors. They are newcomers who have just moved here and older folk who have lived in the neighborhood since it was first established, and multiple generations of a family who live across the street from each other. So, the people who live here share common perspectives from living in this suburb.

There is also a downtown Chicago neighborhood where the people live in apartments, townhouses, above shops, or in grand homes within walking distance of businesses. Larger than either the Cape Cod village or the Bloomington subdivision, it likewise has a distinctive village-like character. The constant noise and flow of traffic crowding its thoroughfares, throngs of people speaking and dressed in ways suggestive of their particular cultural heritages, and density of the housing and shops in this particular neighborhood seem a world away from the tiny village or the suburban subdivision. Yet, looking more closely, we see family members and friends laughing and talking as they stroll along a sidewalk, enter a delicatessen or restaurant, or stop for coffee or at an outdoor market. What may seem at first to be impersonal is nevertheless a village of another sort, in which people forge intimate connections with others who live and work in this place.

Although many people crowd together in this comparatively small area of several city blocks, there is a sense in which they understand their world similarly. Should they meet in another city and discover that they are from the same neighborhood, they would have much to share about the joys and challenges of living in this place. They might discover that they know some of the same people, favorite hangouts, and local claims to fame, and this intimate knowledge helps connect them even though they may at first be strangers.

Despite the evident differences between these three pictures of the village, there are important commonalities. Each also has its own particular character expressed by the people who inhabit it and the ways in which they use this space: for example, the livelihoods of its populace, nature of the buildings and their surroundings, furnishings of living spaces, roads and pathways, and natural surroundings. Its character derives from the people who live here and the ways in which their lives are impacted by the environment that their forebears and they have constructed. Each is bounded in some way as a specific and discrete place. Rather than being entirely isolated, people affiliate with and attach themselves to this place in different ways, some at its center and others at its periphery. Boundaries between one place and another are porous, dynamic, arbitrary, and disputed.

The village is also dynamic and changing. In the Cape Cod village, shops and cafes now line the street in the houses where people once lived. A captain's house is converted into condominiums; a bed-and-breakfast establishment replaces a single-family home. Houses now spread out beyond the originally smaller bounds and dot the landscape that once was wilderness or farmland. The originally quiet suburban neighborhood now faces a traffic problem as people pass through it en route from outlying rural areas and suburbs farther away, and increasing traffic brings greater noise pollution and dangers to children playing in the houses adjoining increasingly busy streets and thoroughfares. Gardens are planted and blossom around homes that once might have been uncared-for, and homes that once were their owners' pride and joy are now untidy and shabby. Students increasingly live off-campus in this neighborhood. Nontraditional families establish themselves in a place originally populated mainly by married couples and their children. Businesses move in and out of the urban neighborhood, property values rise and fall, the nature of the population changes, and all of these changes dramatically impact its character.

There is a fragility about the village brought about by changing political, economic, religious, and demographic conditions that, over time, can work against its relative smallness, compactness, and the intimacy of its population, and that are often beyond its power to contain. The Cape Cod village appeals especially to those from large urban areas and yet, as more people settle here, it is more difficult to maintain the small town feel of intimacy and interconnectedness of the past.

Increasing population burdens infrastructure and services. Rising property values and taxation edge out longtime residents who are unable to keep pace with higher taxes, and the character of the place changes and may become less attractive than it once was. Newcomers may rebuild once modest cottages into large trophy homes that change the character of the village and destroy the very thing that many find charming about historic villages. Villagers who want to preserve their way of life may respond by enacting laws that make it more difficult to change the village, and tensions inevitably pit progressives who desire change with conservatives who want to preserve what they have. Although new, larger, and more expensive buildings might increase the taxes levied on property that is now more valuable, the village may also be less desirable to visitors who come to Cape Cod expecting to see, among other things, modest Cape cottages and historic buildings. Ensuring that the character of the village is preserved, reconciling progressive and conservative forces, and managing growth and development necessitate political action. To this end, on Cape Cod, a pristine landscape is protected by associations of activists, historic preservationists, land banks, conservation areas, and a national park, and land-use ordinances also help to maintain a kaleidoscope of different villages, each with its own character.

COMMUNITY

In proposing that education be thought of as community, Dewey draws on the metaphor of the village, borrowing W. H. Hudson's description of a Wiltshire village in England.[2] He sees education as "a social process," and the school as "community life," and "a form of social life, a miniature community and one in close interaction with other modes of associated experience beyond school walls."[3] The school and the classroom are envisaged socially as groups of people who share various relationships with one another in safe communities, where teachers and their students are empowered to accomplish things that they could never have imagined if left to learn in solitary fashion, and where the happiness of all the participants in education is an important educational end.[4]

Values of safety, intimacy, humanity, collaboration, inclusiveness, equality, valuing human life, and freedom guide the educational community. To briefly sketch them: safety requires that young and old alike are free from physical abuse and violence and have their basic needs met.[5] Intimacy involves friendship, belonging, caring, compassion, and love where self-disclosure is fostered in a safe environment, affection arises out of compassion for others that wants their fullest and best development, and pedagogical love focuses on the interests and needs of others rather than the satisfaction of one's own desire. Humanity is expressed through such means as the arts, rituals, myths, and religions, and people are regarded as precious sentient beings worthy of dignity, respect, carefulness, honor, and justice irrespective of their particular circumstances. Collaboration refers to working supportively and collectively with others in mutually beneficial ways. Inclusiveness asserts the value of incorporating people into collective endeavors; its posture is universalistic. Equality denotes treating all people as if they are of great worth and offering opportunities for all to participate fully and authentically in the community. Valuing human life suggests that all human beings irrespective of their individual circumstances should have the opportunity to participate in general education. Freedom, construed politically, requires that people have agency and can determine the ways in which their lives are lived and governed.

Music. Thinking of music as community emphasizes its social nature and role in identity construction. More important than individual virtuosic performance is the blend of instruments that comprises a whole greater than the sum of its parts—evident, for example, in the collaborative and ensemble musicking among African peoples or in Western classical orchestras, bands, and choirs.[6] The ideal of the many rather than the one contrasts dramatically with the "winner-take-all" individuality of consumption, and, musically speaking, community fosters a different musical aesthetic that values the group over the individual. Although examples of this communal aesthetic abound throughout the history of the Western classical tradition, music educators also look to other vernacular and classical musical traditions to see it in operation.[7] Regarding music as an identifying social marker rather than a solitary spiritual experience, like consumption, community stresses the utilitarian value of music as a means of social cohesiveness and expression. This view of music provides a window into the ways in which music functions socially and its meaning collectively for those groups who share certain musical beliefs and practices. Various "spheres of musical validity" or social-musical groups that form around particular musics contribute to and express group identity.[8] Society is woven into music as meanings inhere in musical expressions and these shared understandings are encoded within music.[9] Although musical meaning is ambiguous and people may disagree about the specifics of this particular performance or its specific meaning, generally speaking, there is also some measure of publicly shared knowledge of music. Who "we" are collectively is understood within the wider culture; music, as an element of that culture, is an important component of this collective practical and theoretical knowledge. Studying music as an area in the humanities reveals the rich web of possible interconnections between music and the other aspects of life, generating a clear sense of a collective "we" beyond an individual "I."[10]

Regarding music within the frame of community also acknowledges its intimate connection to the myths, rituals, and arts of those who make and take it and the importance of studying it as a humanity. For example, Howard Shore's film score for *The Lord of the Rings* film trilogy evokes a distant time, a multicultural milieu, and the spiritual quest of a mythic community and band of brothers. Flawed hobbits and other beings comprise the fellowship of the ring, spirituality is practiced in the midst of others, and as a member of a community, Frodo is inspired and helped by Samwise, Gandalf, and others in his quest for the ring.[11] The multifaceted, complex, and flawed character of a community is played out in its myths and rituals that reveal the various ways in which members act individually and collectively for good and evil. Regarding music narratively, ritually, and dramatically illumines the complex and imperfect character of those who make and take it, and learners better understand themselves and others as they come to know the sonic phenomena and rituals of which they and others are a part.

Teaching. Viewing music teaching as a social phenomenon underscores the teacher's role as a group leader and the importance of the various social structures, functions, and processes whereby the community functions and accomplishes its work. Seen this way, music teachers grasp their roles within the larger educational enterprise and the manner in which they can and should interrelate with teachers of other subjects. Regarding teaching socially focuses on the means by which music teachers create and sustain effective pedagogical groups, fostering and maintaining social processes such as group identity, morale, recruitment, and communication.[12] Thinking of music teaching as a social process also moves the emphasis from descriptive matters of present reality to normative aspects of what should be. The cohesiveness and smooth social operation of the group is the final arbiter of the goodness of the teacher's teaching.[13] As a group leader, the teacher guides the students through the use of "rules" that govern social behavior and musical practice. Learning communities or communities of practice collaboratively construct rules designed to be followed by all of the participants. Social control is exerted when the community collectively disciplines those who transgress these rules.[14] Since rules are crucial for the smooth operation of the educational and musical community, teaching is oriented to transmitting appropriate rule-sets from one generation to the next. Students may at first slavishly adhere to these rules, but later, the rules provide guidance and may even be intentionally broken as new practices are forged.[15]

Teaching is generally conversational or dialogical, focused on questions that prompt learner engagement. Teachers create the conditions for learners to interact with each other conversationally not only through directly questioning students but by establishing environments in which conversations are welcome. The desired conversations are deeply engaging, imaginatively renewing, and potentially transformative, so that participants in them might never otherwise discover some things for themselves.[16] Prompting such conversations requires teachers to be tactful and possess a touch or feel for what needs to happen at a particular time.[17]

Notice that the discourse on community is prone to take an idealistic tack. Since teachers are the architects of their learning communities, their values determine the nature and limits of the ensuing conversation. They are positioned to determine the rules whereby social control will be enacted and freedom articulated. Various teaching styles reflect different ethical and musical commitments and foster all sorts of communities. One teacher may be as group leader, referee, and coach; another may take a more directive stance and through force of example and words construct a very different community of learners. One may elicit conversations through a Socratic style of teaching and another may prefer an expository approach. All may be intense, potentially transformative, and humane, and the nature of the resulting conversations may differ. Although teachers are formally responsible to their students, the dialogical character of teaching fosters an exchange of teacher and student roles as teachers learn from their students as students teach their teachers. This sharing reinforces the knowing of teachers and students alike. The teacher serves as host of a musical, artistic, and cultural feast, mentor of budding musicians, and fellow and more experienced learner who can be counted on for assistance when students find it difficult to construct knowledge unaided.[18]

The lived quality of a musical community means that teachers not only convey wisdom, knowledge, beliefs, attitudes, and skills to the next generation of musicians; they also exemplify a way of life as a musician. From antiquity, teaching has extended beyond the public sphere to include domestic matters. These qualities remain important in today's world where a teacher's example of the musician's commitment and discipline to music is open to view. To live as a musician, as well as knowing musical thought and practice, necessitates that teachers communicate to students the ways in which they should live as musicians and conduct the rest of their lives.[19] Ways of life are complex and construed in familial, religious, economic, political, and musical terms. The particular way of life advocated depends on the institution under whose aegis music instruction is conducted.[20] Some agreement on the community's goals, norms, purposes, and methods is obviously necessary for a community to survive and thrive. Still, because it is comprised of complex and flawed people who do not always get along with others happily, a community cannot be conflict-free.[21]

Learning. The notion of a "learning community" is often portrayed as an ideal rather than realistically pictured as the ground in which people, ideas, and practices interact, sometimes in tension and conflict. What begins as an idiosyncratic grasp of the field of study gradually comes to approximate an exponent's understanding and more public knowledge of it.[22] Unlike consumption, in which students receive knowledge from their teachers, learning in community requires the active and social engagement of students and teachers alike.[23] Since the teacher is charged with the primary responsibility of deciding what shall be studied by students, the learners' construction of the subject matter is delimited by choices that the teacher makes. Within these limits, the "narratives" constructed by the students, specific practical skills they acquire, and learning outcomes that result are likely to be somewhat idiosyncratic and divergent as students appropriate the subject matter in differing ways. Ideally, the teacher's construction of the environment or context for student learning is nurturing, compassionate, and respectful. When all learners are fully present one to another, teachers and students can engage with each other and the material in ways that allow learners to construct their own realities without risk of reprisal.[24] This approach might repudiate standardized learning of the subject matter, but it need not preclude teachers from insisting on certain standards at which they expect their students to work. Different types of content and performance standards require interrogating the particular senses in which standards are used. In contrast to the summative, standardized content, and product-centered approaches to learning in the consumption model, the community model is likely to feature formative, performative standards and processual approaches to learning.

Learning a way of life in community is accomplished in various ways. Since it involves domestic and public matters, formal and informal settings, and active and receptive means, learning through instruction, practice, example, and reflection is complemented by learning through osmosis, participation, observation, and sensibility.[25] Imagination plays a crucial role, since students may not envisage how they might do and think differently until they encounter difference exemplified in the music making and taking of others. Demonstration through lived examples and conversations with trusted members of the community are powerful ways in which students come to know music in communion with others. Participation in the community's musical and social rituals is a means whereby students are gradually socialized and enculturated into its beliefs and practices. There is also an important sense in which learning is collective as well as individual, construed socially as well as psychologically, and egalitarian as well as hierarchical in emphasis. In contrast to the consumption model where teachers position themselves above their students and feed material "down" to them, as teachers become fellow learners with their students, the social distance between them and their students is reduced. So the dynamic, constructive, social, and egalitarian qualities of learning in community stand in sharp relief to the static, receptive, psychological, and hierarchical focus of learning in the consumption model.

Instruction. The community model operates principally through the mechanism of conversation, rather than choice as in the consumption model. Rather than the one-way transmission from teacher to student in the consumption model, a two-way exchange of information between teachers and students results from the interchangeability of teacher and student roles and the mutual sharing of knowledge among learners. The interaction between teachers, students, and subject matter is likely to foster a web of conversation that is richer than the results-driven consumption model, which is less interested in the construction of knowledge by students. This dialogue focuses on the processes whereby learners construct their understandings of music and actively engage music as composers, improvisers, performers, producers, and listeners. The teacher's preoccupation with prompting students' active involvement in music and interaction with other learners in this community translates into a lively environment that is not merely intellectual but also physically and emotionally charged.

The personal interaction between teacher and student and the breadth of learning objectives in this model suggest a profound and transformative process for those involved in it. The subject matter is not valued as a commodity with particular monetary value, as with consumption, but is regarded as of profound individual and collective spiritual worth. There is a sense of mystery, wonder, and awe as fellow learners come to know the limits of their individual understandings and abilities and the possibilities for their personal development. It is sometimes mysterious how groups take on their own personae and the individuals who comprise them are inspired to do more than they thought possible of themselves. Awe may arise when they hear another's brilliant performance that transcends the ordinary and inspires them with its possibilities. This evocative and spiritual quality of instruction may not always be present, and teachers and their students may be surprised or joyful when it appears.[26] Such moments are inspiring, both intrinsically and extrinsically motivating; they help to set up conditions for subsequent pleasurable and successful learning.

Curriculum. The ambiguity of music, and its semantic and syntactic density, mean that music teachers are likely to regard it in various ways and have differing conceptions of the order in or means by which it should be introduced to and engaged by students. This problem is likely to be evident in working out pedagogical issues such as antecedence, in which teachers determine what their students need to know before they can successfully accomplish other things. These ambiguities contribute to the difficulties of achieving consensus among teachers about the scope and sequence of the music curriculum. The myriad ways in which learners construct knowledge result in different curricular beginning points, aims, objectives, methods, materials, and ending points. If learners are to truly engage music in ways that really make sense to them, the musics studied and the ways in which they are engaged by students can also be expected to vary from place to place.[27] Rather than adapting a standard subject matter to particular places, this model goes further to choose musics that express this place and give voice to it and the people who dwell here. Taking place into account requires possibilities for cultivating the understandings and skills that permit music teachers and their students to acquire the specific competencies needed in the particular places in which they are aspiring to teach and learn.

Relating music to the rest of life necessitates treating music as a field in the humanities and regarding it broadly, holistically, and comparatively within the lenses of such fields as ethnography, anthropology, ecology, history, politics, economics, religion, geography, sociology, psychology, and education. Those who make and take this music are validated by its study and performance, and learners need to grasp it deeply as they construct their own musical selves. Acquiring the technical skills to make this music is important, but proponents of the community model also want to transform the lives of its exponents and public. This is especially the case because the people are what this music curriculum is about and for, and because there is a premium on live musical experiences that may be engaged directly by music makers and takers alike.

The rhapsodic, serendipitous, and conversational nature of this curriculum takes it in sometimes unexpected directions. While a teacher might plan for possible developments, a genuinely open-ended conversation is sometimes surprising, requiring that the teacher bring to the conversation an even broader and deeper knowledge of the subject than when instruction is preplanned, as in the consumption model. Because they may detract from the teacher's planned objectives, these rhapsodic and free-flowing developments may sometimes be inefficient in the use of time. However, as learners construct their own knowledge and create, in a sense, their own objectives, the teacher's objectives constitute one set, albeit privileged, in a universe of objectives. Although blind alleys and false leads may divert these musical conversations, such diversions offer possibilities for further learning that, rather than constituting a waste of time, potentially contribute to students' grasp of the subject matter. Learners' intimate engagement with subject matter means that it is more likely to be internalized rather than to remain a static body of knowledge apart from those who teach and learn it.

Administration. This model views the organization of music education dynamically and processually.[28] The centrality of open-ended conversations in instructional settings with different educational ends, and of physical interactions of people in particular places and times, suggests relatively flat and humane organizational structures that permit people in various specialized roles to interact in face-to-face or virtual settings. Some organizations are predicated on the belief that people are naturally lazy and require directives and monitoring to ensure that they work well, while others assert that people are naturally good and need only to be nurtured, supported, and encouraged in their work.[29] Avoiding both of these extremes prompts administrators to realize that some people are naturally attracted to work that is worthy and important, but that others require frameworks to deter them from unscrupulous action and prod them to make positive contributions.[30] Among the organizational approaches to fostering multiplicities and pluralities within the community, a cellular system allows groups of teachers and their students to move in different directions at different rates, to coalesce at some times and to diverge at other times.[31] Organizing communities in cellular ways nurtures flexible conversational networks that are nimble and fluid, so that different groups can take advantage of unexpected opportunities when they appear. In order for all of the individuals in the community to be heard and construct their own realities, administrative units are likely to be relatively small and intimate, and large organizations are challenged to break down large aggregations into smaller units that facilitate members of the community connecting directly with one another and the subject matter. In particular, evaluation functions differently in community than in a regime of consumption. In community, formative evaluation fosters a process of individual and collective development, whereas in conditions of consumption, summative evaluation emphasizes the results that are achieved. The individual and collective diversity that is a feature of community plays out in criterion-referenced rather than norm-referenced approaches, more often informal and qualitative than the standardized measures typical of consumption. Evaluative criteria may also be constructed by teachers and students as a part of the broader construction of knowledge in the community. Over time, these criteria become settled expectations. Should a leader provoke a change in expectations, the community may be quite unsettled until the change becomes more established in organizational policy.

Administering these multiple cells requires particular coordination skills if the organization's general goals are to be met. Rather than top-down manager, the administrator's role becomes that of community organizer. Creating an *esprit de corps* in the organization, fostering high morale, and ensuring that those within the organization work collaboratively and understand the contributions of different others are of particular importance in the community model. Here, the administrator's eye is upon the whole as well as its constituent parts. In contrast to conditions of consumption, where the organizational elements are atomized into their respective parts, community requires a sense of affiliating to some whole that is perceived to be important and worth belonging to. While it is necessary to coordinate the work of the various cells, the administrator acts mainly to foster, encourage, and motivate the organization's members in positive ways. For this to be accomplished smoothly, processes and rule-sets are in place so that administrators can act dispassionately and with consideration to all those in the organization, not capriciously and with favoritism to certain privileged members.

CRITIQUE

Among the benefits of the community model of music education are its social and individual values.[32] The values of cooperation, inclusiveness, empathy, and compassion are absorbed by musicians as they participate together in music making and taking; these values play out in the larger society, temper the pervasive materialism and hedonism of unbridled capitalism, and contribute to more humane and civil societies. Interacting socially and getting along with different others limits unfettered individualism and enables the learning of valuable life lessons that can transfer from musical to other lived experience. Through social experiences one moves gradually from being preoccupied with one's own needs and interests toward greater care and concern for others. The intimacy, domesticity, and caring so central to community join emotional life and physical passion with intellectual thought in a holistic view of knowing that is too often marginalized in educational thought and practice. Joining the domestic and public in community benefits all members of the human family, and the happiness and well-being of those within the community are central concerns.[33]

Notwithstanding these contributions, these values may not jibe with those needed to thrive in today's world; this model may seem too idealistic and unrealistic. Cooperation, inclusiveness, and compassion for different others are noble ideals, but the realities of a competitive, exclusive, and sometimes uncaring world also need to be engaged and students prepared to meet its challenges. Associating particular value sets with community overlooks other possibilities that may be dehumanizing and oppressive, and administrative realities are likely to fall short of their promise. A democratic, egalitarian, and inclusive community is one of a universe of possibilities in which different conditions may prevail. Free-wheeling and open-ended conversations envisaged in this model depend on people being treated civilly and respectfully and free to affiliate with and leave a community.[34] This is not always the case, and social pressures and personal friendships combine to enforce particular ways of thinking, acting, and being. Nor is it clear that the positive results hoped for in this model will necessarily obtain in a world where freedoms are limited or curtailed. Even the most well-meaning people oppress and repress others; dehumanizing forces are at work in every social setting.[35] Those who have suffered oppression may oppress others, and the freedoms assumed in community are fragile and not always successfully attained or sustained.

A romantic view of community sees only its bright side. Dewey's story, borrowed from Hudson, to which I referred earlier, goes as follows.[36] News of the woodsman who has just cut his hand as he chops wood at a house at one end of the village rapidly reaches the houses at the other end. All the villagers are united by "sympathy and solidarity." They understand perfectly how this man must feel and are eager to help him, so united are they in heart and mind. Would that this were always true! In this picture of perfect accord there is no hint of difficulty. Let us suppose that the following additional facts come to light. The woodsman's name is Jack. Fortunately, the cut he sustains is not serious. Jack and his cousin Henry (who lives two doors down the street) are embroiled in an argument over who gets

their aunt Sally's property on the outskirts of the village. Jack has treated his wife
Mary and children Jack Junior and Paulette so badly that they have fled to shelter
with Georgette, Jack's cousin who lives on the other side of the railroad tracks. Jack
has also been making trouble in the village. As a member of a religious sect that is
holding meetings at a house at the other end of the village, he has been preaching
that the church to which Henry, Mary, Sally, Georgette, and other extended family
members belong is evil and this has incurred the wrath of the entire village and its
parson, Father Bill. Yesterday, Jack's daughter Paulette was injured when she fell off
her horse and Jack's relatives blame him for the accident; were he a better husband
and parent, they say, the accident would not have occurred. With these additional
facts in mind, Dewey's rosy picture is more complicated, and it is not at all certain
that all of the villagers' hearts will beat in sympathy to Jack as Dewey supposes.

Notwithstanding these personal differences within the community, there may
still be a sense of "togetherness" in the shared experiences of these people in this
place that cannot be known by a stranger to the village. In Cape Cod, where roots
go down for centuries, these commonly shared experiences are part of the mys-
tique of this place. Nor is this just a rural experience. In suburban subdivisions
in towns and cities across the United States, or in the inner-city neighborhoods
of such cities as Boston, New York City, or Chicago, Dewey's example of the
woodsman's accident resonates with the realities shared by the people in neighborhoods who have a similar feeling of belonging to a particular place. Violence,
fear, and anonymity may also cause city-dwellers to go on with their lives irrespective of the plight of others around them, and Dewey's romantic rural vision
and its village metaphor do not always play out as he suggests. In times of collective trauma, especially, people may reach out to others, as they did in New York
City on September 11, 2001, and its aftermath. As life goes on, however, it is easy
to slip back into a mind-set that is insulated from others' experiences and less
sympathetic of them.

Nostalgia for an overly romanticized vision of the village that may never have
existed in some other simpler time also needs to be tempered by acknowledging its
persistent dark side. Communities can be insufferably closed-minded and intoler-
ant of new ideas and practices. Gossips can destroy reputations, spread falsehoods,
and deny privacy to community members. Well-established, deeply ingrained, and
powerful community traditions can oppress dissidents. Traditionally minded people may be unwilling to change their minds. Unresolved conflicts may fester for
years. Violence may break out. Newcomers may find it difficult to become a part
of the community, and it may become stultified and inbred, literally and figuratively.[37]

To its credit, thinking of music as community emphasizes the widespread musicality of human beings, the possibilities for members of society to participate musically in a host of ways, be they as composers, improvisers, performers, dancers,

listeners, impresarios, or producers. A community-oriented music model enables people to express themselves musically beyond what would be possible where an elitist aesthetic prevails.[38] Musical values of immediacy and accessibility prompt people to participate even if they possess limited musical skills at the same time as they allow others to make music in more esoteric ways and with high levels of musical skills. The widespread participation of musical amateurs, people who compose, improvise, play, sing, dance, and listen to music "for the love of it," is encouraged, and the general music education of young and old alike is devoted to these ends.[39] This view of music as a means or marker of identity construction emphasizes its importance in society and culture. Also, thinking in terms of spheres of musical validity allows us to understand the role that institutions play in inculcating musical beliefs and practices and consider ways in which these spheres may be bridged and musical horizons broadened.

Still, a collaborative aesthetic that fosters ensemble music making and the participation of all members of the community may overlook nurturing solo performers and cultivating high levels of musical expertise.[40] Thinking of music primarily as a branch of the humanities may downplay the imperatives of acquiring musical skills and of performance as a means of coming to know music. Fostering the idea that everyone is musical to the same degree or that music can be experienced immediately and without discipline and effort may perpetuate a fiction, even in those societies that rely on communal music making. Indiscriminate standards of music making may result in a public that is unable to distinguish and cares less about professional training in music, where some of the most adventurous and musically competent musicians find it difficult to be heard in a din of those promoted for other star qualities besides musical ability.

Among the advantages of teaching as community, the rules transmitted by teachers are musical and social; they enable the passage of a musical tradition from one generation to another and prepare people to participate fully and democratically in their civic government.[41] Beyond their musical and political ends, these rules serve important purposes for musical transmission and transformation. In focusing on the principles that undergird practice, teachers systematically help their students come to a richer understanding of music, and the abstract and phenomenal character of musical rules allow teachers to appeal to students' imaginative thought and action. Serving as community organizers rather than dictators prompts teachers toward a humane approach to education that appeals to the differing abilities and aspirations of students and invites rather than commands them to participate in musical life. Fostering musical conversations as places of openings and transformative spaces for growing awareness of self and others opens the prospect for continuing and lifelong learning and professional and personal growth for teachers. Thinking of teaching as presiding over musical feasts is also cause for celebration, happiness, and joy for teachers and students alike.

Among its disadvantages, community may have a limited appeal mainly to those teachers who value social relationships and envision their task in social ways. The collaborative teaching styles required to create and sustain musical communities do not suit everyone, nor are they necessarily appropriate for all subject matter.[42] Teachers who view their task as primarily intellectual and are preoccupied with subject matter that they believe needs to be learned may be more interested in teaching in a subject-focused manner and less interested in the social nature of learning. Such teachers may not find community to be a helpful model, since it potentially diverts their attention away from the subject matter at hand toward the social interactions of students with it. For them, communities ought to emerge as byproducts of good teaching and are incidental to, rather than the principal focus of, their attention. Teaching may also be framed within environments that are hostile to such interactions and conversations, and attempts to create such conversations may threaten those who do not care for a genuinely dialogical education.[43] Not only may the differing teaching styles and value commitments be overlooked in favor of plumping for a narrow type of teaching, but teachers may not hold the specific values or develop the kinds of communities consonant with this model.

On the one hand, music learning in community is about not only acquiring information but being musically socialized and enculturated, living the way of life of a musician, and thriving in the midst of multiplicities and pluralities in wider society. Joining an ensemble or studio class, participating in its social life, learning from other ensemble members, acquiring leadership and organizational skills as one works together with different others, and bonding with other musicians musically and socially are oft-cited benefits of group musical study. The small group lessons that are a feature historically of European music education, while possibly undertaken for financial reasons, also benefit performers by enabling them to learn from others' experiences.[44] The breadth of means of learning that focuses on developmental processes whereby students move from elementary to advanced levels of instruction is an appealing feature of this model for musicians. The fact that people may not think or be able to change except in conjunction with others underscores the importance of group learning experiences in music.[45] Becoming aware of the human dimensions of music and learning more of self and others are also noble educational goals. As music is interconnected with the rest of lived life and the educational enterprise is elevated above the mundane, music becomes an important aspect of human expression and a spiritual experience, and its value transcends notions of music as a commodity of economic value to be possessed as a material thing.

On the other hand, constantly attending to the group's needs and interests may marginalize individual freedoms, initiatives, and tendencies and inhibit individual learning. Focusing on the social nature of music learning may overemphasize interpersonal relationships and fail to value sufficiently instructional content and the important personal and individual engagement of the learner in music making and taking. Some aspects of musical experience are solitary. If one wants to become a solo pianist, it is necessary to spend a great deal of time alone, and this individual experience is not always shared with other students. While group musical lessons provide opportunities to hear other pianists play, they do not necessarily allow systematic attention to each pianist who may be encountering specific and different challenges than others in the class.[46] A teacher's preferential treatment of students may not allow the requisite individual attention to students accorded in solo studio lessons. In general education, the needs and interests of those who are especially gifted musically may not be kept sufficiently in view in the press of caring for the many who are of more normal or average musical ability.

Among its advantages, the conversational or dialogical quality of instruction and the more egalitarian interrelationship between teachers and students foster divergent interpretations of music and different educational ends. Such an approach relies on and develops imaginative thinking that is intuitive, perceptive, felt, and reasoned. While teachers' styles may differ, being in conversation with students opens the prospect of teachers being learners and prompts students to be actively engaged in the learning process. Because they are spiritual as well as sensual and deeply known rather than superficially felt, such experiences may be transformative. Since this type of instruction affects lives rather than merely conveying information, its impact may ripple out into society.

Nevertheless, the conversational and rhapsodic character of instruction in the community model may not be the most efficient use of time. Considerations of efficiency are particularly acute when instruction is expensive and resources are limited. At present, given a pervasive educational environment of choice-driven consumption, a community model of music education may not be regarded by educational policy makers as sufficiently accountable and product-oriented. Attempting to graft onto community the sorts of assessments expected by these policy makers, especially with respect to summative evaluation of instructional products, may also undermine the model's processual, formative, sensual, and spiritual emphases and its effectiveness. Also, the shortage and expense of resources may hamper efforts to establish community models of music instruction.

To its credit, the humanistic, particularistic, holistic, rhapsodic, conversational, constructivist, hands-on, place-centered, time-bound, and diverse character of the curriculum in community contrasts with present educational realities favoring standardized and product-driven approaches to subject matter. Because aspects of the community model resonate and align with the nature of musical experience and it is reasonable to expect consistency between the nature of the subject matter and the manner of its teaching and learning, musicians welcome these qualities. The arts are not the only subjects in which aesthetic considerations obtain; other subjects can benefit from including an artistic approach to subject matter of the sort this model suggests. Cyclical curricular structures point to the importance of room in all subjects for the qualities exemplified in the community model of curriculum.[47] Teaching the social studies, mathematics, sciences, literatures, languages, and the other arts in these ways opens the prospect of seeing music as a metaphor for what might also be accomplished in these other fields of study.

Still, constructivist approaches to curriculum have had their day in the past.[48] Music's semantic and syntactic density and ambiguity make it difficult to agree on a definitive and developmental order of musical study. Scope and sequence charts of musical concepts do not do justice to music's procedural and performative elements, and cyclical curricula end up being overly theoretical even when their architects hope that they are holistic.[49] On the other hand, the method of working from curriculum repertory where the teacher chooses repertoire with performance skills in mind and then integrates theoretical, historical, and other understandings into this framework may suffer from an insufficiently robust theoretical foundation. As the student moves on to more advanced repertoire, it becomes more and more difficult to arrive at a single, overarching, and holistic frame of reference in which a cyclical curriculum may be cast. The place-centeredness and particularity of the community curriculum may also be insufficiently broad to meet the needs of a multicultural society.[50] Although it celebrates various constituent subcultures, a place-centered curriculum may be balkanized if broader threads are not drawn between it and others. Community insularity may also breed disinterest, disdain, and even contempt for different others and contribute to musical closed-mindedness rather than an openness to different others. Further, the curriculum's emphasis on particularity may overlook broader commonalities between cultures.

Among the advantages of the community model for administration, the relatively flat administrative structure it fosters permits decisions to be made close to the places in the educational system that they impact directly. Creative ideas may come from the least powerful in the system, and the community benefits from social climates and procedures that value and enable input from all of its members. Focusing on the various social processes of music education in the institutions with which it is associated allows teachers to frame policies that are attentive to social as well as psychological matters. Being knowledgeable about social processes, structures, and functions enables those responsible for organizing music instruction to make decisions that contribute to the smooth operation of the system. Cast at a higher level of generality than psychological and physiological matters, community's focus on the social nature of music education also contributes importantly to the theoretical and practical foundations of the field. For example, the model's emphasis on communication and conversation throughout the entire system as one of its principal mechanisms alerts music education policy makers to the dangers of top-down thinking that may stifle genuine conversation, and the need to cultivate environments in which such conversations are welcome and heeded. The model's focus on formative evaluation and criterion-referenced evaluation tempers a widespread preoccupation with summative evaluation and standardized measures of assessment. Since evaluation is predicated on certain common understandings and expectations, creating musical communities that enable music making and taking to flourish is an important means of ensuring that musical traditions thrive.

By the same token, the administrative reality with this model is somewhat messy and fuzzy, and its solutions unclear and difficult to achieve. Flat organizations are not necessarily less oppressive than hierarchical ones, and much hangs on the particular values and purposes that drive the organization. Although it is important to interrogate the operative values and the manner in which they play out socially in an organization, it is also crucial to realize that one's place in and perspective on an organization differs from another's, and what may be apparent to one person may be invisible to the other. These differing perspectives may make it difficult to agree on the nature of the social realities observed and what the responses to those realities ought to be. In the absence of the clear-eyed accountability of the consumption model, community may founder on the shoals of unclear objectives and uncertain outcomes, and its persuasiveness may be dampened in an environment in which the value of accountability trumps that of conversation.

SUMMARY

The pictures of *village* and *community* are mixed. We encounter an evocative metaphor, idealistic in theory and more complex in reality, that inspires as well as allows us to imagine music education in particular ways. The associated model also exhibits a theory of music, teaching, learning, instruction, curriculum, and administration that is framed socially and conversationally. Criticizing these pictures allows us to grasp the ways they inform various aspects of music education and notice their theoretical and practical flaws.

4
ARTIST AND APPRENTICESHIP

From time immemorial, musicians have thought in terms of the *artist* and *apprenticeship* pictures to depict the ways in which wisdom is passed from one generation to another. The objective of this musical education is to prepare musicians at the highest level of performance in a particular musical tradition, whether they be professionals—that is, competent and even exemplary exponents of a musical tradition who make a livelihood in music—or amateurs who enjoy music and pursue it as an avocation. School music has historically included singing and playing music, but music's value as a subject of humanities study has been emphasized over the development of musical skills required by competent musicians. Some criticize music teachers for conflating the ends of the musical and cultural preparation of an informed public and the development of musical skills needed by musicians.[1] Others believe that musical artistry ought to be a principal vehicle and end of school music education, and that this artistry has much to contribute to other school subjects.[2] It is important, then, to think about what these pictures mean for the education of professional musicians and for music in general education.

The overlap and slippage between notions of art and craft suggests that when speaking of the artist, one is, in part, thinking of the craftsperson.[3] I reserve the word *craft* for the more or less predictable skill elements that comprise a piece of music and the word *art* for the whole that these elements come to comprise and that is more than the sum of its parts. To pile metaphor upon metaphor, one way to see art and craft is to think of an egg, in which craft represents a yolk surrounded by the white more closely associated with art and both go together. Still, this metaphor does not do justice to the complexity of the art–craft interrelationship, and it might be better to think of an egg broken, beaten, or baked in a soufflé, where the yolk and white combine in different ways. When musicians have done their job well, a piece of music seems to come alive in mind's ear and eye; it appears as something beyond the mere sights and sounds of musicians musicking.[4] In whatever musical tradition, musicians attempt to create sounds and sights that have a unity and meaning that transcend the separate elements that comprise them and that are grasped both with reference to their constituent musical gestures and to other things beyond music. Their public also regularly passes judgment upon them as if they were something whole and discrete from other things.[5] Those who make and take musics grasp their meaning imaginatively.[6] These phenomena are constructed and understood in ways that require skills, techniques, and crafts to do and undergo. The extent to which what is made and taken is regarded as musical or artistic is a judgment call that is made in the context of a socially construed tradition. Music is what people say that it is, both art and craft, and craft plays an important role in art as art does in craft.

ARTIST

Picturing an artist evokes various images. We might think of the cultured and refined aesthete or the bohemian who lives on the edges of respectability, a starving artist in a garret driven by the need to create, or a wealthy artist in a mansion whose work has made a fortune and who can luxuriate in the pleasures of high society. Some struggle to make ends meet, especially when they are not the few highly paid "stars" or when their work does not have wide appeal. Others achieve wealth when their work is appreciated by their public. Such are the differences among artists that these personal characterizations do not get us very far. I want to avoid the romantic vision of who the artist is to focus on what the artist does.

Vernon Howard paints two different pictures of the artist—Athena and Penelope, named with reference to Greek mythic figures.[7] Athena is the channel or vessel through which inspiration that comes from the gods is transmitted to the phenomenal world in artistic artifacts that seem almost "ready-made" when they appear to the artist. The composition comes to Mozart almost fully formed, and all he needs to do is write it out in full and more or less final form. Penelope, on the other hand, struggles to gradually form her artistic project, working tirelessly and patiently to perfect her creation. Beethoven labors over repeated drafts in order to form a composition that, while inspired, requires prolonged and conscious effort to bring the piece to fruition. Notwithstanding these differences in the extent of their conscious labor, Athena and Penelope render that which is initially subjectively felt into something perceptible to and objectively known by their public. Their work is incomplete without their public's imaginative perception and reception of their artistic creations.

The role and importance of the initial inspiration or impulse in the artistic process may differ from one person to another. In studies of creative and exceptional persons, notwithstanding a great deal of variety, artists share important commonalities.[8] Most creative people report some conscious effort that follows upon their initial inspiration. Athena may accomplish more "work" subconsciously or unconsciously than Penelope, who consciously works and reworks the initial impulse. Some practice is necessary in moving from inspiration to finished product. Practice is the process of imaginatively and practically realizing a "vision of mastery" and bringing the requisite skills to bear on this project that enable artists to realize their visions.[9] Artists need to have a command over all of the skills, habits of mind, and attitudes needed in this particular tradition to achieve the particular creations they have in mind. Composing, improvising, performing, or recording require critical examination, and even where composers claim little conscious effort, there are evidences of changes over time. Had Mozart lived longer, who knows whether or how he might have altered works composed in his youth and early adulthood. Even in Mozart's case, one spots changes in his scores along the way; the inspiration does not appear perfectly in all of its detail. The archetypical case of Beethoven as Penelope is likewise suspect. Some passages in Beethoven's sketches reveal few changes while others evidence critical changes; some things seem to be accomplished almost effortlessly while others need work in perfecting or altering a piece or section of a piece. Musicians seem to be betwixt and between the archetypical positions of Athena and Penelope. They draw on inspiration, sometimes more than others, and they think and act critically and constructively in determining how their compositions, performances, and improvisations need to be made.

Musicians work in the midst of lived life and yet apart from it. Creative thought is impacted by life events in various ways. Some creative people report bursts of imaginative activity that follow rest and repose. Others seem inspired by what they see and hear while actively engaged in musicking or in other things. As with other creative people, musicians are also affected by the critical and public responses to their creations; they may be encouraged by acclaim, discouraged by criticism, or able to work on doggedly irrespective of how their work is received. They may lack confidence or face prejudices and family strictures that make it difficult for some to make their voices heard.[10] In becoming artists, they also imbibe a distinctive way of life. In the past, musicians wore a uniform or livery that symbolized their service for the aristocracy. Vestiges of this reality are still found, for example, in the concert attire that musicians wear to performances. The time-consuming nature of their musical activities means that much of their lives are taken up in doing the work of music, whether it be composing, rehearsing, recording, or learning new music. Their homes may feature libraries of books and recordings, musical instruments and recording equipment, and the sights and sounds of music making, after-concert parties, and sundry celebrations extending into the late evenings. Their glittering lifestyles may prompt some people to regard them as eccentric, dissolute bohemians on the fringes of polite society. At the same time, their promoters' efforts or the public's awe of their musical prowess, virtuosity, or ability to give voice to some of the deepest human yearnings may cause others to elevate them as superhuman "stars."

Artists are devoted to their art partly as a result of the process whereby they become artists, and it is difficult to separate the artist from the process of becoming one. To become an artist necessitates imbibing and internalizing values, beliefs, attitudes, and practices that comprise a whole way of life and creating intersecting webs of associations, realities, and relationships between the artist's life and work that persist throughout a lifetime.[11] This protracted and time-consuming process occurs by imitation, little by little over an extended period of time, and often within the context of a tight-knit community. For example, in times past, a youngster I shall call Thomas may begin musical studies under the tutelage of a distinguished musician at an early age. His parents might apprentice him to a relative who is a professional musician and formally contract for the supervision of Thomas's musical education. Thomas might live with his master in order to be able to spend a great deal of time with him.[12] The master musician gradually brings Thomas along, introduces him to more and more difficult music, and he gradually acquires proficient knowledge about music and the ability to do it, makes the necessary connections with other musicians, patrons, and employers, learns what he needs to know in order to conduct himself professionally, gains a reputation for competence, and eventually goes on to make a successful living as a musician.[13]

We see, then, that among the differing images of the artist, there are those like Athena and others like Penelope. Their work is individual and social, subjective and publicly accessible, forged within a social context and yet apart from it, and the process of their preparation is intimately related to their work as artists. Although the things that artists create may be very different, nevertheless all think imaginatively through the means of their chosen artistic media and traditions.

APPRENTICESHIP

The apprenticeship model has its modern roots in the medieval guild and is given contemporary readings by such writers as Vernon Howard and Donald Schön.[14] In earlier times, musical instruction began at a young age, students joined a tightly-knit group around the teacher, copied the master's work and were "corrected" by him, and gradually acquired the ability to assist the teacher until eventually they became musicians in their own right. Rather than just acquire knowledge about music, students were profoundly impacted by their musical study and imbibed a way of life and a commitment to the tradition bequeathed to them at the same time that they gained a command over the necessary musical beliefs, skills, and attitudes for their particular specialty. Their musical education was both specialized, in terms of particular musical or artistic preparation, and general, in implicating an entire way of life. Apprenticeship can also be seen today. Jay Parini describes how he met the poet Alastair Reid in a Scottish pub and showed him some of his poems. He writes: "Most afternoons, I would pedal down the gravel road to Pilmour Cottage, his house overlooking the North Sea. There we'd drink a pot of tea, while he 'corrected' my work, as he put it." He continues: "I would sit beside him at the kitchen table and watch as whole stanzas fell to the stroke of his pen, as adjectives dissolved into stronger nouns, and limp adverbs were absorbed by more accurate verbs."[15] My own experience of going to weekly "lessons" with Hans-Jørgen Holman resonates with Parini's.[16] Armed with sharpened pencil, seated at his piano beside mine, Holman would peer at my markings on my score and make marks of his own, deconstruct my playing, re-finger passages, reinterpret my renderings, and illustrate alternative interpretations, all driven by his persistent devotion to musical veracity. There never seemed to be an end to his search for the more definitive and expressive interpretation, and for richly informed and meticulous performance.

Among its values, apprenticeship requires time, diligence, repleteness, humility, patience, perseverance, and determination. Its breadth requires a protracted and time-consuming process to accomplish. Since it involves insight, students need to diligently expend effort, practically and thoughtfully, in order to attain exemplary performance at every phase of their development. Repleteness suggests that all that is necessary for musical instruction is provided, including the extensive resources of equipment, money, and skilled teachers required to mount an apprenticeship music program. Individual and small-group instruction by expert teachers who are accomplished musicians in their specialties is resource-intensive, and apprenticeship cannot succeed without these resources. Humility on the students' part is required; they must be willing to learn from and place complete trust and confidence in the teacher in order to become musicians. Because the apprentices may meet formidable challenges along the way and need the fortitude to endure even when it is difficult to learn, perseverance is essential. Students must possess determination in order to overcome obstacles and complete a course of study. Given these stringent requirements, it is possible that many students may not succeed; they may lack the willpower, resources, or opportunities or be otherwise unable or unwilling to attain the level of mastery expected.

Music. Viewing music from the perspective of apprenticeship focuses on its nature as a practice, a tradition, and a discipline. A practice refers to the particular commonly held normative expectations about the things that musicians should believe and do, and the collective skills, techniques, and performances of musicians affiliated with a particular set of musical beliefs. A tradition or heritage of practice develops around each music and is characterized by particular instruments, repertoire, performance practice, and exponents. A discipline arises as rule-sets emerge to impose certain limits on, expectations of, and prescriptions and proscriptions for its exponents and public. These rules also encourage musicians to attain particular standards of exemplary composition, improvisation, performance, or criticism, and correct and punish those who depart from these norms. Regarding music as practice, tradition, or discipline intellectualizes music in its requirements of imaginative constraint and self-control and is associated with notions of schooling, training, socialization, and enculturation as the principal foci of musical education.[17] Schooling refers to the emphasis on teaching the student the traditional beliefs and practices for this particular music and the discipline that undergirds this music.[18] Training is a process that extends throughout one's entire musical life and involves the acquisition of the critical, imaginative, or psychomotor skills needed for exemplary performance.[19] This process assumes that frustrating physical and psychological obstacles may lie in the musician's way in rendering what is imagined into a score, performance, recording, or other means of musical expression.[20] Refining a performance toward an ideal envisaged by the musician requires discipline, and the ideal seems to become more elusive the closer one gets to an exemplary performance. Socialization entails the student's acquiring expected ways of interrelating with other musicians. It, too, may happen over a lifetime and experienced musicians may need to be re-socialized when they find themselves in new circumstances. Enculturation requires seeing music as a way of life and as a part of the wider culture; it is ongoing throughout musicians' lives as they encounter other cultures and musics and are changed by them.

Although this view of music may be associated with the classical traditions of East and West, it is also found in African drumming traditions, jazz, and other popular musics; these are also often elitist in their rigorous demands of musicians and requirements for the extensive development of musical powers.[21] Musics that have developed a history, extensive repertoire, complex techniques, and performing and teaching lineage may require years of devoted and intensive study and musical commitment to master and may become less accessible to ordinary exponents. Inevitably, this move separates these musics from the greater mass of people as it puts their performance out of reach and more clearly demarcates and separates performers from audiences.

Teaching. Thinking of teaching within the frame of apprenticeship places a burden on the teacher or master who is charged with training, schooling, socializing, and enculturating students in this musical practice. Like the consumption and unlike the community models, this approach to teaching is directive, and communication is principally from teacher to student rather than conversational in nature. Unlike a consumption-oriented regime, apprenticeship requires teachers to be exponents of the musical traditions they teach and to design approaches that fit the particular students under their care. Teaching is student-centered in the sense that the teacher seeks to bring students into alignment with the beliefs and practices of the tradition, but unlike in the community model, the teacher directs students toward traditional practices and beliefs rather than encouraging them to construct their own disparate realities. Thinking of discipline in terms of encouraging normative conduct and punishing deviance prompts teachers to encourage students' development and ensure their compliance with traditional rules.[22]

Schön pictures some of the ways in which a teacher might go about this process in individual or small-group lessons.[23] In a sort of "backward" or "responsive" teaching, the teacher reacts to what the student has already prepared. Imagine that the teacher has assigned a particular piece for a student I shall call Marie to learn and memorize by the following lesson.[24] What happens in that next lesson is the teacher's diagnosis of the precise nature and problems in Marie's performance and determination of the best approach to the problem. The teacher hopes to balance the claims of critical commentary on the one hand, and the challenge of motivating and inspiring her to practice more effectively and diligently on the other. The teacher begins to take apart various passages of the score, focusing on the most important things first and seeking to make a difference in Marie's performance.[25] Whatever the results, dramatic or marginal, the teacher follows diagnosis with remedial action and prescriptions for further practice designed to improve Marie's performance. This tripartite process of diagnosis, remediation, and prescription is a rich view of teaching that connects past performance with present difficulties and future potential. While beginning with what Marie comes to perform or has accomplished in preparation for this lesson, the teacher focuses on her future development, responds to Marie's capacities and challenges, and points her toward normative practice.

How do music teachers accomplish this work? In short, they show and, sometimes, tell.[26] In terms of showing, they utilize demonstrations that model or exemplify normative practice and require students' undivided attention to intuit. The point of a demonstration is a command-representation for the student to do such-and-such. It shows students how they should do this particular thing and directs them toward the rules and norms that guide the practice of a particular musical tradition.[27] In Western classical music, examples are often accompanied by theoretical analyses of what is happening; whereas in the East, teachers may simply play and/or sing, and students watch and listen intently in hopes of figuring things out intuitively without analyzing them rationally. When demonstrations are accompanied by telling, teachers often employ figurative language and technical discourse.[28] Listening in on such lessons, one might hear a great many metaphors as teachers seek short-cuts to immediate intuitive and imaginative understandings and practices. Later, as a practice settles for the student, a teacher may begin to elucidate the technical language that describes what the student can now do. What may originally be a metaphor may become frozen as a technical term.[29] This teaching is also very gradual, additive, and linear. Unlike consumption, its pace cannot be preprogrammed; rather it follows at the speed at which each apprentice is able to achieve competency at every point in the process. It is necessarily individualized, since students encounter different challenges along the way. This mastery-driven teaching necessitates that teachers design precisely the right challenges for every student at precisely the right times around the principle of antecedence; that is, the teacher attends to whatever is needed before something else can be successfully accomplished.[30] Nor is antecedence necessarily standardized, but the differing individual strengths and weaknesses of students need to be taken into account in determining the precise order of activities.[31]

Learning. How does this learning take place? As a teacher, I confess that how students turn into musicians is something of a mystery. Although I may not fully understand how this process works, I take advantage of the fact that it does occur, little by little over a long period of time. Not all artists in a particular tradition think and act exactly alike, but although they produce divergent creations, they learn how to think normatively in the traditions in which they work. Historically, much of an apprentice's work was spent in copying set exercises and pieces at progressively higher levels of difficulty. Imitation is among the principal ways in which musicians learn their craft and acquire the "know-how" to be able to be guided by rules without the need to follow them slavishly. Since this learning is very practical or "hands-on" and requires knowing how to go on and do such-and-such, a master musician must be able to demonstrate these skills to the apprentice. Howard concurs that the apprentices' task is something of a mystery; they do and don't know what to look for and how to do what is required of them.[32] Still, by trusting the master musician, neophytes gradually come to know and grasp what they need to know. As the apprentices follow their master's example, a transformation takes place that step by step renders them competent exponents of the musical tradition. Since much of the learning is in the context of a community of other apprentices, the process of making the artist is accomplished publicly as well as privately.

Howard describes four types of learning evident in apprenticeship: instruction, example, practice, and reflection.[33] Instruction refers to the wisdom and knowledge that teachers pass on to their students. Teacher talk in this model is invested with great importance, because the teacher stands as a priest or mediator between the student and the tradition the teacher professes. Students are dependent upon the teacher, who personifies the tradition, knows its lore, and brings it and its exponents to life in memorable stories, aphorisms, or proverbs. Examples may be of various sorts, including exemplar, sample, model, caricature, and anti-example. Exemplar is preeminent, because it constitutes a means of directed and directive showing and telling; the teacher expects the student to follow suit. Still, other kinds of examples are also used. Samples, such as repertoire excerpts, enable teachers to introduce a wider array of repertoire than might be otherwise possible. Models are scaled-down instances of scores that can help to simplify an otherwise complex task. Caricatures are sometimes used by teachers to overemphasize a particular point and thereby draw students' attention to things that they are doing or should not do. Anti-example goes even further than caricature, doing the opposite of what is required and thereby pointing the student even more firmly in a different direction.[34] Practice is one of the most important elements of apprenticeship, since it necessitates the learner's active engagement with the music as she or he strives toward a vision of mastery; it requires intentional effort of an imaginative and intellectually concentrated sort in order to improve the ways the student thinks and does, musically, in the quest for ideals that change over time as the student moves to more advanced levels of performance.[35] Reflection is the important intellectual work of calling to mind and pondering what one has performed. It may occur as pre-thinking, in advance of a performance; intuitive-in-the-midst-of-performance imaginative thinking; and critical thinking after a performance.[36]

In counterpoint with this quartet of active means of learning, I have added my own, namely, osmosis, observation, participation, and sensibility.[37] Osmosis refers to the tendency for things to sink deep into one's soul as one undergoes certain events. Observation refers to the learner's copying of salient features of the teacher's example. Participation refers to simply being a member of a group where one does not necessarily practice consciously in a directed way but comes to be able to do certain things as a result of engaging in certain rituals. Sensibility refers to one's physical, emotional, and intellectual engagement with this music.[38] My own contrapuntal quartet reveals a receptive quality to learning that constitutes undergoing as well as doing.[39] Such learning takes time and cannot be hastened according to predetermined timetables. Rather, it is based on the time it takes a particular student, through active and receptive learning, to come to an understanding and expertise characteristic of a particular level of development. In this respect, the values of apprenticeship learning stand in stark contrast to those of consumption learning, in which students are expected to achieve particular predetermined outcomes in order to satisfy the claims of public accountability.

Such learning relies on the learner's insight and is emotional and bodily, driven by intellectual judgment and instinct. Its scope is wide and holistic and it repudiates approaches that would atomize learning into small and discrete components or dichotomize inner and outer, subjective and objective, mind and body, and active and receptive engagement. Given the amorphous and wide-ranging nature of this learning, apprentices are faced with the challenge of getting a feel for doing this musical thing.[40] When learners initially encounter a complex array of ambiguous phenomena, knowing what to attend to is a mystery. All gradually becomes clear as teachers appeal to learners' insights to glean the salient features of interest in particular instances and figure out which specific things they should attend to and do now. In contrast with teacher-directed approaches to learning that regard students as empty vessels waiting to be filled, this model relies on the students' insight and active engagement in imaginatively apprehending what the teacher is attempting to convey and in making sense of the teacher's directions (both shown and told) as they come to their own grasp of knowledge.[41] Whereas consumption learning assumes that the student will "get it" if the teacher finds the right prepackaged program, apprenticeship learning relies on student insight as a learning mechanism.[42]

Instruction. Although it might seem that teacher–student interaction in terms of apprenticeship evokes the community model, communication is mainly from the teacher "down" to the students. The nature of the interaction shifts from a more egalitarian one in community to a hierarchical relationship in which the master welds together an often tight-knit and loyal group of apprentices, much as the king might fashion his court. Apprentices also differ in terms of their experience and the work that they can do for the teacher, and so they, likewise, are hierarchically arranged in order of experience and prowess. It is not unusual for teachers to expect their more experienced students to teach their juniors; this practice allows a master to mentor these assistants as they hone their teaching skills and, through teaching others, gain important insights into their own performance.[43] Respect and loyalty bind apprentices to each other and to their master. These bonds are often life-long, so that students afterward hold the teacher in respect and devotion for what he or she has given them.[44] Although the social distance between teacher and students might be greater than in the community model, the experience nevertheless forges deep personal relationships, grounded in the respect of the students for the teacher. These respectful relationships sometimes grow into friendships later in life.

Teachers and students often affiliate with particular schools and trace their lineage backward through generations of musician-teachers.[45] The longer this lineage, the more outstanding the musicians within it appear, and the more esoteric the knowledge, the more distinguished it is seen to be; by association, musicians claim some of the aura of the tradition to which they belong. Distinctive and particular beliefs and practices characterize Western and Eastern classical schools, and particular "secrets" are protected by its members, sometimes by means of marriage ties as musical knowledge is passed on through family generations.[46] Musicians pride themselves on their particular lineages, and an *esprit de corps* develops among master and apprentices. In our time, schools that were once distinctive are becoming more international; but vestiges of these differences still remain.[47] Likewise, the provenance of musical instruments carries special value whether associated with their particular maker or the musicians who played them. For example, while in London, England, I acquired Clifford Curzon's practice piano, a vintage Bechstein grand.[48] The musician who assisted me in my search for an instrument could name pianos across the City of London that had been played or owned by famous pianists. Having Curzon's piano does not necessarily make me a better pianist, but the aura of the pianist who once played it seems to cover this instrument; it is no longer a mere piano but a special instrument with a distinguished history, and I am its present caretaker.

Curriculum. Since apprenticeship is about the hands-on preparation of practitioners of a particular musical tradition, the curriculum is both practical and theoretical, general and specific. A musical tradition is framed around a repertory of particular pieces or rituals. Knowing the pieces, styles, musicians, and theoretical and historical backgrounds of this tradition, and being able to carry them out, is of central concern to the apprenticeship curriculum.[49] Musicians in today's Western classical tradition draw on a rich musical repertory. Although some orchestral instruments such as the tuba, harp, and saxophone have a more limited repertoire, it is increasing through such means as commissions, arrangements, and transcriptions. Performers on such instruments are also expected to have a broad knowledge of the sweep of the entire tradition. Likewise jazz, which was born in the twentieth century, already has a distinguished line of musicians, tunes, genres, styles, and links with other musical traditions.

The curriculum centers on music, and students engage the repertoire primarily by doing it. They typically begin with the simplest and most basic elements of the tradition and work toward its most complex and advanced elements. Even within a particular tradition, musicians may need to acquire specialized skills as well as skills that they may share with others. For example, although the styles in which organists learn to improvise differ from those that jazz musicians employ, all these musicians need to internalize the formulae, idioms, gestures, and tropes that are passed down orally from teacher to student and attain particular requisite improvisatory standards. They may attain these skills either through undergoing extensive formal preparation of exercises, etudes, and pieces that develop the requisite skills or by taking an informal and even short and direct approach that moves quickly to other things. The individuality of these approaches makes it difficult to mandate which specific things must be in the curriculum and more likely that such a curriculum will be spelled out in terms of general repertoire and traditional standards. The normative character of the tradition requires the student to meet the profession's standards. This position contrasts with a community curriculum, in which the student may have more freedom to diverge from the norm. At first glance apprenticeship seems more akin to the consumption model, where curriculum is conceived primarily in terms of subject matter to be learned rather than knowledge to be constructed by the student. On further reflection, there is an important difference in the attitude to the subject matter between these two models. Rather than a commodity for consumption, subject matter in apprenticeship is regarded as invaluable and of inestimable spiritual worth, and the curriculum takes a mythic approach to the musical tradition that emphasizes its great value.[50] This curriculum also encompasses living a way of life and covers subject matter some of which can and some of which cannot be fully codified. Without living the musician's life, one catches only a part of the understanding needed. For this reason, many teachers expect their students to live with them or in close proximity, to perform, compose, or teach at the same time as they undertake their formal studies, and to spend time learning things that go beyond the formal curriculum. Artist teachers often expect their students to attend concerts and other cultural events, socialize together, and undertake special courses of instruction that are not necessarily mandated in their curricula.[51]

Administration. Since the founding of modern European and Western conservatories in the late eighteenth and nineteenth centuries,[52] the apprenticeship model has been in common use in conservatories, music schools, and colleges. Administering musical apprenticeship in large organizations is obviously more complex than the simpler administrative arrangements of earlier times when a teacher might found an independent studio and accept private pupils. Now, musicians are typically trained in sometimes large conservatories designed principally for the preparation of performers in classical traditions. In the United States as in other countries, university faculties, departments, and schools of music sometimes bridge the traditional university role of preparing musicians academically and the conservatory role of cultivating music performers. This marriage is not always easy; the conservatory brings to bear professional music standards and the academy applies its own scholarly standards, and these interests are sometimes in tension. For example, while a performer might wish to spend extensive time practicing, the academy makes other intellectual demands that curtail the time available for practice; whereas the scholar might prefer to spend time in research, the conservatory makes practical demands regarding musicianship that limit the time available for intellectual pursuits in music.

Organizing music education according to the apprenticeship model is a complex undertaking that needs to be done flawlessly in order to ensure a smoothly operating school. Alongside individual and small-group performing classes are a host of theoretical, historical, pedagogical, compositional, and technical classes and small and large ensemble rehearsals. There are also the challenges of operating performance facilities that showcase solo, chamber, and large ensemble performances, operas, musicals, and ballets. Even for a small music program, scheduling all of these musical activities is a daunting task, especially as the self-same music teachers and students are likely to be participants in multiple events. Apprenticeship makes particular demands on administrators. They must provide for extensive individual or small group teacher–student interaction; a prolonged and significant time commitment; dedicated spaces that permit a sense of distinctiveness, even isolation from other subject areas, and where students can regularly gather inside and outside of formal instruction; and a curricular organization that permits extended contacts between music teachers and students throughout the entire calendar year. Such spaces and times need to enable formal instruction to meld into informal settings in which teaching and learning can continue. Because apprenticeship extends over a prolonged time and relies on the close bonds forged between teacher and apprentice, it is important to arrange settings in which students can work with the same teachers for long periods of time. This musical instruction is also necessarily organized around qualified musicians who are specialists rather than generalists.

These stringent requirements necessitate a sympathetic administration with the resources and will to ensure that the music program receives strong support and all the needed resources are in place for the musical education of professional musicians.[53] American conservatories that revolve about performing music of the Western classical tradition typically focus on the advanced development of musicians; they sometimes have preparatory departments that allow the early training of musicians on their campuses; and students advance by passing courses of instruction provided by their faculties.[54] In a different vein, the British conservatory tradition (extended to Australia, New Zealand, Canada, among other parts of the former British Empire and Commonwealth of Nations) provides for graded instruction from elementary to advanced levels where advancement is by means of examination. Here, students can study with private teachers of their choice and are examined at various sites by conservatory faculty or affiliated examiners. This widespread system of graded instruction is organized around set repertoire and theoretical, aural, and historical skills that are prepared by students for examination.[55]

Standards play an important formative and summative role in apprenticeship, and it is essential to evaluate teachers and students in performance settings. This differs from the accountability of the consumption model, where music is evaluated with reference to fiscal and other criteria. Rather, accountability is assessed in terms of the purposes, methods, and ends of musical education; it is construed musically and determined with reference to particular musical traditions. This intrinsically musical evaluation, by musicians, and where the musical standards are specified by exponents of this musical tradition, is a very different matter than the sort of evaluation conducted by those who are not necessarily expert musicians and where other extra-musical considerations come into play. Given that apprenticeship is conducted within the framework of a tradition, such standards are presumably public; that is, common expectations are more or less shared by its exponents. This common sensibility reveals itself, for example, in audition rating scales that widely use some of the same criteria, including intonation, note accuracy, interpretative aspects such as dynamics, phrasing, tempi, and articulation, and global categories, to assess overall impressions of the performance-as-a-whole. It is also common to see groups or panels of musicians adjudicating recitals, juries, competitions, and auditions in the hope that a broader sense of the quality of this performance may help to mitigate idiosyncratic evaluations by any particular judge. When musicians evaluate performances, compositions, or papers, they act as the gatekeepers of their traditions so as to protect the profession from usurpers or others who would undermine its work.[56] As an apprenticeship system concerns itself with ensuring that the musical tradition prospers in the future, evaluation serves the dual purpose of helping students to become musicians and weeding out those who ought not be musicians.

CRITIQUE

Apprenticeship forms the model for much music teaching, particularly that focused on composition, improvisation, and performance, and it is clear that musicians value its contributions. This is a musical approach to music education conducted for the sake of music and adjudicated primarily with reference to artistic values. Its practical emphasis, necessarily skill-centered in its focus on the ability to do or make music rather than just think about it, ensures that music is continually brought alive and that traditions continue from one generation to the next.

Notwithstanding its widespread influence, its musical tradition-centeredness also means that it transmits wisdom from the past, rather than transforming that wisdom in the present and into the future, and this orientation may make it prone to excessive conservatism. In this respect, it may be less effective in prompting innovative approaches to music making when change is needed. Its practical thrust may also downplay the importance of intellectual or abstract aspects of music that are evident, for example, in listening to or researching music.

Among its advantages, teaching within the apprenticeship model relies on a personal transmission from teachers to students from one generation to the next. Its emphasis on training, schooling, socialization, and enculturation encompasses a broad preparation in musical and artistic practice. Since teachers also need to be expert in what they teach, music education is not left to amateurs, generalists, and those with little care for, appreciation of, and skills in a musical tradition. Rather, students have access to expert knowledge, and the expectations of them are raised as a result. Teacher expectations significantly impact student performance, and so it is likely that knowledgeable music teachers have high expectations of their students, who may then achieve more than they might otherwise do.

Nevertheless, not only does this approach to teaching leave insufficient opportunity for student construction of knowledge and divergence from normative standards, but it may be the wrong model for teaching in circumstances where student purposes are simply recreational. Think of the difference between becoming an athlete who can compete in the Olympic games and becoming physically fit to live a life directed toward other goals. Using this model indiscriminately for all students in general education may be like expecting all students to prepare to become Olympic athletes; this is obviously unrealistic. Since it is conceived mainly in terms of training requisite skills required for musicianship, the time and effort required may be off-putting to amateurs who wish only to dabble in music or learn about it and who are less interested in acquiring the skills for doing it at an advanced level. This is especially the case where the skills taught are more or less inaccessible to students because of the sheer amount of time needed to practice them. Classical guitarists have expressed to me their frustration at the attitudes of many of their students who may be interested in learning the guitar mainly for recreational purposes such as accompanying popular songs and who are reluctant to practice and develop the technique required for classical guitar performance. Since the violin, viola, cello, and double bass likewise require considerable technical prowess before they produce good sound, students who do not want to put in the time and effort may resist a teacher who wants to develop a solid technique in these instruments and a knowledge of some of the best repertoire for them. It is easy to understand why instruments that require the serious purpose that apprenticeship demands are less popular than those that are much more immediately grasped and for which an extended apprenticeship seems less pressing. These disconnects between teachers who rely on apprenticeship and students who have little use for it may be part of the reason why string teaching lags behind the teaching of other instruments in public education even though artistry may be a desirable attribute of general education. Life-long learning may also be jeopardized when young people are excluded from musical education too soon, or come to believe early in life that they do not have the requisite abilities or interests to succeed as professional musicians.

On the bright side, the active elements of learning through instruction, practice, example, and reflection, complemented by "passive" or "receptive" elements of learning—namely, osmosis, participation, observation, and sensibility—provide a wide variety of ways by which to learn music. Students have the example not only of their teachers but of their more advanced fellows, and this learning deepens and broadens their experiences and reinforces the skills needed to succeed musically. Contextualizing learning in this way, by approaching the subject through a need to know it, is motivating to students. Gradually taking over more advanced and complex musical tasks as students are able (taking advantage of readiness to learn) seems suited to the learning of practical endeavors. As they advance, students are more apt to think of their teachers as mentors or coaches and regard their musical lives dynamically, in the sense of "becoming" more skilled in and knowledgeable about music.

On the dark side, one might criticize the elitist stance of this model that demands high levels of aptitude, ability, and devotion on the part of students. It is possible that the best teachers and students will find each other, but, for a host of reasons, this may not always be the case. Those students who cannot choose, do not have the requisite ability, or choose not to commit the time and effort are ejected from the system, fall by the wayside, or imagine themselves to be "unmusical." The directive nature of apprenticeship teaching may foster student apathy or excessive dependence on the teacher. In such circumstances there is also the possibility of student powerlessness, especially where teachers are abusive, inconsiderate, or inhumane. Values of student patience, perseverance, and effort toward future hoped-for rewards may be out of tune with contemporary society and lived life.

To its credit, apprenticeship is also a broadly based and holistic instructional approach. When combined with the search for musical wisdom, its practical thrust constitutes a potentially holistic approach with broad instructional objectives. Sharing elements of a community view of music teaching, apprenticeship relies on direct contact between teacher and students, and among students as more senior students show their more junior fellows how to go on in music. As with the consumption model, this approach is driven by teacher and student choice, since apprentices (or their guardians) choose those experts from whom they wish to learn, and teachers choose those students they wish to teach. As I have shown, the nature of the interaction may differ from both the consumption and community models, in that it is guided by musical values and the teacher is in the position of master in relation to disciples, rather than a more egalitarian position as a fellow learner in the community. The shift to mentoring or coaching as instruction unfolds is also a time-tested means of working with experienced and talented students. Its hands-on character vests instruction with importance and relevance to the rest of lived existence.

Still, instruction is problematic in several respects. The teacher–student relationship is a mainly one-way communication that may not provide sufficient feedback to the teacher. As such, it may be insufficiently nurturing of students. Without students being able to express their ideas and feelings, a teacher may miss important cues about what should be accomplished next. The model's reliance on some measure of teacher and student choice and the privileged musical knowledge and wisdom possessed by this teacher means that only those the teacher believes to be worthy may come to know it. This possibility vests enormous power in the teacher's individual determination of student abilities, aptitudes, and potentials. Its hierarchical and masculine character may be less appealing to some girls and women (as well as some boys and men) who might prefer and thrive in more egalitarian and less daunting approaches and environments. Like all human relationships, the personal interconnections between teacher and student are also fragile. Much wisdom is embodied in the teacher, and a tradition may be lost when this personal connection is severed; precious knowledge is lost with a generation's loss. This fragility of musical transmission in apprenticeship requires constant attention to ensuring that music education remains strong across the generations.

Among its advantages, the curricular focus on repertoire and skills entails knowing how to go on as a musician and do music. Aside from these practical skills, the subject matter is also treated broadly with reference to historical, theoretical, aural, and other technical knowledge and wisdom. The teacher is steeped in a tradition and conveys to students its preciousness and the importance of fidelity to it. Since the objective of this curriculum is to help students to attain competent and even exemplary practice, expectations of students are undeniably high and even grueling. They demand commitment and insight as well as a grasp of the things that are conveyed by the teacher. Students' construction of learning is constrained by the normative claims of traditional practice as they are brought to internalize its myths, rituals, beliefs, attitudes, and techniques. The arrangement of musical subject matter from elementary to advanced levels is construed performatively and rationally according to the pedagogical principle of antecedence; that is, the teacher determines what needs to be learned (and done) before something else can be learned (and done).

As to its disadvantages, apprenticeship may not be attractive for students for whom acquiring skills to become exponents of a tradition is not their motivation for musical study, and those who might wish to experience it in more accessible and immediate ways. Not bent on marketing its attractiveness to consumers, apprenticeship may appeal only to a limited group of students whose purpose in studying music is serious and who are ready for its discipline, patience, and hard work. Its curriculum also risks becoming too technical and atomistic; its focus on musical skills can render it inaccessible, because it is often more time-consuming to come to know how to do something than know about it. Should the tradition in which the teacher is grounded differ from those to which students subscribe, it is possible that the subject matter that teachers wish students to learn may be unattractive to them. Surrounded by a pervasive climate of consumption, this curriculum may seem out of date and irrelevant to students.

Administratively, the cellular organization of apprenticeship contributes much to music education. It shares a great deal in common with the community model, although each of the cells may be more hierarchically organized than in community. Historically, this structure has been an effective means of musical transmission. It relies on extended personal contact between teachers and students. This intimacy allows teachers to carefully plan an instructional process that keeps students' interests and needs at its center while also pointing them toward the practice of the tradition's exponents. These small groups also enable the development of friendships and networks of colleagues that may be carried into later life. Notwithstanding the hierarchical organization of each cell, mutual respect rather than mutual affection is relied upon as a basis for musical instruction.

By the same token, apprenticeship is expensive in terms of the resources needed to carry it off successfully. Organizing cellular instructional units is likewise problematic. The attrition from music programs built on this model may undermine music education by suggesting that it is really for the few rather than the many. Also, the disjunction between what students generally want and are willing and able to do musically and the heavy demands of an elite music profession is not lost on administrators who are not musicians. When teachers in some musical specialties are in short supply, administrators may second teachers who are not experts in these areas to fill the vacant positions. Music teachers are often educated in institutions in which musical considerations are not always preeminent, and even though there is some measure of independence on the part of the music school, conservatory, or college, apprenticeship is often vulnerable to the claims of a more general if not also superficial study of music by many students. Accrediting agencies to which musical institutions are often beholden may also be politicized, and their standards do not always benefit conditions of apprenticeship.[57] To the extent that conservatories and schools of music are located within institutions with other academic or religious ties, the primacy of musical considerations may be challenged. Clashes or tensions between musical and other purposes and ends occur whenever and wherever music education as apprenticeship is situated within larger organizations whose ends are not necessarily musical. A tug-of-war for control over the music programs may pit musicians against other areas of the academy. For example, in denominationally affiliated liberal arts colleges in the

United States in which music serves religious as well as musical ends, there is a tension between its strictly musical aims and the college's legitimate claims on music as a functional aid to worship. Likewise, in state-supported schools other political objectives may come into play that challenge the primacy of musical objectives. Practically speaking, the resource-intensive quality of apprenticeship music education places particular burdens on administrators charged with securing the needed resources for their conservatories, departments, faculties, and schools. Where administrators refuse to supply the necessary resources, the musical program is jeopardized and, to allow it to function optimally, it becomes increasingly necessary to create an independent endowment. My own school employs a professional staff whose purpose is to generate additional revenue and financial support for the music program, and the dean is judged especially regarding his ability to generate sufficient funding for the school's offerings. These realities place music administrators in a bind; they seek to protect the musicians in the school so that they may do all that is deemed necessary musically, and they must also demonstrate accountability to other administrators for whom musical considerations are only a part of their concern.

SUMMARY

In sum, the pictures of artist and apprenticeship are evocative especially of the preparation of music professionals. Seen figuratively and literally, they contribute to and detract from music education. Much hangs on the particulars of the situations they illumine. While these pictures doubtless have been important to music education historically, they give us pause concerning how we might think about and do music education in the future. In particular, they raise questions about the extent to which the artist and apprenticeship pictures should be reserved solely for the preparation of professional musicians, or how they might be applied more broadly to music in general education.

5
REVOLUTIONARY AND TRANSGRESSION

The *revolutionary* and *transgression* pictures depict sometimes violent moments of history, upheavals of the accepted order of things, dislocation, violence, suffering, death, grief for what has been lost, and fear of what the new order may bring or of the retribution those who work for or resist change may exact. These pictures are heroic in their larger-than-life quality that is heightened with a brightness and darkness and drawn in starker contrasts than ordinary lived life. They are emotionally and morally charged in the revolutionaries' commitments to enacting ideals that would dramatically change the present state of things and turn it on its head. Even in the absence of assurance that they will succeed in their quest, revolutionaries struggle to achieve their ideals.[1] Their struggle has a moral imperative, especially when cast between the forces of good and evil, light and darkness.[2] The possibilities of tragedy and revolutionary heroism and selflessness in the face of almost certain defeat imbue these pictures with an emotionality that is gripping and even inspirational. Their sometimes disturbing images and powerful intellectual and emotional associations draw us in to contemplate them.

REVOLUTIONARY

A revolutionary is a radical who departs from tradition and introduces a major change, often political in its challenge or resistance to a powerful establishment. Beyond thinking of the revolutionary as merely *against* the accepted order of things, we should also recognize the revolutionary as being *for* a marked change in a dramatically different direction. The revolutionary believes in particular ideas that are articulated rationally as an ideology by which to live. Not driven by passion alone, he or she is intellectually committed to a particular vision, a new order of things, a better world, and ideals that may even be impractical and utopian.[3] This is true of revolutionary moments in American music education, such as the introduction of musical instruction into the public schools of Boston in the nineteenth century, and the Tanglewood Declaration and original MAYDAY "manifesto" in the twentieth.[4] Although they met with mixed success, these politically charged and ideologically grounded movements illustrate revolutionary thought and practice that resisted the status quo and sought to create a better reality.

The revolutionary seeks a wholesale transformation of the present order of things. Where there is oppression, the revolutionary seeks freedom; where there is disempowerment and disenfranchisement, the revolutionary seeks empowerment and enfranchisement. Feminism, for example, revolts against the entrenched power of patriarchy, while civil rights activism rebels against the pervasive exclusion of people of certain color, age, religion, ethnicity, political affiliation, language, or sexual preference parameters. Both movements seek the full and equal participation of all the members of society. The changes envisaged are so profound and pervasive that the revolution necessarily implies a wholesale redistribution of power. Since powerful people do not relinquish their power willingly and are difficult to dislodge, rising against them and their interests and institutionalized beliefs and practices risks retaliation, punishment, and even death.

Among musical revolutionaries, I think of Fred Ho, jazz musician and composer, avid "Marxist," and "self-described 'radical, revolutionary artist.'"[5] Ho's edited essay collection, his opera *Warrior Sisters* (he believes that a matriarchy should replace patriarchy as a stage toward the establishment of true communism) as an "homage to female rebels," his lifestyle, in which he repudiates mass-produced clothing and capitalism in favor of his own personally designed clothing or body-painted nudity, his performances (with the Brooklyn Jazz Quartet among his various bands), and his rejection of monogamy (except in relation to his baritone saxophone) evidence a lived life devoted to musical and social revolution.[6] The sounds he produces are, according to Myra Mayman, "among the most aggressive, awakening music I've ever heard in a concert hall" that "grabbed you by the back of the neck. He was trying to explode things, to tear tops off of ordinary experience."[7] Pictured in green against a green backdrop, clad only in specially designed boots with saxophone strategically placed in front of him, he is quoted as saying,

"I prefer to live my life as if I lived in a rain forest."[8] He sees himself as carrying on the work of revolution and challenging the musical status quo.

The revolutionary's commitment to particular beliefs and practices goes well beyond mere intellectual assent to take on an almost evangelistic fervor that plays out in the phenomenal world. Since revolutionary ideals may be held as *a priori* and self-evident truths, belief is in search of reason. Revolutionaries are passionately attached to particular ideas that they regard as self-evident and that, while justified rationally, they feel to be true irrespective of supporting argument or evidence. For example, the assumption that all human beings are precious and worthy of dignity and respect may seem obvious to a revolutionary and require no justification. The emotional attachment to this, among other, ideals may make it difficult to disprove assumptions that are taken as self-evident. These passionate commitments readily become dispositions to act in particular ways. Since reason may be overcome by emotion, it may be difficult to temper and restrain the revolutionary process. As the revolution takes on a life of its own, revolutionaries can be caught up in extremist action and swept into a current that goes far beyond what they originally intended in repudiating and overthrowing the old state of affairs, sometimes violently.

Revolutionaries are the prophets who articulate certain ideals and utopias and defy the powerful others who stand against them. Given the normative character of the ideals and even utopias to which revolutionaries aspire, they evaluate actions in the phenomenal world with regard to these ideals. Where the values of liberation, personal and collective empowerment, compassion, and fidelity are absent, the revolutionary sets about to implant them in the phenomenal world. This inevitably leads to collision with supporters of the status quo.

Revolutionaries are often surrounded by like-minded others with whom they work collectively and collaboratively.[9] Working collaboratively is a source of mutual support, solidarity, and assistance in carrying forward the work of radical change, overthrowing often widely accepted traditions and shibboleths of the past, and ushering in a hoped-for world. The ideal of the "promised land," a place where evil is overcome by good, where justice, mercy, freedom, and truth prevail, and where pain, suffering, evil, and death are no more, is often to be seen in revolutionary thought. American slaves, for example, longed to "cross over Jordan" into a place where all would be made right. They not only articulated this vision in their songs and spirituals but fought and died for it; they struggled over centuries to overcome the tyranny of their enslavement and the oppression of their second-class status. Had they been alone, they might never have gained the insight or courage to persist until their enslavement and marginalization in society was overcome. The long march of people of color and their supporters from Selma to Montgomery, Alabama, to demand the right to equality with white Americans is a high moment in this drama.[10] The American project of freedom is still unfinished, and ongoing civil rights struggles play out in public and private spaces, in familial, economic, political, musical, and religious institutions.[11] As I write, three crosses have been burned near Durham, North Carolina.[12] These burnings (historically associated with the white supremacist Ku Klux Klan, infamous for its persecution particularly of people of color) demonstrate the persistence of bigotry and hatred against people of color. Some fundamentalists would like to return women to the domestic sphere and reempower men in the belief that the subjugation of women is a divinely appointed state of affairs. Those of differing sexuality who are presently contesting the right of all people to be fully present and participate fully in society without discrimination have been strongly rebuffed in some state legislatures in the United States, even as they have been supported in some others.

The violence that often characterizes revolutions arises because passions run deep and resistance is often strong. Revolutionaries may be fighting for their very lives, and they see the sacrifices they make as a small price to pay for ideals and values of such moment and importance. The powerful with whom they struggle may also consider the status quo worth preserving and may be unwilling to give up or share their power or rearrange a present order of things that benefits them. Although some revolutions may be nonviolent (witness the late twentieth-century and early twenty-first-century uprisings in the Czech Republic and Ukraine, respectively), others involve force. There is also a sense by those embroiled in the conflict that the impact of the struggle on those not immediately involved but nevertheless caught up unintentionally in it is unfortunate but unavoidable; to some extent, the end justifies the means. This "collateral damage" is evidenced in the major political and cultural revolutions of the modern era. Although Martin Luther King Jr.'s nonviolent civil rights movement in the United States contrasts with Malcolm X's espousal of violence as a tool for persuading the white establishment in the United States to repudiate discrimination against people of color, violence still ensued.[13] This violence, exemplified in the assassination of King and others connected with this struggle, illustrates that even if the revolutionary's intention is to act nonviolently, casualties may result, and those who are not directly involved may be implicated nonetheless.

The risks of revolution are often high, and isolation, violence, imprisonment, and even death may come to those who propagate, participate in, and resist it. Punishment and destruction take various forms. Beside physical retribution, attacks on a revolutionary's reputation may result in humiliation and discrediting. The establishment's power is such that the odds of succeeding at the revolution are small. Revolutionaries require courage and persistence in the face of concerted opposition, but these qualities may not come easily to people. Refusing to acquiesce to the status quo and withstanding punishment for one's beliefs and practices may conflict with a desire for a happy and peaceful existence. Few may have the independent-mindedness, heart, and stomach for it. Revolutionaries feel deeply about those things for which they struggle, and they are willing to count the cost, accept the risks, and act courageously in spite of the consequences.[14]

TRANSGRESSION

Transgression of the status quo is a powerful theme in the work of such educational writers as Neil Postman and Charles Weingartner, Ivan Illich, Paulo Freire, Maxine Greene, Jane Roland Martin, bell hooks, and Nel Noddings.[15] It is also to be seen in the music educational writings of Thomas Regelski, Elizabeth Gould, Patricia O'Toole, Julia Eklund Koza, Randall Everett Allsup, and Cathy Benedict.[16] Among its principal advocates, Freire portrays liberatory education, in which educational policy makers act to liberate oppressed people and teachers work with the populace to educate them regarding their oppression and empower them to rise against their oppressors. Revolutionaries are *conscientized* (that is, their consciences are moved to action as they become radicalized and conscious of the evident wrongs of the past, including the patent disregard for such values as inclusiveness, fidelity, compassion, freedom, and equality, and they act to bring "what is" into line with "what should be").[17] Educational revolutionaries have caught a vision of a transformed reality, sometimes utopian, other times idealistic, to which they aspire. Rising up like prophets, they defy the powers that be and work tirelessly to bring about change, no matter how difficult. Although sometimes alone, they seek to empower others to collectively overthrow the shibboleths of the past and usher in a new and better reality. Notwithstanding their sometimes differing perspectives, educational writers on transgression such as Greene and Allsup evoke Freire's liberatory vision and share the common objective of re-visioning education and music in ways that challenge the status quo, pressing it toward a more humane and civil society.[18] In a similar vein, Ivan Illich advocates the "deschooling" of society, the dismantling of educational institutions that exploit and degrade teachers, learners, and educational stakeholders, monopolize access to knowledge, and objectify people and knowledge. By replacing the present system of compulsory formal education in schools with institutions that rely on "self motivated learning" and that provide access to "available resources at any time in their lives," Illich hopes to construct informally operated communities formed around common interests. He seeks to "empower all who want to share what they know to find those who want to learn it from them" and "furnish all who want to present an issue to the public with the opportunity to make their challenge known."[19] These liberatory and hope-filled networks of institutions treat teachers, learners, and knowledge as subjects rather than goods and services to be produced and consumed; they enable learners to be their own teachers and locate and access the necessary educational resources to develop the desired skills.[20]

Although transgression may be regarded in the negative sense of committing evil or breaking moral taboos that require punishment of the offender, the word also has a positive sense of breaking the expectations and rules of the status quo, challenging and subverting the establishment's power, and seeking to create other realities. Etymologically, transgression derives from the Latin, *transgredī*, meaning to "to step beyond or across."[21] Figuratively, one steps across the threshold from generally acceptable educational and musical thought and practice to unacceptable ways of thinking, being, and acting.[22] Although the step from the acceptable and expected to the unacceptable and unexpected is fraught with difficulties, looking at things differently opens possibilities that otherwise might not be apparent.[23]

Transgression appeals especially to the idealistic, those who think of themselves as ploughing new ground, exploring new territory, and effecting change in the lives of people engaged in the work of education and more widely in society. It is transformative in its commitment to ideas and practices. Assent to a particular belief does not suffice; transgression requires action on one's convictions, because one grasps that change is needed and feels a moral imperative to think, be, and do differently. Ideas consequential to the future of humankind, such as the creation of a just and civil society, prompt thought and action about how they can be realized in the phenomenal world. Such ideas take on a normative character as ideals for which those who believe in them strive. In education, such ideals serve to inspire teachers, students, and other educational stakeholders and prompt desire for a better world. As these beliefs are internalized as commitments, those involved in the work of education seek to live by them.

Music. Throughout musical history, transgression has played an important role in musical transformation, just as it has served as a vehicle for forwarding political and religious revolutions.[24] Among the musicians to step beyond the taken-for-granted borders of their musical traditions, Hildegard of Bingen composed religious chant evocatively in ways that were well ahead of others of her time, Ludwig van Beethoven ploughed new ground in pianistic and orchestral writing, Igor Stravinsky challenged the sensibilities of audiences of his day with his driving rhythms, Arnold Schoenberg reached beyond tonal traditions toward new musical scales, Duke Ellington and Billie Holiday put jazz in the same league as classical music, the Beatles developed their own approach to rock music, Paul Simon borrowed from other vernacular musical traditions in his popular recordings, Carole King wrote and recorded popular songs and put them to political ends, John Williams developed film score writing into an important genre in twentieth century music, Marin Alsop followed Sarah Caldwell as one of the most important women orchestra conductors, and Butch Morris conducted his avant garde New York–based improvisatory ensemble by telling them "how to play, not what to play."[25]

Musical transgression relates not only to the musical genres, forms, styles, scales, structures, timbres, and constructions of particular musical pieces but to an array of contextual assumptions and expectations in which music is made and taken. For a man we shall call Philip, who plays a piano piece by Clara Schumann at an open air concert at Tanglewood, the summer home of the Boston Symphony Orchestra, a critic judging his performance will assess it in terms of particular expectations concerning this piece. Beyond the music, dress codes and other expected modes of concert behavior invite transgression, should Philip decide to press the limits of acceptability or seek to develop new expectations.[26] One musical transgression may spark another, and determinations of which musics are transgressive also depend on the particular musical traditions that are normative at a particular time and place. Revolutionary aesthetics that prize music's utilitarian purposes, simplicity, and accessibility may transgress Western classical ideals of complexity, esotericism, and elitism, just as Western classical music may transgress certain revolutionary aesthetics.[27] Likewise, popular musics may transgress normative classical expectations, just as classical musics may transgress ascendant popular music beliefs, values, and practices.

Teaching. Regarding teaching as transgression recognizes the teacher's agency in transforming past tradition and creating change. In this view, rather than simply transmitting received wisdom to their students, teachers filter wisdom from the past and interpret it for present realities. This process of interpretation and reinterpretation, of construction and reconstruction of beliefs and practices that are suitable for this time and place, is systemic rather than superficial. Over time, received wisdom is altered from one generation of teachers to the next; the resulting musical tradition is transformed by successive generations of musicians and teachers.[28] Such teaching is a moral and intellectual undertaking grounded in the teacher's beliefs and assumptions. Idealistic and sometimes utopian ideological commitments of transgressive teachers toward changing present realities, righting past wrongs, and creating better realities are communicated to their students through talk and action. Such teachers are passionately committed to particular ideals and critical of traditional and taken-for-granted assumptions and practices. They embrace change and follow their best lights irrespective of what others think they should do; they seek to live their beliefs in the hope that their example will inspire their students, in turn, to affirm, internalize, and exemplify them.[29] They resist corporate influence in music education, rework gendered music educational ideas and practices, subvert the hegemony of particular music traditions in music education, and seek to reconstruct the ways in which teaching and learning is conducted in music education.[30]

Among the particular techniques required of such teachers, setting up conversations requires a style that invites openness, divergence, mutual respect, and risk-taking. As in the community model, teachers are concerned about their students' engagement with and construction of musical knowledge; subject matter is not simply something to be packaged, marketed, and "sold" to students as in the consumption model, or non-negotiable as in apprenticeship. Teachers focus on creating openings or opportunities to critically engage in discussion about and practice of music, rather than closings, or the achievement of certain "right" ideas and practices. Opening dialogues between teachers and students is unpredictable, in that students may wish to travel in directions that their teachers may not expect or in which teachers may not be prepared to lead them. This rhapsodic process requires that teachers be able to improvise strategies to take advantage of these openings, necessitating a wide preparation on the teacher's part. The open-endedness of this teaching results in divergent outcomes that transgress efforts to standardize, normalize, and domesticate educational outcomes. Questioning serves as a primary tool for teachers in transgressive teaching, as they challenge students to engage important issues relating to musical beliefs and practices for themselves.[31] This requires that teachers formulate real questions for themselves and their students, and value questions as instructional ends as well as means to other ends. Teachers also need to be skilled listeners, able to focus a discussion, intuit what needs to be said and done or not said and done, how and when, and articulate and summarize understandings that emerge throughout the conversation.

Learning. Like community-style and apprenticeship learning, transgressive learning is holistic in its intellectual, emotional, spiritual, and physical quality that merges into the rest of lived experience. It is formal and informal, active and receptive, individual and collective, and occurs particularly through example, observation, osmosis, and participation.[32] Example here refers to the teachers' lived commitments to certain ideals that model ways in which students ought to live musically, invest the subject matter with great importance, and convey the imperative of a musical life.[33] Observation occurs as students seek to think and do as their teachers do. Osmosis depicts the process whereby students gradually absorb or internalize the wisdom and commitments exemplified by their teachers. Participation denotes the ways in which teachers and their students learn through simply being members of this revolutionary community and taking part in its various rituals. Construed as a lifelong endeavor, learning is often informal and takes place outside schools. Examples of this informal learning may be found in performing ensembles where formal instruction is often incidental to other social and musical objectives.[34] Notwithstanding that informal learning is couched within broader social, performative, as well as pedagogical situations, it may transform the minds and hearts of its participants and broaden and also deepen their musical understanding.

Learning in conditions of transgression is also manifestly dialogical and action-oriented. As in community learning, it requires that students be free to name their worlds and construct their own realities.[35] In contrast to the consumption learning model, in which students passively receive subject matter that is already named and organized, transgression learning provides freedom for students and teachers to actively engage with the subject matter and construct their particular under-standings.[36] As they do this, students grasp the relevance of this subject matter to their lives, and their musical impulses and interests are woven in the fabric of the pedagogical situation. What they learn is a matter of transaction between teachers and their students and between students and other students. Learning is particularly compelling for teachers and students at those pedagogical moments when student interests move the conversation in unanticipated directions. This is a rhapsodic, improvisatory, and possibly idiosyncratic process.[37] Importantly, it is framed not only in intellectual terms but through the development of dispositions to act differently as students internalize particular ideas, commit to them, and are disposed to or want to live by them.[38] Although the effects of some learning may not be immediately apparent, the tendencies toward certain types of action indi-cate that learning is taking place.

Instruction. In transgression as in the community mode, since the purpose is to alter student behavior, instruction is dialogical; that is, a special sort of conversa-tion takes place between teachers and their students in an atmosphere of mutual respect, affection, and safety.[39] Individual dignity, mutual concern and regard, and restraint characterize the conversations that unfold within the frame of rules that are respected by teachers and students alike.[40] Strong attachments may develop in the pedagogical situation, but these attachments do not impose on the mutual respect, openness, dignity, sensitivity, and equality with which all are treated. The conversations in which teachers and their students engage flow out of clearly ar-ticulated subject matter that is regarded as genuinely important by, and relevant to, the lived experience of all of the participants. The opening and conduct of these conversations depends on genuinely hearing the other, questioning one's self and others, framing one's own conclusions, and interpreting those of others. These dynamic processes stand in stark contrast to the consumption model, in which teacher directives render students passive recipients of received wisdom. In its fo-cus on process and divergent results, this approach transgresses the consumption mind-set in education.

Musical conversations are central to musical instruction. They are not restricted to verbal discourse but can be conducted through the performative means of com-posing, performing, improvising, and listening. Just as a musical idea can be criti-cally examined by the teacher and students, they may also compose, improvise, or perform a piece of music together, listen to it, and reflect on it critically. The acts of composing, improvising, performing, and listening can be forms of musical conversations even if they are not accompanied by critical discourse about these events. Although closings are also implied in musical openings, creating openings eschews rigidly predetermining the ends of these conversations or overly restricting them to a narrow range of outcomes. These pedagogical conversations are thought of as dynamic yet developmental, as students broaden and deepen their understandings of music. Listening to such a musical conversation, one might hear the hum of voices, sometimes raised and sometimes not, silences, bursts of laughter, musical pieces replayed or resung, and, when students and teachers emerge afterward, little knots of people playing, singing, or talking earnestly as if reluctant to let the conversation cease.

As in community instruction, teacher and student interaction proceeds formally and informally (in settings centered on other things besides pedagogical purposes). Instruction encompasses the entire life cycle, all aspects of human life, and all of the societal institutions within which music is made.[41] In repudiating the sharp delineations between pedagogical and other interests, the transgression model offers a wider array of possible instructional settings and means to include those that are not purposely pedagogical. Including informal as well as formal instruction raises the possibility that informal musical instruction may assume particular significance.[42]

Curriculum. The subject of instruction in transgression is problem-centered; that is, it concerns questions that require resolution, particularly in the lived experience of the participants.[43] For musicians, although musical problems are of a different sort than those in propositional discourses, music is presented to students problematically with a view to students also solving the distinctly musical challenges they face and creating and undergoing music through such ways as composing, improvising, performing, producing, and listening. For students, these include such accomplishments as mastering instrumental technique and musical notation, and interpretation of musical repertoire. Procedural understandings are initially something of a mystery to students, but things gradually become clearer as they acquire the necessary critical thinking and performing skills and habits and achieve progressively greater competence in the direction of exemplary performance. Whatever the emphasis, whether on knowing about music or knowing how to make and take it, both aspects are needed in a broad grasp of music that transgresses narrow musical interests.[44] When musical problems are also contextualized within the rest of lived experience, students can engage music more meaningfully and vitally. Exploring these myriad musical and cultural connections leads students to frame problems, come to know music in various ways, and make better connections between their own lived experiences and those of different others.[45]

This view of curriculum has a distinctly political twist.[46] When music education serves democratic purposes and evidences consistency between its means and ends, its means are likewise democratic. Although esoteric and arcane musics and their study have been associated with elites, music teachers in the service of democracy seek to democratize music as they also democratize the means of its study. Criticizing the canons of masterworks in Western classical music, jazz, and other vernacular and popular traditions renders visible the politicization of music and the musics that have been hidden from general view.[47] These canonical criticisms constitute criticisms of the power brokers and gatekeepers of musical traditions. Affirmative action on behalf of those who have been marginalized, excluded, or rendered invisible is likely to be resisted by the musical establishments of those traditions. In widening the canons of exemplary works, the transgressive curriculum defies traditional canonical expectations and creates new ones as it also reaches beyond the borders of a particular tradition to others. "Border crossings" or movements over the "threshold" of one tradition into another cultivate a "cosmopolitan" approach to music, in which one comes not only to understand the music of different others but is able, at least to some extent, to critically hear and see the music that is one's heritage from the perspective of others for whom it might be foreign.[48] Border crossing not only widens one's understanding but makes one more critical of one's own as well as another's point of view.[49] Although regarding music as an essential subject of general education transgresses narrow politically and economically driven educational interests focused on what politicians consider to be "essential skills," it develops qualities that are often devalued in general education and promotes well-rounded and psychologically well-adjusted and happy people.[50]

Administration. Some proponents of educational transgression suggest an informal "cellular" mode of organization whereby its work is forwarded [51] Others propose a radical rethinking or even dismantling of educational institutions associated with the formal credentialing and certification of learning, with the substitution of grassroots or informal bottom-up organization structures whereby educational and societal transformation can spread broadly throughout the society at large.[52] Still others envisage educational transformation as a top-down process in which a coordinated and systematic approach is essential, especially when conceiving of large-scale or national education systems.[53] The large scale of modern musical and educational enterprises suggests that although cellular organization may be necessary in certain circumstances, especially those that facilitate dynamic groupings of teachers and students, relying solely on this form of organization as a principal administrative tool is impractical. I cannot imagine successful and large-scale musical transgression without situating cellular mechanisms within some sort of overall administrative framework that makes them viable. Taking this view, administration in transgression may be directive and systematic from the top down even as it is cellular and scattered from the bottom up. Hierarchical structures are likely to exemplify some aspects of the organization, while "flat" organizational structures may be typical of other aspects. To work successfully, combining these approaches requires certain agreements concerning the rule-sets that govern music education. In a university music department, for example, in addition to administrative and faculty guidelines approved for university-wide use, special procedures followed by the music department afford opportunities for students and faculty to organize themselves into ad hoc groups from time to time.

Cellular organizations require the exercise of choice if they are to work effectively. The possibility of choice allows people to join groups that benefit from the particular interests of those within them. Although this emphasis on choice might seem to evoke the consumption model, in which it also plays an important role, its purposes here differ. In the case of cellular mechanisms or learning webs in conditions of transgression, choice is intended to allow the exercise of individual liberty in the educational process and foster communities that can provide mutual support in the work of revolution rather than direct the consumption of educational products. Choice is thereby linked to activism and the individuality of learning styles, personalities, and other attributes that bring pleasure to teachers and their students. It is exercised not on behalf of particular curricular products so much as to enable teachers and learners to find and engage with each other and the subject matter in effective and transformative ways.

The assessment of music education in the transgression model cannot be entirely formative and processual but also needs to be summative and product-oriented. Transgression is partly adjudicated with reference to the results it produces in the phenomenal world. As in the consumption model, stakeholders in the transgression model insist that music education deliver the results desired: they are interested in actions, not just words. Still, the results are adjudicated differently from those of the consumption model. Whereas in the consumption model, its procedures and results are measured primarily in economic terms, in the transgression model, its objective is the creation of a more just, humane, egalitarian, and inclusive society.[54]

CRITIQUE

Notions of freedom and liberation that dominate much of the recent writing about educational transgression often assume that transgression is always in the direction of the good. Here, the status quo is cast as oppressive, evil, and dehumanizing, and the transgression is construed as liberating, good, and humanizing. Such a construction pits the forces of good against those of evil, light against darkness, and liberation against enslavement. The clarity of the ethical contrast between these alternatives demands a similarly clear stance on behalf of goodness and humanity and against evil and dehumanization. These obligations carry into ordinary lived life in directions that point toward the good. The clarity of the alternatives, painted in blacks and whites rather than shades of grey, is comforting to people, since it does not demand the critical engagement of a more nuanced perspective.

Still, transgression may have a dark side even when it may appear initially to be for the good of the public at large. Sometimes revolutions are mounted in the cause of evil—for example, the "purification" of a population and genocide of people of differing religions, ethnicities, and gender orientations. Although the Nazi Third Reich was cast originally as a revolution toward a better world order, the ensuing holocaust graphically demonstrates how misguided, wrong-headed, and evil this cause was. Its ideals were not in the best interests of the public or society at large, and those brave souls who resisted the radical changes its revolutionaries wrought were right in their opposition to its inhumanity. I was reminded of the awful character and consequences of this revolution when I stood with two friends at a memorial site just opposite the Dammtor railroad station in Hamburg, Germany. We had stopped earlier at a spot marked by small plaques in the pavement of a sidewalk near the University of Hamburg memorializing the deportation of members of a Jewish family. Now, at this site, tens of thousands of Jews were deported during the period from 1933 until the end of World War II. Under sunlight-dappled trees in a small park where new spring-green leaves rustled in the breeze, I tried to imagine what it must have been like for those who waited, afraid and distressed, at this very spot. They waited to be sent away from their homes, families, and work, all because of who they had been born. As we bowed our heads in remembrance, one of my friends commented that this was no black-and-white photograph of the sort we had seen in the past that seemed disconnected from reality, but a lovely world in rich and living color. It seemed incomprehensible that on a spring day such as this, any human being could do what was done to these people. Yet it was done. This memorial park remains a stark reminder that revolutionaries may work in the cause of evil, and it is imperative that their ideals and values be examined critically.

Musically, among its strengths, transgression serves to revitalize traditions by promoting new or fresh beliefs and practices, introducing music from the margins of the tradition or from other traditions that enrich it, and ensuring that the tradition remains relevant to the particular times and places in which it is made and taken. Without transgression, a musical tradition may die, especially if society is changing all around it. If its proponents insist on ensuring its purity and remaining faithful to it, it could become increasingly irrelevant to new societal and cultural realities. For example, technological advances in instruments, electronic sound generation, and manipulation permit new ways of composing, performing, and experiencing music. When taken advantage of, these inventions may transgress previous expectations, offering new and different ways of being in music that may eventually become an accepted part of the tradition. Thinking of music in democratic and utilitarian ways could also strengthen the links between music, education, and society to ensure that music remains a vital part of cultural life. Embracing change offers a means of guaranteeing that musical traditions remain vibrant and relevant to lived life rather than moribund and isolated.

By the same token, transgression as an ideal may also be very uncomfortable to the high priests of a musical canon and those who are more inclined to follow a tradition rather than to transgress it. A prized tradition may be lost if it is not preserved. Traditions are forged according to rules. If these rules are constantly transgressed, traditions may disintegrate. Failing to attend sufficiently to a musical tradition's beliefs and practices and transmit them more or less faithfully to the next generation can also cause a tradition to wither from lack of carefulness and interest. This is particularly the case in music, because it involves procedural knowledge that needs to be brought to life constantly and passed on orally from one generation to the next. Where revolutions are repressive and restrict musical expressions, composers are unable or unwilling to test the limits of the accessible and write more esoterically, raising the possibility of a resultant barren and prosaic musical culture.[55]

In terms of teaching, the transgression model has several advantages. It stresses a holistic approach that emphasizes skills needed to begin and continue musical conversations between teachers and students. Teachers take a critical perspective on classical and vernacular musics with a view to bringing together theory and practice and exemplifying a thoughtful and careful approach to music in their own lives. As with the community model, they are particularly interested in engaging students actively rather than purveying content to them in prepackaged forms. Transgression necessitates independent-mindedness and courage on the teacher's part in challenging taken-for-granted beliefs and practices together with judgment in assessing what to keep of traditional wisdom. Such an approach to teaching is both passionate and clear-eyed, weighing carefully the received wisdom from the past and the claims for change in the present. Regarding teaching as a calling, as does transgression, evokes notions of teaching as apprenticeship and community.

Nevertheless, many teachers are conservatives and conformists by nature, more anxious to fit within the norm than to challenge it. Given the possibility that the revolutionaries may be misguided or even evil, or their hopes and dreams unrealistic or utopian, teachers' natural conservatism and caution may help preserve traditions that might otherwise be overthrown hastily. Over time, and in leisure, their caution leads them to weigh the claims and counter-claims of revolutionaries. The fact that many music teachers are often trained as apprentices and steeped in musical traditions may also make it difficult for them to try on new ideas or practices. Even should teachers seek to change things, it is easy to succumb to the old ways of thinking and doing because these ways are ingrained in minds, hearts, and bodies. Transgressive music teaching is also less safe, since teachers must traverse new territory. Engaging in transgression almost inevitably positions teachers out of the mainstream. There is also the risk of punishment and retribution from powerful others if the sacred idols and groves are destroyed. This is not an easy path, and many may prefer not to walk it. What transgressive teachers do is necessarily political, and this may not appeal to those who are devoted servants of art. Fear may likewise bind teachers in inaction.[56] Nostalgia may make them reluctant to relinquish the comfortable beliefs and practices of the past.

On the bright side, learning in transgression is active and holistic. It involves mind, heart, soul, and body—that is, one's intellectual, emotional, spiritual, and physical self. This active approach, as with apprenticeship and community, contrasts with learning as a passive recipient of knowledge, in a form of consumption. It is also liberating in its possibilities for learners to construct and name their own realities. This approach to learning relies on insight, or one's seeing into things as a necessary element of understanding. Since it situates musical learning within political, religious, and other social and cultural contexts, music is more comprehensible, interrelated to other knowledge, and relevant to the student's lived life. Musical practices can thrive when students learn through example, imitation, osmosis, and participation, follow what their teachers do and say, and seek to become competent musicians. This is also transformative learning that deeply impacts the lives of those engaged in it. Where it is also politicized and learning is critical, learners are empowered to carefully negotiate the political processes that are now unmasked for their view. Understanding the politics and economics of musical production and distribution, for example, students are in a better position to criticize and resist the power and control of the corporate, political, and religious institutions that dominate production and distribution—to give voice to their individual musical interests and find ways to be heard in the public spaces.

On the dark side, if transgression is repressive rather than liberatory, learning may be very directive and allow little room for the learner's construction of subject matter. Unlike apprenticeship, which conserves traditional thought and practice, transgression boldly sets forth to break the rules and create new beliefs and practices even if this is accomplished in restrictive or authoritarian ways. Although transgression is intended to be liberatory, learners may pay insufficient attention to traditional ways of thinking, being, and acting musically. Not only may students fail to become sufficiently familiar with the musical traditions they are transgressing, but what they learn of these traditions may be caricatures of them. This is so because teachers are concerned to establish rationales for the new ways and may be inclined to overdraw the problematic aspects of the old ways. Musical practices, while ambiguous, are precise; learning a musical tradition requires certain understandings that are not open for interpretation. For example, scales, notational systems, instrumental ranges, and tempo markings may be quite unambiguous. Relying entirely on student insight and individual constructions of music may be insufficiently directive, especially when these relatively unambiguous aspects of music would seem to require a more directive treatment by the teacher. Since this approach is unsuited to learning some aspects of music, it may be too limited to serve as a general theory of musical learning.

To its credit, the dialogical character of instruction in transgression provides a potent means of liberation in thought and practice. As in instruction in the community mode these conversations model ways of negotiating ideas peacefully and democratically. There may be various conceptions of democracy, some more free-wheeling or inclusive of minority perspectives and driven by differing values than others. Still, in free societies in which all citizens are enfranchised and regarded as persons of worth, instruction that prefigures democratic societies is particularly relevant to general education. It serves as a metaphor for democratic societies and a means of inculcating democratic principles in the young. In today's multicultural societies, constructing bridges between one culture and another through conversations in which the young learn to treat different others with respect is a particularly important aspect of general education. Such a climate suggests that educators attend especially to employing means of dialogical instruction that cultivate respect for different others. It is also important to exemplify ways of negotiating conflicts and tensions that arise between people from differing ethnicities, religions, languages, colors, and gendered ways of being so that we may all live together peacefully. Conversations of the sort fostered in transgression go some way toward these ends.

Still, the possibility of transgression's dark and even repressive side suggests that instruction may become indoctrination, in which alternatives are not genuinely explored and conversations between teachers and students are heavily scripted. In such circumstances, the hoped-for kinds of rhapsodic discourse and interaction found in transgression oriented toward liberation are supplanted by constricted question-and-answer dialogues in which teachers ask approved questions, students memorize approved answers, and instructional ends are convergent rather than divergent. Even in the best of worlds, dialogical instruction may take insufficient advantage of teacher expertise and be less suited to some learning than to others. Aspects of learning a musical instrument, for example, may be better accomplished through apprenticeship, whereas learning about the philosophical and historical aspects of music may be appropriately approached dialogically. Since the nature of the interaction between teachers and students seems better suited to some subject matter than others, it may be insufficiently broad a perspective to cover the entire sweep of musical instruction. Where complex musical matters are under discussion, or where students are inclined to learning styles that respond well to directive teacher approaches, this instruction may be inefficient and even ineffective.

Among its advantages, curriculum in conditions of transgression is generally construed as a dynamic process whereby learners interact with music directly and construct or make sense of this engagement for themselves. As such, it shares much in common with the curriculum in community. Rather than passing unchanged from one generation to the next, the tradition is transformed in the process of criticism and intersection with music on the margins of the canon or from other musical traditions. Although conversations end in certain achievements, the focus of the curriculum is upon the process rather than the product. This dynamic and constructivist view of music curriculum permits learners to follow their individual interests and results in divergent rather than convergent outcomes. Such results are consonant with the nature of music, which is likewise ambiguous and understood imaginatively in differing ways. The connections between music and the rest of lived experience, as well as music's politicization, also make it relevant to contemporary culture and amenable to critical examination as a cultural artifact. Music's accessibility and the connections between theory and practice allow students to grasp its importance in their lives and its role and meaning as an aspect of contemporary culture.

Among its disadvantages, totalitarian regimes may employ a top-down and directive curriculum. It may be difficult to see how the Kodály system of music education, developed for use in a totalitarian state, cultivates democratic thought and practice and is consonant with education for democracy. Nevertheless, music teachers regularly use it in American schools and invoke it as if this were the case.[57] Some may see it as liberatory in the hope that sequentially organized musical instruction can permit successful achievement at every level, ultimately bringing freedom by virtue of the mastery that students can demonstrate. Still, in post-Communist Hungary, it would not be surprising to find that Kodály's approach is also tainted by virtue of its association with the previous totalitarian regime; teachers who continue to follow it because they find it an effective approach to musical instruction might well find themselves engaged in transgressive acts of a sort. Even when transgression is intentionally liberatory, the divergent aims and methods of musical study may clash with present societal realities. Rather than deliver specific identifiable ends, such as consumption, this curriculum may result in open-ended, diverse, and sometimes unclear purposes and methods. Since it is likely to be painted in strong colors, it may be an insufficiently nuanced treatment of music. Its boldness is captivating and its distinctions riveting, yet it might better be cast in more muted or subtle tonings. The very qualities of fearlessness and boldness in staking out new territory render revolutionaries less interested in the subtler nuances. When a farmer first clears the bush and scrub, builds a cottage, and plants a crop, the very first clearing is pretty rough; the house may be thrown up quickly, and when the crop is first planted, roots of trees, brush, and undergrowth may still be in evidence in the fields. Over time, this roughness dissipates as attractive fences, buildings, and plantings replace the initial hasty and often makeshift construction, and roots and undergrowth and decay are removed. Gradually, this clearing comes to be a well-established farm. I see transgression as the initial clearing—bold but less nuanced, rough rather than smooth, essential for dramatic change yet lacking in subtlety. There is also the possibility that the curriculum is insufficiently conservative and more heavily weighted on change than on tradition. Tradition may be caricatured or even demonized, and transgression may not be sufficiently faithful or even generous to received wisdom. Where music is used as a revolutionary tool, it may be too prosaic and insufficiently esoteric. Since its focus is on the contextual and social aspects of music, this curriculum may be unsuited to preparing musicians who are practicing exponents of particular traditions.

Regarding the strengths of administration, the cellular organization of instructional units can encourage teacher and student choice, and this choice permits considerable self-selection of what is taught and learned, and how this happens. In a conservative mind-set, the reliance on individual choice in transgression resonates with its value in society at large. Its close intersection with practical matters and the variety of its purposes and methods renders it prone to the exigencies of particular times, places, and people, and it seems reasonable to conclude that a meld of top-down and bottom-up organizational processes is appropriate. This ambiguity and open-endedness in organizational possibilities suggests a particularistic rather than universalist view of administration.

There are other potential administrative problems. Dictatorial top-down administrations would seem to be insufficiently divergent to allow or foster the divergent action that this model promises. Revolutionary leaders may face day-to-day supervision that restricts their freedom to act and stifles change. Organizations may be forged around transformational ideas that erode over time or become passé.[58] The potential instability of its administration also suggests that a transgression-oriented educational system may go out of control and overshoot its mark, and it is unclear whether the proponents of transgression will be able to keep control of the process while it is under way or be swept away by forces out of their control. In 1967, the members of the Tanglewood Symposium began an effort to secure a place for vernacular musics in the school curriculum.[59] As I write, their movement has become so successful that popular music has become a mainstay of American school music education, while classical music has been largely sidelined and relegated to the status of a musical subculture in society at large. I do not know whether the participants in the Tanglewood Symposium anticipated this state of affairs or whether they would have been entirely comfortable with the results of their declared ends. What is clear, however, is that the ideas gathered a momentum of their own, until we have come to a point where a music teacher might well transgress by focusing on Western classical music rather than popular or vernacular musics. Similarly, I recall Patricia Shehan Campbell's worry in 1990 that multicultural music education would become yet another bandwagon onto which music educators would climb and ride until the horse fell in its tracks, the wagon broke down, or the passengers tired of the journey.[60] Her worries turn out to have been justified; once the advocates of multicultural music education began their push for including international musics in general education and the idea caught on, this movement likewise gathered steam to become an unstoppable phenomenon beyond the power of any one individual, or a few, to rein in. Why is this the case? My sense is that the passions involved in transgression are so great that reason can fly to the winds, the movement becomes largely uncontrollable, and leaders find themselves helpless to restrain or contain it. Understanding transgression is to grasp why music education has been so prone to a bandwagon mentality. Still, this knowledge is cold comfort if one cannot prevent transgression from overshooting the mark and prompting a possible and equally extreme reaction in the opposite direction.

SUMMARY

In sum, I have briefly described the revolutionary, sketched the musical, teaching, learning, instructional, curricular, and administrative aspects of transgression, and noted the contributions and flaws in these pictures. Notwithstanding their occasional and brilliant flashes of light and freedom, they may also be dark and repressive. Passionate commitments and actions make the revolutionary unpredictable, and transgression is difficult to steer as it tends to overshoot its intended targets, arrive at extreme positions, and invite a backlash against its excesses. It is in the interest of music education policy makers to find ways of organizing music teaching, learning, and instruction so as to harness transgression in the interests of a humane and civil society and maintain its best features while repudiating its worst.

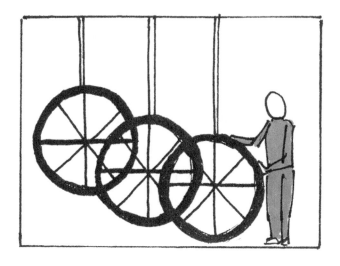

6
FACTORY AND PRODUCTION

The pictures of *factory* and *production* date especially to the industrial revolution that impacted Western societies and, now, the industrialized world. In the United States, although small-scale factories of the nineteenth century that employed skilled artisans have been largely replaced by large factories where economies of scale flow from streamlined and highly mechanized and automated manufacturing operations, some factories have gotten smaller as niche operations and technology make them competitive.[1] Since antiquity, the factory has been a place in which goods are manufactured or assembled with the use of machinery for the purpose of selling them to others and breaking even or making a profit. Its roots lie in the Latin *factōrium* meaning an oil press.[2] Before the industrial revolution (and even today), factories were operated by craftsmen responsible for all aspects of manufacture from start to finish. For example, various Italian families made violins with the help of apprentices learning the trade.[3] Their operation included all aspects of violin manufacture including the selection of wood, drying, varnishing, cutting, gluing, and final assembly of the instrument. This small-scale operation was more like the artist-apprenticeship pictures in its reliance on the artist's craftsmanship. Some of the most prized violins are still made by craftsmen, but as with other musical instruments, factories now account for much of their manufacture. The earlier small-scale and individualized operations seem far removed from modern factories that predominate in our time.

In this chapter, I sketch some of the important features of the modern factory and its related production model. This powerful metaphor and model pair is influenced by and shapes society and cultural life, especially in the West, where capitalism is a pervasive ethic.

FACTORY

I think of a factory located not far from where I write these words. Its purpose is to manufacture potato chips. Hidden from a major thoroughfare by a wooded area, it is housed in a relatively new, modernist, industrial structure near other similarly styled buildings, surrounded by parking lots and laid out with an eye to the delivery of supplies and transport of finished products. Inside, the manufacturing process is organized so that the raw materials are gradually turned into potato chips. Each day, as a siren blast marks the beginning and end of each shift, workers arrive and depart the factory at predetermined times, and they count on income earned there as an important source of their livelihood. The smells of the chips cooking, wafting out into the surrounding area, remind those who travel nearby it of its existence.

Factories are ubiquitous, and despite its specialized purpose, this particular factory is likely to operate much as other potato chip factories around the world, or even other factories making different products. The manufacturing process is segmented, specialized, and atomized into small steps of the whole process. By segmented, I mean that each step in manufacturing this product is discrete from every other step. This segmentation permits workers to specialize on attending to specific parts of the operation, so that one individual's skill does not need to extend over the entire manufacturing process but each worker can develop expertise in particular parts of the operation. Multiple repetitions of particular tasks suggest that the quality of a potato chip made by a team of specialists may be more uniform than one made entirely by generalists who may be better at some things and worse at others.

Assembly lines require the use of standardized machines, parts, processes, and products. Breaking down the manufacturing process into constituent parts and developing specialized machines and skills to focus on each of these parts requires that inputs, processes, and outputs are standardized. As a linear process, all of the parts of the process need to be coordinated so that they all eventually fit together. Workers must also work at the rate at which the assembly line moves. The more closely all elements are calibrated to the standard, the easier it is to assemble them. This is especially the case in complex manufacturing operations in which precision is imperative. Ensuring that all of the ingredients and nuts and bolts of the machinery are of the exact specifications allows the factory to make potato chips seamlessly according to the pattern of normative specifications. The spread of standardization from this factory to others necessarily follows; it needs standardized inputs, and others require standardized outputs, in turn, from it. For this reason, standardization in one industry rapidly spreads to others and becomes normative not only in one society but throughout the world. As the infrastructure of standardization develops, it becomes more and more difficult to change the standards since they are institutionalized and relied upon by factories everywhere.

In order to ensure that the same process is followed exactly and the same results are achieved in every repetition, factory workers become cogs in a machinery of manufacturing standardized products. Machinery is central to the manufacturing process and may be preferable to humans; people are prone to do things idiosyncratically and think about their work reflectively, whereas machines can be programmed to do certain work in exactly the same manner and to produce standardized products. Although this machinery needs to be designed, programmed, operated, and repaired by people, management replaces people with machines wherever possible and relegates a relative few people to the work of caring for machines. Instead of a human-intensive operation, the factory becomes a mechanized operation in which people mainly deal with machines and work at the rate at which machines are operating, and robots perform tasks that once might have been done by people. This mechanization of the workplace renders standardization even more powerful and forces people to work in situations that are machine-like. It also dehumanizes factory workers, co-opting them in the service of inanimate objects, forcing them to work like the machines created by other people, but without the freedom to change or to do differently than these machines have been programmed to do. Such a situation creates a gulf between those who design the machines and program them and those who carry out largely repetitive tasks in the factory. Even though this reality is subverted when groups of people work together in teams, the nature of the manufacturing machinery largely dictates the ways in which all must work, and their freedom to act idiosyncratically is curtailed.

Predictability and reliability are of greatest importance in a closed system in which standardized inputs, manufacturing processes, and outputs are clearly specified and constructed to perform flawlessly. If the planning for the potato chip factory has been thorough, all aspects of its location and manufacturing system have been considered and accounted for, and management is certain that all that needs to be known is known before the factory is built. Simulation systems may also be constructed in order to better visualize how this factory will actually operate and to ensure that the best possible system is constructed. All of this rational planning suggests that unexpected consequences represent a failure in the system, and the manufacturing process is flawed and needs to be fixed. Standardized potato chips are expected to be manufactured exactly as specified and their predictability and reliability are to be as high as humanly possible. Ironically called "quality control," the process whereby potato chips are manufactured requires that outcomes can be predicted with a high degree of certainty and produce the same result for every test.

Factory managers are absorbed with the efficiency of the process, that is the production of the greatest quantity of potato chips at the greatest speed and for the least cost in terms of money, labor, and equipment. Assessing the efficiency of the process of potato chip manufacture as objectively as possible and increasing profitability can be accomplished by quantifying various measures of the factory's performance. Profits (or break-even points) are measured numerically, and quantifying all aspects of the manufacturing process, especially in fiscal terms, is consistent with the factory's objective. Counting such things as "person-hours" necessitated in potato chip manufacture, or costs per machine and per day of factory operation, can generate statistical measures of the factory's efficiency. These allow objective and statistical assessments to be made about such things as how well the factory is presently performing as opposed to how it has performed in the past, and to extrapolate how it might be expected to perform in the future. This principle of quantifying assessments of the factory's operation extends even to those things that are not as easily quantified. For example, the company's "goodwill" is an educated guess of what its reputation or contribution to the community are worth.

The manufacturing process whereby predictable inputs are rendered into predictable outputs is a central consideration. This process is predicated on the notion of antecedence; that is, what must precede something else in the manufacturing system so that products are produced with the greatest possible cost efficiency. To this end, management's decisions are data-driven and rational. The factory has to do with material things, and workers' happiness and contentment in the workplace are taken into account only insofar as they are demonstrated to contribute to the factory's output, profitability, and goodwill. Finding the most efficient manufacturing process requires testing alternatives to determine the best system. Once in place, this system drives the factory's operation for some time. This is true especially when the investment in machinery, materials, and personnel required to operate the machinery is predicated on these initial decisions about the manufacturing process. Retooling a manufacturing process is a costly enterprise that the factory undertakes as infrequently and efficiently as possible.

Worker remuneration and morale are important considerations. Each worker has skills and accumulates experience and expertise that may be thought of as factory assets. Piecework and bonuses are among the means by which management seeks to align worker interests with its own. Piecework is particularly seductive, since it entices the worker to work just a little harder, faster, or longer for additional financial reward. Especially where workers are paid poorly, these marginal income increments may make a significant difference in worker income and quality of life. Historically, management has exploited workers' willingness and need to work and their relative powerlessness in the workplace, and so laws and regulations control such aspects as working conditions, minimum wages, child labor, hours of work, and rest breaks. Since labor costs are a significant element of manufacturing costs, factories now relocate to low-cost environments where labor can be contracted more cheaply. Workers may be exploited by management, especially when their interests are not sufficiently protected and they fear the loss of their jobs. Excessive exploitation can boil into labor unrest, sabotage, and violence.

The factory's purpose is functional rather than aesthetic; its design aims explicitly at manufacturing particular products. Parts of the factory, especially its front office and public spaces, may be decorated with gardens and attractive interior and exterior spaces. Often, the factory is hidden from public view by earth berms, treed areas, and other means of camouflaging otherwise ugly and unimaginative spaces. Some factories have an eye on form as well as function, but, typically, form follows function and considerations of whether this building promotes efficient production override aesthetic considerations. As a result, factory workers often labor in crowded and often unaesthetic spaces and are cooped up so that their work can be readily observed. The lack of privacy and such attractive features as finished walls and roofs, interesting architecture, painted surfaces, attractive floors, and abundant natural lighting with outside views combine to focus workers' attention on the manufacturing process and its machinery. Humdrum functional spaces contribute to the dehumanization of workers, underscore the often prosaic character of their work, and result in ennui, illness, and accident.[4] Although workers seek to escape these working conditions in time away from work, the functionality of their workplaces often translates to their expectations regarding all the other places in which they live, worship, shop, eat out, attend movies, watch sporting events, and otherwise spend their time.[5] So workplace functionality spreads throughout the rest of lived life and workers may not realize that anything is amiss.[6]

PRODUCTION

The production model is pervasive in music education, and, at least in the United States, is one of the most important models of music education in the last two centuries. It is also evident in the modern European conservatories established during the nineteenth century that were designed to produce large numbers of professional musicians to perform in regular and publicly supported concert and opera seasons.[7] In the United States, the efficiency movement in education of the early twentieth century spearheaded by Franklin Bobbitt, among other curricularists, drew directly from industrial values.[8] This educational movement is illustrated in the latter part of the century in the "competency-based" music educational approach of Clifford Madsen and Cornelia Yarbrough.[9] Other music educational methods such as the Kodály and Suzuki approaches likewise analyze elements of ear training and violin performance, respectively, into systematic programs in which students must master each respective level.[10] The same goes for examination systems developed by the Australian Music Examinations Board, the Associated Board of the Royal Schools of Music in the United Kingdom, and the Royal Conservatory of Music in Toronto, Canada, in which each subject is broken out into its constituent parts, organized into a systematic set of objectives and levels of performance, and tested to ascertain if pupils have met the requisite standards.[11] The long-standing fixation with positivistic premises in music educational research, instructional methods, and national standards of music education also reflect a data-driven management approach.[12]

Music. Standardization of musical composition, performance, instruments, and the transmission of musical knowledge, along with specialization among the various aspects of music making and taking, are characteristic features of the production model.[13] Historically, in the Western classical tradition, the conductor's position changed from that of leader of a chamber orchestra to maestro of a large ensemble. Rather than participate in a collaborative process whereby musicians improvised on and interpreted the composer's musical sketch of what they were to play, the conductor directed the ensemble's interpretation of a complete score.[14] Improvisation was marginalized as composers began to write out their scores in full rather than allow musicians to make their own impromptu, idiosyncratic, and extended improvisations. The impact of technology on music making and taking became an important element of contemporary musical life.[15] The increasing standardization and mass production of musical instruments opened the prospect for mass musical study and fueled growing numbers of amateur and professional performers. Separate worlds of music historians, theorists, pedagogues, composers, early music aficionados, and contemporary music enthusiasts and of each of the orchestral and other musical instruments emerged that were often formalized in professional societies.[16] Today, early musicians are often a different crowd than contemporary musicians; the harp world is a different entity than the piano world; the classical guitar has its own world; the various orchestral percussion, string, brass, and woodwind instruments likewise attract different people; and the operatic and singing worlds are yet other realities.[17] Orchestral audiences may find little interest in wind ensemble concerts, those interested in chamber music may be uninterested in orchestral performances, and opera lovers may have little time for instrumental music.

The pervasive technologization of music in society has altered the possibilities for musical performances through such means as electronically synthesizing and reproducing sound, recording technologies, manipulating acoustic environments, amplifying sounds, and using "prepared" instruments, and has prompted an instrumental rather than vocal approach to music. At first glance, singing may be more natural and less interesting to young people than instrumental technologies, but even singing may also be co-opted by technology, especially by the use of the microphone that amplifies acoustically produced sound and creates a sense of intimacy and presence encouraged in today's popular music. The microphone also impacts vocal production and fosters timbres that sometimes differ significantly from a bel canto vocal sound.[18] This electronification or mass mediation of music also enables the widespread sharing of musics in which different forms of vocal production can be heard.[19]

Professional institutions also govern the conduct of music in production. Modern musicians unions have their roots in the musicians' guilds of medieval times.[20] The medieval guilds presaged contemporary musicians' unions by setting particular standards of musical education and strict rules of musical and professional conduct. They formed a sort of musical monopoly for guild members and ensured that there was not an oversupply of qualified musicians. Although their influence was often undercut by musicians outside the guilds, they still held considerable power. Today's musician unions negotiate contracts on behalf of musicians, set suitable fees for musical services rendered, provide continuing education, and help to ensure that musicians are treated respectfully by management. These union rules for rehearsal and performance limits, rest periods, and payment of musicians help to protect musicians from exploitation and standardize the nature and length of musical performances and recording sessions. In the twentieth century, associations and accrediting agencies were created to oversee the conduct of these standardized programs and ensure that their operation met established standards.[21] The creation of formal courses of study to replace earlier and somewhat rhapsodic, idiosyncratic, serendipitous, and unsystematic approaches to musical study in earlier times was a response not only to the increasing numbers of students wishing to study music in the nineteenth and twentieth centuries but to a desire for a more standardized preparation whereby students would be trained efficiently to reach particular musical standards. Such programs might also be credentialed as university degrees and conservatory diplomas, and comparisons made between one educational institution and another. Systematizing knowledge transmission from one musical generation to another required breaking down musical knowledge into its constituent parts, notably history, theory, ear training, instrumental study, and ensemble participation, and requiring all students to take the self-same programs by which they are credentialed as musician-teachers.

Teaching. Under the production model, instructional materials and objectives are predetermined, and the music teacher assumes a technical role of delivering information and organizing and conducting musical activities that achieve specified ends.[22] Teachers are responsible for ensuring that students meet, and if possible exceed, the prescribed standards, so they need to determine the program of work that will enable their students to meet these standards within the available resources at hand. Specifying certain standards may also mandate additional teacher preparation and materials beyond those already in place. When this is the case, since the standards are normative, teachers need to secure whatever training and resources are needed in order to attain them. Music teachers in conditions of production are often specialists and, theoretically, no one teaches every aspect of musical study. Each teacher may see only a part of a student's overall musical and educational development. Even in elementary and secondary school music programs where there may be one music teacher at the school, music education goes on outside the school in various ways, and school music teachers see a part of a larger whole. The control by powerful people and organizations over music programs is dehumanizing in its removal of teachers' freedom of choice, especially concerning crucial curricular decisions.[23] Although teachers may be prepared to make independent professional judgments, they often find themselves unable to do so because they are hemmed in by the decisions of more powerful others. In the absence of power to exercise their own professional judgments, they may see themselves as technical and exploited workers and unionize in order to gain collectively what they cannot gain individually.

Teaching proceeds by means of "impression."[24] Just as a computer disc is burned, so the teacher serves as the agent of im-pressing the student. This is a very directive approach that regards the transmission of wisdom and knowledge as a one-way process from teacher to student, where the teacher gives and the student passively accepts. The teacher's methods need not be reinvented constantly; the most efficient methods are utilized to produce the best results. Rather than rely on the student's insight, which might affect what is learned and how, authority figures in the field of study determine what should be taught, why, how, when, and where, and teachers serve as intermediaries to ensure that the directives they receive are in turn received unquestioningly by students. Theirs is not to ask or interrogate but simply to do exactly as they are bidden. The result of this process, it is assumed, is the production of competent musicians and music teachers that fit the norm.

Learning. In the production model, learning is a "one-size-fits-all" approach. It is assumed that learners share common traits and, especially in large group instructional settings, some approaches are likely to be more appealing and effective than others. Certain outcomes are predicted on the basis of research findings and specified in advance, and those approaches that successfully enable the greatest number of learners to produce the desired results are selected. The learning of the majority of students, rather than the outliers or the minority who do not fit the norm, is the focus of attention. Efficient approaches that enable the largest numbers of students to progress the most and with the least cost in resources are fostered. This approach to learning deemphasizes diverse learning styles in favor of accommodating to the particular learning approaches that meet the needs of the greatest number of students. Predicting learning outcomes is bound to emphasize the learning of the great majority of students and to focus on measures of central tendency. Such a convergent approach downplays the role of surprise and serendipity in learning, focusing instead on the more predictable aspects that are likely to follow a particular course of instruction.[25] Some might suggest that "mastery learning" predominates in the production model.[26] I suppose if one is willing to refer to mastery in its soft and relative sense, hedged about by caveats, the notion of demonstrating competence in progressively more difficult tasks seems appropriate to the production model. This approach depends, of course, on the ability to build one set of progressively more difficult tasks that all musicians and music teachers can agree on. Still, in production teaching, it is presumed that they can agree, and this knotty problem is assumed away.

Learning in the production model, as in apprenticeship, is mostly receptive, as students are im-pressed by and receive knowledge from their teachers. Even in performance, composition, and improvisation, teachers often direct their students. For example, ensembles of musicians are taught to sing and play exactly as the teacher desires, and there is little room for students' musical interpretations of pieces. The teacher's objective is to produce musicians who can play standard repertoire in standard ways and at standard levels of competence, so students focus on the models and examples provided by the teacher and seek to imitate them. In the studio lesson, for example, the teacher's performance is regarded as exemplary and definitive. Students are expected to perform like the master; their interpretations are "corrected" by the teacher, whose judgment is regarded as infallible and normative. Rather than divergent approaches to musical pieces, students learn certain interpretations, fingerings, articulations, and phrasings that are regarded as definitive as they seek to come as close to the master's rendering as possible.

Among the ways in which learners make decisions and discover new knowledge as performers, teachers, and researchers, the scientific method has primacy in this model because of the rationality of its procedures, the quantification of its observations, and the objectivity and generalizability of its findings.[27] For example, approaches undertaken under clinical trial conditions that demonstrate statistically significant advantages for musical learning over control conditions may be preferred, even if they are employed in widely different conditions than those under which they were developed and tested. Ethical questions concerning the validity of particular approaches to learning may be downplayed when statistical manipulations reveal a clear advantage of one over another. When what works in prompting student learning is considered to be of greatest importance, the end justifies the means and efficiency trumps other criteria.

Instruction. In circumstances of production, as in apprenticeship, the student's task is to receive the teacher's wisdom and emulate it, and music teachers and their students interact in predictable, hierarchical, and unidirectional ways. Instruction is hierarchical, because the teacher is invested with the authority and responsibility to deliver certain outcomes—notably a certain level and sort of student musical achievement. It is also unidirectional: teaching is directive and learning is a receptive process whereby the student listens, watches, copies, and thereby learns. It is further designed to enhance predictability. Serendipity, synchronicity, and the possibility of surprise at the unexpected and joy in the verification of fulfilled hopes fly out the window. Instead, the subject matter to be studied is broken down into its constituent parts and introduced to the student in a step-wise fashion, enhancing predictability. Analyzing those things that are needed in order to succeed in other things enables teachers and students who are focused on the ideas and practices of the subject matter to move systematically and consecutively through the material. The methods of presenting this subject matter are tested to determine and confirm the one best method. As a rational process, instruction relies on time-tested methods of conducting the interaction of teachers and students; it is driven by data that ground the methods whereby the subject is treated. Since the system relies on empirical demonstration and is worked out rationally, teachers and students are assumed to interact predictably and rationally. As instruction is research-based, systematic, and geared to student musical achievement rather than intuitive, disorganized, and unclear in its objectives, musical instruction is rendered less mysterious and spiritual than it might otherwise be. Teachers' empirical observations of the behavior of their students further reduces the unpredictability of the pedagogical situation.

Teachers and students have scant freedom to deviate from the standards imposed on them by the musical and educational establishment. To regard someone or something as a subject is to respect and honor that person or thing as of inestimable worth, to imaginatively feel what another's actions mean, wonder what is not said, or approach another tactfully in ways that are respectful to and sympathetic of the other.[28] By contrast, treating someone or something as an object takes a dispassionate approach that relies on reason rather than emotion and on what is seen rather than not seen; much depends on the value of the object in question as to how it is treated.[29] For example, teachers who value musical expertise may treat students who are talented musicians as of higher worth than those who possess little demonstrable musical aptitude or ability; musical knowledge that is considered of greater worth may be accorded more attention and respect than that of lesser worth.[30] Production also fosters autocracy at the same time as it undermines individual freedoms and disempowers those who work to forward democracy. Freedom and choice may be sacrificed for expediency, but this is considered to be a small price to pay.[31] As powerful, goal-oriented, and widely established norms, standards enforce widespread compliance as they also maintain the musical establishment's power. The establishment's power leaves little room for divergence from these standards and for individual choice on the part of teachers and their students regarding all aspects of their interaction with each other and the subject matter. Their use demonstrates music teacher and policy maker accountability to their publics at the same time as it controls the terms on which this accountability is demonstrated.

Curriculum. Thinking of curriculum systematically, the teacher addresses matters relating to the objectives of instruction, the nature of the specific subject matter to be studied, the specific instructional strategies to be employed, and the assessment procedures to be followed in measuring the instructional outcomes.[32] Conclusions arising out of this evaluative process feed back into the next cycle as the teacher considers what should be taught. This approach is appealing in its simplicity, in the seemingly self-contained and systematic character of curricular decision-making; it leads naturally to conceptions of curriculum in terms of systems theory, flow charts, and information processing and management.[33] Such models are typically comprehensive and closed, rather than incomplete and open, in order to allow for their scientific study and the design of the most efficient systems. Data generated by empirical studies provide bases for objective and rational decision-making on the part of educational policy makers and teachers. In music education, this systems approach is exemplified in competency-based music teacher education curricula in which instructional outcomes are broken down into their constituent parts.[34] These competencies emerge from professionally agreed-upon standards of music education. Each category is operationalized in terms of demonstrable behaviors that define when particular levels of competency have been met. A program of studies is then designed to prepare students to demonstrate these competencies. When students have demonstrated all of these competencies, they are deemed ready to be certified as teachers, and having been trained this way, it is likely that they will take the same approach with their own students.[35] Teachers confront technical challenges in rendering prescribed objectives and materials into instructional programs that demonstrate when prescribed objectives and competencies are met. The rational and objective criteria of curriculum and the difficulty of observing students' emotional attachments and commitments also suggest that the curriculum is likely to focus on developing students' mastery of specific competencies and producing musical products rather than on the holistic process of music education or its emotional and spiritual elements.

Articulating and focusing on specific competencies in the curriculum relies particularly on summative evaluation to demonstrate whether competencies have been met. In contrast to the formative emphasis in community and transgression curriculum, a summative emphasis is needed because the entire program of studies is comprised of the mastery of specific competencies all along the way. Rather than assisting students in attaining competencies, a principal task of formative evaluation, this summatively oriented approach tells students and teachers whether or not they have attained the required competencies. Teachers and students view this continuous evaluation in the curriculum differently. For students, the curriculum is strewn with barriers to be surmounted; for the teacher, this evaluation provides regular feedback on the program's success and students' progress. If students succeed in demonstrating the requisite competencies, this process may be encouraging and motivating; if they do not succeed, their lack of success thus far may be discouraging and become a self-fulfilling prophecy.

Administration. The environment in which much music education is situated is pervasively oriented to production, especially in the mass media and in the general education of young people, and this context is predominantly functional, with little emphasis on artistic form. Think, for example, of the often industrial-looking school buildings lacking architectural interest and designed mainly for educational production. The administration of music education is also organized hierarchically and segmented into specialized departments. This is accomplished partly through the use of space, but it is also formalized in self-contained administrative units that work independently of others. As with elementary and secondary school education, today's corporately oriented university administration evidences a top-down organizational structure governed by a powerful class of professional administrators inclined to dictate to their faculty and students on important issues.[36] As administrators control the financial resources, faculty and students are rendered relatively powerless. Workers are treated as means of production, and administrators are inclined to reduce the costs of human capital wherever possible even though education is a human-capital-intensive undertaking. An administrator's interest is naturally in getting the most talent for the least cost; faculty are the means to the end of efficient education, and so they are paid accordingly.

A data-driven management approach emphasizes rational decision-making and aims for clarity of objectives and an efficient and seamless production process. Quantifiable evidence is preferred, since it can be manipulated statistically and seems most objective. This leads, inevitably, to the enumeration of all aspects of the production process. In the academy, for example, there are the number of applicants to a program and the ratio of accepted students to applicants; the teacher–student ratio; the number of courses per teacher per academic year; the number of performances, articles, books, recordings, compositions, commissions, and other indicators of creative output per teacher; the grade point average and cumulative grade point average received by students individually, comparatively, and aggregated per school; the size of the school's endowment comparative to competitors; and the amount of money raised by a dean per year compared with other deans in this and other universities and over time. Within elementary and secondary schools, data are also generated on student results on standardized and nationally administered tests or ratings at musical competitions. The result of all of this enumeration is that those things that resist counting, such as the quality of the work done, the happiness of teachers and their students, and the morale of all involved in music education, are inevitably out of the public eye, while matters that can be quantified take center stage. Since all these data are often rendered into monetary terms, "bottom-line," cost-benefit, and financial thinking become facts of administrative life and drive administrative decision-making. In such an environment, undertakings that are most efficient and contribute most to the institution's financial well-being and musical prestige receive emphasis and financial support, and those that do not are marginalized or removed.

CRITIQUE

The production model offers important advantages for music. In a world in which large musical institutions with global reach are a fact of our contemporary life, its product orientation and mass-production emphasis ensure a large and predictable supply of competent musicians and a public who can be expected to support them. Its product orientation is also a good fit with pervasively materialistic and secular societies and capitalistic economies, where its values accord with the broader society and culture. Its large scale of operation is also suitable for those societies in which the many rather than the few are accorded the right to an elementary music education and to know their respective cultures—a right supported by the United Nations Convention on the Rights of the Child, which grants every young person the right to a cultural education that includes music.[37] Musical specialization also fosters the development of virtuosi in their respective fields, sophisticated instruments, technologies, and methods of instruction that enable a systematic and advanced system of music making and taking. Standardized instruments, expectations concerning musicking, and facilities permit large groups of musicians to play together, as well as the internationalization of music making and taking across political borders. Ideas and practices can thus be readily shared in ways that would be otherwise impossible. The emphasis on quality control of all aspects of music making is advantageous to all involved in music making and taking, and this is particularly the case in music education where most have the opportunity for musical instruction at a specified minimum level or above. These minimum standards remove chance from the system insofar as possible and prompt those who are performing below par to improve their work. Predictability and standardization of music making and taking also motivate administrators, teachers, and students by serving as musical "sticks and carrots" to punish those who do not perform well and reward those who do.

Among the disadvantages of the production model, however, emphasizing normalization, standardization, and canonicity overlooks musical diversity, even within a particular musical tradition. Improvisation is likely to be sacrificed in the interest of performing composed pieces that give performers less scope for musical expression,[38] opportunities for which are likely to be downplayed in the search for definitive readings or pieces. Also, the press for large-scale and mass music making and taking inevitably marginalizes and even compromises salon music and chamber music in the interest of filling large concert halls and opera houses. Because the intimacy of chamber concerts is difficult to achieve in large concert spaces, it is hard for chamber music to be competitive in a musical world oriented to mass production. Music critics may be reluctant to cover concerts in less prestigious locales, and local papers may be uninterested in carrying reviews of them. Repeated performances of canonical pieces leave less room for the composition and performance of new pieces. Large-scale musical performances requiring substantial forces require conductors to direct them, and conductors can become tyrannical and uninterested in securing musical performances that all the musicians can help to shape. Silencing dissent and stifling transgression undermine the very forces that can renew a musical tradition and make it relevant to changing times, places, and circumstances. Also, pushing for least-cost production goes counter to the nature of art—namely, its employment of all desired resources regardless of their cost—and contributes to exploiting musicians, especially those who are not "stars."

Regarding teaching, on the bright side, production employs tested methods that are regarded as efficient. This saves reinventing new teaching methods with every generation of teachers, so that those approaches that have been found to be efficacious in the past can be used in the present and future. Focusing on efficiency is particularly important where resources are scarce, as they often are in education. Musical instruction is among the more expensive subjects of study, given its high cost of personnel, musical instruments, and acoustic spaces suitable for musical rehearsal, performance, and recording, and teachers are naturally concerned to make the greatest use of resources at their disposal. In competency-based teaching approaches, teacher accountability is demonstrated in quantifiable terms; this seeming objectivity may be particularly persuasive to policy makers who are driven by such considerations. Specialist music teachers who possess a systematic understanding of music instruction and know what they are doing can be expected teach well, and their students should also do well. As teachers attend to traditional and normative musical beliefs and practices and seek to achieve certain results, unlike in the transgression model, they are likely to foster the continuance of those musical traditions that are the subject of their teaching.

On the dark side, the emphasis on methods elevates the means over its end. It reduces the teacher's role to that of a technician who applies particular methods in specific circumstances. Teaching to the central tendency takes insufficient account of the differing and individual needs and interests of learners, especially those at the ends of the spectra of student ability, achievement, and interest. Thinking of teaching as impression may be the wrong metaphor for learning; it can fail to take sufficient account of student insight and imagination and the importance of learning the rules that underlie this musical practice so that students develop habits of mind that permit them to become independent of the teacher. Teaching in standardized ways for convergent learning outcomes can fail to employ imagination and cultivate different and even better ways in which to make and take music. Regarding teaching as a one-way process of knowledge transmission from teacher to student does not envisage sufficiently the opportunities for teachers to be fellow learners with their students fostered in other models, such as community. Treating teachers as technicians and paying them low salaries also demeans their work and social standing and exploits their efforts, which are so central to music education. By constantly looking to powerful others for instruction and guidance, teachers may become passive, insufficiently independent-minded followers of others. Expertise in subject matter is no guarantee of teaching quality. Nor does specializing in particular fields of study allow sufficiently for the generalization and integration that other models such as community, apprenticeship, and quest foster. Rather, teachers are left in a relatively powerless position, since their specialties can leave them insufficiently cognizant of the general field. It is natural for administrators to fill this vacuum with their own global perspectives even though such action may further disempower teachers and students.

On the one hand, learning in the production model emphasizes qualities of receptivity and docility that are valued in many workplaces where there is a clear chain of command and those in control give direction to those below them and expect to be obeyed. Constantly and successfully surmounting obstacles and demonstrating competencies can motivate some learners, who desire continuing feedback and evidence of their increasing power. Learning is also the subject of careful planning and thoughtful and continuing assessment of student progress. This systematic approach enables students to take advantage of teacher expertise in a comprehensive way that attends to all aspects of musical development and is not "hit-and-miss"; that is, important aspects of student preparation are not left to happenstance. The possibility of quantifying important markers of student learning provides important evidence of accountability to stakeholders in music education.

On the other hand, the model's reliance on teacher direction breeds passivity, docility, and uncritical thought and action in students, as in their teachers. This learning fosters neither freedom nor democracy.[39] The trivialization of much subject matter and the drumbeat to create tests and measures focused on atomistic bits of knowledge and specific skills harms students when it fails to develop higher-level critical thinking skills and a holistic grasp of the subject. In competency-based music education, the focus is upon observable behaviors, and important spiritual and emotional learning that defy ready measurement are sidestepped. Some learners may not be able to keep up the pace of production, fall behind others, and may be discarded from the system. Fostering learner passivity is likewise potentially exploitative in its rendering students easy prey to autocratic regimes, unprepared to think critically and act to change society where necessary. Its one-size-fits-all approach fails to foster individual differences that make human society so interesting. Setting constant and trivial roadblocks in students' way creates a "busy work" syndrome, or a preoccupation with doing things that are not necessarily of value, and a student mind-set focused on meeting the minimum standards and obtaining the credentials of musical study. Students become skilled test-takers, able to successfully demonstrate competencies, but not necessarily better musicians and teachers. Since musical and pedagogical learning is more than the sum of its parts, one may learn the host of conducting skills and still not be able to effectively lead an ensemble. Effective musical leadership is holistic and elusive, difficult to quantify, and emotional, spiritual, and intellectual in character, and these more holistic qualities defy a productive approach to their development.

Concerning the benefits of instruction, interaction between teachers and their students in this model is results-oriented and appeals particularly to those who are motivated by directive environments. Its hierarchical structure clarifies the roles and responsibilities of participants and their respective powers, thereby creating an unambiguous environment in which to relate to others. Those who value such clarity of roles, responsibilities, and relationships are likely to find this situation congenial. Standardized instructional methods designed for use in large as well as small group instructional units are also likely to fit well with the internationalization and globalization of today's world. The hierarchical and specialized organization of instruction also focuses on teacher and student "on-task" behavior, permitting a direct, no-nonsense approach to teacher and student interaction.[40] By on-task behavior, I mean conduct that focuses directly on the specified objectives of instruction. The continuing assessment of teacher and student interaction, organized systematically from most elementary to most advanced levels of instruction, can help to ensure and even insist that the specified objectives are met.

Nevertheless, the standardized, hierarchical, and unidirectional nature of instruction renders it impotent to foster the kinds of conversations possible in the community model. When teachers are preoccupied with purveying knowledge to students in the framework of specified objectives, outcomes, and often materials, there is insufficient room for exploring differences, creating alternatives, and teaching for openings. Rather, it is the closings that are of primary concern, and students need to arrive at similar understandings and skill sets if they are to successfully demonstrate the specified competencies. There is little room for teachers and their students to construct knowledge divergently, and instruction is much more a process of ensuring compliance to norms than of suggesting and creating new possibilities. The use of standardized instructional methods leaves limited space to engage students in their multiplicities and pluralities, to focus on students' grasp of the subject matter rather than ensure that they fit into a particular musical mold. All is predicted wherever possible; serendipity and synchronicity are dispatched from, rather than welcomed into, the instructional process; and instruction is object-centered rather than subject-centered. Also, the instructional atomization, specialization, and objectification dehumanizes the music and the people when they are treated just like widgets to be analyzed into little pieces and reconstructed bit by bit.

This standardized and systematic music curriculum in the production model is beneficial in various ways. Its rationality emphasizes the nature of the subject matter as understood by experts, who then design ideas and practices that enable students to grasp the subject matter intellectually. In this vein, the Manhattanville Music Curriculum Project exemplifies a carefully articulated program of study that systematically progresses from elementary to advanced levels of understanding.[41] Here, music's rhythm, pitch, dynamics, form, and timbre are revisited spirally at ever increasing levels of sophistication. At every level, students perform, listen to, improvise, and compose music as they also relate music to the other arts and sciences. They produce products that can be evaluated publicly. Such a curriculum avoids idiosyncrasy and serendipity but seeks to forecast as clearly and accurately as possible the intended outcomes following instruction. Its use of scientifically demonstrable approaches grounds the teaching of this subject matter in a body of research and theory that is thoughtfully considered by policy makers and teachers. Its use of "proven" methods that can be readily assessed with reference to clearly articulated objectives and data-driven decision-making demonstrates how the curriculum is meeting the prescribed objectives. Taking a normative and standardized approach that focuses on the canonical also provides a common body of shared musical knowledge for students to learn. In multicultural societies, this common knowledge (including skills) provides a basis for conversation between different others as musics among other aspects of culture are contested in the public spaces.

More problematically, the atomized, systematized, and objectified knowledge purveyed to students in this curriculum is a static product, rather than a dynamic process wherein learners construct knowledge in diverse ways. Its presentation is likely to constitute knowledge that is "inert" and seems not to live or to be relevant to students' lived lives or constructed by them.[42] Such subject matter may be learned for the purposes of demonstrating competencies, but it is not necessarily to be lived by or internalized in the hearts and minds of students. Since wisdom is the capacity to make sense of information and ask compelling questions about what is known and not known, this preoccupation with atomistic bits of information and specific skills in standardized ways does not allow for the development of musical wisdom. Its lack of engagement with complex and important matters can leave those involved in this sort of music education without spiritual satisfaction, constantly needing refreshment and new ideas provided at workshops, clinics, and other demonstrations. Lacking critical thinking skills, teachers and their students are unable and even unwilling to forge different approaches to music making and taking for themselves—the very skills that would enable them to be their own teachers and find satisfaction in their teaching and learning. The preoccupation with summative rather than formative evaluation may also discourage teachers and their students when they are unsuccessful in meeting prescribed standards because, unlike formative evaluation, summative evaluation does not provide the means whereby they can be helped to succeed. Objective and quantified assessments of behavior also downplay subjective and qualitative approaches that might be helpful to teachers and their students in improving their work and attending to its spiritual and emotional rather than material aspects. The objectivity of these assessments may be more illusory than real; the meanings of the numbers ascribed may be more ambiguous than the precision they suggest.

Among the administrative advantages of the production model, the rationalization of instructional resources, personnel, time, and space according to functional criteria assure that times, places, and means of musical instruction are deployed in circumstances for which they are designed. These functional criteria make it possible for the system to work smoothly: the elements needed for successful music education are all in place. For example, rehearsing in spaces designed for rehearsals can be musically satisfying, effectively use instructional time and teaching expertise, and permit high musical expectations of music teachers and their students. Working in circumstances where there are clear lines of authority and unambiguous roles and responsibilities can also contribute to a smoothly operating music program. Focusing on the system's fluid operation not only permits an efficient use of scarce resources, especially time, space, personnel, and money, but enables limited resources to be used so that music education can have the greatest impact on the most people.

Among its disadvantages, exclusively rational, object-centered, efficiency-oriented, and fiscally driven administrative decision-making can be dehumanizing and exploitative. Making administrative decisions mainly on the basis of bottom-line and cost-benefit assessments and standardizing behaviors and procedures is dehumanizing in its treatment of people and music; it also misses the point of art, which is often extravagant and delights in differences. In the United States, the free market conditions in the academy result in inequitable teacher salaries and an increasing reliance on adjunct and part-time faculty in music teaching; this practice can be exploitative, since piecework inevitably results in lower payment than the work is worth when compared to the remuneration received by full-time faculty. Part-time workers are readily seduced by what additional income increments can mean for their quality of life and are inclined to work as much as possible even at the cost of their health and happiness. In European countries, a paucity of professorships in music education creates competitive and inequitable situations in which only a few reach the best positions and garner the greatest rewards and privileges. At this time, few women have reached such positions, notwithstanding that they do much of the work, and many others subsist on the margins by cobbling together music teaching livelihoods. The primacy of function over form also means that music education is often conducted in humdrum, prosaic, and shabby surroundings that dull the human spirit; were form also important in these environments, there could be greater harmony between music education and the context in which it occurs. Focusing on musical products likewise diverts attention away from the process of music making and taking. Being preoccupied with techniques and instruments of music teaching, learning, and instruction can miss its heart and soul. As most teachers and students see only a small part of the whole, production makes it possible for administrators to grasp power and create environments in which there is little freedom of thought and practice.

SUMMARY

In sum, the pictures of the factory and production are powerful and pervasive in music education. On the one hand, they offer advantages of large-scale operation and efficiency, and on the other, they undermine the power and life of musical traditions and those who practice them. Such is their overwhelming presence in the West that some may wish to remove them or altogether displace them to positions of less prominence. Still, there they are, looming over the gallery, and as we gaze upon them, we consider what we should do.

7
GARDEN AND GROWTH

The *garden* and *growth* pictures are of ancient vintage. Their subtle character, muted tones, and naturalistic themes are appealing especially in an industrial or postindustrial age. The dissonance between these images and technologically dominated lived life evokes nostalgia for a sometimes-forgotten and long-lost Paradise expressed in myths, musics, arts, and religions. In societies shaped by monotheistic religions such as Judaism, Christianity, and Islam, these images are evoked in the story of Adam and Eve once living in the Garden of Eden but expelled from it, or in a citrus orchard cultivated within the courtyard of a mosque-turned-cathedral symbolizing how the desert may bloom as a garden in Paradise.[1] At every hand, the garden reminds us of our limitations and fallibility and the power and promise of the natural world. Sketching the metaphor of the garden construed both as noun and verb, and its related model of growth, prompts a critical examination of the bright and dark sides of these pictures as they impact music educational thought and practice.

GARDEN

As I write, I look out upon a cottage garden. Hostas, astilbe, lobelia, cimicifuga, hydrangea, lenten rose (*Helleborus*), petunia, ivy, geraniums, red hot pokers (*Kniphofia*), heliopsis, coreopsis, daylilies, daffodils, and hollyhocks (*Althea rosea*) planted in beds, baskets, and pots flourish there. This little garden is quite new, having been established last spring in the moraine of which Cape Cod is comprised. This year's perennials seem to be twice the size of last year's and are filling in the beds nicely. Several plants that grace the border have been transplanted from a much larger and more well-established garden in Indiana. I recall the delight of first putting spade to moraine and finding the digging so much easier than in the heavy clay soil of Bloomington to which we are accustomed. Pouring bags of topsoil, peat moss, and mulch into the beds and mixing them with this sand resulted in a lovely rich and light soil in which these plants thrive. Repeated watering and natural fertilizer applications left this little garden a mass of greens highlighted by spots of color. From where I sit, astilbe flowers are forming, the cimicifuga has almost finished flowering, and the impatiens are growing nicely. Flowers on the little hydrangea bush are just setting, and the lenten rose seems to have tripled or quadrupled in size since being brought from Bloomington as a tiny cutting a year ago. In the midst of the garden beds, a patio table and chairs invite one to sit in the garden. The garden beds curve into a grass swath leading to the woodland beyond. Looking out on the verge of the woodland, I see in mind's eye an extension of this garden as it might yet be. Located privately, at the rear of the cottage, this garden was established not in order for others to see but to extend an interior living space into the out-of-doors. A front garden is likewise simply designed with tubs of impatiens, hanging baskets of petunias and coleus, and a brand new little holly bush by the front door, with stepping stones over mulched beds to a little garden shed. For now, it is full of possibilities awaiting realization. In its latent state, as a place of beginnings, it is already a source of joy.

Thinking about the garden, not only is it an ambiguous word, but there are at least two contrasting philosophies of gardening. One looks at gardening as creating a landscape constructed from the outside in, as if one were standing outside the garden viewing it from beyond its borders.[2] The other designs a garden from the inside out, and from the perspective of someone standing in the garden looking around. Whatever the perspective, gardeners create something subjectively appealing whether it be a riot of informally arranged plants, a formal garden with trimmed hedges, a rose garden with arbors arranged around a pool with a fountain playing on it, or sinuous lines of borders anchored by native grasses, shrubs, and trees. Each gardener brings a personal perspective to the character of the garden, differing knowledge of plants, and imagination as to what the mature garden might look like. For most gardeners, the project is never complete but always in a state of becoming. To my mind, the outside-in approach seems closer to a production or consumption mind-set, in which the garden is valued for the other things it brings rather than for itself. The gardener in me is drawn, rather, to the inside-out approach, since it is being in the garden that brings me most joy. In a real sense, I cannot fully "see" it from the outside, but I must also be in it.[3] An inside-out approach to gardening shapes my discussion of this metaphor, and I think of the garden's outside-in benefits as by-products of thoughtful inside-out thinking and planting.

To plant a garden is to dedicate a particular plot of ground or indoor space to the creation of a whole that, like art, seems more than the sum of its parts. Historically, a garden was laid out adjacent to a house, often within the walls or enclosures of the house so that it became a part of its yard.[4] Its roots are domestic, as they are also public in the parks and gardens adjoining prominent civic buildings and land set aside for recreational purposes. The garden is a part of the rest of lived experience, yet apart from it. It refers both to the creating and creation. Within a greenhouse or inside a building, its climate may be artificially constructed so as to create an environment in which particular living plants may flourish. It may have a functional purpose—for example, an indoor garden dedicated to the growing of vegetables or fruits. Within a city square, the public garden may create a cool and quiet oasis in a busy metropolis. It may serve as a space of natural beauty as plants flourish and bring color, texture, and form into an otherwise sterile environment. On a rooftop or in a tiny patio, it may feature tubs of plants or landscaping to provide vistas of plants at different levels. Or it may include statuary, fountains, monuments, sculptures, and other artistic and human artifacts. Pathways may wind through the garden, and a bench may invite us to remain a while. In all these myriad ways, it is a place in which people linger and socialize, and it is attractive because of its sheer natural beauty.

Art and science come together in the garden. Even though it may utilize native flora, the garden is dressing/dressed and arranging/arranged. It has primarily to do with the natural world, and is the means and end of designing and cultivating this particular place in which living things thrive.[5] Whatever the specific philosophy that undergirds the garden's design, and irrespective of whether plants are in profusion or accents in the landscape, it is a living thing. Natural forces of earth, wind, sun, and water govern which plants can survive and thrive in this particular situation, and developing a garden entails the art of providing appropriate differentiated conditions for the plant life within the garden. Although it is possible to create artificial conditions in which specialized and sometimes exotic plants can grow, whenever gardens are located outdoors, natural forces constrain and limit the plants that can live and thrive there. Matters of place and the situation of the garden, its orientation toward prevailing winds, soils, sunshine, shade, and climatic zone are prime considerations in designing and cultivating a garden. Growing these plants in this space necessitates that a gardener understands their particular characteristics in order to site them to best advantage. Science profoundly affects the garden through such means as the botanical names and classification of plants, chemical tests and treatment of soils, propagation of new varieties of plants, and horticultural practices of plant placement and cultivation. Plants in the garden evolve, sometimes helped along by human intervention.[6] Year after year, the garden changes, and although these living things are rooted in the ground, it is a place where change seems to be the norm.

Making a garden involves a commitment to this place that has a long-term impact on the land.[7] Anyone who has gardened knows that plants seem to have a mind of their own. Each grows differently than the rest. In the absence of continued care, plants would develop in ways or to an extent that may not be desired by the gardener. Even under the best of conditions, nature is so prolific that gardens invariably reach a point where it is necessary to thin out the plantings in order to keep them within bounds. Beside thinning, weeding, pruning, and the sometimes necessary destruction of plant life, vulnerable and sensitive plants that take longer to establish may need special care and fertilizing. Native species can be overcome by invasive plants from other places, and a gardener may spend a great deal of time encouraging and providing space for these otherwise endangered species. Some plants become sickly and die, and it is sometimes hard to accept the fact that plants also have a finite life, need to be replaced from time to time, and some do better than others simply because of the particular conditions of plant stock, soil, sun, wind, and rain in this garden. The cost of continuing labor in preparing the soil, planting the plants, watering and nourishing them, trimming and pruning them, weeding them, preparing them for winter, or readying them for spring is of a scope that a novice gardener could scarcely imagine. In our own garden, this sometimes back-breaking work requires patience and caring for this place and these living plants (and the other living things that dwell near them). Years of composting and mulching this soil gradually build a thick layer of organic material where worms and other earth-enriching creatures thrive. Rabbits, skunks, raccoons, squirrels, chipmunks, and foxes are among the animals that now call this garden home or visit it for the "mixed greens" it affords. Birds such as cardinals, blue jays, woodpeckers, finches, robins (of the thrush family), wild turkeys, nuthatches, titmice, juncos, doves, hummingbirds, and chickadees visit the garden to bathe at the birdbath, partake of the seeds, insects, or worms in the garden, or nest in its shrubbery. Not all of the living things that inhabit the garden are equally attractive, yet this little place becomes a refuge and haven for wildlife as well as family pets. Our own cat, Tilly, adores the garden and is often to be found resting in the sunshine or stalking wildlife with murder in mind. When we have made a garden, we want to see these living things flourish in the place that has also become theirs. Neighbors may also establish their own gardens, and so one garden becomes many.[8] One day, this garden will eventually pass to others. In the best of worlds, the newcomers would love the garden.[9] In the worst, this soil will still be different for years to come, even if others neglect or destroy the garden.

So, the garden is a place and activity where the natural world and human intention, mind and heart, theory and practice, art and science intersect. It speaks across the borders of our technological and mediated world as a reminder of a mythic past when there was time and space to have a garden, and when it served a necessary role in a family's survival. Its dynamism, incompleteness, diversity, and dependence on natural conditions, human imagination, and effort seem to mirror our human selves. We commune with living things beyond our ken in a garden. Those who love to garden may not imagine living happily without dwelling in one.

GROWTH

Among the proponents of this model, Plato believes that the "right" musical modes need to be employed in education so that the music that is learned and performed will sink into the souls of the young and help to cultivate the character needed by the republic's citizens.[10] As a student of the natural world Aristotle classifies things into their parts, and through this analysis leads the young toward wisdom.[11] Rousseau argues for the importance of allowing the young to develop naturally throughout childhood until puberty, when they add to their understandings the study of ethics so that they may live their lives morally as well as naturally.[12] Friedrich Schiller can be read to view human nature and morality dialectically, with the arts forming a crucial means whereby balance is maintained and morality is attained.[13] Johann Heinrich Pestalozzi advocates a natural approach to education viewed as growth.[14] More recently, John Dewey, Maxine Greene, and Nel Noddings forward notions of education as growth and caring relationships.[15] In music and music education, Michael Chanan documents the evolutionary history of musical change in the Western classical tradition, Shinichi Suzuki establishes a plan of musical instruction based on growth, and Randall Everett Allsup views musical change figuratively through the lens of Darwinian evolutionary theory, noting its implications for music education.[16] Given this long-standing interest, how does growth play out in music, teaching, learning, instruction, curriculum, and administration?

Music. In the growth model of learning, music is regarded as a changing and evolving phenomenon. A case in point is the evolution of the Western classical tradition from Gregorian chant into present-day electronified music.[17] Changes in scale systems, in musical forms, changes from pervasively liturgical music to secular music and from improvised to composed pieces, all instance this transformation over a long period of time. Growth spurts are complemented by periods of stability and consolidation as the possibilities of new styles and genres are worked out. Many changes are incremental rather than radical, although music history is punctuated by dramatic transformations such as the social and musical movements in the twentieth century.[18] Seeing music in a dynamic state of becoming and mutating through the process of acculturation, as musicians and their publics absorb aspects of other musical traditions, is to view it quite differently from envisioning a static stock of knowledge and wisdom to be passed on inviolate from one generation to the next.[19] Changes emerge from the contest of musical ideas and practices in the public spaces and the survival of those best able to thrive under different circumstances. Those musical traditions that become fossilized or unable or unwilling to adapt and change in response to new realities are either marginalized or disappear. In this respect, musics seem to respond much as civilizations and the sociomusical groups formed around them ("spheres of musical validity") evolve in "life-cycles" from formation, expansion, maturation, regression, to cessation, or rejuvenation (if social and musical renewal occurs).[20] Some musics are esoteric, their appeal is more limited, or they require extraordinary preparation and commitment on the part of music makers and takers alike. These may be deemed more fragile than others and cultivated through formal education. For example, classical musicians are trained in the possibly artificial and hothouse environments of conservatories, and classical traditions are the subject of formal instruction in schools. Such training and schooling typically focus on a musical canon and systematic methods of theoretical and ear-training instruction and instrumental pedagogy.[21] Over time, schools of instrumental performance and pedagogy develop around particular teachers and institutions, and despite changes and the trend toward internationalization of the various instrumental sounds and performance practices, varieties of instrumental sounds are preserved and fostered.[22]

A continuing search for new musical knowledge and a humanistic approach to music are also characteristic of musical growth. Instruments are modified and new ones are introduced. Composers compose new music and performers seek out repertoire that is largely unknown.[23] Scholars research and publish their studies of various aspects of music and the ways in which people come to know music. Professional and scholarly societies are formed to disseminate knowledge about music and musical instruction. In these and other ways, lost pieces are recovered and new musical ideas and practices are forged. Musical values undergird traditions that are preserved and enhanced for their own sake, not necessarily for any utilitarian purposes they serve. Musics are prized as expressions of human ingenuity and as integral elements of human culture. To know one's culture is also to know oneself; a pervasively humanistic ethic that dignifies humanity prevails and is evident in writings about music since antiquity.[24]

Teaching. The teacher's primary tasks in the growth model are to set up the environmental conditions that enable students to develop musically. This interconnectedness of the classroom to the past and the context in which it is situated is essential for student development since it provides a firm and seamless basis on which students can construct knowledge.[25] In order to prompt student insight, teachers set up frames of reference in which students can grasp interconnections between past and present and make sense of what they are doing in the rehearsal, classroom, or studio. By taking advantage of students' impulses or natural inclinations to learn, teachers transform these initial impulses into desires for and commitments to longer term development.[26] Teachers also construct the kinds of instructional situations in which there is the greatest possibility for student development, in such a way that each end becomes a means of further development in a lifelong learning process.[27] Whether assisting students in making connections between things or removing obstacles to their understanding or both, teachers seek to help students do what it is assumed comes naturally to them, namely, learn. These connections are practical as well as theoretical and are evident in the cultivation of dispositions to act in particular ways; that is, teachers treat ideas in ways that students are inclined to live by them.[28] When these dispositions are directed toward ensuring democratic principles and practices, they are assumed to tend toward the good.[29] This view presupposes no insurmountable difficulties in relying on the student's natural desires to learn and to grow.

Teachers focus on an array of differing educational purposes: training, schooling, eduction, socialization, and enculturation.[30] Of these, eduction is of paramount importance, because it focuses on prompting and assisting students to take the necessary steps in active doing and receptive undergoing. To educe is to bring forth that which is already there, and to foster, elicit, and "draw out" capacities that may have been latent but are now made manifest.[31] Training systematically analyzes musical skills into their constituent parts and provides the means whereby students progressively acquire them.[32] Schooling is a matter of learning the discipline of a particular subject and coming to know and do it comprehensively. Socialization and enculturation focus on broader matters of the ways students are brought into conformity with social norms and become a part of the wider culture. The teacher's work is cast comprehensively and transformatively in an educational process that is both general and specific, social and personal, objective and subjective, doing and undergoing, formal and informal, holistic and atomistic.

Providing these conditions for natural development on the students' part necessitates that teachers know their students and establish and maintain rules for the conduct of instruction. Doing this requires a careful study of children in order to ascertain their particular backgrounds, impulses, desires, aspirations, and other circumstances of their lived lives.[33] Teachers' informal observations of students are complemented by empirical research into how children see the world and the pedagogical approaches best suited to their continued development. Moreover, the necessity of teachers' grasping their students' present musical development requires developmental theories of music and their empirical testing as frames through which teachers can identify their students' present intellectual, physical, emotional, and musical progress.[34] Primacy is accorded to scientific approaches to knowledge in which hypotheses are formulated and systematically tested, and researchers seek to establish a solid evidentiary basis for teachers to decide how best to foster student development.[35] Teaching is also a matter of establishing freedom and social control, whereby all of the participants in the pedagogical situation are mutually bound by rules that are constructed conversationally.[36] The preeminence of rules as the means of self-government necessitates that teachers are fair-minded and also agree to be bound by the rules that are set. Like apprenticeship, music making and taking is a rule-governed system. Teachers are experts in what they teach; they assist their students to grasp the rule-systems that characterize their musical traditions, and they foster student growth in those musical traditions.[37]

Learning. In the growth model, learning is a matter of nurture more than nature; that is, the environment in which it takes place is most important in students' development.[38] When obstacles to learning are removed and students' natural propensities to learn are encouraged by their teachers, the entire process enables learners to progress successfully at each step along the way. Students' individual insights into the challenges that teachers set for them at their particular stages of development enable them to grasp what they need to know and be able to do.[39] Gradually, what at first seems mysterious becomes clear as students observe and intuit their teachers' instruction and example, practice their instruments, participate in music making, and absorb, reflect on, and sense the import of this instruction. Learning is a matter of being helped by one's teacher to find one's own way and to evidence what is latent within oneself. Because people are different, this learning is bound to result in divergent outcomes as students construct their own understandings of music. Since music is practical as well as theoretical, learning is necessarily psychomotor as well as cognitive and affective and a matter of maturation.[40] By psychomotor, I refer to the connections between mind and body required in music performance. It is not surprising that matters of skill development are of paramount importance to music teachers, because skills are essential to being able to make and take music, and musicians recognize the limiting role of musical techniques in preventing those who do not possess them from musicking.[41] By maturation I mean the process whereby learners go from being neophytes to competent musicians. This process has often been described in terms of developmental theories drawn especially from psychological research, for example, Piagetian theories.[42] While these perspectives are important, students' specifically musical development—for example, their progress on their instruments—is also of particular interest to music teachers. At each stage in the process, students may demonstrate musical competence appropriate to that level, and as their development proceeds, so musical expectations of them naturally change.[43]

Learning is not cast as delayed gratification for some imagined end; rather, the circumstances in which learners learn contribute directly to their present happiness.[44] Students experience happiness within a caring environment in which all are treated with affection, sympathy, and respect. My own term—pleasure—signifies the compassionate and enjoyable elements of learning that make for a joyful experience.[45] Thinking figuratively, learning is conceived of as drinking the "water of life." What is learned is vital, refreshing, and renewing in its influence. Water symbolizes energy imbibed by and energizing to learners as they come in contact with this subject matter. A chorale's performance is energizing, as singers are moved emotionally and inspired by what they have collectively created to dream of further possibilities, of "what if's," and to wonder how they might make their imagined realities come true. In these ways, knowledge lives for students and energizes them, and music takes on "vital import," or the meaning that seems to be full of life and enlivening as music is done and undergone.[46]

Instruction. Teacher and student interaction in the growth model is conversational and individualized, yielding diverse consequences. Like instruction in conditions of community, it is conversational in fostering interchanges between students and teachers concerning issues of moment. These conversations are framed within rule sets that govern teacher–student interaction musically and pedagogically and are arrived at collectively by teachers and their students; they help teachers understand the particular needs, capacities, interests, challenges, and experiences of their students and tailor instruction to them. As in the apprenticeship mode, teachers and students interact in ways that permit instruction to be individualized and its ends divergent. Rather than situating teachers as fellow learners in the community of learners, teachers are the senior partners and leaders in instruction, responsible for engendering learning in their students who are able to take advantage of their expertise and guidance.[47] In particular, teachers act as referees to ensure that the group's rules are upheld.[48] Democratic ideals are crucial in instruction. When rules govern conversations that are conducted in civil and humane ways and focus on divergent rather than convergent outcomes, the classroom becomes a public space in which multiplicities and pluralities may flourish.[49] Still, musical rules take a long time to acquire and master, and performing competence necessitates an extended time to mature. There is a difference between slavishly following the rules as neophyte performers and knowing when and how to be governed by, bend, or even break these rules as accomplished performers might do. At first, students depend on their teachers to help them develop the musical skills they need. Even when they have acquired the requisite skills, there are further artistic requirements in creating musical compositions or performances that are vital and compelling to listeners and performers alike. In gaining these more advanced interpretative aspects, students are likewise helped by the teacher's expertise.

The success of instruction hangs, in large measure, on the "atmosphere," social climate, or quality of interpersonal relationships between teachers and their students. Growth relies on evoking rather than impressing student progress and requires positive rather than negative reinforcement, helping students rather than hindering them; it hinges on mutual respect and sympathy of all the participants in music instruction for each other.[50] We speak, informally, about people "being on the same wave length" or "seeing eye to eye," and these are ways of expressing the holistic, receptive, and positive way of seeing and being in tune with the other.[51] The point here is that the pedagogical situation is a safe place for learners to risk trying out new ideas and practices, students' best interests are central considerations for the teacher, and all those involved in the instructional situation treat each other civilly, humanely, inclusively, and respectfully. Arranging the conditions that collectively constitute environments in which to educe learning is a tall order for teachers.[52] They need to be creative and responsive to their students, and their students need to be willing and engaged learners in constructing their own understandings of music. The sheer diversity of ways in which teachers and students are, think, and act makes it challenging for teachers to settle on a single plan that will suit all of the participants equally well, and they are faced with doing the best they can under the particular circumstances.[53] Still, music is especially efficacious in stimulating imaginative thought and action and affording means whereby openings can be created and explored.[54]

Curriculum. In the growth model, curriculum may best be seen as *currere* in its emphasis on the experiential nature of and dynamic engagement of the student with the subject matter.[55] The process works as follows.[56] Children come to the subject matter with their own idiosyncratic, intuitive, and psychological constructions of it, and the teacher's task is to bring the child's initial experience of the subject matter to a more mature grasp approximating an exponent's.[57] Each step in the process becomes an end that, when reached, becomes the means to yet other ends. The nature of musical study is interrelated with other school subjects being studied contemporaneously, as well as within a more general cultural context. This integration of music with the rest of lived life constitutes process as well as product in the sense that the musical performances and the like that emerge from musical study are linked together in means-ends chains of developing expertise. Rather than build the entire system on inherently musical concepts (designed by musicians), the teacher initially approaches music as children might see it, for example, through such activities as musical games that enable them to experience music before they learn the concepts and terms to name these experiences.[58] The challenge is to move from an initially intuitive and "romantic" grasp of music, through the achievement of musical skills and techniques, to "generalization," where the initial romance is informed by a subsequent instrumental grasp of music and integrated into a mature understanding of music as its exponents know it.[59] Along the way, the teacher needs to "change gears" without losing music's "romance" while still enabling the student to move to a more systematic and mature understanding.[60]

In contrast with modernist accounts of growth that seem conservative in terms of a single canon of masterworks in a particular musical tradition, postmodern writers in the later part of the twentieth century have interrogated the establishment's knowledge claims. Today, we are acutely aware of the extent to which the canon is politicized and ideological and the plethora of musical traditions and pieces of music that are also worthy of notice. Exponents within a particular musical tradition disagree with each other; knowledge is subjective, constructed, partial, and fallible; and a single, homogeneous, fully agreed-upon expert grasp of music seems impossible.[61] Rather than *either/or* thinking, conservative and progressive views of the curriculum are required.[62] Students need to grasp the commonly held beliefs and practices in music as they also embrace the renewal and transformation that comes when their teachers engage both tradition and students' interests, impulses, and backgrounds. This synthetic or dialectical approach is bound to transform the canon (sometimes incrementally and other times dramatically). Music is in the midst of change even when musicians are not consciously subverting and changing it.[63] Focusing on the student as well as the subject matter, present and past, and classical and vernacular traditions requires finding a pathway between extreme positions, even though this may be a complex and challenging position to hold.[64]

Curricular assessment is likewise both formative and summative. It is formative in the sense that students can be helped to develop in ways that motivate them to improve and summative in its concern for demonstrating accountability to its public, making the best use of limited resources and attending to those whose possibilities show most promise. Avoiding the pitfalls of evaluating students' performances too harshly or too leniently is a challenge for teachers who want to balance the two extremes. Teachers are fallible, work in the context of incomplete knowledge, and may err in their judgments of their students. Knowing their students as well as possible can help them more accurately assess their students' effort, progress, and achievement. Their interest in, and commitment to, their students' long term development also leads them to also take a long-term view of assessment. Unlike in the model of production, their interest centers on the process of development and on long-term rather than only immediate or short-term results.[65] It seems clear that throughout compulsory schooling or elementary and early secondary school, formative rather than summative evaluation is regarded by many music teachers as more important because it aids in musical development and resists a too-exclusive approach to student musical development.

Administration. Organizing music education in the context of growth requires dialectical top-down and bottom-up mechanisms that permit direction to ensure the group's cohesiveness, yet allow and foster spaces in which initiatives may arise at a grassroots level and filter up to administration. Accomplishing this feat requires the organization to balance ideas and practices that foster its own development while also enabling individuals to develop in divergent ways. Instead of the closed system of the production model, growth-based administration is an open system in which surprise, serendipity, and synchronicity are welcomed. The rules that govern the system's operation are interpreted by the organization and individual members and are regularly subverted and transgressed. New rule-sets emerge as they are contested in the public spaces. Integral to this holistic approach to education are surprise and the joy of verification, among the cognitive emotions experienced by members in an open system, along with emotional cognitions experienced particularly in the arts, religions, myths, and rituals.[66] Such a stance requires administrators and music teachers to treat music instruction as an important element in general education.[67] The fallibility of administrators, teachers, students, and stakeholders, and the ambiguities surrounding beliefs and practices in the arts, religions, myths, and rituals require teachers and policy makers to approach their work with humility, since there are definite limitations to what they can accomplish with others who have minds of their own. I suspect that administration in circumstances of growth probably flourishes best in a relatively flat rather than hierarchical organizational structure.[68] As in community and apprenticeship administration, organizing individual and small group instruction requires the possibility of some student and teacher choice. It is hard to see how arranging for individual development could be accomplished solely within the purview of large group instruction. Rather, some combination of large and small group and individual instruction would seem to be needed.[69]

Planning for growth also requires critical thinking skills in navigating the interests of the one and the many, the large and the small musical traditions, the cultural and the technical, the theoretical and the practical. Dialogical decision-making requires finding a way through the claims of consensus, compromise, agreement, and disagreement that result when those involved in music education think critically. Given the prospect of multiplicities and pluralities, divergent musical beliefs and practices, commitments to ideas and practices, and their emotional and physical ramifications, while peaceful coexistence is a possible ideal, practically speaking, tensions and even conflicts are likely to arise. Creating humane environments that are inclusive and respectful of various ideas and practices and that provide and foster public spaces where ideas and practices can be debated is a primary concern for administrators. Fostering critical thinking, especially when it is critical of administrative decisions; sharing power with those involved in the music educational enterprise; creating a humane administration—these efforts necessitate secure, broad-minded, and humane leadership. I suspect that teachers and students are likely to thrive and be happy when these circumstances prevail.

CRITIQUE

Among the musical advantages of the growth model, music is related to the rest of life and the present is related to past traditions. The arts are central to education, and the artistic and aesthetic aspects of all subjects are explored. Musical change is often incremental. Musical traditions are respected and cultivated even when they are fragile or out of the public consciousness. Traditions also change as musical knowledge is mediated by teachers and constructed by students in differing ways. Such change serves to renew music traditions and subvert and sometimes replace their primacy with others. Acculturation results from musical traditions coming into contact with others, and musics (and those who make them) are enriched and changed in the process. Sometimes dramatic changes occur, and the survival of musical traditions depends on the cultivation of musics and the responses to these shifts in the musical landscape. This dynamic view of music as a "living tradition" accords well with the historical evidence of the Western classical tradition that stretches over millennia. Propagating various musics also necessitates engaging the changing social and cultural contexts in which musics are made and taken. An idealistic view of music prompts a search for ever more satisfying performances and different ways of doing and undertaking music.

Still, it may be tempting to take too literally the parallels between the natural and social worlds, thereby oversimplifying the situation in music education.[70] Musical values are of central importance and cover many things. It is not always easy to distinguish between performance programs that are self-serving or oriented toward other external ends, such as the teacher's or program's reputation, and those that are focused mainly on the process of affording students the opportunity to develop as musicians. In situations where production or consumption are prevalent educational models, teachers' interests may readily shift to results that accrue from performance rather than the value of preparing to perform, or performing for its own sake. Nor can it be assumed that music instruction creates better people.[71] Rather, the evidence suggests that evil people also enjoy music making and taking. The dialectical character of growth and its inclusion of training, schooling, eduction, socialization, and enculturation may also make it difficult to achieve a balance between these means. Musician-teachers may be too traditional, dictatorial, and directive, instead of oriented toward the tradition's renewal and open to helping and conversations with their students. When this occurs, a musical tradition may become stultified and students may not develop in the ways the model envisages.

To its credit, teaching in growth is rhapsodic and conversational as teachers engage each of their students differently so as to prompt their long term development. This long view of the impact of teaching is driven by teachers' nurturing and caring for their students, as well as their carefulness for the subject matter they teach. Qualities such as tact are also manifested in the tender and sensitive way in which teachers treat their students and contribute to the humanity of the educational process.[72] Teachers' recognition of the limitations of what they are able to do in prompting student learning and their reliance on and trust in their students' willingness to learn focuses attention on those things that teachers can affect—namely, the environment in which students learn. Systematic and naturalistic studies of students also make sense in designing programs of instruction that are likely to interest students and enlist their effort in learning. As in the community model, the model's attention to individual differences and divergent outcomes allows teachers to teach for openings that allow students the fullest range of possibilities for development and the opportunity to follow their own inclinations, interests, and aptitudes. Its democratic character in caring both for the common good and for individual development serves to model and foster democratic behavior in society at large.

Nevertheless, teaching in this model is a more difficult undertaking than more directive approaches in the production and apprenticeship models and may be too rhapsodic and insufficiently committed to particular ends for some tastes. The assumption that human nature is good and that people naturally want to learn is flawed; the evidence shows that not all students are motivated to learn, and some of the best teachers have evil students.[73] Insight may also be the wrong metaphor for education, since it places too much onus on the students, who cannot always grasp what their teachers are saying and doing.[74] Likewise, tensions between the model's emphasis on insight and its orientation to rules, individual understanding, and collective behavior require teachers to reconcile, at least practically, the various approaches to teaching.[75] As in community learning, the model's lack of emphasis on the teacher's role as fellow learner inevitably places the teacher in a directive or mentoring role rather than as a fellow learner in search of truth. Consequently, the conversation ultimately seems a one-way rather than genuinely two-way dialogue.[76] Teaching for openings may also fail to address sufficiently the closings on which production is focused. This is especially the case in the arts, where closings are as important as openings.[77] Teachers may also fail to see their role as requiring the destruction of habits and patterns of thought and practice that are sometimes required if the student is to develop musically. Given the constraints on and conditions of their work, teachers may be unable to attend sufficiently to the divergent and individual development of their students.

Among its benefits, learning in the growth model relies on student insight, imagination, and willingness to learn. This model takes account of the differing styles, developmental levels, and modalities appropriate to each learner, grounding impressions in empirical observations that are systematically described and tested. The conversational character of instruction prompts critical thinking, and students are encouraged to engage the subject matter in deep as opposed to merely superficial ways. Learning is helped by the attention to learners' happiness and a holistic approach that attends to their spiritual, emotional, physical, social, and intellectual maturation. Developing dispositions to democratic thinking and practice, a generous spirit toward those who think and act differently, and humanity and civility in dealing with different others ensure broad outcomes in students' lives. Reinforcing learning in positive rather than negative ways not only helps to cultivate happiness but is likely to constitute a more successful way of motivating students than punishing them when they do not do well. Including propositional and procedural knowing provides for a broad, holistic, and integrated theoretical and practical approach to learning music that is in keeping with the nature of music making and taking.

Learning in the growth model may also be flawed. Focusing on environmental conditions and taking insufficient cognizance of individual capacities, abilities, and potentials may lead to unrealistic expectations of students. Their potentials are not necessarily open-ended but are also shaped by physical and psychological characteristics, opportunities, and choices made by students and their guardians.[78] Happiness, pleasure, and positive reinforcement as means of encouraging students to learn may also overlook the power of sometimes painful, unhappy, and unpleasant experiences and punishments. Nor does this idealistic world mirror the realities and vicissitudes of life, in which learning often takes place when one is confronted with what one cannot or may not do. The ideal of happiness as an end of education may also cause teachers to pander to students rather than putting them to the test and confronting them with what they cannot now but could do.[79] Even though growth is oriented toward the long term, its lifelong possibilities may be forgotten in the press of short term thinking and immediate results, sometimes driven by a fear of missing immediate opportunities.

Instruction, or the pedagogical interaction of teachers and students, has various advantages with this model. Among them, it is both active and receptive. Its humanistic character permits critical examination of musical ideas and practices and civil discourse within a climate of mutual respect and caring for the other as well as the subject matter. Its dialectic and democratic nature guided by rule-sets prepares students for full participation in a democratic society. Integrating possibilities for choice in individual, small group, and large group settings with situations in which choices are limited prepares students to participate fully in home and public life.

Still, the interaction between teachers and students is a more complicated matter than in the production model, where a much clearer and more directive communication from teacher to student obtains. Establishing rules for the conduct of instruction in democratic ways may not suit some activities, such as conducting ensembles that are often product-centered and constricted by limitations of time, space, and personnel. Musicians might argue that since the ensemble, by definition, needs to be a musical whole and large forces are often involved, democratic procedures are inappropriate; the ensemble's musical interpretation needs to be shaped and unified by the conductor. The ensemble is, in effect, an instrument, and just as one would hope that the various keys of the piano do not go on their own independent ways (or we would call in the piano tuner if they did), so the individual players and various sections cannot go on independently but need to be brought together. Conductors may have high expectations of their musical forces, insisting that their wishes be carried out exactly how and when they command, and yet they may also treat their musicians with respect, humanity, and caring.[80] Democracies can also be tyrannies of the majority. Although an ensemble is typically not organized as a democracy, the conductor needs to ensure that all the ensemble sections are in balance so that the violas are of equal worth to their often more visible cousins the violins and cellos, and the solitary English horn player is heard over the myriad strings or the other winds. In short, too readily equating democratic means of governance with humanity and civility fails to grasp the complexity of the musical and instructional enterprise and the various ways in which civility, respect, humanity, and caring can be demonstrated. There also need to be places for the more directive approaches typical of training and schooling and exemplified in apprenticeship. Every orchestra rehearsal is not a musical conversation between director and players, nor is every studio lesson a conversation about the particular pieces that need to be learned or skills that need to be mastered. There are moments in a choral rehearsal when a conductor, wanting a particular interpretation or tone, insists on it, and the singers, having achieved what the conductor wants, have their ears opened when they hear the result. The limited time for rehearsal may constrain the extended conversation that might otherwise ensue. A more practical interpretation might be to think of a musical group as striving for a performance with finesse while also caring about and for each other and the music they perform, and a conductor who takes every opportunity to dialogue with the performers and inspire them to think musical thoughts and do musical deeds they might not otherwise think and do. Openings and divergent outcomes may need to be taken sometimes literally and sometimes figuratively, according to the particular circumstances.

On the bright side, curriculum in the growth model enables students to first approach music idiosyncratically, individually, subjectively, and intuitively, within the context of their lived worlds, and gradually come to the musician's more objective and systematic knowledge. Cyclical curricular approaches, moving progressively from an intuitive, instrumental grasp to a more generalized musical understanding, offer a holistic and dynamic approach. Here, curriculum is process as well as product, and each end becomes the means to yet another. This view contrasts with the stock-of-knowledge approach typical of the production curriculum and opens the prospect of divergent outcomes on the part of teachers and their students. The model's emphasis on the present, on happiness, enjoyment, or pleasure in the moment rather than delaying gratification until some future time make musicking more a matter of play than work. Studying one's students also makes it more likely that the strategies employed in bringing them into contact with music will be more successful as students experience music positively. Meeting student interests while also attending to the subject matter enables teachers to find a balance between these differing claims and avoid either/or thinking. Focusing on short-term formative and long-term summative evaluation allows assessment to serve as an agent for the student's immediate and long-term musical and personal development.

On the dark side, balancing the differing objectives of music education is difficult to achieve, and teachers may place too great an emphasis on one aspect or another. When they find it difficult to achieve a balance of sometimes diverging, competing, and even conflicting ends and means, teachers may turn to the development of skills, since these are straightforward and more clearly articulated than the otherwise more ambiguous spiritual, emotional, and intellectual ends and broadly conceived cultural purposes. Fostering skill development may cause teachers to lose awareness of the whole cloth of music education and afford insufficient opportunity to explore music's cultural and social context. Focusing on providing positive environmental conditions for learning may result in pandering to students' present impulses and interests and losing focus on the long-term ends of music education. In this way, teachers may not sufficiently challenge their students or bring them from initially intuitive and idiosyncratic understandings to the more sophisticated musical understanding of musics well beyond their initial experience. Linking music to the rest of lived life may not pay enough attention to those more esoteric musics that are out of the public eye and not immediately accessible. Teachers may too readily excuse an emphasis on popular musics at the cost of other less accessible musics when their students resist learning about or how to do such musics. It may be easier to put pleasure and ease ahead of the more challenging task of constructing an effective plan whereby students' musical horizons are broadened and their knowledge is deepened. Emphasizing musical processes rather than products may be difficult to accomplish in a social and cultural milieu in which products are especially valued. This may be the case because, practically speaking, teachers may have little choice over their purposes and plans, so constrained are they by regulations and administrative directives. Moreover, the conversational character of instruction may allow for a less systematic view of music than that possible in the consumption and production models.

Concerning the advantages of administration, creating humane and pleasant environments in which teaching, learning, and instruction are forwarded contrasts with conditions in the production model and may impact music education positively. Modeling a democratic society, respecting differences among teachers and their students, thinking critically, and ensuring that minority perspectives and the voices of those who are most vulnerable are heard enable music educators to positively impact the society at large. The ambiguities and tensions in this model require negotiation, reconciliation, and even resignation, and these skills potentially benefit the wider society. When all have a vested interest in decision-making, all are likewise empowered and liberated and may find greater satisfaction in the educational process. The administrator's principal responsibility lies in assembling the resources required for music instruction, and vital aspects of time, space, personnel, instruments, and money are not left to happenstance but are actively planned for and secured. In this way, administrators fulfill an important part of the music educational process and are needed by their colleague teachers, just as leaders need the help of those they lead. Such a collegial view contrasts with the sometimes dictatorial and confrontational relationship between management and workers in production.

Nevertheless, among its disadvantages, leaders may be charged with undertaking tasks with which they have not had prior experience. If they have not experienced first-hand the sort of education the growth model suggests, it is difficult to imagine how or why they would seek to create an organization like this. As a result, there is a "chicken-and-egg" problem in which it is difficult to know how best to intervene in order to provide these experiences. Administering an organization in which it is necessary to meld, balance, compromise, or choose between alternatives is a challenging undertaking and an elusive goal. Some seize upon the processual aspects of music education to the detriment of articulating the ends and products that ought to emerge, thereby overshooting a balanced approach. Where the environment in which music education takes place is pervasively product-centered, it is likely that well-meaning music administrators, teachers, and students may sacrifice the process in order to produce the product, be it a composition, performance, recording, publication, competition win, positive teaching evaluation, or high grade in a course. For some, the ambiguity and subjectivity of this model's aims are simply too amorphous and unclear for their taste. Democracy may be more apparent than real and democratic procedures can mask corruption, greed, and the desire for power over others. It is possible, for example, to arrange many meetings in which teachers and students express their views and democratic procedures may seem to be in place, and yet administrators do what they want to do or plan to do anyway. Thinking of music education in this way may also unduly politicize the undertaking and fail to attend sufficiently to the claims of music making and taking; it may misinterpret musical traditions as undemocratic in political terms that musicians do not intend and would repudiate were they to realize how their actions are being interpreted.[81] Since actions are symbolic, their meaning is ambiguous and it is possible to interpret them variously. Musicians may be uncomfortable with unduly politicizing their work because they see it artistically rather than politically. Administrators may also be foiled in their attempt to secure the necessary resources for music education because the values of growth in music education are not aligned with those of production and consumption in which music education is situated. They rely, in turn, on others with more power and control of the time, space, money, personnel, musical instruments, and equipment of various sorts, and they may fail to convince these others of the importance of providing them for music education. Their task might be easier were the values of music education to mesh with those in the larger environment. So, although administrators are responsible for creating the immediate environments in which teachers and students do their work, they have limited power and work, in turn, within other constraints. Not only is the concept of environment an elastic and murky one, but it is possible to fault the environment for what one cannot accomplish, an ultimately self-defeating proposition, yet one that cannot easily be challenged exactly because of this murkiness. When administrators believe that they are not able to "compete" effectively for scarce resources, it is a short step to moving from a growth orientation to a production or consumption orientation, where music educational values may better synchronize with environmental conditions, ambiguous though these be.

SUMMARY

In sum, the pictures of garden and growth, although initially heart-warming, pose significant challenges for music teachers and those interested in their work. Notwithstanding their potential contributions to humane and civil discourse, fostering individual development in the context of the wider public and teaching for musical openings that foster creative and divergent musical makings and takings, they have a dark side. Among the issues of concern to musicians and educators are prospects of turning democratic purposes and means on their head and creating tyrannies of the majority; failing to focus sufficiently on nature rather than nurture; overshooting the mark of balancing differing aims and methods; pandering excessively to students' present interests; misconstruing the differences between the natural and social worlds; and failing to attend sufficiently to musics beyond the ordinary lived lives of students. One ponders how these pictures can impact those in capitalistic societies who are devoted to the production and consumption of material goods and services, and what might be done practically to conserve the best of what these pictures might offer while guarding against the worst.

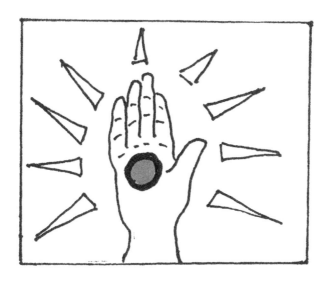

8
THERAPIST AND HEALING

The pictures of *therapist* and *healing* may have a special resonance with studio teachers who conduct individual and small group music instrumental and vocal lessons.[1] These situations permit an intimacy between students and teachers that is not always possible in large classes and ensembles. Rather than urge that music education *become* music therapy, I offer the therapist as a *metaphor* for music education; clearly music education and music therapy need to remain distinctly different fields in order for the metaphor to work. The word *therapy* comes from the Greek *therapeia* meaning "healing."[2] Taken in this sense, the therapist is one who "practices in therapy" one or more of a wide range of medical, physiological, and psychological skills that "have a good effect on the body or mind."[3] By "good effect," I mean that these skills foster health and well-being. I use the word *healing* to indicate "restoration to health" and "recovery from sickness," related to the Old English word *whole,* and in its archaic senses of "mending" or "reparation," "restoration of wholeness, well-being, safety, or prosperity," "spiritual restoration" or "salvation."[4] I might have called this model *integration* or *restoration*, since its emphasis is upon bringing together or restoring parts that have been separated into a unity that represents a comprehensive view of the person in music education. Still, I prefer the word *healing* for its humanitarian connotations, its figurative usage, its re-dressing of an old idea, its sense of re-mediating, restoring, and making whole, its use by writers in music education, and its reclamation of what may have been lost through circumstances of birth, family upbringing, religious and moral teaching, and socioeconomic status. Following a sketch of the therapist drawn intuitively from the perspective of a recipient of a therapist's skills and attributes of the related model of healing, notably, music, teaching, learning, instruction, curriculum, and administration, I examine briefly this model's advantages and disadvantages for music education.

THERAPIST

Long before I met Katina, I had heard about her from many friends who believed her to be a "healer." I first went with a friend whose condition, these friends thought, would be helped by Katina. After making the appointment, my friend received a multi-page questionnaire to be completed before her first appointment. This questionnaire, which I would later receive too, constituted one of the most comprehensive medical and family histories I have ever been asked to complete, including many details stretching back to birth that I had never before been asked by a physician to disclose.

When I arrived at her office located in an old sunlit building full of light and an abundance of plants, a ritual was in process such that as one person came out of the treatment room, another in the waiting area went into the treatment room. Seated in the waiting area and hearing groans and moans emanating from the treatment room, I wondered whatever was happening, only to discover, later, that it is often Katina who makes these sounds—although sometimes her patients do so too. My friend emerged some time later with the news that Katina would want to see her every week for the next few months, and by then, she should feel real relief. Katina also came out to meet me and I was enveloped in a bear hug before she disappeared back into the treatment room. Gazing around the waiting area, I saw one person curled up in a fetal position under a blanket; another was reading, and still another looked very agitated. These women and men looked as if they might have come to Katina as a last resort after ordinary medicine had failed them. As the weeks passed and Katina stretched knotted muscles, did chiropractic adjustments, and probed for "sore spots" that relieved pressure and tension, my friend gradually began to feel better. She joined the congregation of those who recommended that I might also be helped by visiting Katina. When friends chatted together, the subject of Katina inevitably came up, and I heard how she had healed people who had endured pain for years but found great relief in the treatments Katina prescribed. One person told of how she had been pumped full of chemicals and given little time to live. A friend had urged her to go to Katina who, she believed, had saved her life. She had never felt better, she said, as Katina had put her on natural remedies and on the path to wellness. Her brother had likewise gone to Katina, who had freed him of long-standing pain.

I am naturally a skeptic and a doubter. The academic in me found these stories hard to believe. This was not traditional medicine but almost magical, spiritual, and physical, of a sort I had only read about in accounts of medicine women in archaic societies. The groans emanating from the treatment room were unnecessary, I reasoned, and this talk of "healing" must just be in the mind. Surely, in the twenty-first century, all such healing was a matter of superstition; maybe the pain had not really been there at all but was a figment of the person's imagination. So, although willing to go with my friend to her treatment, I was reluctant to try it myself.

The first crack in my armor came when I sought relief for incapacitating headaches. Rather than just taking powerful pills, I wanted to get to the bottom of what was causing these headaches, but I could find no answer in my physician's office. A colleague suggested that chiropractic treatment might help me. Now, in my well-ordered universe of medical treatments, chiropractic fell into the category of marginal and alternative. Still, I thought, if there is something that would rid me of these headaches, I would try it. I visited John, who, after examining me, said that there was a physical reason for them and the problem could be corrected. Rather than follow his usual practice of gently moving through the problem, John decided on a more dramatic approach. With two enormous cracks, I thought at that moment that my head had become disconnected from the rest of my body. As I sat there staring at him in disbelief, he asked me to move my head, and for the first time in years, I was able to move it freely. That was the end of those debilitating headaches. I now had to admit that there was medical knowledge beyond the normal reach of medicine, and doctors of medicine do not possess all the knowledge worth knowing. I had been healed of my headaches by someone who is a fringe dweller in the universe of traditional Western medicine. Judging this treatment by its results, I had to admit that it worked.

I was curious about the uncanny powers of observation that Katina seemed to possess. One of her patients told of arriving at her office after being berated by a member of her extended family. As Katina approached her, she wanted to know, "Who has been criticizing you?" and continued, "There are all these gnats biting you?" How did she know this? I wondered. What visible signs was she reading? Why did she groan so deeply as she worked? Was this really necessary? How would her work measure up to John's?—the new standard by which I measured chiropractic skill. Were her medical powers real or imaginary? Doubter, that I was, I decided to put her work to the test for myself.

Katina has eight treatment beds in a large room and adjoining anteroom on which her patients lie or sit. On one side is a shrine with candle burning, while background music plays. An accredited chiropractic doctor, Katina also practices other healing arts related to acupuncture, deep massage, and spiritual meditation. All around the room are pictures of bodily systems. Rather than perform quick chiropractic adjustments, she prepares her patients, runs her hands over an aura that she feels, and mutters prayers, proverbs, and sayings. Working on me one day after I had just returned from an overseas trip she said sharply, "Come back into your body." I thought my body was already there and I was in it, but her metaphors have a way of getting you thinking about yourself. Sometimes she presses various sore parts of the body, finding them immediately, and unerringly. "Have you been having heartburn?" she might ask, and I wonder: however does she know? "This will help," she says, moving things, and the digestive tract problem subsequently dissipates. Other times, she moves her hands over the body and flicks them away uttering sayings as she goes. At still other times, she seems to wrestle people into various postures and groans as she makes an adjustment. Her patients laugh or cry either with the relief of tension, distress released, or pain gone. Rather than treat her patients individually, Katina believes in group therapy. Some patients, she says, have "good energy" and they laugh and chat together happily. Others have "bad energy" and seem miserable and in pain. I take it that these are the ones I have seen curled up in the waiting area. They are situated strategically between those with "good energy" so that this good energy can be transferred to them. How can this possibly be?

Several visits to Katina later, doubt overcame sense. Surely, most of this was sheer pretense, psychic mumbo-jumbo amounting to a way to extract money out of well-to-do patients. Did I really need to attend Katina any more? "Give it one more chance," said my friend, planning to keep following her treatment. "It takes a while to really make a difference." So I agreed. On this visit, Katina decided that it was time for a dramatic treatment. She had determined, apparently, that I needed to stand more upright in a new way that would affect my entire posture and go to the root of why I had developed headaches in the first place. Working far from my neck, she pulled and twisted at the base of my spine, and rather suddenly, I found myself sitting upright in a way I had not experienced in years. Moreover, I sailed from her office like the Queen Mary in full steam, with a feeling of freedom and well-being. Looking beyond the incantations, groanings, sayings, and other elements that I had mistrusted, I saw a person who had an intuitive, spiritual, and profound understanding of the human body, and a grasp of things beyond that of traditional medicine.[5] I saw someone who, in earlier centuries, might have been regarded as a wise woman or a medicine woman, or would even, perhaps, have been burned at the stake as a witch.

What is Katina up to? She is intent on using her skills to relieve suffering, be it physical, psychological, or social. She relates to the other with sympathy and respect, seeking to at least ease through palliative means those things that are causing the suffering and, if possible, restore the person to physical and mental health. To this end, she employs an array of skills for the benefit of the other, a caring expressed through actions that are helpful to the "one-cared-for."[6] Her skilled knowledge is not only propositional, in the sense of knowing that such-and-such is the case, but procedural, or knowing how to go on and do such-and-such.[7] She knows a body of wisdom not understood by those who have not been initiated into her particular therapy. The healing arts she practices are based on theoretical frameworks of assumptions that guide these practices. This knowledge sets her apart from others who do not possess her particular therapeutic skills.

The character of contemporary life leaves many people sad, sick at heart and in body, and sometimes unable to carry on without therapeutic help. Physical diseases and their often interconnected maladies are exacerbated by the toxins in the environment and the nature of the ways in which people live in the contemporary world. Notwithstanding physical predispositions to particular diseases attributable to genetic and other developmental factors, our contemporary lived lives can also have a detrimental impact on our spiritual, emotional, and physical well-being. Today's wired and technologically oriented world is stressful in its constant and unremitting demands, leaving insufficient time for rest, recreation, and reflection. The fast pace at which life is now lived leaves us constantly running to catch up with what others seem to be accomplishing. Economic pressures, lack of a sense of safety and caring relationships, and absence of trust in others may leave us without the calmness, safety, affection, and assurance that contribute to personal well-being. Trading depth for superficiality and things of lasting value for the next new thing, today's popular culture may leave us dissatisfied and on a perpetual merry-go-round whirl of activity trying to keep up with the latest fashionable practice. Sensitivity, intuition, spirituality, introspection, restraint, calm, and peace are subverted by a pervasive inhumanity, rage, violence, mistrust, emotional exhibitionism, and physical aggression that play out daily in the mediated public spaces.

Given the breadth of the problems generated by living in such a world, it is difficult to conceive of effectively treating those who suffer in any other way than by using holistic and time-consuming approaches. Katina takes time to appropriately diagnose her patients' problems, especially since she seeks to dig deeply for root causes, and determine, carry out, and follow up on a course of treatment. This process cannot be hurried; it takes as long as required to carefully diagnose the cause of the patient's symptoms and for the patient to feel the benefit of therapy or be restored to health and well-being. She understands that people respond to treatment differently, and it may be necessary to adjust treatments in order to find the best approach for this particular patient. In seeking to understand her patients, Katina hears and gazes upon them. Dealing with suffering others constantly, she needs to become "hardened" to their suffering if she is to do her work effectively, dispassionately, and professionally.[8] Although she is sympathetic to her patients, she must also distance herself psychically from them in order to effectively see and hear them, and thereby grasp the nature of their maladies. Her compassion must be of a certain sort—an attunement and resonance with her patients, and yet a distancing that may be in tension with her desire to sympathize. So she must struggle to reach compassion of a depth needed to converse or work with her patients while also preserving her own sense of balance, so as not be swept into a maelstrom of agony, from which position she could not help others.

Katina is both scientist and artist. Trained to observe and with knowledge of ways to treat particular conditions, she grasps the intellectual and empirical foundations of her particular practice. Her work is grounded in intuitive and empirical observations, and she speaks in metaphors. She is like the medicine men and women of old who sometimes possessed encyclopedic knowledge of plants and their properties in treating victims of accident and disease. Her medical wisdom, skill, and power in confronting disease in nontraditional ways may also threaten patriarchal power. Like an artist, she diagnoses her patients' symptoms, fashions appropriate treatments if possible, effects a cure, and otherwise seeks to create people as integrated wholes who are then free to live happy and well-balanced lives.[9]

HEALING

Among the writers who think in terms of music education as healing, June Boyce-Tillman argues that a holistic approach remedies an otherwise unbalanced approach to life, music, and education.[10] In her view, Western societies often subjugate the arts, religions, myths, and rituals, and restoring people to wellness and wholeness requires embracing and expressing those qualities that are subjugated, thereby restoring physical and psychical harmony, balance, and order.[11] Abraham Maslow also writes concerning the ways in which music education can answer human needs for spiritual fulfillment and transcendence.[12] Among those who attend to the spiritual aspects of education and music, Nel Noddings examines the role of happiness as educational means and ends; Anthony Palmer reflects on the common threads of human spirituality that unite human beings and their expression musically; Deanne Bogdan reflects on the place of spirituality in embodied aesthetic experience in the academy; Iris Yob forwards the notion of the school as sacred space, a place in which children's needs for transcendent experiences may be filled; Bennett Reimer posits the importance of experiencing transcendence in music education and the wonder, awe, and reverence evoked when one experiences musical profundity; and I apply Paul Tillich's theoretical analysis of "ultimate experience" in the arts to music education and speculate on the various musical and religious experiences evoked in music.[13] These writers are after a holistic approach to music education consistent with healing, and their ideas prompt an examination of how healing plays out in music, teaching, learning, instruction, curriculum, and administration.

Music. The concept of music as healing rests on arousal theories that music triggers particular physical and psychological effects. Since antiquity, music has been employed, among other things, to soothe troubled minds and to encourage soldiers to fight.[14] Music intensifies ordinary lived life; it is thought-about-emotion, or subjectively felt "inner life" that is also intellectually known.[15] To consider music as healing is to take a comprehensive view of the ways in which music impacts mind, emotions, and senses and potentially restores one to health and wholeness. Arousal theories of music are taken to be helpful in examining and testing empirically music's effects. These effects on mind, emotion, and senses go beyond conscious control as music directly impacts heart rate, skin response, and brain waves in ways that can be observed and measured.[16] Postulating that music impacts health and well-being opens the possibility that some musics may actually do physical harm and make people sick.[17] This possibility requires excluding or censoring music that is demonstrated or presumed to be harmful and including and encouraging that which is conducive to health. Healing suggests that musicians adapt their instrumental techniques to ensure the most natural positions, avoid excessive stress through too-prolonged practice sessions and repetitive tasks, and learn to sit, stand, and move in ways that do not place unnecessary stress and tension on their bodies.[18]

Thinking of music as healing also evokes music's association with religious and spiritual rituals and the integration of musical form and function.[19] Music functions across a wide spectrum of religions as an important element of ritual in heightening and intensifying the experience of the sacred, whether of transcendence or imminence; it engenders the religious transports of believers in Pentecostal Christianity and the excitement of participants in the Corroboree of the Australian aboriginal peoples. Musical artistry fulfills particular functions, and music can only have the desired effect when it is performed authentically.[20] For the Shoshone people of North America, for example, music is also judged with reference to the success of its contributions to social purposes.[21] Music's therapeutic use as a means of affecting mood, relieving depression, helping autistic people communicate, rehabilitating prisoners, or providing physical therapy is consistent with these religious and spiritual functions.[22] In these and other ways, music constitutes a means of connecting with the phenomenal world while at the same time accessing whatever lies beyond. This holistic, broad, and integrated view of music requires a contextual study of music in terms of the social roles it serves and the nature of the sounds themselves; it is performative and theoretical, doing and undergoing, and has intellectual, emotional, and sensory appeal and effect.

Teaching. Viewing teaching through the lens of healing supposes that people are out of balance and need to be restored to a natural state of health and happiness.[23] Teaching is concerned with meeting the specific needs, musical and otherwise, of particular students. Since many of the world's children live in poverty, are ill, and lack even the basic necessities of food, shelter, safety, and affection, the teacher is faced with a broad task that covers much more than purveying knowledge of particular subject matter. Restoring this balance also goes beyond the classroom to impact the lived lives of children in ways that also affect their food, shelter, safety, and affection. Before teaching these children, healing supposes that a teacher also ensures that these children are fed, properly housed in a safe environment, and treated with love and affection.[24] The dysfunction in much of contemporary society is remedied by emphasizing those things that are typically lacking in it, notably, a sense of order, calm, caring, and respect.[25] Order is expressed in the teacher's emphasis on the smooth organization of the classroom. Predictability and ritual provide a sense of safety that can be comforting to the young, who often live their lives in circumstances of disorder.[26] The calm of a classroom in which a teacher need not raise her voice and in which students are able to reflect quietly stands in sometimes stark contrast to the lived lives of agitated, uncertain, and anxious students. Her caring for her students is empathetic and compassionate.[27] She regards her students as subjects, and her work is oriented toward people as much as toward the transmission and transformation of subject matter. Her caring demeanor is evidenced by her tact in engaging with her students, interest in their well-being, and carefulness about the ways in which the subject matter is studied and the musical instruments are handled. A sense that they are persons of worth and are respected by their teacher, the subject matter they are studying is important, and the instruments they play are precious communicates itself directly to these students. This teacher's work in the classroom fosters the very qualities that students need to experience by way of restoring them to well-being and remedying societal dysfunctions.

Three central tasks comprise this teaching: analysis and diagnosis of problems; re-mediation of problems; and assessment of the success of the protocols employed. Regarding analysis and diagnosis of problems, teachers carefully assess and analyze the issues and problems that stand in their students' way of success and determine which things need to be attended to. At first, they ask, "What needs to be done with these particular students?" Diagnosis is accomplished by studying the symptoms presented by the students.[28] As in the community model, teachers then design and implement specific treatments for these students that meet their needs and interests.[29] Following these interventions, students' progress is assessed and a determination is made about what procedures to follow next. Teaching through questioning and conversation are important strategies in addressing each of these tasks. While questioning, teachers attend to their students carefully, focus on their students' actions and words, and seek to understand insofar as possible what their students are attempting to express in order to assist them to better articulate their thoughts and feelings musically and in other ways. Soliciting students' ideas plumbs the sometimes difficult to explain reasoning behind their musical ideas and practices. At times such questions may be unsettling, yet the moments when students stretch themselves afford the possibility of quantum leaps in understanding and a sense of transcendence, peak experience, or flow.[30] Although a challenging undertaking, teaching through questioning prompts critical conversation and dialogue of the sort typical in the community and transgression models. Such conversations result in differing outcomes according to the particular circumstances and people involved.

Learning. The holistic nature of learning that includes body, mind, and spirit is potentially transformative. A case in point is el Sistema, a government-funded classical music educational program begun in 1975 by José Antonio Abreu in Venezuela to "change the lives of lower-income, at-risk, and special needs children." This program has been described by Simon Rattle as "the most important thing happening anywhere 'for the future of classical music.'"[31] The serious study of classical music in lessons taught every day by musician teachers has helped thousands of youngsters to learn music and, anecdotally, transformed and healed broken lives. Accounts attest to the fact that teachers in this program care about their students and treat them as persons of worth, and the music their students play is among the finest and most challenging of the Western classical repertoire. The caring approach of teachers has made a deep impact on their students that has not only raised the sights of disadvantaged young people but benefited their families and society at large. Among the success stories, Lennar Acosta had been arrested "nine times for armed robbery and drug offenses"; he was fifteen when a music teacher came to the state home where he was a resident to offer free lessons and instruments. He tells of the transformative impact on his life of this musical training. In his words, "Before, nobody trusted me, everyone was afraid of me. I was a discarded kid. The teacher was the first person who understood me and had confidence in me." At the time of this writing "he plays in the Caracas Youth

Orchestra, studies at the national Simón Bolívar Conservatory, and is paid to teach younger clarinetists." Another young musician, Wilfrido Galarraga, plays trumpet in the Simón Bolivar Youth Orchestra; he earns more at twenty-one than the combined incomes of his mother and father and is helping to lift his family out of poverty. While students study their various musical instruments, other needs are also taken care of, such as stipends for the older students, musical instruction and instruments provided free of charge, a safe place to study, and the affection of their teachers and fellow students. Learning music is contextualized within the frame of other basic needs, and students are more able and motivated to learn than if these other needs were not also met. Opportunities for peak experiences or moments of transcendence and imminence arise as students perform music at high levels of expectation and intensity, and practice and receive musical instruction year-round.

Learning is also a matter of self-understanding or insight that is carried into action. As in the transgression model, ideas need to be put into practice in the phenomenal world. Coming to know music and oneself and experience moments of transcendence and imminence are complemented by opportunities to express oneself musically.[32] This learning is practical as well as theoretical as students sing or have instruments in their hands and performance is a principal vehicle of musical learning.[33] Performing music provides opportunities for moments of awe, and wonder, and a deep awareness of self. It constitutes an important means whereby music is brought alive in the present moment and opens musical moments of intensity, focus, and concentration that are potentially inspiring and life-changing.[34] Performing is only one of the ways musicians express "inner life"; we think also of the composer who plans how the music will sound, the improviser who composes in the moment of performance, the performer who brings alive a score, the producer who records a performance, and the listener who takes it all in. All of these aspects are important vehicles of musical learning. What is the "inner life" that is illumined and expressed by these means?[35] We can say, at least, that it is imaginative, amorphous, spiritual, emotional, and sensual. By imaginative, I have in mind that when perception, reason, intuition, and feeling are present together, imagination is presumably at work.[36] By amorphous, I mean that this thought-emotion-sensation is in some flux, sometimes loosely formed and sometimes chaotic; it is not clearly worked out and one is not always fully conscious of it. By spiritual, I suggest a lived reality that lies beyond the sensory and physical. By emotional, I refer to the presence of feelings, such as rage, abandonment, sorrow, guilt, love, joy, and hopelessness that dwell in the mind and body and sometimes require the services of professionals to unravel. By sensual, I think of the power of desire and the wish for fulfillment. Words fail to do justice to this inner life, and one turns, inevitably, to music, the other arts, religions, myths, and rituals to *enact* or perform it and thereby make it manifest in the phenomenal world. This subjective life—a web of thought-emotion-sensation—is a subterranean and driving force toward making and taking music. Music performance along with composition, improvisation, production, and listening are valuable ways of musical learning and of discovering and communicating these subjective realities.

Instruction. The dialogical and conversational character of music education is a beginning point in thinking about the interaction of teachers and students within the mode of healing. Such conversations, as in the community and transgression models, are grounded in mutual respect, affection, and caring. A dialogical relationship suggests that the conversation partners genuinely listen to each other— that teachers love their students as students love their teachers.[37] By love, I am thinking of the deep interest, enjoyment, and happiness each finds in the other. Desire is rooted in our sexuality and affects our attraction and attractiveness to others. If we are to be truthfully present to other participants in the conversation, desire cannot be obliterated or sanitized; it needs to be acknowledged and embraced as a source of the "sparks that fly" between people. Nor can desire be relied on as the sole source of teachers' interaction with others in pedagogical situations; it needs to be tempered with integrity, dispassionate interest, empathy, compassion, and caring for all students, no matter how unlovable, uninterested, or even hostile they might be. We also think of love expressed within the framework of other human needs, including safety and freedom from exploitation. As in the community model, when teachers and students respectfully, carefully, and sensitively engage in conversations with one another, not as bits or pieces of characteristics but as whole people, and the tasks on which they are engaged are regarded as consequential and of great value, happiness can flourish in the classroom, studio, or rehearsal. Happiness simply ignites teaching and learning. This improvisatory and rhapsodic conversation illustrates a genuine "give-and-take" between the teacher who is an experienced guide, mentor, and coach and students who, as in community, are all in this situation together. The questions that prompt instruction—for example, "What would you like to start out with today?"—are means whereby teachers lead their students while also giving them opportunities to shape the directions in which the instruction goes. If the students should falter, or if a teacher senses that these students might benefit from studying or performing a particular piece, he might ask, "Shall we play this piece?" The answer to the teacher's inquiry about the piece to be played leaves the solution ambiguous. Students might see that they need to play something else first while keeping in mind the teacher's suggestion, or they may follow his open-ended suggestion. Such questions as, "Which pieces shall we sing?" and "How shall we play this piece?" are conditional. There is no one final answer to them, and they are at the crux of the instructional predicament and situation.

Musical conversations also play a crucial role in the interaction between teachers and their students. Meaning is to be found in the interplay of voices in musical performance.[38] Music making can also be a metaphor for the sorts of dialogue that are pervasive in notions of education construed as healing. Thinking of conversation as enacted musically evokes a kind of holistic interplay that is at once intellectual, passionate, spiritual, and physical. Such a conversation goes beyond words to include the gestures and movements required in making musical sounds and the passion and spirituality that nuances and gives them life. In music, all of these elements run together into a whole that seems more than the sum of its parts, and this very quality of music as a vehicle for conversation among differing voices allows teachers and students to experience the conversation even before they realize, and can name, what might be happening. In music, the people and the music are also integrated, interwoven, and inseparable. The "conversation" between the musician and the score, musical idea, or tune to be improvised on demonstrates how the focus on those involved in instruction as subjects and the subject matter (in this case, the music) are, practically speaking, inseparable and together comprise a whole. The healing model goes further than those of community or transgression in its holistic approach to musical instruction. As students and their teachers enact this integration and holism, they are changed in the process, find themselves as whole persons, and discover well-being.

Instruction in this model is both formal and informal. It is carried on formally within institutions such as schools, colleges, universities, and conservatories, and in classroom, rehearsal, and studio settings that are purposely pedagogical, and it arises informally in the context of activities that are focused on other things, such as performance, where teaching and learning may be incidental. It involves formal means of teaching and learning through such processes as instruction (in the sense of passing on wisdom or giving directions), practice, example, and reflection, and informal means such as osmosis, participation, observation, and sensibility.[39] This active and passive, didactic and serendipitous approach to teacher and student interaction is likewise holistic in the sense that all are interwoven together.[40]

Curriculum. In the healing model, music as the subject matter of study is integrated with and infuses other subjects, just as it is integrated with the rest of the students' lived lives. From the students' and teachers' points of view, music is not delimited by strictly musical considerations but impacts the study of history, geography, economics, politics, mathematics, science, languages, religious studies, among a host of other fields of study.[41] These sorts of intersections blur the borders between individual subjects and make it possible for students to travel back and forth across their boundaries, thereby enriching their understandings of music and other subjects. Since teachers and their students construct knowledge in differing ways, curriculum is viewed as the process whereby learners make sense of the subject matter. When repertoire is suited to their individual needs, interests, and strengths, they are enabled to turn their weaknesses into strengths. This integration of music with other subjects and between students and subject matter enables students to encounter music and other fields in unified ways, and gain wisdom that emerges from this broad and holistic view. As music becomes a way of life and is integrated with the rest of lived life, teachers and their students likewise become whole. Individual differences among students and the various musical meanings that they construct necessitate choices about what and with whom to study music, resulting in divergent outcomes of musical study as each student follows a different path.[42] In contrast to those of the consumption and production models, this curriculum, as in circumstances of growth, community, and transgression, is dynamic in its process and divergent in its ends.

The curriculum's integration with lived life also affects its accessibility: as in conditions of community, students directly engage it, and the teacher's objective is to ensure that it is relevant to and within the experience of students to encompass. Particularly when music is used for other functions—for example, in religious rituals, political events, or family gatherings—it needs to be immediately accessible to ordinary people.[43] In order for students to achieve success all along the way, the curriculum is carefully graded, as in the growth model, so that students achieve success at every level and music is studied consistently throughout the year. Happiness is both a means and end of music education, and so students encounter music in positive ways and are encouraged and validated as they progress in their musical studies. Performance-based, compositionally oriented, or improvisatory programs that focus on students making music in a variety of ways are also undertaken continuously throughout the year rather than offered in intensive blocks of time at one part of the school year and not at others.[44] When students are young and unskilled, they need to practice music regularly and study it every day if they are to make significant progress and remember what they learn in their lessons. Even in high schools, students can make excellent progress when they study music on a daily basis throughout the entire school year.

This dynamic and divergent approach to curriculum and its emphasis on the individual construction of knowledge results in musical performances, improvisations, compositions, recordings, dances, films, theatrical pieces, writings about music, among a host of products. Since these outcomes are experienced by others, they are adjudicated and assessed both formatively, in the process of developing understandings and skills, and summatively, in evaluating the achievements of these teachers and students. Viewed from a holistic perspective, evaluation is a means whereby students and teachers come to better understand themselves and others. Students and teachers need to understand how their efforts fit within the larger scheme of things and what their particular strengths and weaknesses are.

Still, evaluation is also humane and transparent; teachers judge the performance of their students just as students assess the work of their teachers. As in the growth model, assessment is hopeful, affirming, and challenging rather than destructive of another's sense of self and well-being. Since the aims of musical instruction include its role in fostering happy and well-rounded people, students' and teachers' efforts are evaluated on musical and other criteria.

Administration. The holistic nature of music education in the mode of healing is imbued with humanity and has at its heart the health and well-being of all students, faculty, and staff. As a humane and civil learning community, music education cannot stand in isolation. It is integrated within the larger whole of general education, which is in turn incorporated into the wider lived life and society. A music educational program with healing as its purpose and in its programs may prefigure the healing needed more generally and, to some extent, its effects may ripple into the wider society.[45] Still, the more broadly grounded the plan, the more likely its success as an agent for healing. When the plan is broadly supported and institutionalized, it can have the kind of extensive and intensive support needed to implement it in transforming ways. This is so because administration construed as healing requires broad-minded, liberal, and visionary administrators to foster the integration needed for such a holistic approach to music education. Without this vision, healing seems impossible. I recall, for example, the comprehensive musicianship movement in United States in the latter half of the twentieth century.[46] Its purpose was to integrate all aspects of music study in ways that blur the boundaries between the various music specialties such as performance, history, theory, pedagogy, composition, and improvisation. It floundered, in part, because administrators could not persuade their musician colleagues to integrate their specialties with others. Despite farsighted faculty and administrators, there was too much fear of, and pessimism about, what the effects of this holistic approach to musical study might be. It subverted and transgressed entrenched, specialized, isolated, and atomistic approaches to music and its integration of theory and practice challenged the academy's preference for theoretical over practical endeavors. Musicians may also have been skeptical of its challenge to their tenuous toehold in the academy, because regarding music as theory/practice might prompt more theoretically oriented academics to regard it as inferior. Given this resistance, administrators seemed powerless to effect the kind of radical integration that would have eventuated from implementing comprehensive musicianship.

Circumstances of healing suggests different forms of organization, flat rather than hierarchical administrative structures in which all of the participants in the system have an interest, and humane working environments. I imagine, for example, nimble, flexible, task-oriented, and functional organizations rather than those organized strictly and inflexibly around academic disciplines.[47] Administrators are responsible for creating with their colleagues organizational climates that foster humane approaches, wholeness, wellness, and healing. Where people are happy, challenged, and feel valued, there are grounds for fostering healing. It is easier to be motivated and find meaning and value in what they do when they see things as wholes rather than as atomistic bits. The practice of just policies, respectful attitudes to and from administrators, teachers, and students, warmth and friendship to others within the musical community go a long way toward creating a musical organization that is healing to all those within it, as it is healing to the society beyond. Healing cannot take place where teachers demean their students, colleagues unfairly criticize their fellows, and administrators mistreat their staff. This does not mean that the emphasis is just upon creating a friendly and warm environment in which little is accomplished and music education is not held accountable to its public. Rather, as in the mode of growth, this is a place where significant musical challenges are met successfully. The performative and enactive nature of music promoted in healing intensifies musical experience, prompts moments of wonder and awe, and opens a deeper and wider understanding of self, world, and whatever lies beyond. As the public experiences this transcendence and imminence in musical performances, these experiences constitute compelling justifications for music in general education.

CRITIQUE

Among its musical benefits, the healing model's emphasis on the contributions music makes to health, well-being, and happiness and its role in expressing feeling reveals music making and taking as useful activities. In an industrialized world that so often represses such values as spirituality and introspection, it also helps to create more psychologically well-rounded individuals. The model's integration of science and art provides empirical data upon which to make musical decisions and recognizes the role of imagination and artistry in music making and taking. Its intersection with rituals, myths, and the other arts takes a broad and holistic view of music as art and humane endeavor, prompts wonder, awe, and reverence, and opens many avenues through which the musics of the world may be approached.

Still, its detractions include the possibility that the model of healing may center insufficiently on coming to know music for music's sake rather than for the sake of other things. This reality may make it less effective in training professional musicians than other models such, as apprenticeship. Its emphasis on intimacy, caring, and nurturing may not prepare students sufficiently for the pervasiveness of pain and suffering in human existence and a world of professional musicking that is too often raw, competitive, and uncaring. Music's use as a means of personal and communal development is not the only solid basis for music education; the same claims may be made regarding, say, the arts and religions. As healing presumes that something is amiss or awry and needs to be "fixed" or made whole, it may be the wrong picture of or basis for music education in cases where students come to music education happy, healthy, and well-adjusted.[48]

Regarding teaching, to its credit, like the community model, the healing model fosters the view of the music teacher as a fellow, although more experienced, learner. All persons are regarded as precious and treated with respect, sensitivity, and affection. Their well-being is fostered as teachers seek to treat their students and colleagues holistically rather than atomistically and demonstrate tact, tenderness, caring, integrity, and affirmation in their dealings with others. The centrality of questions and the conversations they open allow teachers to explore things that may be mysterious, awesome, and wonderful and, while exercising reverence, nevertheless seek to demystify and deconstruct these things, and render them plain. Listening to and hearing, gazing upon and seeing students—these acts also provide important windows whereby teachers can gain clues about how they should proceed. The model's dialectical nature, in which teachers cultivate respect and reverence and deconstruct and demystify knowledge, resonates with the nature of music making and taking and opens what can be known, while also admitting what eludes understanding. In the face of these realities, teachers exemplify honesty, integrity, and humility. The possibilities of divergent outcomes of music education and the individual needs, interests, abilities, and backgrounds of students suggest that teachers need to be skilled in arranging for these multiplicities and pluralities in group and individual instruction.

Among its problems, again like the community model, the conversational and dialogical character of teaching-as-healing may provide insufficient leadership and direction on the teacher's part. This is the case especially where teachers are required by their administrators to present their students for competitions, examinations, juries, and other public performances. Its focus especially on the music educational process may also render it insufficiently focused on common measures of musical achievement and shared products of music education. Spending time in counseling students, attending to other than musical needs, and solving personal problems may cause music teachers to assume, literally, the roles of therapists for which they are not necessarily trained. Taking valuable time away from musical instruction to attend to these student needs and interests outside music may also fail to provide the sometimes necessary "tough love" for students; that is, students are not both loved and also challenged to make the progress of which they are capable. Such teaching may focus less on students' musical development than on their immediate feelings of personal well-being and happiness, thereby pandering to them unnecessarily. Individual and small-group instruction may also be an inadequate means of mass music education. The affection, intimacy, and trust between teachers and students may be misinterpreted, especially in a world in which exploitation is all too common; teachers and students may take advantage of each other and feel safer if they are not fully present to each other. Under the guise of seeming to help students, teachers may subjugate and disempower them, thereby contributing to the very dis-ease they seek to remedy.[49]

On the one hand, since learning in healing is a matter of self-awareness and knowing one's self, its affirmation motivates and helps students as it also inspires them at moments all along the way. Its holistic and atomistic, serendipitous and systematic, abstract and practical emphases also provide a broad base for coming to know music, self, other, and whatever lies beyond. Its engagement of body, mind, and spirit, subversion of narrow intellectual approaches to music, validation of the body and spirit as vital areas of educational focus open ways in which students can come to know music. Its holistic approach to valuing individual learners challenges ways of thinking of them as objects in production and consumption. The healing model's focus especially on individual learners fosters divergent learning outcomes and the possibility of integrating special-needs learners in general education rather than isolating them in special classes and institutions. Music's impact on mind, soul, and body affords opportunities for working through sometimes difficult personal issues that other subjects may not offer.

On the other hand, as with learning in community, the model's reliance on insight may pay insufficient attention to the importance of rule and impression as means of fostering learning.[50] By rule, I mean that students need to acquire an understanding of the norms that undergird music education as their teachers exemplify and instruct them in these systems and insist that they follow and are governed by them. By impression, I refer to the importance of teachers instructing their students directly and insisting that they practice the things they have been taught. Impressing students means making it clear that they *must* do things in particular ways; they have no choice in the matter. Healing's emphasis on affirmation may also neglect the importance of experiences that seem at first to be negative but may turn out to be transformative. For some learners, such negative experiences constitute a "wake-up call" to action on their part. It may also be important to tell students what they cannot do or what they are not capable of doing, at least at present, so that they make realistic decisions for the future. Learning may be facilitated when learners recognize the limits on their freedom to choose what to think and do musically and in other ways. Such is the frustration and even pain of such moments that students may excuse their lack of self-discipline, preparedness, and practice or attempt to sidetrack their teachers rather than directly confronting and rectifying these problems.

Among the advantages of the interactive and interrogative nature of instruction in the healing mode, conversations are opened that focus not only on the systematic nature of the subject matter, but on student needs and interests. In this way, students construct knowledge through grasping its relevance to their lived lives. The caring nature of relationships that are forged is affirming and helpful to all participants in the situation. Intimacy and trust created among teachers and their students are crucial in humanizing the process of music education, and in rendering teaching and learning less antiseptic and devoid of life and affection. Also, regarding the teacher as a more experienced learner, guide, and mentor—someone they trust to keep them safe—enables students to take risks as they unmask taken-for-granted assumptions and explore new ideas and practices. Being in this group as a fellow learner also helps relieve teachers' fears as they are affirmed by their students and released from the necessity of demonstrating omniscience when they are, in fact, fallible. As teachers and their students come to the limits of their knowledge and skill, there is always the prospect of awe, wonder, and even reverence at what still remains to be understood.

Nevertheless, relying on questions and conversations may be insufficiently directive or efficient a means of music education, especially in the context of large ensembles often focused on musical performances, of classes centered on achieving particular results, and of product-oriented educational environments. Finding a way in the midst of sometimes conflicting purposes and methods may also be difficult for teachers and their students to accomplish. A teacher focusing on matters of student well-being, happiness, and morale may be tempted to pander to present student interests rather than challenge students in ways that they need to be challenged. There may be insufficient focus on the music as the subject matter of instruction in the press to satisfy other personal and collective purposes. In contrast to naturalistic ideas of growth, thinking of instruction in restorative and remedial terms may take too negative a view of human nature. Since education and therapy may be interrelated in the minds of some music teachers, at least practically, it may be easy to literalize what is merely figurative, and rather than grasping the nature of healing in the special sense of restoring to wholeness and well-being, come to see it in literally as the practice of a medical therapy.

Among the advantages of curriculum in the healing model, its student-centeredness and the construction of knowledge by learners foster diverse outcomes; these are in keeping with musical ambiguity and affirm the particular learners involved in the music educational process. Also, its dynamic character of learner engagement with music is helped by the continuing affirmation learners receive as they progress successfully at every stage of the process. Arranging for a seamless progression necessitates careful planning. Curriculum in the healing model is like that in the growth mode: this planning requires analyzing the subject matter into its constituent elements, generalizing it so that students encounter wholes as well as parts, and integrating music with other subjects of study. Still, the healing model cannot wait until later to secure generalization and integration but includes them at every point in the educational process. In this way, the learner sees the wholes as well as the parts at every stage of education. This broad view of music education energizes students, who can immediately make the connections between the subject matter and their lived lives. Its insistence on accountability, both formative and summative, renders music education transparent to its policy makers, participants, and public—a benefit especially important where production and consumption are pervasive in education and society in general.

In emphasizing the functional purposes of music education, however, the music curriculum may insufficiently emphasize musical understandings, technical "know-how," and esoteric and less accessible musical beliefs and practices. Blurring the boundaries between musical specialties and between music and other subjects may mean that students may not come to understand the differing and particular characteristics of these various subjects. Thinking of music so performatively may not highlight sufficiently the characteristics that might contribute to wholeness and healing, namely, those reflective and receptive aspects of musical experience in musical listening. The curriculum's pervasively functional thrust may have an insufficiently musical emphasis. Its process-orientation may focus on formative over summative evaluation, thereby proving less compelling to music educational participants and policy makers with a production or consumption mind-set.

Regarding the model's advantages for administration, focusing on the broad and humanitarian ends and means of music education fosters well-being and happiness on the part of its leaders, teachers, and students. When the environment in which music instruction is situated is pleasant and peace and tranquility prevail, teachers and students are more able to teach and learn effectively because there is less stress, conflict, and disorder. The collegial nature of decision-making imbues all participants in music education with a sense that their ideas and practical efforts are valued and acted upon. Dialectics within the organization prompt it to consider and search for ways to integrate multiple and differing beliefs and practices. An intersecting flow of top-down and bottom-up initiatives within the organization helps balance the tendencies when encountering change to become either needlessly indecisive and unresponsive or insufficiently reflective and firm.

Among the model's administrative limitations, planning for large-scale music educational institutions requires agreeing on certain organizational frameworks, and given its divergent practices and ends, it is likely to be difficult to administer. I have noted the Venezuelan experiment in music education designed to remediate social ills. Since it assumes the primacy of orchestral music in the Western classical tradition (as a result of the particular perspectives of its founders), and even though it is organized nationally, a relatively small number of students study music under the plan and it does not impact directly the majority of Venezuelan children.[51] Agreeing upon and designing a national scheme that is both holistic and inclusive of musical and artistic multiplicities and pluralities is even more daunting. Healing requires close attention to individuals, and so music instruction modeled as healing is also expensive of time, space, personnel, and money. Should musicians and educators mistakenly read the metaphor of the therapist literally, and think of their work as medical rather than educational, critics may counter that therapy and healing are the province not of the school but of the medical profession; they may limit music education to strictly musical and educational rather than other functional ends.

SUMMARY

In sum, the pictures of *therapist* and *healing* shed important light on music education. They are also flawed in one way or another and do not suffice when taken alone. Nevertheless, their humanity in embracing well-being, wholeness, and happiness, and in integrating such binaries as theory and practice, mind and body, the material and spiritual, the whole and the parts, subjectivity and objectivity, is laudable in a world in which spiritual, subjective, and introspective qualities are often overlooked in general education and society at large. Detractors may criticize the underlying assumption that people are sick and in need of healing, the focus on music's functional purposes rather than musical attributes, and the possibility of teachers pandering to personal and present interests, inclinations, and needs. They may also point to the practical difficulties in balancing atomistic and holistic approaches to subject matter and creating a sufficiently broad-based and integrated organization in which healing may take place. These pictures nevertheless invite our imagined reflection about how these ideas might be applied practically while avoiding the pitfalls that lurk on every hand.

9
COURT AND RULE

The pictures of *court* and *rule* have a somber, stern, and dignified character. Evoked in much educational thought and practice in the past, they might make us think of the English poorhouse where Charles Dickens's Oliver approaches the authorities seated on the rostrum to ask for more food, or the schoolmaster standing on a dais before his class caning an errant student into submission.[1] We encounter these pictures in twentieth-century educational writing by Israel Scheffler and in notions of discipline-based arts education in vogue during the latter part of the twentieth century.[2] In music, we see them evidenced in the maestro conducting his ensemble or the opera house manager directing his singers and orchestral musicians. Far from being outmoded, these pictures have a very modern and authoritarian edge and appeal. Designed for and by privileged and educated men, they may be hostile to women, people of color, the poor, and the disenfranchised.

COURT

I think of the courthouse in the county in which I reside in the United States. Located in a prominent stone building constructed for long-term use, imposing in its grandeur and situated prominently in the city, it inspires us to approach it with some awe. Passing through security systems that detect firearms and other dangerous weapons, we are cleared to pass into the foyer, where we wait with others until permitted to enter the courtroom by one of the guards in attendance. Entering a high-ceilinged and spacious room, we observe the judge's bench, front and center on a raised dais, flanked by flags of the country and state by which authority cases are tried. Below the judge's bench and to one side is a witness stand where those who bring evidence and speak to the court are sworn to tell the whole truth and nothing but the truth. There are rows of benches to be occupied by the jury. Beneath and directly in front of the judge's bench sit the court reporter and clerk, who record the court proceedings. Facing the judge's bench are two sets of benches, one occupied by the plaintiffs, or those making the charge, and their counsel or the lawyers prosecuting the case, and the other for the defense or counsel defending those who are being charged.[3] Since, in the United States, anyone charged is presumed innocent unless shown to be guilty beyond reasonable doubt, those charged sit beside their counsel at this bench. Behind these two sets of benches and facing the judge's bench sit those who have an interest in the case being tried. In a criminal proceeding, the lawyers, dressed in business attire, have assembled; the clerk of the court prepares to record the proceedings; the bailiff escorts the defendant to a place beside counsel for the defense; the prosecution lawyers are in readiness; the jury members, already empaneled, are ushered to their seats; and the hushed gallery of observers awaits the judge's appearance. All rise as the bailiff announces the judge's name and credentials and that the court is now in session, and the judge, clad in black robes settles on the bench and calls the case.

The court now gets down to business. The American legal system, as with its British antecedent, is a common-law system in which cases tried in the past and legal decisions regarding them become the precedent for the present case. Lawyers take adversarial positions; some argue the case for the defendant's guilt beyond a reasonable doubt, while others defend against the charges being made and rebut the prosecution's case. Each set of lawyers calls witnesses to testify on relevant matters. Lawyers for the prosecution ask their witnesses questions designed to provide evidence of the defendant's guilt. Lawyers for the defense then cross-examine the witnesses and, wherever possible, cast doubt on the veracity or reliability of the witness's testimony. After the prosecution has made its case, it rests; that is, it brings to an end its argument that the evidence against the defendant suffices to show guilt. Lawyers for the defense now mount their argument against the prosecution's case and seek to show why it must lead to reasonable doubt about the defendant's guilt.[4] All through the process, the judge rules from the bench on procedural matters, resolves disputes between the lawyers for either side, and keeps order in the court. After the defense has rested, the prosecution and defense lawyers sum up their arguments for the jury. The judge then issues instructions to the jury members about their specific responsibilities in rendering a verdict, and they leave the courtroom to debate their verdict on the defendant's guilt or innocence.

Time elapses, the jury returns to the courtroom, and the foreperson gives the jury's verdict to the judge. The defendant rises to hear the verdict. A hush descends as the foreperson reads out to the court the jury's verdict concerning each charge against the defendant as to guilt or innocence. Exclamations of distress or joy may be heard in the courtroom, especially when the charge is serious and the stakes are high for the defendant, either found guilty and facing punishment or acquitted and free to go. Should the defendant be acquitted, the judge issues particular rulings and adjourns the session. If the defendant is guilty, the judge may, at a later date, determine a sentence appropriate to the defendant's guilt and the circumstances of the case. Either party, if dissatisfied with the verdict, may make an appeal to progressively higher courts, where the judge's ruling is either sustained or overturned. Eventually the case may reach the Supreme Court, which may or may not decide to take it. Its decision is final.

There are moments of high drama in trials that arise from the unexpected developments during the course of the trial and the high stakes involved. Tales of sixteenth- and seventeeth-century trials still hold interest for our time. In Shakespeare's play *The Merchant of Venice,* Portia, disguised as a man and learned legal scholar, defends her husband against Shylock's accusations before the court; Martin Luther pleads his innocence of the religious charges brought against him before the jury of those gathered to try him at the Diet of Worms.[5] Today, television audiences watch to see what will happen next and theorize on the guilt or innocence of those being tried. When witnesses falter, or dramatic developments occur, or surprising evidence turns up, hordes of reporters and other commentators remark on every twist and turn of the proceedings and analyze and speculate on the prosecution, the defense, and the guilt or innocence of the defendants. Such is the appeal of some highly publicized trials that they provide material for theatrical dramas, television channels broadcast trials live with accompanying commentary, and where cameras are not allowed in the courtroom, actors play the trial's transcript.

The judge's power in the courtroom is absolute. His or her decisions may later be appealed, but while the trial is ongoing, the judge's rulings must be obeyed. Seated above all the other participants, addressed as "Your Honor," referring to her or his own decisions in the voice of the institution as "the Court," and clad in and surrounded by symbols of authority and power, the judge inspires fear, respect, and sometimes awe. Everyone in the courtroom stands when a judge enters and leaves. All of the other participants in the courtroom are beholden to and dependent on the judge's rulings. They dress, speak, and conduct themselves in particular ways that suggest dignity and restraint. Should they fail to do this, they can be held in contempt of court and summarily punished.

What do judges do? Since not every case is decided by a jury, in some trials, plaintiffs or their attorneys make the case, defendants or their attorneys rebut, and the judge rules from the bench. In appeals courts, where the decisions of the lower court are reviewed, a panel of several judges may decide the case. Split decisions among such judges may also result in minority reports that contest the majority's verdict. All of this legal opinion and the rulings themselves become part of the legal precedent on which future cases are decided. Judges interpret the law, govern the procedures in the courtroom, admit or deny certain evidence, and limit attorney freedom in prosecution or defense. One or the other side brings motions to the judge's bench for a ruling, and the judge acts to ensure that the defendant receives a fair trial. The judge's rulings also take into account the law's spirit as well as its letter. Mitigating circumstances may be considered, and the judge balances the claims of mercy, when required, with those of justice, which demands equitable treatment of all persons before the law. In a jury trial, since the plaintiff's case against the defendant may be a matter of interpretation of certain facts, the judge ensures that the jury members understand the complexities of the case, the nature of their task, and the evidence before them. Although the trial by jury system can be manipulated by commercial and other political and legal interests, the judge seeks to keep the process as fair as possible to all of the parties to the case.[6]

The court is about the ideal of justice. Justice has its roots in the Latin word *jūstus* meaning "righteous, equitable, rightful," and the French *jūs* meaning "right, law, justice."[7] The quality of being just refers to notions of fairness, equitable treatment, and moral rightness. Although practical realities do not necessarily match their theoretical ideal, the court exacts the penalties required under the law. Since the law is framed in abstract statements and cannot deal with the particulars and complexities of every practical situation, judges and lawyers need to interpret the law and the specific circumstances of each case. In legal notions of justice, the laws written by legislators constitute the standard and measure by which actions are judged, and it is necessary to interpret the particular words framing the laws and the intent behind the words. The ideal of a just and civil society looms large over legal claims to justice. Behind legal notions of justice are problematic questions of morality, virtue, and caring for all persons, irrespective of circumstances of their birth or other aspects of their lived lives. Although some laws may be unjust in failing to provide equitably for all persons and ensuring their civil rights, and the carriage of justice may be imperfectly realized in practice, the ideal of justice remains.

Money and politics play an important role in the American judicial system. The rich can afford a much more vigorous defense than the poor, who may not be able to afford to hire the best legal counsel or must rely on over-worked and possibly less self-interested legal assistance that is provided for them. Becoming a judge can also be a matter of money and political influence. Judges may be experienced trial lawyers, but they may need to be elected to the office. As people with differing ideological leanings, they interpret the law or the facts of the cases before them variously and rule in different ways. In the political process, the judge's ideology on crucial matters may be a deciding factor in who is elected. Mounting a political campaign is an expensive undertaking that can preclude otherwise excellent candidates from running for the position of judge. In those courts in which judges are nominated by elected officials and must be confirmed by politicians, the process is also politicized.

The appeal to judge and jury is emotional as well as rational. Argument is designed to move people to sympathize with a position, or at least be willing to understand it fair-mindedly. The judge dispassionately assesses the evidence or the law, but he or she also has particular beliefs, hopes, dreams, fears, prejudices, and predispositions.[8] The jury may be particularly susceptible to thinking emotionally, as its members may be less skilled in rhetoric and in sorting through the complexities of a case than the judge, with her or his expert knowledge of the law. Much depends on the judge's ability to be dispassionate while also able to understand the nature of the complaint to be decided. The judge is expected to listen intently and with equanimity in the face of the evidence, and to rule dispassionately according to the law and the evidence in the case. Still, it is natural for the judge to feel some measure of wrath or compassion for the perpetrator, as well as concern for the victims of a crime.

Watching the court reporter and clerk of the court carefully taking notes and supervising any live recording made of the proceedings highlights the evidentiary nature of the court's work and the importance of the transcript of proceedings, the record of the trial, and the physical and other evidence on which decisions are made. The judge and members of the jury often take notes as they listen and observe the presentation of evidence and the process of the trial. The lawyers may also study the trial's transcript while reviewing their daily performances and preparing their next strategies. The members of the jury, too, examine the facts of the case in the light of the law to produce an evidence-based verdict. They may come to an immediate agreement after relatively little deliberation or they may debate for days. When judges also serve as jury, they likewise evaluate the evidence, examine precedents, and determine a verdict and sentence accordingly.

Other activities beside the prosecution of evil-doers take place in the court. I think of the momentous and happy occasion when, along with other new citizens, I took an oath of allegiance in front of the court. One by one, the judge welcomed us as new citizens and gave us our certificates of naturalization that marked our new standing in the United States. We came from all walks of life and many countries; our knowledge of the English language and the governing principles and history of the country had been examined and found to be satisfactory, and a gallery filled with friends and well-wishers gathered to congratulate us. In his homily on the rights and responsibilities of citizens, the judge lamented that there were not more happy occasions such as this one over which he might preside in his courtroom.

RULE

The word *rule* comes from the Old French *ruele* and from the Latin *rēgula*, meaning a straight stick used in measurement.[9] In our time, rule is defined in ordinary discourse as "a regulation or principle governing conduct or procedure within a particular sphere," or the "normal or customary state of things." We also use a ruler or "a straight-edged strip of rigid material, marked at regular intervals to draw straight lines or measure distances."[10] Rule encompasses, then, not only the principles and regulations governing conduct but also their measurement and assessment. I want to preserve this ambiguity in thinking about the various aspects of music education construed as rule. In music education, and education generally, rule is an important model. Educational writers such as John Dewey, R. S. Peters, and Israel Scheffler are among those to invoke notions of reason, schooling, and discipline, and pedagogical models that emphasize procedural systems and methodical and ethical conduct.[11] In music education, rule plays out in the discipline-based approaches to music and arts education and is invoked variously by such writers as Vernon Howard, Bennett Reimer, Ralph Smith, Paul Woodford, and Marja Heimonen.[12] Whether rule is thought of broadly as a governing principle of music education, or construed more narrowly to refer to a particular kind of governing principle, reason and critical thinking play important roles in music education. Notions of justice and rights to music education are also implicated.[13] The transparency of the process is evident in its accountability to all those with an interest in music education.

Music. As a practical tradition with theoretical associations, music operates on the basis of rules that constitute the yardstick against which artistry is measured.[14] These rules often emerge out of practical tradition rather than ahead of it.[15] Musicians can have various relationships to these rules.[16] A beginning student is governed by them and learns faithful and slavish obedience to the letter of the rule. Later, the developing musician learns to follow the spirit of the rules, not necessarily and always literally obeying but invoking them as needed, and interpreting or even rejecting them in favor of other rules.[17]

Musical belief and practice are also traditional and conservative. Following rules suggests a systematic study of a musical practice and lends itself to a progressive study of the sort typical in the apprenticeship mode. Gradually, new musicians move from elementary and most obvious rules to more advanced and sophisticated understandings, and from scrupulous and legalistic adherence to rules to being governed by, following, or even transgressing them. Musicians also revere and respect the authority and traditional basis of the rule system, looking back to musical belief and practice of the past even as they invent new rules and work by them. All of the details of a musical practice derive their importance from their relationship to certain underlying principles, and there is considerable room for musical interpretation and flexibility in maintaining a practice as a living tradition.

Music construed as rule operates somewhat ambiguously.[18] For example, one performer seeks to ascertain the musical import in the score and in what is known about the composer and the work, whereas another feels freer to interpret it more idiosyncratically and personally. Each is rule-following to some extent and in differing ways. One takes a more conservative position and stays closer to the letter of the rule (suggested in the score and in historically informed practice) while the other is more progressive, less bound by its letter and more by its spirit. Both may be disciplined in the performance of their instruments and their faithfulness to the marks in the score, but each sees the rule differently. Each exercises judgment in deciding how to interpret the score. Making these musical judgments necessitates some "psychical distance" from the music in order to grasp it more objectively, although this may be more the case for the conservative performer than the more progressive one.[19]

Teaching. Viewing teaching as rule emphasizes the teacher's logical reasoning, dispassionate thought, restraint, and fair-mindedness in exercising judgment.[20] At the root of this view of teaching is the ideal of justice.[21] Teachers are expected to treat their students dispassionately, fairly, evenhandedly, and with restraint so that all have, at very least, equal access to the teacher's time, attention, interest, and help. In seeking to arrive at just decisions, teachers also agree to be bound by their own rules just as their students are. Thinking through their rules for teaching practice requires teachers' intellectual engagement and critical and constructive thought.[22] The teacher employs reason in all decision-making, not in unfeeling intellectuality but as a clear-eyed exercise of judgment that is also emotionally tinged.[23] By dispassionate thought, I mean the teacher's ability to deal at some psychical distance with ideas and practices that are laden with affect and moral valency. Psychical distance refers to the capacity to separate oneself from what one is observing so as to see the situation objectively and logically—to assess it more or less across the board, without favoring a particular point of view or practice over another. Attachments are held in abeyance as the teacher thinks through this situation as dispassionately as possible. Such qualities as moderation and self-control give evidence of restraint.[24] Teachers exercise restraint by acts of mind and will. They are disciplined and controlled in the ways in which they think, speak, and act; they are even-tempered in their dealings with others. Their emotions and passions do not control their decision-making. Fair-mindedness is the quality of giving each idea and practice its due and recognizing its strengths and weaknesses. Implicit in fair-mindedness is the ideal of equality, that all persons are precious and ought to be treated equally rather than some regarded more favorably than others. Although notions of what is meant by equality and how it is to be adjudicated are complex matters, teachers in the model more or less agree with the general principle that there ought to be, at very least, equality of opportunity for students, even if they differ on the specifics of how this is to be accomplished.[25]

As a form of schooling, taken literally to refer to a particular place in which instruction is given or figuratively to indicate a set of beliefs and practices that are inculcated in the next generation of musicians, teaching is disciplined, contractual, and evidentiary.[26] By discipline, I mean a "system or method for the maintenance of order; a system of rules for conduct," and "the practice of training people to obey rules or a code of behavior."[27] Obedience to particular rules (and the punishment of those who disobey) situates the task of teaching as developing specific skills (ranging from habits to critical thinking skills) and techniques appropriate to this practice. Students are brought into conformity with the underlying principles of the musical practice not for the sake of developing standardized products (as in production) but in order to sustain a musical tradition and foster its core beliefs, values, and practices. So obedience, or the willingness to be brought into conformity with the tradition's principles, is at the heart of rule, especially at the early stages of instruction, when the student is very dependent on the teacher and begins to form habits of mind and action. Cultivating obedience is quite a different matter from teaching students to deconstruct, subvert, and transgress the rules they are being taught, as may be the case in the transgression and community models. As the heir of a musical tradition and an expert or exponent of it, the teacher rules the classroom, rehearsal, or studio and may be honored and beloved by students.[28] Such teaching is often contractual. A contract is a way of formalizing the teacher's and student's obligations and clarifying the specific aspects of the program of musical instruction to be followed and the rule-sets operative in it. Such formalities may be prescribed in course syllabi that serve as implicit if not explicit contracts concerning the times of classes, requisite out-of-class work to be done by students, and rewards and punishments for following or not following the prescribed plan. This teaching is also evidentiary in its reliance on arguments justifying the purposes and methods of music education, demonstrating empirically those approaches most effective in governing the classroom and, wherever possible, refuting bogus approaches and ineffective plans. Such an approach, as in the production model, values studies of "best practices," although for quite different reasons. Here, the emphasis is on providing bases for teachers to make judicious and wise decisions, whereas, in production it is on establishing the most efficient, cost-effective, and standardized means of teaching.

Learning. In the rule model, learning is grounded in rights and responsibilities. The United Nations charter grants to all children the right to know their culture and, by implication, music as an element of that culture.[29] Although the United States is not at this time of writing a signatory to the United Nations Convention on the Rights of the Child, music has been adopted as a classroom subject in the nation's elementary schools since the nineteenth century, lawsuits brought against school districts for not providing music education have been settled in favor of including musical instruction in the public school curriculum, and there is congressional support for school music.[30] Still, as a practical matter, music instruction for all children is predicated on state and local decisions, and the quality and spread of music education in the nation's public and private schools is uneven.[31] Regarding musical learning as a matter of justice from the perspective of equality of access to music instruction suggests that every young person, irrespective of conditions of birth or socioeconomic status, ought to have access to cultural knowledge and participate in music as a part of general education. This is a broad claim, and the devil lies in the details that are the subject of debate in the public spaces. Nevertheless, a debate framed within rule begins with notions of justice and explores ways in which it can be practically implemented in regard to music learning.[32] Among the responsibilities of students, critical thinking is important not only for musical thought and practice but for the active and full participation of citizens in a democracy.[33] In particular, critical thinking in music is one of a range of skills that cover the gamut of musical theory and practice, and its development requires cultivating a respect for the rules that undergird a musical tradition.[34] When learning music, students tend to begin with a somewhat slavish adherence to the rules, gradually come to the point where they negotiate them more critically and judiciously, and later reach the stage where, although rooted in a musical tradition, they are also its critics and architects of new rule-sets.[35] This stress on reason gives learning an intellectual edge as students learn to think as well as do in a particular tradition. Still, imaginative and intuitive thought are also present in the midst of making and taking music, and the immediate, holistic, active, and receptive thought-in-the-moment-of-performance brings together mind and body, emotion and cognition, in an approach akin to learning as healing.[36]

This is a serious and directed approach to learning.[37] Given presumably wide differences between those who are content to approach music somewhat superficially and the relative few who are initiated into its deeper secrets, the rule model supposes one sort of musical education for the masses and another for the few musicians, with the caveat that all students should receive some of both.[38] In this view, all students shall have access to broad musical, historical, and cultural understandings that enable them to better grasp their musical worlds and broaden their horizons. Although not primarily directed at developing musical skills, they are still to perform, compose, and improvise in accessible ways. Those who demonstrate musical aptitudes and abilities are to be encouraged by an equally serious development of musical skills, keeping in mind music's broader cultural role.[39] In this way, those students who wish to study music in great depth can do so seriously, unhindered by those who would rather learn about and do something else.[40] The roles of teacher and learner are clearly differentiated; rather than teachers engaging students in open-ended conversations, students are expected to receive their teachers' instructions and obey their dictates. Students are challenged by competent musician-teachers to follow the rules set forth by the teacher. Punishments and rewards are unambiguous, immediate, and measured, so learners know exactly where they are and what they need to do and not do. This clarity of objectives and models for imitation relies on their insight into the nature of music and requires that their teachers "im-press" and shape them so that they exemplify the desired ideas and practices.[41] Gradually, they come to grasp the underlying principles of thought and practice that frame this particular musical tradition and, if they study several traditions, see how the rules governing one tradition differ from others. Seeing their teacher model musical judgment according to these rules also prompts them to develop skills to judge music themselves. So they, in turn, use the same criteria as a frame in which to think critically about this music.

Instruction. Teacher–student interaction in the rule model is quite lopsided, contributing to a wide social distance between teacher and student and formal interaction between them. Teachers do the teaching; students receive knowledge from the teacher and do the learning—a relationship similar to that between a monarch and a subject or a referee and those who are playing a game. As in the consumption, production, and apprenticeship models, the teacher is presumed to be the powerful one-knowing, in possession of knowledge that the student does not have. The teacher conducts the lesson by imparting, explaining, directing, and showing the student what to do and insisting that it be done as directed and shown.[42] This sort of lesson provides no opportunity for students to shape the direction of the class except insofar as the teacher determines. The powerlessness of students and their dependency on their teacher for opportunities and advancement mean that they are liable to be on their best behavior, eager to please their teacher, and apt to work diligently in the intervening times between lessons and rehearsals in order to prepare for their lessons. Employing rule democratically as a means of social control is likely to ameliorate the social distance between teacher and student and change the quality of the interaction.[43] Under these circumstances, the teacher acts as referee and adjudicator of the rule system, governs how the group works socially, and ensures that these rules are followed. This teacher–

student relationship may be less formal because students or musicians have a greater stake in forging rules that apply to classroom and rehearsal procedures. Still, the teacher shapes the content of instruction and formally instructs the students, and the socially constructed rules control or limit their behavior.

In the rule mode of teaching, teachers direct, explain to, and exemplify the musical tradition to their students, and so instruction is necessarily and primarily formal. Informal, haphazard, idiosyncratic, and serendipitous means cannot be relied upon, because students cannot be presumed to know what is important or good for them to know. Although their approach to instruction may be dictatorial or monarchical, teachers are assumed to be benevolent and have their students' best interests at heart.[44] Such teachers reason that some students are more apt musicians than others, and the sooner they learn this lesson, the better it will be for them. Instruction is also bound to be systematic and rationalized. As in the production and consumption models, preparing musicians requires the comprehensive and specific knowledge and ability that rule-sets embody. Rather than the divergent and idiosyncratic repertoire fostered in the community model, teachers ensure that their students come to know about, and know how to play or sing, exemplary works of the canon that musicians in this tradition share. Instructional systems work toward this end, and teachers participate together in passing on a body of musical wisdom to the next generation of musicians. Over time this process is rationalized, and conservatories, schools, and faculties of music are organized to train musicians according to agreed-upon musical rule-sets.

Curriculum. When rules are construed musically, the musical subject matter for students is viewed as a body of knowledge they need to come to know about and know how to practice. This requires, in turn, a focus on acquiring musical skills. Accordingly, as in the growth model, subject matter is organized systematically and sequentially so that students are able to successfully acquire these skills. Unlike the apprenticeship curriculum, however, in the rule model these skills run the gamut from critical thinking skills and habits of mind to the skills required in musical performance and the habitual dispositions to make and take music in particular ways. Emphasis is on the organization of the subject matter rather than its construction by learners as in the community, growth, and healing models. Among examples in school music, *Discipline-Based Music Education,* as with *Discipline-Based Arts Education*, focuses on the things that musicians and arts need to know and be able to do, takes music and the arts seriously, and regards the "high arts" as normative.[45] In contrast to the growth model, where students grasp the nature of music in their own ways and only later approach the subject matter as experts would see it, the rule model favors organizing subject matter according to strictly musical considerations and presented to the students, who are then not faced with constructing knowledge for themselves. From the earliest grades, music teachers help their students learn the content as it is arranged pedagogically and musically by musical experts.[46] Teachers emphasize the musical discipline from the very first, seeking to ensure that the students respect its norms and obey its rules. There are no open-ended opportunities for little children to sing and play musical games and simple instruments without the necessity of these activities also being of some conceptual use in articulating the discipline of music as experts understand it. In similar vein, the National Standards movement in arts education can also be read, most sympathetically, as a traditional approach to music's underlying structures and functions, literatures, principal figures, knowledge basis, and skills.[47] School music curricula introduce students to the rule systems and structures of Western classical music; explore its musical instruments, notable musicians and composers, and other musical traditions such as jazz; and foster direct musical experiences through songs for classroom use.[48]

Whether construed mainly in regard to musical rules, social rules, or both, this curriculum is contractual. Music teachers in publicly supported schools develop two quite different skill-sets—musical skills at the basis of the discipline of music, and social skills at the root of the discipline of democratic government. Where the two rule-sets intersect, the interests of music and political values sometimes collide. Still, teachers engage them both as they determine what they need to accomplish in their classrooms and how they can bring their students to a deeper and broader understanding of music as well as these other things. Thinking of the classroom as a game played by participants within sets of rules suggests that whatever rule-sets apply, all agree to live by and be bound by them.[49] Teachers and their students act as if the curriculum is binding, and academic policies are often framed on this basis. Once a curriculum is approved and published, students expect that it will be delivered and that there will be no substantial changes going forward, and teachers presume that students also understand this when they take a course. The intended curriculum tends to become quite set and fixed, and it is less possible to make substantial changes along the way without the agreement of all of the participants.

Administration. In the rule model, policies govern the conduct and evaluation of all aspects of the organization's operation. A systematic and disciplinary view of music requires the organization of departments, each with its head, and of committees and councils that formulate and legislate the policies, procedures, and regulations that govern the school's operation. This policy-based and regulated organizational structure permits the system to operate smoothly within rule-sets by which all the members are bound. Administrative tasks entail interpreting and carrying out the school's policies, regulations, and procedures. Where problems arise, they are adjudicated with reference to existing regulations and rules, and if these prove inadequate, new legislation is required. By examining the existing interrelationships among participants in music education and the policies and procedures in place, it is possible to grasp underlying symbolic meanings of the observed phenomena.[50] Rule systems are understood not only in terms of what they say but what they intend and represent. For example, the differences in power between teachers and their students are reflected in teachers' use of informal means of communication with their students.[51] Even though academic policies may require teachers to notify their department heads or other personnel officers when they are absent, students may not challenge those who do not follow these rules, because they are dependent on their teachers and fear retribution should they complain when their lesson times are altered. Summative evaluation is likely to play an important role in assessing the specific performances of all of the participants in music instruction and the degree to which contractual obligations are met. Even though formative evaluation may be used as a means of helping participants improve their performance, the rule model, like the production and consumption models, emphasizes summative evaluation because it provides a more or less objective assessment of the situation so that appropriate rational judgments may be made. Given the emphasis on rationality in this model, it is likely to prefer quantitative assessments because of their claims to objectivity and generalizability.

Courts of inquiry and rights and procedures to appeal administrative decisions are also characteristic features of rule. Typically, these features cover every aspect of the school's organization, handling such functions as resolving contract disputes and scheduling conflicts, and holding hearings to determine student progress or to discipline teachers, staff, and students. Curriculum policy committees and councils also integrate courses taught in multiple sections and determine courses of study, degrees and diplomas awarded, and public examinations and recitals. Resolving disputes and settling grievances of one sort or another is accomplished with reference to these social and musical rule-sets. Sometimes, the rules and regulations oriented to past tradition and precedent prove insufficient and no longer apply to present realities. Since the personnel in an organization and the context in which it is situated also change, from time to time, it is necessary to review the organization's policies and procedures and develop new and more appropriate rule-sets.

CRITIQUE

Among its musical advantages, the rule model emphasizes musical and related social processes and their symbolic meaning and musical products, be they performances, research publications, compositions, improvisations, or recordings. Regarding music as a practice driven by certain expectations, which are based on a systematic body of knowledge, enables a comprehensive view, akin to that of the apprenticeship model, that covers the gamut of critical thinking and physical skills and habits. The model's exponents honor tradition and exemplary practice, help to keep alive musical knowledge and wisdom from the past, and emphasize the intellectual character of musical knowing at a time in which sensual and affective elements are often the focus of culture. This model also relies upon musical and artistic judgments in evaluating musical composition, performance, and criticism. It predicates these judgments on systems of rules rather than deriving them idiosyncratically or impressionistically.

Among its disadvantages, the underlying musical rule system may be so emphasized that the tradition becomes backward looking, stuck in its veneration for past practices, and unwilling to change. As rules and norms are difficult to change, it may be difficult for composers to have new music accepted, performers to program music outside the canon, and audiences to adjust to the changing sounds of music. Critics and other tastemakers may forget that rules simply confirm past practice and regard them, instead, as immutable and obligatory on present and future practice. Focusing mainly on musical rules may lead to a preoccupation with training and schooling, leaving the musical tradition bereft of musicians with a broad and integrated view of music as a branch of the humanities and an art, who lack the courage to transgress its rules, push it in new directions, and thereby revitalize it.[52] Those who focus on the social and political character of musical events may likewise fail to notice sufficiently the specifically musical rule-systems that shape musical belief and practice.

On the bright side, since this model bases teaching on reason and judgment, rendered in terms of rule-sets that govern either the subject matter and/or the ways in which instruction is organized, it is possible that teachers' decision-making may be less capricious, incoherent, and extreme than might otherwise be the case. Its systematic, measured, and reflective approach suggests that teachers both think critically about what they are doing and take appropriate steps to carry out their ideas in practice. As expert musicians in the traditions they teach, teachers impart competent knowledge about music, and about how to make and take it to their students, from the very beginning. The value teachers place on what they teach is communicated to their students, and the seriousness of their purpose and the importance of what they are doing together can inspire students to take their learning seriously. The idealistic character of learning by rule, whether in democratic principles of justice, equality, and self-determination or musical principles of exemplary performance, as well as its devotion to musical artistry, constitute imperatives for teachers who seek to realize these ideals. Aspiring to these ideals dignifies teachers' tasks and raises their sights to accomplish extraordinary feats with their students, exemplifying the best of this musical tradition in their explanations, directions, and demonstrations.

On the dark side, the lack of ambiguity in the roles of teacher and student and their relationship to the subject matter in the rule model situates the teacher as a giver of information and the student as the recipient of it, thus failing to take sufficient notice of the construction of the subject by each learner. Such a view falls short of acknowledging the importance of teachers as learners and students as teachers, and the possibilities that might arise from a more conversational approach of the sort evident in community and healing. I see a tension between the focus on teaching for obedience and conformity on the learner's part and teaching for reasoning; one would seem to undermine the other, and it would be difficult, in the practical sense, to accomplish both ends if both are desirable. Either students may learn too well the lessons of obedience, or they may be prone to dismiss too quickly the tradition's practices as they think critically about them. Emphasizing the intellectual elements of music may prompt music teachers to overlook music's emotional and physiological aspects. Given their focus on the subject matter of music, teachers may fail to be sufficiently cognizant of their learners' predicaments and the often idiosyncratic and intuitive ways in which they approach music. So preoccupied are teachers with telling, showing, and directing that they may fail to question, listen to, and observe their students. Nor do they always act benevolently toward their students or have their best interests at heart.

Among the advantages of learning in rule, the focus upon students' grasping the principles and procedures of a musical tradition empowers them musically as they systematically attain its requisite skills and knowledge. As teaching is very directive, students have clear purposes; their role is to acquire a knowledge of the theories and practices of this tradition. All along the way their tendencies to diverge from the norm are curbed, and they approach, by successive approximation, the know-how of competent musicians, grasping the musical wisdom to which they are heirs. This curbing process also requires that students learn self-discipline, since they need to acquire a knowledge of the rules undergirding this musical tradition. In the context of formal instructional settings, much devolves on their own diligence in studying and practicing their music and their own will to learn. Attending to general principles as well as specific skills also offers a comprehensive approach to musical learning. Their teachers, while sometimes authoritarian, may also have their best musical interests at heart and be devoted to their success as musicians. When social control is emphasized as well, students can learn important skills in practical judgment that prepare them for social and public life.

Nevertheless, there are several possible difficulties. In the serious purpose and systematization of music education, teachers and their students may forget to play, and thereby miss the serendipitous and open-ended opportunities to learn in the unexpected ways hoped for in the community and growth models. Unlike the production model, although certain normative ideas and practices undergird the instruction, learning in the rule model presents possibilities for divergent and for unexpected outcomes. Still, if the learner's experience of music is rendered so systematic and conceptual that play is overlooked, the reign of rule may destroy the very quality it hopes to foster, namely delight in the unexpected. Any sense of control that students may seem to have over how the subject matter is approached may be more illusory than real. New and generative ideas prompt a range of rich ideas and practices to be explored, but eventually the doctrinal experts codify and render entirely systematic the idea's possibilities and wear out the generative idea, so that it becomes a shadow of its former self.[53] This is precisely the danger I see in musical learning based on rule. If the rules come to assume a prominence out of all proportion to their place in the overall musical scheme of things, they can destroy the power and possibility of learning in this model. Excessive normalizing and curbing creative thought and expression are soul-destroying, creating technicians who know the rules well and can apply them brilliantly but have forgotten their spirit. Should the system of musical learning be set up to foreshorten the opportunities for general music education before weeding out those with insufficient musical ability or demonstrable achievement, there is the risk that rule may result in eliminating too many students too soon from opportunities for music learning.

On the one hand, setting up instruction according to rule underscores the importance of ideas and ideals in shaping practice and the possibilities for developing systematic approaches to music education. This serious purpose and its formality are especially important at a time in which music education may be regarded cynically, and as something of tangential importance in general education and where informality is pervasive in society. If music education is a serious undertaking, it necessitates the expenditure of significant resources to do it properly. It also requires more than the too-often minimal resources presently provided in terms of instructional times, places, personnel, equipment, musical scores, and instruments. Its formality reawakens ideas of civility, etiquette, and sensitivity to others; and the sense of order it provides is comforting especially to those who live their lives in disarray and disorder. Where it is directed toward principles of justice, equality, inclusiveness, freedom, mutual respect, and affection, it approaches transgression in its liberating and empowering influence on all those involved in music education. As a metaphor for the conduct of civil society, its impact is functional as it is also musical and artistic. Since it is organized systematically, it also provides a basis for carrying out programs of mass musical education.

On the other hand, thinking of instruction as rule also raises important issues that may detract from music education. Regarding the process of interaction between teacher and student so contractually may suggest too legalistic an approach to music education. Excessive dotting of i's and crossing of t's, counting of points, and focusing on trivial aspects of instruction may deflect teacher and student attention away from the central issues of music instruction—aspects that resist easy prescription and assessment. Thinking of instruction so seriously as work may detract from the delight teachers and their students may take in the process of musical play, removing possibilities for affection and joy that might otherwise be present. Such emphasis on formality neglects the important informal ways in which music is regularly taught and learned and contributes further to the alienation or social distance between teacher and student. This mode of instruction seems excessively cold, cerebral, and task-oriented; it yields a narrow view of music instruction. Even where social-control notions obtain, thinking of music instruction in terms of athletic games or judicial dramas fails to notice the power of teacher and student interaction on a personal level that cannot be reduced easily to rule-systems. So rule may be a limited view of music education, as it is also limiting to those who may undergo and even endure it.

Curriculum seen within the lens of rule is beneficial in several ways. Its focus on developing students who can think in musical traditions gives them the kind of grounding that allows them to make musical judgments intelligently. Its intellectual emphasis values mind as the "life of feeling" and contributes to a broad and humane education of the sort especially needed if citizens are to have a stake in their own government.[54] Thinking in musical traditions constitutes the basis of musical practice as actions flow from ideas. In this view, atomistic and specific skills become integrated within more general systems of thought and practice. Where curricula are designed in terms of the underlying structures of musical knowledge and practice, students may gain a comprehensive view of a field as expert musicians see it. As students are also in the position to construct knowledge for themselves, they are enabled to grasp a musical tradition's norms while venturing off in their own ways as their knowledge becomes more established. The possibility of moving from slavishly following rules at first to a more flexible following and even transgressing of them from time to time has the advantage of building on normative understandings and practices rather than too quickly disregarding them.

Still, curriculum in rule is also flawed. The static body-of-knowledge view of the curriculum takes insufficient account of how learners construct knowledge, and it may be too staid and motionless to deal with the dynamic realities of music education. Regarding music as a systematic structure of rule-sets overlooks the particular differences between musics. Each music has its specific rule-sets; assuming that one structure of rule-sets ought to provide the basis for the curriculum privileges a particular music. Aside from the inevitable ethnocentricity of such an approach, there are the practical difficulties of determining whose music is to constitute the basis for the music curriculum or how the various musical rule-sets are to be contested and negotiated. Keeping the focus throughout the entire development of the student from young childhood to old age on these musical rule-sets does not enable young and old alike who approach music as neophyte musicians to simply experience music and make their own constructions of it before they move on to more systematic understandings. For example, discipline-based approaches may be effective in some reaches of music instruction, but they cannot suffice for the entire gamut of it. The possibility of emphasizing musical concepts and abstract rule-sets before students experience them is doomed to practical failure, just as was the attempt by early American singing masters to provide the musical rules before the musical practice.[55] Such approaches may be arguably inappropriate for the very young, the musically inexperienced, and all those who undertake music for other than strictly musical ends. Privileging past tradition rather than creating new approaches to music making may also doom a musical tradition and fossilize it. When musical skills are constantly broken down systematically, the danger lurks that they may not be subsequently integrated as they are in curriculum as healing, and students may never experience music's transcendence and imminence or know wonder and awe in the face of exceptional musical experiences.

Administration in the context of rule also presents benefits. Among them, a social view of the musical organization provides an important perspective on musical events cast at a higher level of generality than physiological and psychological perspectives. The clarity of roles and responsibilities, structures and functions, organizational systems and their underlying symbolic import are insights that help make the nature of music instruction more transparent to its participants and public. Possibilities of drama, conflict, negotiation, and resolution reflect the practical realities faced by music teachers and their students. Working through sometimes intractable dilemmas and riding on the crest of euphoric moments are the lot of all those who work together with others in social situations. Policies, procedures, and regulations oil the wheels of the musical organization and permit difficulties to be overcome and happy circumstances to be celebrated. As administrators oversee the formulation of rules and interpret them fairly, indiscriminately, dispassionately, and transparently, they can also command the respect and admiration of their colleagues and contribute, as in the healing model, to making this organization a happy and satisfying place in which to be.

Among the drawbacks of this model for administration, it is possible to develop systems, regulations, and procedures that appear to be civil, just, and humane, but are, in fact, oppressive, unjust, and inhumane; they may have a form of democracy but lack the spirit thereof. Predicating a system of music education on rules is only as civil, just, and humane as the rules themselves and the people who interpret them. Too many rules may destroy an organization just as they can destroy a music. When the organization's administrators, teachers, students, and staff are hedged about by rules and regulations, they may have insufficient freedom to move, think divergently, and act creatively. Every rule requires policing that diverts resources from other activities; these resources are not well spent when they demoralize those whom the rule impacts. Relying on rule systems to "instrumentalize" or "technologize" administration so that decision-making is more or less automatic removes important possibilities for the exercise of judgment. Systems-theory approaches to administration seem too akin to the standardized and technocratic thinking of production and may fail to take sufficiently into account the many ways in which personal circumstances demand more nuanced and humane ways of acting than the rule prescribes. For example, a deadline looms and a teacher cannot produce the required documentation in time in order to be paid. Appealing for an extension due to mitigating factors beyond his control, the teacher is told that the deadline cannot be moved and he will be punished for failing to meet this deadline by not being paid for the period in question. The administrator may be technically right; the prescribed deadline has been missed, and the rules call for this teacher's punishment. Still, if the administrator grasps the circumstances and the teacher's desire to do the right thing, and if she wishes this teacher's affection and loyalty in the future, she may waive the letter of the rule in this case, and in its spirit, arrange for the teacher to produce the requisite documentation at the earliest opportunity. What is the long-term effect on this organization of such a comparatively minor matter? If the administrator acts legalistically, the teacher's morale may be undermined; he is likely to tell his story to friends and family members; they are likely to be dismayed, knowing how hard he works; and they may grumble about the administrator's heavy-handedness. If the administrator acts more considerately and exercises judgment regarding the spirit if not necessarily the exact letter of the law, she may gain influence with this teacher and engender his trust and gratitude, and the ripples of her kindness may also travel out into the wider organization. The danger of the rule model, as with administration as healing, is that musical organizations may take on the trappings of the metaphor and what is intentionally figurative may be interpreted too literally.

SUMMARY

It is clear that the pictures of *court* and *rule* offer much for music education. Their dramatic, social, reasoned, measured, and systematic character are appealing, yet the prospect of their stifling imagination and innovation, failing to welcome play and serendipity as much as work and system, valuing tradition over change, privileging reason over intuition, mind over body, and formality over informality, distancing administrators, teachers, students, and staff from each other, and taking too literal and legalistic a perspective on music organization, reveal the dangers that also lurk on every hand. Yet I cling to ideals of justice, inclusiveness, love, reverence, respect, tact, and the preciousness of all people regardless of their birth and background in the hope that ways might be found to avoid these detractions wherever possible.

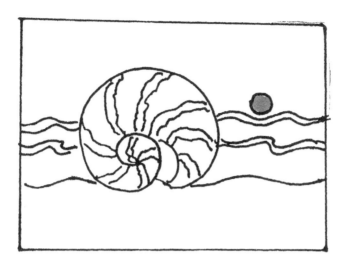

10
SEASHORE AND ENERGY

We come upon the pictures of *seashore* and *energy* in differing moods, hues, colors, and contrasts that resonate with musicians. The ocean is "a magnet in all seasons," and there is something evocative, spiritual, majestic, calming, fearful, and wonderful about "Neptune country with its ancient rhythms and mysteries."[1] Walking along the shoreline between land and sea and writing on Cape Cod surrounded by ocean remind me of the long-standing philosophical and scientific interest in the relationship of music, education, and energy. The ancient philosophers believed that music was the stuff of which the cosmos was made.[2] Modern scientific notions of energy, contemporary understandings of musical acoustics, mathematical foundations of music, and speculative approaches to music breathe new life into these ideas by pointing to ways in which wave motion and vibration of which music is comprised undergird the known universe and constitute a fundamental principle of all matter.[3] Susanne Langer and John Dewey describe musical and artistic experience as psychologically perceived movement connected with the nature of life itself.[4] The dust jacket for Nel Noddings's book, *Happiness and Education,* depicts three laughing children splashing through the waves at the seashore.[5] Now, I reflect on the seashore, describe aspects of music education construed as energy, and sketch the positive and negative attributes of these pictures.

SEASHORE

I grew up near the sea, and some of my earliest memories are of family holidays by the ocean. My parents would rent a cottage by the sea, we would pack up all the things that we would need, and along with the family pet pile excitedly into an overloaded car. Our days were spent swimming and playing by the seashore. In the evenings, we would walk along the beach to nearby shops, buy our supper, and afterward, walk out onto a jetty stretching into the ocean. By day the bright sun burned fiercely hot, and by night the moon turned the Indian Ocean silver. Sometimes, huge rolling waves crashed so fiercely that it was easy to be knocked unconscious. As youngsters, we learned to swim almost as soon as we learned to walk, and what to do if we were in trouble in the water. I recall the regular shark warnings as we fled for our lives from the ocean. It seems like yesterday when, having gone to the ocean on a blustery day, a fellow college student was taken by a shark, and we stood in a miserable group and watched helplessly as life-savers did all they could and a small coast guard plane flew overhead in a fruitless search. We went to the beach as happy singles and couples and returned home that evening sorrowfully to mourn a terrible loss. To write about the seashore, then, is to remember happiness and sorrow, desire and release, friends and strangers, storm and calm, spirit and body, danger and safety.

Yesterday, I sat thinking by Nantucket Sound on a grey and windy afternoon. An almost monochromatic scene melded sea and sky and veiled it in mist. A choppy sea rolled waves onto the shore, I could barely make out sailboats not far away, with a boat pulling a parasailor almost lost from view, and the world seemed to shrink to an intimacy typical of this locale. The day before, at this same place, the world was bathed in brilliant sunshine, the sky almost cloudless, the sea calm and a beautiful blue as gentle waves lapped the shore. Sky and sea were clearly delineated at the horizon, and the vista was so expansive that it seemed to go on forever. These two worlds could not be more different, and yet more the same.

Or, I think of a salt marsh beside Cape Cod Bay. After a winter nor'easter, a snowstorm with hurricane-force winds that beat on this place for three days, we strolled on a boardwalk that led out over the marsh. In the freezing cold, this was a world of white, huge ice waves and snow drifts, tree limbs laden with snow, and winter sky showing pink-red at sunset. Nothing could be more different than when, at summer's height, we again walked this same path. Today, at high tide, boats floated, the deep-green grass of the marsh was bathed in sunlight, the water sparkled, a group partied on the beach across the estuary, crabs scurried and fish swam in the clear water of the channels, and above the marsh, an osprey pair fed their young. Where snow and ice had reigned, the world was now sun-dappled green and blue.

Those who dwell by the sea know these contrasts. It may be that people are drawn to the oceanside because it is so varied. Constant change is evident in the sky fire-red at sunset turning blue water gold, the ocean whitecaps and waves pounding white froth on sand in a storm, great breakers rolling onto golden beaches, crashing on rocky headlands and spouting water high into the air, phalanxes of pelicans skimming across the waves, sunrise breaking pink and the sea shades of pink-grey to blue, porpoises cavorting, birds scampering along the shoreline, seagulls mewing, and the coming and going of people. We may see white sand, turquoise water, and grass-covered sand dunes on one day and billowing stormclouds, driving wind and rain, whitecapped waves, and roiling surf on another.

At the seashore, wind and water shape the landscape in powerful ways. Walking a beach shell-shocked after a hurricane, we are moved to tears by the devastation nature has wrought as ocean escapes its normal bounds, floods the land, breaks through a barrier island, and changes the normal course of things. Houses upended from their foundations, thrown about like matchsticks, piles of debris, shattered glass, and household effects like so much trash. All of this is so very capricious— one building standing and another not. In the face of nature's wildness, some buildings people have constructed on the land are blown away and devastated by the power of wind and water. Although this magical place is turned into a disaster for the people who live here, somehow the animals and birds seem to know and are safe. Two proud swans and an accompanying flock of ducks still swim in the lagoon. Where were they when the winds blew and the waters rose? They must have been in some safe place, because here they are swimming.

Notwithstanding its dangers, the possibilities of rip currents, shark attacks, bites from other sea creatures, and destructive storms, people are drawn to the seashore, which becomes at some times a hive of activity. Looking around, I see several children building a sand castle and debating details of its construction. A family plays a ball game. Relatives and friends are reading, talking, laughing, sleeping, eating, walking, swimming, board surfing, sailing, kayaking, and fishing. Some have built shelters to protect themselves from the wind. Others have put up umbrellas under which to shelter from the sun. Some have brought coolers with supplies of drinks and food and folding chairs and chaises on which to sit and recline, and there is a long line at the nearby concession stand. Parents are keeping a close eye on their little children as they play at water's edge. There are people of all shapes, sizes, and a rainbow of colors. I wonder at all of this activity and the evident happiness of those who have come to spend time at this seashore today.

There is romance at the seaside. A couple of young lovers lie nearby murmuring softly. I see an older couple hand-in-hand strolling along the shore. Friends laugh and giggle together. There is time to talk, gossip, reflect, enjoy the present moment, and be restored and re-created. Here, very close to the natural world, often stripped-down to essentials, we dwell in the present moment and yet seem to be a part of something bigger than ourselves. The lure and romance of the seaside for those who love it is physical and spiritual. It is a place of pleasure and of play rather than work. Those who earn their livelihood at the seaside are often looked upon as fortunate for having the privilege to spend so much time here. It is also a place of escape from ordinary life and those who enjoy the seaside come here of their own free will. I suppose that many who enjoy this seaside today live and work at other places. As I reflect on the fact that I shall soon return home, a thousand miles away, I am sad that my sojourn here must come to an end all too quickly. I treasure every moment that I have to spend at this place.

Thinking of the constant ebb and flow of the water, the tides that daily mark points on the seashore where the sea advances and retreats, reminds me that much of life is inevitable and unstoppable. As the tide comes in, it lifts all of the boats along the pontoon, large and small, and as it goes out, they are all left stranded. There is a sense of inevitability in these natural forces that resist human control. William Shakespeare thinks of tides when he thinks of human life. He writes, "There is a tide in the affairs of men / Which taken at the flood, leads on to fortune; / Omitted, all the voyage of their life / is bound in shallows and in miseries."[6] Opportunities are like the tides; if one seizes them, they may lead to glory; and if not, they leave one stranded. Ideas and practices also have their times and tides, their ebb and flow.

As a place of becoming, the dynamism, movement, and changes of the seashore resonate with our lived lives, which have their own ebb and flow, coming and going, and ongoing movement. The landscape is constantly shaped and reshaped by water, wind, and human action. Even on a calm day, in which there is profound stillness and silence, we know that this is but a brief moment in which change is the norm. Although we might wish that time would stand still in order to allow this moment by the sea to last forever, the sun moves across the heavens and eventually sets on this day; night falls, and another day begins. Time does not stand still, nor does the moment last, except as it is treasured in memory for a lifetime. The natural world seems very near at the seaside, and, here, we may be especially conscious of how precious each moment is in our lived lives.

The sea's attraction for people prompts some scientists to wonder if humans came from the sea. As I write, the IMAX film "Volcanoes of the Deep Sea " has been pulled from some theaters in the "Bible Belt" of the United States.[7] Fundamentalist Christians have criticized the film's references to the similarities in DNA between the "tube worms" that live in the ocean depths and that of humanity, suggesting "that human evolution may have begun in the deep sea." Sidestepping the debate

over fundamentalist Christian belief in the literal truth of the biblical story of creation, I am intrigued by scientific theories of human origins and the power of the
oceans in shaping human destiny. From antiquity, civilizations and cultures spread
across the seas from one continent and island to another. Throughout recorded
history, people have gone "down to the sea in ships."[8] Wondering what might lie
beyond the horizon led to epic voyages of discovery. Now, scientists explore the
ocean depths and, finding there remarkable similarities to human life, wonder at
our origins. They may also think of what they do figuratively in terms of the sea. As
Isaac Newton aptly stated: "I do not know what I may appear to the world, but to
myself I seem to have been only like a boy playing on the sea-shore, and diverting
myself in now and then finding a smoother pebble or a prettier shell than ordinary,
whilst the great ocean of truth lay all undiscovered before me."[9]

This link between the seashore and science is interesting on all sorts of levels.
Most particularly, our encounters at the seashore are not the stuff of romance,
legend, or myth alone, but also of science. Whether it be the study of wave motion,
erosion, marine life, or geologic forces beneath the oceans, scientists see the seashore as a place for wonder of a very different sort than that an ordinary beachgoer
might experience. For example, at the Oceanographic Institution at Woods Hole,
Massachusetts, scientists press the boundaries of their knowledge about the ocean
and the living things in it.[10] Using scientific methods and the insights from various
scientific specialties, they seek to establish knowledge about the sea and its shore.
As the IMAX film illustrates, scientific findings and religious dogma may clash
now, as they have clashed in times past. Still, it is important not to confuse one
way of knowing with another. Science wants to refute ideas, religion teaches faith
in and obedience to them, and art focuses on other than propositional discourse.[11]
It is important to distinguish these different ways of wondering, see value in scientific, religious, and artistic perspectives, and grasp their respective contributions
and limitations.

ENERGY

The word *energy* refers to qualities of "strength and vitality required for sustained activity" or "physical and mental powers."[12] Looked upon physically, from
the Greek *energeia*, energy is "an ability or capacity to produce an effect."[13] Among
the word's ambiguities, there is an etymological connection to work and its use as
a means of musical play, and it can be thought of physically and spiritually, literally and figuratively. Energy is so all-encompassing that, looking through its lens,
it reveals education's interconnection with the rest of lived life. Carl Seashore, Carl
Orff, Susanne Langer, Edwin Gordon, Anthony Palmer, Mary Reichling, Eleanor
Stubley, Krista Riggs, Deanne Bogdan, and Iris Yob are among the writers to ex-

plore music and education as energy.[14] Research studies of music teacher personality reveal the importance of a conductor's charisma and appeal to musicians in
large ensembles and corroborate public perceptions of the importance of a music teacher's personality.[15] Charismatic music teachers such as Eunice Boardman,
Julia Ettie Crane, Frances Elliot Clark, Mary Goetze, Lowell Mason, Mary Ellen
Richards, Robert Shaw, and Eugenia (Jean) Sinor dominate the history of practical
music education.[16]

Music. Regarding music as energy takes us back to acoustics and the properties
of sound and its perception. Still, it is more than this.[17] Beyond the sum of the
physical elements of which it is comprised, music needs to be understood holistically as well as elementally.[18] Figuratively speaking, there is a sense in which the
elements that comprise music seem to "disappear" as we grasp a "moving plastic,"
or a dynamic and living form that is psychologically and imaginatively construed
and inheres in music but also seems of greater significance than its constituent
elements.[19] Instead of the singer's separate pitches, we hear a song full of meaning
and nuance. Were we were to be distracted by separate elements that seem not to
fit together smoothly, we might declare this music to be off-putting and of poor
quality. To say that music is more than its elements is not to disparage or belittle its
constitutive elements. Musicians continue to rely upon them as essential to their
work, whether it be the nature of sound waves in organ pipes, the harmonic series in brass, woodwind, and string instruments, or the acoustic properties of the
spaces in which music is performed. The resonance of the sonic waves upon which
music is predicated, vibration of atomic particles that comprise the human body,
and waves emitted from distant stars may help to explain music's widespread appeal throughout the world and in every culture of which I am aware.[20] Music is,
literally and figuratively, energy; it is valued by people for that quality because
humans are, in some sense, in tune with it. This view of music connects sound
with human beings on a variety of levels—acoustic, physiological, psychological,
and social—and thereby relates the phenomenal and the spiritual, body and mind,
individual and group, primal and intellectual. Despite the many differences among
the musics of the world, we may, to some degree, interpret musics that are not
our own and recognize them as what, in the West, we think of as music.[21] Those
who have made and taken music know that we may come to a concert agitated
and worried and leave lighthearted—such is the power of making and taking music communally and individually. Whether this energy is to be understood literally or figuratively, the experience of music can be energizing, as it may also be
enervating.

Notions of music as movement are intriguing in the performative sense of what
is happening as music seems to ebb and flow, rise and fall in intensity, arrive at
points of climax and drop away to less intensity, sometimes smoothly and other

times sharply articulated, sometimes calm and serene and other times stormy and agitated.[22] This sense of dynamic movement through time is central to our musical interest; we may be as interested in the particular qualities of energy that music seems to embody as we are in the particular sounds we hear, and we dress up these sounds and senses imaginatively and playfully. Although we might seek to explain what we are up to, eventually words fail and we rely on the music itself.[23] Simplicity is often a feature of such music making. This utter musical simplicity, profundity, and accessibility can move individually and bring people together collectively in community.[24] Such music is often intergenerational, and thinking of folk music in this way prompts pictures of two, three, and sometimes four or five generations of family musicians playing and singing together.[25]

Making and taking music is also a matter of mental concentration. It does not suffice to simply hear music; one needs to attend to it.[26] Attention requires focusing on it, whether on its general interest or the specific character of its melody, text, texture, rhythm, timbre, or function. Among performers absorbed in their music making, the "virtual time" of performance may approach zero (that is, little clock time is perceived to have passed). The better the composer (and performer) the more apt at riveting attention on this music and the less the awareness of other things.[27] To focus in this way is to expend effort and energy, and the musician and listener, with this unawareness of time, may be exhilarated but also feel drained afterward. These moments when we are utterly absorbed in and concentrated on the music seem almost effortless, work merges with play; this intensity transcends ordinary lived experience, and there is a quality of being that psychologists have described as "peak experience" or "flow."[28] Here, a psychic and socially derived "energy" seems to be at work that impacts people individually and communally. Such moments when music takes on a life of its own seem to be intuitively and even instinctively caught and can be utterly captivating.

Teaching. Thinking of teaching in terms of energy evokes notions of charisma and mental concentration. The word *charisma* denotes the quality of a person's "attractiveness or charm" and comes from the Greek *kharisma,* from *kharis,* "a free gift or favour"; "a grace, a talent"; or "the capacity to inspire devotion or enthusiasm."[29] One is drawn to another as a magnet to its pole, such is the appeal and grace that the other appears to possess. In this view, teachers are not compendia of specific attributes but whole persons who attract or repel others because of who they are and how they think and act. Charisma is often found in leaders who are able to attract others to follow them into sometimes difficult situations. As leaders of young and old alike, teachers seek to attract the attention and trust and even command the obedience of their students, especially when the challenges they face are difficult to surmount. They are often attractive, well-adjusted, positive, and enthusiastic people who love the students with whom they work and enjoy what they are doing. Concentration connotes diligence, focus, and an intensity of effort and will as the teacher excludes other, personal distractions and gives his or her entire attention to these particular students and music(s).[30] Teaching is a process of giving and receiving energy; it is not so much the particulars of what teachers do and say as their preoccupation with and absorption in working musically that energizes these students. A teacher's engagement, enthusiasm, caring, and commitment to music draw students to her or him and the music. Like education, this approach to teaching works on the principle of attracting students and happens naturally as the teacher's persona and example prompt students to want this for themselves.[31] It is as if the force of the attraction of this music and this teacher, like magnetism, pulls students into the music making and taking sometimes in spite of themselves; students cannot resist trying this out for themselves.[32] This model of teaching is not just about teachers energizing their students but about being open to receiving energy from students as well. It is also sometimes the case that teachers and conductors draw energy from the ensemble, just as their students and musicians draw energy from them. Teachers may go to meet a class feeling anything but enthusiastic, but as the students bursting with life and energy begin to bubble, teachers may be inspired and energized. Still, much hangs on who teachers are, what they do, and how their students respond to them. As this is a teacher-centered rather than subject-matter-centered form of music teaching, it is important to find the kinds of people as teachers who have what it takes to attract and energize students.[33]

Some energy is negative. Sourness, criticism, arrogance, angst, disdain, destructive competition, ego, darkness, and rejection may be felt but difficult to put into words or explain.[34] Teachers may evidence this negative energy. Some lie, cheat, double-cross, gossip, undermine others with whom they work, and otherwise grasp for power. They are like bad apples that can sour the entire barrel. Negativity and unhappiness can develop when one or two unsettle the rest, poisoning the atmosphere so that the entire group comes to exude negative energy. By negative energy, I mean effects that are harmful, hurtful, and evil, and where unhappiness and conflict prevails. It is not surprising that those who desire happiness flee from such situations. Still, experienced teachers know that these situations arise from time to time and that it is sometimes difficult to escape them. They hope for relief, and it occasionally comes. Given the possibility for negative as well as positive energy, some degree of choice is needed for the best teaching and learning, so that those students who are repelled by some teachers can find others to whom they are attracted, and teachers can likewise find students they can more effectively teach. Recognizing the holistic nature of the teacher and student attraction requires an understanding that teachers cannot dramatically alter their inner self, age, ethnicity, or personality. Even gender changes are not so much a matter of changing one's inner self as making appearance accord with reality.[35] Recognizing the prejudices that others have toward teachers because of who they are frees teachers from thinking that it is necessary to be all things to all people and allows them to work with those students who respect what they have to offer and value their help.

Learning. In energy, learning is receptive and active. Among its receptive qualities, osmosis, participation, observation, and sensibility are important means whereby learning occurs.[36] Osmosis, or the student's absorption of the teacher's teaching much as the salt in boiling water passes through the porous shell of an egg, is particularly important.[37] Osmosis depends on the student's receptivity and capacity to absorb what the teacher conveys. Without such openness, energy cannot pass from teacher to student. Participation suggests that learning occurs simply by being in a situation with others, even if one is focused on other than pedagogical activities. In these circumstances, a person learns even without necessarily being aware that learning is taking place. Observation suggests that the student copies the teacher, not only in respect of specific musical skills but in a wide array of respects that extend to the rest of lived life. Sensibility refers to learning through means of feeling and sensitivity as much as by reason. Such learning is inherently subjective, and yet transforming in its impact. Here, students actively receive their teachers' musical wisdom and are influenced and moved by their example as much as by what they say. This idea of seizing the present moment and catching the teacher's spirit is found in various musics around the world where breath is an animating spirit as energy is transmitted from teacher to learner.[38] When a song is taught to others, it carries the spirit of its creator.[39] This teaching is an active transmission; students are engaged in activities that involve doing as well as undergoing music. These activities are both basic, in terms of the nature of music making and taking, and simple, so that students can directly experience music without being distracted by irrelevant or unnecessarily complex details.[40] When activities are regarded as play, they are enjoyable and engaged in imaginatively. Since students directly make sense of what they learn, this learning is subjective and idiosyncratic. Although students partake of common activities, their ends diverge as they construct musical meanings in differing ways.

Such learning is also contextual and intergenerational. The context of musical learning affects the manner and extent of what is learned and how students feel about what they learn. Students are happy in their learning, and teachers construct learning environments that are full of life, vitality, pleasure, and play, and in which learners can work and play happily as they face and surmount obstacles that naturally arise in learning new skills.[41] Rewarding and encouraging students predisposes them to learn naturally and appropriately at the various stages of development. Whatever they learn in such circumstances is tinged with the affect resulting from the positive feeling they have toward this subject matter and those with whom they engage in this pedagogical situation. Learning is also intergenerational, in the sense of one generation learning *from* and *with* another. As the young learn from and with parents and grandparents, they connect with other times and places. Life-world approaches that begin with students' lived musical lives and move beyond immediate and extended families to friends and strangers energize the different generations.[42] Sometimes, the young learn from older family members.[43] In musical projects that map family musical traditions and songs, older family members are energized by the enthusiasm of the young in learning their music, while young people are excited to learn the songs of their elders. This singing can catch fire among young and old and bind them together socially as well as musically. Taking such approaches means journeying musically backward and forward in time as well, as from place to place, thereby broadening musical learning well beyond narrow and contemporary musical cultures.

Instruction. Instruction in the energy mode works as follows.[44] Imagine two poles—reciprocal empathy (++) where teacher and students are mutually attracted to each other and reciprocal antipathy (--) in which both are repelled. Where teachers engage with students who are receptive to them under conditions of reciprocal empathy, they are able to do their best work because they receive positive energy from their students that reinforces and supports them. Happiness results from the positive interaction between teachers and their students and positive feelings about the subject matter. Where students are not receptive, teachers cannot do their best work; they are resisted at every hand, the energy they expend is not reciprocated, and they are not supported when their own energy is at a low ebb. The possibilities of four types of musical instruction, ranging from Type I (++) to Type II (+-), Type III (-+), and Type IV (--), where the nature of the intersection of energy between teacher and student is variously positive and negative, impact the ways in which teachers and students interrelate and the nature and effectiveness of the instructional process.[45] Type I instruction is likely to be optimal, because both teacher and student have choice in the matter and are likely to choose the student and teacher, respectively, who are the "best fit." If this situation does not work satisfactorily, both parties can terminate the instruction. In Type IV instruction, however, neither has choice, and if the situation falls within their zone of tolerance, teacher and student may both collude at less than optimal levels of effort and time; if not, they are likely to reduce the effort and time committed to instruction even further, thereby exacerbating the situation away from optimal positions. Types II and III instruction fall somewhere between these extremes. Type II may be less optimal for students than Type III, since they do not have choice in Type II, whereas they can choose in Type III. The reverse is true for teachers, who may find Type II more optimal than Type III because they have choice in Type II and no choice in Type III. In group instructional situations, teachers are likely to pitch their instruction to those students most in tune with their expectations more than with those who are neutral, antipathetic, or out of tune with them. In these ways, the nature of teacher and student choices and expectations affect the energy (indicated by the effort and time devoted to teaching and learning) expended on music instruction. Where teachers and students cannot choose, and reciprocal and mutual antipathy exists, the energy or effort devoted to teaching and learning is significantly lower than optimal, and teachers and their students combine to subvert instruction. Type I instruction is normative; teachers seek to make Type II and III situations as much like Type I instruction as it is in their power to accomplish; and Type IV instruction is less desirable, since it prevents the exercise of teacher and student choice and the happiest and most congenial "fit" between teachers and students. In circumstances where teachers and their students are happy working together, they are willing to expend more energy in instruction because they "see eye to eye" with each other, feel comfortable in this instructional situation, and agree on their expectations of music instruction; they are more apt to be absorbed in music making and taking; and they are likely to be energized by the process.

This is a fragile and sometimes emotional approach to music instruction. Its fragility is evident in the teacher's breath exhaled and inhaled by the student "in the present moment." This present-centeredness in music instruction resonates with the nature of music that is likewise a moment-by-moment phenomenon.[46] Figuratively, the transmission of knowledge from teacher to student can easily be broken if this interpersonal relationship is severed.[47] When teachers and students are preoccupied in the moment of engaging in music making and taking, they are thinking and doing intuitively and almost instinctively.[48] The present moment is fragile and quickly gone, and teachers and their students are eager to catch it and make it count. This urgency in the encounter is driven by the preciousness, potentiality, and fragility of the "now" that is invested with significance. The differing degrees of choice or perceived control over the situation, and of intensity of attraction or repulsion from one person and situation to another, mean that it is unlikely that every student will feel the same interest in, or attraction to, even the most charismatic teacher.[49] Where negative relationships exist, as they surely must from time to time, disagreement, contention, and conflict are likely in group instructional settings, especially where feelings run high either way. The possibility of choice is counted on as a means for teachers and students to escape from those instructional situations that repel them or in which they are uncomfortable.

Curriculum. Rather than the prepackaged and "teacher proof" curricula of the production and consumption models, the curriculum under conditions of energy requires the teacher's intervention to make this curriculum work. Simple and accessible means are used as ways to enable individuals and groups to engage in music making and taking in various ways and to different ends. Activities need to pass the litmus tests of allowing both active and receptive learning; they need to involve mind and body, and be both accessible to all yet allow for various sorts and levels of musical skills to be expressed and developed along the way. For example, teachers in the American "little red schoolhouse" of bygone days simultaneously taught eight or so grades comprised of children ranging in age from five or six years to fourteen or fifteen years. Even within a single-grade classroom, students may range in musical ability from beginners with little musical experience to competent instrumentalists and skilled musicians, and the music teacher engages all of these young people in activities in which they can participate, albeit in differing ways and levels of musical accomplishment.[50] Carl Orff and Gunild Keetman used accessible classroom instruments that could be played at differing levels of proficiency and approaches to the development of improvisational skills; these were musical and accessible to all, open-ended yet progressive from archaic forms, modal music, and speech-song to more contemporary tonal music.[51] Texts formed the framework for songs that were improvised by the class and linkages were made to a mythic past and with other musical cultures.[52] As in the community model, happiness and learning are fostered when students engage in an activity in different ways and their learning leads them in a plethora of directions, some further than others. Under these circumstances, students rejoice in the brilliance of their fellows as they also learn the capacities and limits of their own powers and interests.

Play is central to the music curriculum because of its attractiveness to students and its importance in human life, and curricular activities can be expected to include play and be play-like.[53] The imaginative quality and intensity of demands on all participants of play suggest that musical expectations are high. In teaching instrumental skills, musicians speak of "playing" their instruments, and teachers seek to keep the delight suggested by this notion of playing.[54] Teachers also ensure that the presentation of the subject matter is attractive to students, so that there is consistency between the teacher's persona and the subject matter and both are attractive to students.[55] As in the consumption model, teachers present material in appealing ways so that students want to engage it.[56] Such a curriculum would likely differ from one school to another and one teacher to another, and the resulting musical knowledge would be divergent. Basing a curriculum on activities to which students are attracted and in which they are interested invites them to invest their energy and identity in this music making and taking. One way of accomplishing this is through musical games that often blur the borders of music to include art, dance or movement, drama, story, and poetry. Learning their own traditional dances and songs, wearing their traditional costumes, telling their traditional stories, and reciting their traditional poems or rhymes can bring them together in musical games. Competition may also be involved in the musical games that children invent for themselves, and they develop particular skills in these games.[57] Employing games in the curriculum enriches children's repertoire of games and provides a means of connecting with their lives where play is a vital part of learning. As adults also enjoy games, there is reason to believe that musical games also work well with adults.

When students become excited by music making and taking, their energy may spin out of control; the curriculum is a way of guiding and keeping this energy at optimal level. Experienced teachers know that when their students are working energetically, they may be difficult to contain. In their excitement at what they are doing, students tend naturally to become noisy; they noodle on their instruments and otherwise distract others. Keeping this energy within bounds is a teacher's principal challenge and the curriculum is one way of accomplishing this. This curriculum is punctuated by periods of tension and release, intensity and relaxation, effort and respite, action and reaction.[58] All the while, evaluation is largely formative and ongoing. Teachers are constantly assessing what their students are accomplishing and their levels of engagement so as to make course corrections along the way in the event that student energy falls or their own interest flags. They are looking for moments when the studio, class, or ensemble comes alive and the energy bubbles up; this is seen in eyes dancing, intense concentration, smiles, laughter, and a sense of group cohesion as this activity takes on a life of its own and captivates all involved in it. There are also important moments for summative evaluation, although, generally, this is less potent than in the production model. As in the community model, since ends are divergent and the process may be as important as the product, qualitative and descriptive assessment procedures and criterion-referenced measures may be more important than quantitative procedures and normative tests.

Administration. In the energy model, as music educational ideas and practices gain momentum and take on a life of their own, certain societal and cultural forces become almost unstoppable, and music educational leaders must take into account these movements in making their plans and developing their policies.[59] Coping with change and danger are particularly important administrative challenges. The societal and cultural milieus in which music education operates may shift in directions that may or may not be helpful to the work of music education. These particular challenges may differ from place to place and from time to time, and administrators need to be alert to the opportunities and dangers they present. For example, in a conservative age, music educators may be concerned about the fate of liberalism, just as in a liberal age, they may be concerned about the denigration of conservative values. Even though music educators may wish to find middle ground, it may be difficult to accomplish this when society is moving in one direction or another. Administrators may bide their time, ready their plans, and work actively to subvert the most extreme ideologies. They may seek to curb present excesses and move musical culture toward the middle ground or more liberal and humane points of view. Once an organization becomes established and reaches maturity, it is more difficult for it to change or be changed, so institutionalized are its beliefs, values, mores, and practices.[60] Under these circumstances, the challenge for administrators is to involve teachers and their students in developing responses to these changing circumstances, and to offer opportunities for reflection about what the organization's posture to changing realities ought to be and how changes can be implemented practically. Typically, leaders work with incomplete information; it is not always clear what they should do. Some are cautious and wait for others to clear a path, and others press forward immediately to adjust the organization's course. Dangers lurk in responding too quickly or reacting too slowly. Astute leaders carefully consider the missions of their respective institutions, consult with their colleagues, students, and stakeholders, and move forward boldly when they sense the time is right. Because opportunities often present in brief moments of time, leaders need to be ready to move when the tide comes in or goes out. Whatever position they take, their stance is not adopted for all time, but considered within the context of present or foreseeable realities. Administrators need patience to realize that the "tide in the affairs of men [and women]" eventually shifts, and they need to be ready to seize opportunities when they come.[61]

Among their important tasks, administrators release the energy of all those in an organization so that all work intently and optimally, the entire organization is energized, and its effects ripple out into the wider society. Administrators' energy and commitments to music education are communicated psychically, whether or not they are aware of it, and their engagement with music education affects the commitment and effort of others in the organization. Flat organizational structures in which teachers and their students contribute to the formulation and conduct of administrative policy are characteristic of the energy model, because they allow for the necessary kinds of choices. As human energy is finite, it is imperative that the energy expended on the running of the organization be used efficiently so that teacher and student energy can be directed to music teaching and learning. As in the healing mode, administrators endorse teachers who are psychologically suited and professionally prepared to attract students musically and provide them with the resources of time, financial support, equipment, musical instruments, and space needed to undertake their work with integrity. The energy model requires teachers to be expert musicians. Under conditions of choice, the best teachers are likely to generate the greatest interest on the part of students and the poorest teachers are likely to generate the least interest. Student enrollments and assessments of teachers are among the ways in which administrators assess teachers' work and teachers demonstrate their professional competence to administrators. Administrators are invested in the organization and in facilitating the work of music education. They approach their work without pretense or affectation but with simplicity, directness, plainness, artlessness, ease, and a sense of duty.[62] As they lead by example and inspiration, they are personally interested in the organization's people who are at the center of music education.

CRITIQUE

Seeing music in the frame of energy has several advantages. It highlights the importance of music's accessibility and simplicity in attracting a wide public. Focusing on the ways in which music gives pleasure and contributes to happiness in individual and group contexts downplays the intellectualization of music in the rule and apprenticeship models. This approach recognizes that music can be delightful and may simply be enjoyed rather than just contemplated intellectually. Links between music, the other arts, and the wider culture are forged as people dance to music, paint their bodies, dress in various costumes, and employ music in dramatic rituals. In this way, music seems close to other aspects of lived life. Returning to "elemental" or early music or to the musics of previous generations provides mythic connections to people of earlier times, relates sophisticated classical and other esoteric traditions to their vernacular roots, and enriches, intensifies, and deepens otherwise thoughtless, banal, and superficial musical experiences.[63]

There are several difficulties with this view of music. Emphasizing music that is accessible and simple may neglect those more sophisticated and complex musical traditions that engage participants intellectually more than emotionally or physically. Thinking in terms of moving from "primitive" or simple musics to those that are modern and complex suggests that complex musics are normative and is reminiscent of evolutionary models of music that promote the "rationalization" of music from "primitive" musics to the epitome of Western classical music.[64] Ethnomusicologists have long debunked notions of "primitive music."[65] Defining complexity in terms of one particular musical culture leads to an ethnocentric and narrow view of music that defeats this model's purposes of multiple and divergent outcomes.

Regarding the advantages of teaching, the energy model focuses on teachers' attractiveness to students and the importance of their passion and enthusiasm in moving their students musically. Historically music teachers have acted as if the teacher is crucial to music education, and this model validates what teachers already know and do. Such an approach likewise focuses on teachers' caring and humanity and their efforts to make this subject matter "live" as they also physically live and breathe. Thinking of teaching as communicating psychic or spiritual energy suggests that what is communicated cannot be separated from the personhood of the teacher. So, as in the growth model, the teacher's task becomes one of eliciting, prompting, encouraging, and helping students to exercise their own choices and will to learn. Teachers need to be expert in their fields in order to attend to individual student capacities and interests, and they know what they are doing as they transmit and transform musical knowledge to the generations who come after them.

Teaching also suffers from distinct limitations with this model. Among them, focusing on teacher-generated energy and charisma may rely too heavily on the teacher's personality. Teachers have varying degrees of attractiveness, and such a view of teaching may end in popularity contests among teachers. The most popular teachers may attract the most students while those who are less popular end up with fewer students. Given that some teachers are not as attractive as others because of what they teach or their high expectations of students, rewarding and recognizing the most popular teachers does not necessarily reward the best teaching. Charisma may mask a laziness and lack of expert knowledge. Nor is all energy equally productive; some teachers may be very energetic and needlessly so, and thus it is also important to ask how the energy is directed and what impact it has on students. The fact that energy can also detract from student effort and future development may be overlooked in emphasizing the goods presumed to flow from teacher enthusiasm. Teachers may not always be as cognizant of the toll such expenditures of energy take on their own health and that of their students. While valuing energy output, teachers may forget the importance of calm, rest, quietness, and time and space for reflection. They may throw so much effort into their teaching that nothing is left for their personal lives, families, and friends.

On the one hand, thinking of learning as energy has important advantages. It recognizes the important role of the learner in learning. Unlike in the production mode of learning, students are not impressed by the teacher, but construct their own realities. Their musical potential is, importantly, a matter of their own choice.[66] The teacher can invite learning and offer encouragement to students, but it is finally the students' choice to receive what the teacher offers and make of it what they will. Learning depends greatly on students' openness and sensitivity to the teacher's desire to communicate wisdom. There is a sense in which learners "breathe in" this wisdom and "catch" it. In so doing, this teacher's spirit is likewise imbibed as students remember the one who brought them to the point of deep engagement with the subject in sometimes life-changing ways. The notion of musical learning as recapturing the archaic and traveling forward, as it were, through time, roots musical learning in the mythic and provides an important frame in which contemporary musical culture and culture may be seen. Its divergent means and ends enable learners to exercise choice and develop in more or less unique ways that are respected by others in the instructional situation. This approach to learning cultivates humanity and models a civil society to which education needs to attend.

On the other hand, among its difficulties, the model's reliance on student concentration, will, and effort in learning may fail to acknowledge sufficiently the important ways in which music teachers may affect that concentration, will, and effort. The mushrooming of syndromes that affect the ability of students to concentrate is a worrying fact of modern life. Not only do parents and teachers need to find ways to remedy these difficulties, but training and schooling also affect students' ability to concentrate and will to learn, and the approaches typical of apprenticeship and rule are not sufficiently invoked in this model. Where students are unable or unwilling to exert the effort, will to learn, and concentration needed, sometimes over extended periods of time, they are likely to be dismissed too soon as having insufficient musical aptitude and ability.[67] Relying so much on directed student activity may also place insufficient emphasis on reflection and play that is not focused on the learning tasks at hand but exists for its own sake or for the sake of other things.

Advantages for instruction also follow. The concept of teacher and student interacting holistically (as in healing), and in terms of the teacher's inspiring presence, focuses on trying to secure a positive and supportive learning environment. Relationships may sometimes be stormy; nevertheless, instruction is most enjoyable when teachers and students have choice in the matter and the best "fit" between them is achieved. Although teachers are able to transcend their natural predilections, the natural and personal inclinations on the part of teachers and their students are still respected, and situations are constructed in which they are most comfortable. Where conditions are most conducive to learning and teaching, teachers and students are able to do their best work and the atmosphere can be more playful and enjoyable. Consistent with historical practice, focusing on energy also highlights the effort required in music education.

Instruction is likewise problematic in the energy mode. Privileging the most attractive teachers and students who have the greatest choice, and thus marginalizing the least attractive teachers and students who have the least choice, may exacerbate the differences between potentially happy instructional situations and those that are unhappy and in which resistance and conflict is more likely. Such an approach favors a few, and the great many teachers and students must then teach and learn in less than optimal situations. This approach may also confuse teacher-centeredness focused on teachers inspiring their students with teacher-dominance whereby teachers manipulate students. Rather than invite multiplicities and pluralities, teachers may confuse their attractiveness to students with power over them, become dogmatic, and fail to allow or encourage their students to develop divergently. In these ways, it is possible for popular teachers to abuse their hold over students and, rather than caring genuinely for them, serve their own interests rather than their students'. Focusing on how energy plays out in what teachers and their students do may also benefit extroverts and downplay the importance of introversion and introspection.

Concerning curriculum, the energy model has important advantages. Making knowledge live rather than focusing on "inert ideas with their accompanying 'mental dryrot'" is crucial.[68] This liveliness resonates with the nature of the musical experience and its vitality for music makers and takers. Such knowledge also animates those who encounter it, and so, as learners construct it, they are also energized. These inspirational and imaginative encounters between people and knowledge possessed and received seem artful in their personification; that is, knowledge is both separate or apart from those who make and take it, and a part of and inseparable from them. Since the curriculum is based on musical activities, learners are actively engaged rather than passive recipients of ready-made knowledge. The simplicity of the musics and their accessibility to a wide public enables many to come to know music directly and immediately. Possibilities for divergent curricular outcomes, as learners construct musical knowledge for themselves in differing ways and value each learner's perspective, multiply the possibilities for musical engagement and suggest changes in musical practice in the future. This curriculum is playful and enjoyable, and evaluation is more likely seen to be formative and helpful to future development rather than summative and discouraging to students.

Among its potential flaws, the activity-based nature of this curriculum may mean that insufficient attention may be paid to developing thought as well as practice. Objectivity rather than subjectivity may be valued as music teachers seek to be accountable to their public. If there is insufficient opportunity for reflection, it is also possible that curricular activities may contribute only superficially to the development of musical understanding, whether it be of theory or practice. Without measures of the degree to which apparent busyness and effort pay off in effective teaching, learning, and instruction, it is possible that this activity may be inconsequential. In the event that the curriculum values musical accessibility and popularity, teachers may also fall into the pitfall of pandering to present student interests and impulses rather than working for their long-term musical development. Sorrow and disappointment are a part of ordinary life. If the curriculum stresses only the student's happiness to the exclusion of these other existential realities or cultivates a sense of guilt when success does not come immediately or easily, it may be unrealistic and even harmful to personal and collective well-being. Focusing only on play may exclude the importance of work as a means whereby education is achieved. As the objectives of this curriculum are prone to be, at least to some extent, idiosyncratic and indeterminate, it may be difficult to plan curriculum on the large scale needed for publicly supported school music programs.

Administration in the energy model is also advantageous. The collegial, communal, and egalitarian approach to organizing music instruction in ways that enable choice are humane and contribute positively to the nurturing and caring instructional situations that teachers foster in their studios, classrooms, and rehearsals. Organizing the work of music education in the context of flat organizational structures enables teachers to contribute in important ways to the organization's objectives, policies, and procedures. As in the growth and healing modes, teachers' roles are regarded as primary; leaders are supportive of their work and collaborative with them rather than hostile to their interests. Such attitudes are prone to engender teacher happiness and encourage teachers in their work. Change is acknowledged as a central element of this dynamic model, as for those of transgression and healing, so administration in the frame of energy focuses on ways in which change can contribute to the musical traditions that are taught and learned and the well-being of those who make and take them. Organizations, just like classrooms, studios, rehearsals, and performances, have "atmospheres" that are intuited by their participants. These subjective realities are readily understood and taken into account by music leaders, teachers, students, and staff in their practical work and relations with others.

Nevertheless, among its difficulties, as in the community and growth models, arranging for teacher and student choice may be cumbersome and difficult to achieve practically, especially in large organizations. Protecting the interests of less popular subjects and teachers and ensuring a broad student access to the best teachers may lead administrators to curb the working out of this model to its logical end. Basing teacher evaluations on popularity may also penalize those whose evaluations are not high, make unrealistic demands on them, and otherwise discourage them. The appearance of energy on the part of teachers and students may also disguise incompetency on their part. In rewarding the expenditure of energy, it is possible that administrators may wear out those who work for them, such that administrators, teachers, students, and staff members may have insufficient rest. Given the seeming inevitability of societal and cultural movements and particular ideas and practices, it may be difficult for administrators, practically speaking, to know when to make a course correction in the organization and when to wait until another, better time. As these are intuitively perceived moments, there is the risk that administrators trained in objective systems approaches may fail to catch the opportunities when they present and to move in directions that benefit the organization in the long term.

SUMMARY

In sum, thinking about these pictures of the seashore and energy allows us to grasp their possibilities and perils for music education. On the one hand, we notice a dynamic view of music education that is subjective and objective, congruent with much music teaching and learning experience, and actively engaging of teachers and their students in the moments of music making and taking. On the other, there lurk perils of privileging some teachers and students, insufficiently challenging students beyond what seems playful and immediately attractive, failing to emphasize reflection as well as action, unduly penalizing those who are on a path that Robert Frost describes as the "one less traveled,"[69] and missing or not taking advantage of opportunities along the way. It is also challenging for music educators and those interested in their work to rescue the best and avoid the worst of what these pictures suggest.

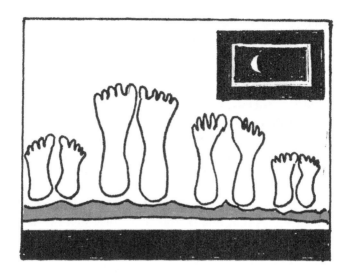

11
HOME AND INFORMALITY

We encounter pictures of *home* and *informality* that are rooted in antiquity, pervasive in practice, and more recently commented on by music educators. Musically, they are invoked in the work of Sophie Drinker; educationally, in the writing of Maria Montessori, Maxine Greene, Jane Roland Martin, Max Van Manen, and Iris Yob; and music-educationally in the writing of Patricia Shehan Campbell, Lucy Green, Marie McCarthy, and Shinichi Suzuki.[1] Since women have often been relegated to the domestic sphere (derived from the Latin *domesticus* or from *domus*, house, thought of in terms of home, family, and country), it is not surprising that these pictures are often by women.[2] Still, I want to think of them inclusively, as referring to women and men, girls and boys. In focusing on the home and its interrelated model of informality, we think, then, about music education in the private rather than public sphere.

HOME

The camera pans over a sight of devastation. Where once houses stood, now all that is left is a jumble of building materials. Looking upon this scene, a man is cry-ing inconsolably. Disaster has struck, his wife and children have been killed, and he now looks at the remains of what he once counted as home. What do we mean when we say that he has lost his home? He has lost not only a place where he once lived but also the people who made it a place where he loved to be. Their love and affection can no longer be returned, and he is bereft of their company in the daily living of life. He regarded this as a safe place where he could escape the pressures of coping with all of the public aspects of life and be at rest. Now he faces the world alone, without a safe haven and a home, physically or spiritually. We might just as well have pictured a woman or child in his predicament, so pervasive is this loss to people all around the world. Our hearts go out to all those who have lost their homes.

Against the backdrop of the profundity of this loss I think of my present situation, where nothing could be further from the terrible scene we have just witnessed. I write at home on Cape Cod and look out onto a sun-drenched world. This is a temporary home. We live simply in this little house built in keeping with the architecture of the area, with its upstairs bedrooms, study, and bathrooms, and downstairs kitchen, great room, and bathroom. Before the window, the desk and chair where I am writing are comfortable rather than elegant, and this goes for the home's furnishings generally. At this moment, I am alone, yet not alone if we include the family cat, Tilly, who is exploring the garden on her lead. The great room in which I sit includes an open space for dining, sitting, and visiting with family and friends. As I look around, I am reminded of the one with whom I live and the history of how we transformed this somewhat dilapidated townhouse into a space that we now call home and undertook (with the help of professionals) its renovation and repair, painting, and installation of floor and window coverings. The fireplace across from where I sit kept us warm in the winter, and its crackling of an evening was a delight. Now, in the summer, doors and windows are flung open wide; geranium-and-ivy-filled window boxes bloom luxuriantly and delight the eye. Inside, a profusion of plants beside my desk, a plant potted in an oversized teacup and saucer on a stand across the room (a funky note of pure fun), and another plant on top of a cupboard enliven this space. Two pictures that we commissioned from an artist whose work we loved, an Australian tapestry scene worked by a family member, and a handmade quilt found years ago in Ottawa, Canada, grace the walls. I look across to the bright galley kitchen, newly restored, and think back to the dark room it once was. A candle holder screen stands on one wall and a round dining table and bent-wood chairs lend a cottage-like air. I notice that the cupboard and occasional tables are overflowing with books and realize that we shall need to think about getting some bookcases in the near future. In short, our home is special to us, filled with meaning and delight, history and hope. It matters not whether it meets the discerning eyes of interior decorators or home-fashion editors. What is important is that it is a happy place to be and for family and friends to visit and stay.

Homemakers turn houses into homes. Thinking about the different kinds of spaces that count as homes evokes a plethora of images. All the way from mansions to shacks and huts, people around the world construct different spaces in which to live. Sometimes, the home may be a simple clearing with a lean-to designed to keep out wind rather than rain, a portable tent that can be carried from place to place, or a permanent dwelling, whether a simple hut with thatched roof and bare earth floor or more complex construction of natural and man-made materials. Each of these spaces is a function of cultural and societal traditions, geography, and wealth. Irrespective of the particular nature of the home, whether communal or individual family, apartment, condominium, townhouse, free-standing house, or mansion, in the city or countryside, these places can become homes. Our focus here is the making of homes.

Distinguishing between house or living space and home emphasizes aspects of intentionality, spirituality, commitment, and caring. Making a home involves "staying put" and living in this place at least for a short time.[3] We speak of people "putting down roots" and being identified with particular places. Even nomadic tribes who carry their tepees or tents to their hunting grounds or move around in forest, grassland, or desert must look forward to the times when they can pitch their tents, erect their shelters, sweep the earth, spread their mats or rugs, build their fires, and eat, sleep, and socialize with others in their household for a time. Intentionality refers to the aims and purposes of this space as one where people dwell together. In industrialized societies where the population is settled, homes are often regarded as investments, built and decorated by others, and not always committed to as places in which to dwell. In the sense in which I think of home, however, one feels rooted to this place, safe, contented, and at peace in staying here. This view of home sees it as more than material possession, focusing rather on its personal and collective benefits—intellectual, emotional, and physical. Commitment is also a matter of one's dedication and loyalty to this place and to those with whom one dwells. Homes are made by individuals as well as collectively by those who live together with others. Caring refers to one's concern and devotion to others and for this place, and one's willingness to invest oneself in, pay attention to, guard, and preserve these persons and this space. As such, home is construed figuratively and literally, physically and spiritually. Such is the importance of the spiritual and figurative idea of home that even if this place is destroyed, those who survive can still make another home in another place.

Who comprises the home? Although some may think of homes in terms of married couples with children, many people live alone and in nontraditional families comprising lovers, friends, or other, institutionalized groupings, as in homes for the elderly and those with various physical and mental challenges. Although in the West many families are small, in other parts of the world extended families often live together. Some live with others in communal homes around particular religious and political affiliations. Many children grow up in single-parent families or live with grandparents or other guardians, or in orphanages and homes for disadvantaged and troubled young people. Other living creatures sometimes live with people, including pet birds, fish, cats, dogs, rabbits, and reptiles. Thinking of the role of these other creatures in the home reminds me of how much we share with them. As a grey, short-haired, domestic tiger, Tilly the cat has a will and a soul, and she is just as happy when we return as she is distressed when we leave. She is committed to us and we are the center of her world, taking care of her needs for food, water, comfortable places to rest, and companionship. Just as we care for her, she comes to comfort us if we are ill, and she is often eager to be petted and to enjoy the various rituals that comprise our life. Blurring the lines between the human and the other creatures allows us to view the world compassionately (as it may also cause some of us to be vegetarians). Home is also thought of figuratively, as comprising those who share our interests, attitudes, commitments, passions, beliefs, traditions, rituals, and practices. For me, this invisible and spiritual home consists of musicians and scholars around the world who share an interest in music, education, and the philosophy of music education, friends I have met in the various countries in which I have lived and visited, and relatives in different countries. Sometimes, when we meet again, it is as if no time has passed since we saw each other, so "at home" are we with each other. Occasionally, when I read a book by an author I shall never meet, the communion and fellowship of mind and soul is such that I feel that I have come home.

Homes are as varied as the people who create them. I think, for example, of this group of townhouses in which I live. Each one is more or less the same, with similar architectural features, interior layout, doors, and windows. What we make of these spaces, however, is remarkably different. They are so individualized in terms of use of space, furnishings, colors, floor materials, and wall coverings that when I visit a neighbor's townhouse, I seem to be in a very different space. One neighbor might collect antique furniture, another books, and still another artifacts from around the world. The various beliefs, passions, and interests of those who live in these townhouses are clear. One fills the walls with family pictures extending over multiple generations; another is a British expatriate with pictures of various English scenes; still another is a cat fancier with pictures of cats all over the walls; one is a keen fisherman with nautical scenes and model boats all around; another is a music lover, and state-of-the-art audio-visual equipment feature prominently; and still another is an avid gardener with a riot of plants inside and out. In these spaces, although externally somewhat similar, homemakers express themselves in a host of differing ways. Each space reflects those who dwell there.

Homes are created around ideals. They are places where love is preeminent. Although difficult to define, love entails friendship, desire, affection, and steadfast faithfulness. Such love, when reciprocated by others, is a source of deep joy and contentment. Love is grounded in the preciousness of human beings, and such preciousness is manifest in civility, kindness, and thoughtfulness.[4] It is also evident in words and deeds, thoughtful acts and expressions of kindness. Values such as respect, tact, safety, intimacy, and happiness are also important. Respect connotes valuing, esteeming, and prizing those with whom one lives. Tact is a matter of intuitively grasping what needs to be done in this moment.[5] One may need to listen or act; knowing what to do now necessitates being sensitive and open to the other and responding with the other's best interests at heart. Safety is the important matter of being free from danger and injury and in a place of refuge. Intimacy refers to friendship and closeness to others. Happiness is a state of joy, pleasure, and contentment. Although conceptually discrete, these values are practically interrelated. Abuse, violence, incivility, anger, and hostility go contrary to the ideals on which home is predicated. When people live together intimately and privately and their pets share their quarters, they are especially vulnerable to the others who live with them, since their strengths and weaknesses are well known. Their interdependency and vulnerability make incivility and inhumanity especially undesirable and an anathema. A person who abuses a spouse, child, or pet is rightly prosecuted or punished when this comes to light.

Those who comprise the home have roles and responsibilities. Domesticity concerns private aspects of living and loving; there are mundane, ordinary, and sometimes even distasteful aspects to daily life, and a drudgery and daily grind to making and keeping a home. Activities such as cooking, cleaning, sewing, marketing, eating, tidying, sleeping, dressing, shaving, nursing, making beds, washing, bathing, repairing, painting, renovating, decorating, gardening, mowing, building, working, playing, and socializing, while sometimes enjoyable and rewarding, are sometimes tedious and not valued in public life. The difficulties of accomplishing these tasks are also exacerbated when one cares for the very young or the feeble. Constant distractions and unexpected developments also demand courtesy and care. Where earning a livelihood requires long hours, these ordinary tasks may become even more irksome. In some societies, roles in the home are gender-specific. In others, tasks are undertaken by various family members according to their interests and abilities. Whereas in one society it may be a woman's role to do the marketing and cook, in another a man may assume the role as household chef and chief marketer. In some homes there is a clearer organization of responsibilities than in others. One home may run like clockwork, with all the family members assigned their particular duties. Another may run in chaotic fashion.

The home is situated in religious, political, economic, and cultural contexts and is subject to external influences, as it also impacts society. As a place of dwelling, sleeping, eating, playing, and sometimes working that consumes a great deal of our lives, the home concerns private aspects of living. Still, public policies impact home life in determining such matters as who may marry whom, matters of birth control, rights to live and die, and taxation. These limit the extent to which a family can stray from traditional and public expectations of its roles and responsibilities. Religious precepts also influence home life, and religions may assume a central role in family life as centers of socialization, play, and worship. Economic factors also affect what work is available to sustain the family and the times at which that work must be undertaken. The mass media also impacts the culture in which the family lives. The home likewise affects society. Some children arrive at school ready to learn, with a clearly established sense of moral and spiritual values, and the advantage of previous musical and other artistic experiences. Others come from dysfunctional homes in which abandonment, crime, and violence are a way of life.

INFORMALITY

I use the word *informality* in its sense of "relaxed, friendly, and unofficial."[6] Its root "form" refers to its shape and configuration or the way things seem or appear to be.[7] Rather than a tightly articulated structure, informality connotes an easygoing approach, not necessarily authorized by a public authority or agency but rather a privately held belief and practice. As such, music education is not considered to be a part of the public sphere—that is, the collectively held beliefs and practices representative of people generally and on whose behalf music education is carried on within publicly supported schools, colleges, and universities.[8] I go further than this ordinary-usage sense of informality to think of it in the more specialized sense of music education conducted under the aegis of families, religions, businesses, and various musical events organized by musicians. It also occurs in the framework of other activities, such as musical composing, performing, improvising, producing, dancing, and listening, where music instruction is not the primary focus and other activities are preeminent. With these points in mind, I sketch the various aspects of informality.

Music. Informality is found widely in vernacular and classical traditions. In folk and popular traditions, music is often accessible to ensure the widest audience and participation. Its simplicity should not be taken for a lack of profundity, and its role in giving voice to a people's experience means that it may be deeply moving and inspiring. It is within the ordinary experience of most if not all the people, and at least listeners or dancers, if not also singers and instrumentalists, can participate in it. Its accessibility requires little formal training, so that people can expect to be able to do it within their normal day-to-day activities of living.[9] Classical musics are often intended for the initiated and are elitist rather than universalistic in their appeal; listeners, performers, and composers often require formal education in order to participate in this music and grasp its meaning. Even in these musics, however, much is learned by young musicians from the lives that musicians lead socially and musically. Where musics are organized according to families of musicians as a means of preserving their livelihoods, they are somewhat exclusive, and certain musical knowledge may be secret from one family to another.[10] Such families might foster soloists and ensemble performers, singers and instrumentalists, and listeners who are present at family gatherings and informal music making. Particular musical knowledge might be known within the family, but others would not necessarily possess it. So this musical informality is exclusive in one respect as it is inclusive in another.

Music, in the mode of informality, is regarded mainly as a matter of practice. This performative approach also values music's contribution to social and artistic life. High degrees of skill may be picked up in informal settings by musicians, some of whom become virtuosi, and who contribute to traditions that are esoteric as well as accessible to the initiated.[11] As performers become specialists and professionals, they may set a high level of practice that excludes all but the most devoted amateurs, and this reality contributes to creating a wedge between professionals and amateurs.[12] Music is thought of practically; this reality obviously influences the training of musicians and emphasizes keeping the musical tradition alive. It is also thought about, reflected on, and criticized.[13] Thinking of music in terms of enacted rituals focuses on its social purposes and roles whereby music functions as a part of ordinary lived life rather than apart from it.[14] In this view, music is described mainly in terms of the social events in which it is made and taken rather than just as a sonic phenomenon.

Teaching. In the informality model, those who teach may not be designated as teachers per se but may assume the role because of their more advanced knowledge, experience, and expertise. As teaching is performed by those who possess the required knowledge rather than only by those who have been authorized to transmit knowledge, the roles of student and teacher may be blurred, fluid, and interchangeable. Students also teach themselves the necessary skills for this tradition and act as their own teachers. Such teaching is more like mentoring in the sense that one is "an experienced and trusted adviser" who is not responsible for the musician's progress.[15] It is egalitarian in the sense that teacher and student are often fellow musicians, the one being more experienced in this particular respect than the other and assuming the role of teacher at any given time as circumstances require.[16] More experienced musicians assist and pass on helpful knowledge to less experienced musicians in the midst of musical activities that are not intentionally pedagogical.[17] Although incidental and complementary to other musical activities, teaching is urgent, because certain skills need to be mastered in order to compose, improvise, perform, or produce this music. Demonstration is a principal means of teaching, and it occurs in the midst of making music. Much teaching is through self-instruction and imitation of exemplars, including performances and recordings, so much hangs on the nature of the examples teachers provide as well as on what they say. The teacher asks the student to observe and do rather than analyzing what is happening, and expects the demonstration to suffice.[18] Teaching may be indirect in that the teacher is not necessarily directing the student's attention to what is happening, but is simply composing, improvising, or performing. It is up to the student to notice those things that are important, because a ritual may be ongoing and there may be no time for the teacher to stop and explain his or her actions.

Teachers selectively enculturate, socialize, school, and train their students, and these processes are often indirect, rhapsodic, and serendipitous. Enculturation, or absorbing one's culture and coming into contact with others, takes in the arts, humanities, sciences, and practical aspects of making a living and a life as a musician. The ways in which knowledge is communicated by teachers to their students encompass lived life, and teachers embody a way of life and a tradition that goes well beyond musical knowing. Exponents may not specifically give instruction, but their example is imitated by students who seek to copy it and interpret what they have learned in their own ways. This approach puts the onus on the student's observational powers and the clarity of the teacher's example. Socialization is also at work as students learn how they ought to believe and act through participating in family, religious, political, and musical rituals. Schooling, or acquiring the discipline of music making and taking, may play a role as students learn the rules that undergird this musical tradition. Training may also be involved in the necessity to cultivate skills of various sorts.[19] In the classical traditions these aspects are more likely to have a definite formal twist; but even in vernacular traditions that are historically more informal, some schooling and training are involved.[20] When music is associated with power, secrets, and the supernatural, those who teach music often do so in order to preserve a tradition and a way of life. As a source of livelihood musical knowledge carries power, and the family's power is related to its musical preeminence. Musical connections to religious ritual and the supernatural make the musician a powerful person in the society.[21] The claims of secrecy are important in a teacher's determination of whom to teach and which students are presumed to be "worthy" of receiving a particular tradition. Experienced musicians in the family, tribe, or clan watch for talented youngsters who can be encouraged and assisted in developing their musical skills, while others are deliberately discouraged from undertaking further musical training.[22]

Learning. Informality in music education relies particularly on osmosis, participation, sensibility, and observation.[23] Osmosis is seen in other models, such as growth, healing, and energy. As in the energy model, the teacher seems to breathe life into the student, and the student absorbs knowledge by attending to and receiving instruction from the teacher.[24] Participation refers to the learning that takes place by virtue of being with these particular people in this place as one undergoes as well as makes and takes music. By repeating these musical rituals, people come to know them without being aware that they are learning them.[25] When children follow the models set by their parents, grandparents, or other older family musicians, music education involves at least two generations. Sensibility involves the senses as students are engaged bodily and as they listen to, play, sing, and dance to music. Observation means that when young children constantly hear and see exemplary intonation, interpretation, and articulation, their hearing acuity in this musical tradition is sharpened and these attributes become part of their own musical personae. Traditions and examples are taken to be normative, because the young imitate exemplars and pick up a tradition largely idiosyncratically and by themselves. Learners may come to know the tradition with the benefit of somewhat limited formal instruction, and the onus is on their picking up knowledge on their own as they copy the examples they hear. Learners engage in some trial and error and successive approximation as they gradually come closer to these models.[26] Emulating the music they hear means that learners are constantly looking back at what is and has been in the past. Many never get beyond the stage of emulation to construct their own ways of making and taking music.

Formal learning may reinforce informal learning and curb idiosyncratic outcomes.[27] Talented youngsters might live with their older family members so that formal education through instruction, practice, example, and reflection is intimately tied with informal education. This intersection of formal and informal instruction is vital in helping to integrate musical knowledge with the rest of life.[28] As an extension of what is experienced daily by the young, formal learning reinforces informal learning and gives it added meaning.[29] At first glance, this approach to musical learning may seem egalitarian, but this is not always the case. Contrary to images of inclusiveness and an egalitarian ethic, vernacular and traditions, like classical traditions, may be selective and elitist. Exceptionally gifted students may be chosen to pursue music seriously, while most people learn their musical limitations and are content with a more elementary musical knowledge.[30] Although this exclusivity may appear more benign because of its place within families, clans, or musical groups, it is still there.[31] In families of professional musicians just as in musical ensembles, the family's or group's reputation and livelihood is at stake; it forwards its best musicians and redirects those who are not so gifted musically into other pursuits. So, informality is a means of filtering out those who are not as talented just as it is a matter of encouraging those who are gifted musically. Much depends on learners' insight and intuition into the musical tradition, and this reality may lead to idiosyncratic and non-standardized outcomes. Still, the power of the examples and their normative character curb these idiosyncratic possibilities and shape them in traditional ways. Learning is conservative in its prizing of examples from the past. Although learners discover musical knowledge in their own ways, their musicking is evaluated by other exponents and the music's public, and they are pressured to conform to the tradition's norms. Even in their play, which constitutes an important means of learning, the players insist that the rules be followed. When the young participate musically with their elders, they are expected to conform to rules that have their source in the musical traditions in which they participate.

Instruction. The interaction between teacher and student in the mode of informality is one of love, caring, tact, and duty. Family members and friends are often involved as teachers and learners, and the model begins with assumptions of love and affection that bind them together and help to shape the ways in which they interrelate. This warmth of interrelationship goes beyond the subject matter and focuses on those who are undergoing this interaction in the context of music. Informality is people-centered and process-oriented, and a sense of the preciousness of all those involved drives this relationship. Caring derives from love and concern for others.[32] Rather than self-centered relationships in which people are interested only in themselves, caring focuses on the needs, impulses, desires, and interests of others and helps and assists rather than directs and forces them. The quality of this interaction is potentially humane. Still, the fact that musicians have chosen to play together and have committed to the success of this group means that their learning is driven by collective self-interest. Their individual and collective reputations are on the line when they perform. The expression of tact is like parenting in many respects.[33] The older person is sensitive to the young ones and presents new things to them as they are ready and able to benefit from them. The teacher is diplomatic, measured, and thoughtful about what the young need and the differences between what they need and want. Duty proceeds even when inclination falters.[34] The obligations of each to the other are felt even though one may not be disposed to do what is needed. Having undertaken teaching and learning responsibilities, teacher and student are each indebted to the other in following through with what they have started to do. Having accepted to train a nephew as a musician, a family is obliged to feed, house, and care for this boy as he grows up to be a musician. The teacher is obligated to the boy's parents and immediate family, the extended family or clan, the musical tradition the boy aspires to learn, the boy himself, and the teacher's own sense of honor; the boy is obligated to the teacher, who expects him to take heed and actively participate in his own learning, and to his own emerging sense of honor as a person. Irrespective of the difficulties that arise along the way, each is bound to honor the contract between teacher and student (or the student's guardians who act on his or her behalf).

Much instruction is informal, occasional, and less systematic than, for example, in the production, rule, or apprenticeship models, and it is sometimes competitive. It is conducted within the lives of musicians engaged in things that are not primarily or intentionally educational, and the situations in which teachers and their students engage contribute to regarding music as a way of life. These myriad contexts, whether it be at a family social gathering, religious ritual, political event, musical concert, journey, or in ordinary life, requires students to glean what they can and engage in musical and other activities vitally. Opportunities for passing on wisdom are relatively scarce and so instructional moments are invested with significance. Although there may be less formal instruction, it is valued more highly than if it were common and pervasive. Teachers and students pay special attention to formal instruction when it comes, and this more limited time is more likely to be used in compelling ways and reinforce the generally informal means of instruction. The occasional nature of instruction enables connections between music and other aspects of life and, as with instruction in the healing model, it contributes to a holistic approach to teaching, learning, and instruction. These connections motivate teachers and their students to teach and learn while also making and taking music.

Instruction in informality is driven by the exercise of teacher and student choice. As in the community, healing, and energy models, teachers and students are drawn to each other differently. When they are free to engage with like-minded others, the sparks fly, the "chemistry" between the musicians is right, they think similarly about music, the repertoire they like to play is more or less consistent, and they blend and meld together because of the ways in which they perform. Choice is a means whereby compatibility is established and affection, caring, tact, and duty are fostered. One cannot care for everyone and everything, and there are practical limitations on one's duty. It is also easier to be tactful when one is drawn to the others in the ensemble. In joining the ensemble, members accept the responsibilities of membership and the commitments of time, effort, and sometimes money involved. Although the outcomes may be of varying success and differ from those that might be hoped for, nevertheless, what at first glance appears to be a built-in inefficiency affords opportunities for imaginative and artistic expression. As teachers and students can exercise choice, it is likely that teacher and student interaction will tend toward reciprocal empathy and contribute to a happy atmosphere. Sometimes teachers communicate information to students; often instruction is driven by the student's need and desire to know such-and-such. Here, the student's questions prompt the teacher to show or tell in response. This dynamic, then, is much more student-driven than in the case of the consumption and production models. The relationship between teacher and student is likely to be more egalitarian than, say, with the rule, apprenticeship, or production models, because student and teacher are fellow participants in musical rituals, and these bonds narrow the social distance between them. By virtue of their privileged knowledge and experience, teachers have greater power than their students, who desire to know what they know. Informality is not always cooperative and, as in conditions of community, various individuals and groups compete for the teacher's and group's attention. Where instructional resources are scarce, students may vie with each other even in the context of musical rituals in which music instruction is not the focus.[35]

Curriculum. As with the rule model, informal curriculum emphasizes tradition and follows rather than challenges traditional beliefs and practices.[36] It is mainly practical and focuses on what musicians do and are. Music is related to the rest of life and, as with the healing model, there are no arbitrary boundaries in music; the subject matter extends to the rest of life. Knowing how to go on in music, as well as knowing about it, are central to the curriculum in informality, because music is often taught and learned in the context of musical rituals typical of this tradition. Besides playing or singing this music with its exponents, listening to musicians talk about the people they have known permits learning this music's lore and better understand its practice. Earlier generations of musicians become mythic figures to the young and those who are in the midst of coming to know this practice. Watching accomplished musicians perform, studying the scores of composers from the past, and participating in musical events develop expectations that allow students to evaluate their own and others' music. Tradition provides a clear understanding of the ideas and practices that characterize this music, and in looking backward, learners are better able to bring their own particular perspectives to bear in an informed way. This tradition is not only taught didactically or formally; rather it surrounds the student and pervades the entire culture in which the student is immersed. This consonance between formal and informal approaches that rely on incidental, unplanned, and serendipitous events allows students to gain an integrated, holistic, and broad experience of musical study and music. It may be difficult to know which aspect is of greatest importance—the formal or the informal instruction.

The curriculum is grounded in exemplary repertoire and approached within the students' frames of reference from multiple points of view. Students are invited to study some of the best of musical repertoire in a particular tradition in various ways, especially through performing, improvising, and composing music. Constructing a music program informally requires many opportunities for making and taking musics, often in contexts that are not inherently pedagogical, and the leisure to enjoy, reflect on, and ask questions regarding them. Instead of filling every waking moment with activities directed toward formal instructional settings, such a curriculum values leisure, play, and the freedom to construct the particular meanings that seem appropriate to each participant in the process. Informality values certain shared performance-based knowledge and opportunities to diverge from the norm in individual ways as the tradition is mastered. This shared knowledge can be gained through performing the characteristic repertoire of the practice. Musical pieces and traditions appeal to students in various ways, and students' approaches are individualistic as they pick up this music by themselves. When students engage music from a variety of perspectives that are sometimes quite specialized and limited, they come to different understandings depending on the ways in which they approach it. Rather than constitute a systematic conceptual approach, informal music educational curricula build on students' ability to self-select their approaches to music. Such a curriculum may be a specialized and even narrow way into the music for each person, and yet when it is conducted in groups, learners can experience a wider array of music than they could accomplish alone. Their specialized instrumental skills and techniques also allow them to participate with others in music making and taking. Attaining comprehensive musical knowledge is not as important as students finding their own ways into the music, taking particular roles, and making and taking music individually and communally. Although often self-taught, students may also have access to expert instruction and example. Much hangs on the modeling and repertoire studied. If the music is technically demanding, students can become virtuosi without really thinking about the difficulty of what they are doing. In not being overly concerned about acquiring a comprehensive and systematic knowledge of the tradition, as in apprenticeship, students learning in informality mode can attain quite specialized knowledge and high levels of skill appropriate to the tradition(s) studied.[37]

Administration. Providing for alternatives and times and spaces in which individuals and groups can participate musically in ways that reflect their own desires, interests, and musical proclivities is a central administrative focus in conditions of informality. Informal instruction also bubbles up spontaneously in musical organizations.[38] Whatever the particular organization, there are serendipitous and unexpected happenings when students come together informally with musicians from various traditions. Accomplishing this in music schools requires building informal components into every music program so that informal occasions are not overlooked in the press of formal instruction. Administrators also need to plan for some looseness in the system if students are to have the time to plan and participate in various musical and social activities outside their regular courses and ensembles and other groups are to emerge of their own accord.[39]

It is particularly important to preserve the distinction between the home considered literally and informal agencies of music education in the phenomenal world.[40] Students are central to informal music education, and teachers who are regarded *in loco parentis* treat students respectfully, sensitively, compassionately, and tactfully. In large organizations, leaders might organize "houses" so that small groups of teachers and students can know each other intimately and teachers can give individual attention to students in ways that are difficult in large, impersonal groups. This principle might also be applied to music ensembles and studio lessons where conductors or studio teachers form tight-knit communities of students who become families that nurture and sustain each teacher and student. Beyond integrating informality into formal music educational institutions, policy makers also foster other informal organizations and ensembles beyond the borders of schools and in the everyday lives of people in the community. Garage bands, family musical groups, community music ensembles, religion-affiliated musical groups, and business-supported musical clubs are among the informal organizations that exist for other musical and social purposes but are central to the work of music education. In these ways, the borders of the music educational "home" are enlarged to encompass a host of other organizational possibilities for music education.

CRITIQUE

Informality offers important advantages for music education. Regarding music, informal music making and taking keeps alive a musical tradition. Its focus on such practical aspects of music as composing, improvising, performing, and listening ensures that the skills of live musicking are passed on from one generation of musicians to the next. Learning music in the midst of the rituals of which music is a part also relates music to the rest of life. Music's often ancillary or supportive role in rituals devoted to other things, such as religious worship and family sociality, emphasizes its societal function and instrumental value as well as its value for its own sake, thereby helping to ensure music's importance in society. Informality's role in classical and vernacular musical traditions also reveals something of the similarities and differences between and among them and emphasizes the often serendipitous ways in which music is transmitted from one generation to another. Its conservative and traditional focus is complemented by possibilities for change as new understandings emerge, sometimes unexpectedly. This model balances the need for some selectivity in regard to advanced musical knowledge with accessibility in terms of at least making an elementary musical understanding widely available.

Among its musical disadvantages, its conservative emphasis may be insufficiently forward-looking and transgressive and may curb creative endeavor.[41] Given its pervasively practical emphasis, music education in informality may be insufficiently reflective about, or critical of, this or other musical traditions. Stereotyping and prescribing or proscribing musical instruments by gender, race, ethnicity, size, or other delimiting factors can limit people musically. Approaching musical traditions uncritically may also fail to take more humane and inclusive approaches to musical theory and practice when justified, or implement change when warranted.

Teaching music in informality has several advantages. Those who teach are expert practitioners, skilled in musical tradition(s). The roles of teacher and student are sometimes interchangeable, and those who teach do so because of their authority and expertise in regard to particular matters. Techniques involved in showing and telling involve an array of ways to help students understand music, not only "knowing that" but also "knowing how"; that is, both propositional and procedural knowledge about music. Informality's humane approach to interpersonal relationships requires that teachers treat their students as persons who are precious, respect and value their questions and insights, and exercise their duty to keep their word and provide safe places for learning to take place. Teachers' exercise of tact emphasizes their sensitivity, imagination, and carefulness in regard to music and the students with whom they engage. Much teaching is student-initiated, and teachers' roles as mentor and responder to student inquiries are more in the line of helpers than of dictators. Teaching also takes advantage of unexpected events and employs a rhapsodic approach to meeting students' needs, interests, and desires and responding to their requests for help. This approach removes the necessity for teacher infallibility, since teachers respond to student inquiries and actions from their own somewhat limited expertise. Teaching is also more collegial, because the social distance between teacher and student is lessened, and conversational, because the roles of teacher and student are often interchangeable.

Teaching in this model may also be flawed. By relying on students' motivation to learn within contexts that are not inherently or mainly pedagogical, informality may create too rhapsodic and idiosyncratic and insufficiently systematic an approach to ensure that musical traditions continue. It may also suffer from being too directive on the one hand, when students rely entirely on what the teacher says and does, or insufficiently directive on the other, when students receive only superficial or fragmentary advice that does not effectively assist in developing the skills in question. Much hangs on the examples provided by teachers, and what is taught is only as good or as expert as the teacher in question. Since groups of neophyte musicians may be engaged in teaching, inexpert teaching may result in establishing poor techniques and bad habits that limit musicians later on. The resulting quality of teaching may be very uneven—sometimes very good and other times very poor.[42]

Among the advantages of informal learning, the possibilities inherent in the wide array of life circumstances that are not primarily or intentionally pedagogical are taken advantage of by learners, thereby broadening their opportunities for learning. Much music education occurs outside formal schooling in music, and informality highlights the possibilities for lifelong learning from babyhood and early childhood through to maturity and senescence. Thinking of music education as a multigenerational process, like growth and healing, also focuses on its contextual and environmental aspects. This model emphasizes consistency among the various societal institutions in forging musical environments for the young and those who are older, and also helps to explain why music education may not be as successful when musical beliefs, values, and practices are inconsistent. Among the important means of learning, play features prominently here, as well as more formal means of "work." Through taking advantage of such ancient approaches as trial and error, successive approximation to modeled performances, and rote learning, informality relies on students' inherent motivation to learn. Its reliance on receptive aspects of learning such as osmosis, participation, observation, and sensibility stresses the "undergoing" aspects of musical learning.[43] It also co-opts student insight into what is happening.[44] Learners' surprise and the joy of verification that may arise in informality foster their personal engagement and commitment.[45] As in the energy model, learners in informality can become their best teachers and cultivate the qualities needed for lifelong learning.

Still, several problems emerge with this model in regard to learning. Not only may learning be unsystematic and insufficiently formal, but if it is driven mostly, if not entirely, by student interest and desire, when this interest and desire falters, informality may be too narrow an approach. There may be insufficient emphasis on what others know and do, and learning may be tied, too closely, to the expertise of one or a few exponents rather than the wider community of teachers. Since it relies on sometimes indifferent expertise, learning in informality may cultivate amateurism masquerading as professional expertise.[46] Learning also depends on the particular nature of the music employed in ritual. For example, in some Christian traditions, musical tastes are actively cultivated to encompass an array of sometimes sophisticated musical traditions.[47] In others, simple choruses based on repetitive melodies of limited range are sung in unison, often pitched at the lower end of the female voice and the upper end of the male voice, and in keys that make part singing difficult.[48]

On the one hand, among the strengths of informal instruction, as in the energy model, teacher and student choice allow the "best fit" of people who are likely to work well together and enjoy each other's company—a situation likely to engender happiness for both teacher and student. When teachers and their students know each other intimately, teachers are able to suit responses to students in ways that are most effective in eliciting learning, and their feedback reinforces a positive response to instruction. Instructional situations that seem so much a part of other things, be they musical performances or rituals of other sorts, may be less likely to carry the negative connotations sometimes associated with formal schooling. Students' need to know and teachers' specific tailoring of teaching to particular practical situations give instruction an urgency and invest it with importance. Its connection with power and a possible livelihood motivates teachers and students alike.

On the other hand, among its difficulties, informal instruction may be too egalitarian (since the roles of teacher and student are sometimes interchangeable) or too directive (when musicians tell students how to do such-and-such). Not every musician is a good teacher, and much rides on the assumed natural gifts of the musician as teacher and the student as learner. Students may not know what they need or what to look for, and this process may become one of "the blind leading the blind." The model's reliance on choice may privilege some and disadvantage others; those with least attractiveness and know-how may have less choice or may choose less effectively and wisely than those who are most gifted, personable, and musically educated. Such a system privileges some and marginalizes others. Although families and other institutions in which informal music instruction occurs may be thought to be humane, this is not always true, and abuse and violence may work against the model's assumptions of love and caring. Some teachers and students do not feel a sense of duty and commitment to music instruction and do not always persevere when they are disinclined to teach and learn.

In the mode of informality, curriculum has several advantages. This is a broad approach to musical knowledge that takes in far more than formal means of instruction. Knowledge is constructed by the learner and contextualized within practical situations to which it can be immediately applied. As in the apprenticeship model, the subject matter is approached from the learner's perspective rather than formally in a logical and sequential fashion. Musical knowledge can be construed from differing perspectives, and learners decide which knowledge they most need at this particular juncture. Serendipity also plays a role, and an experienced musician may spot a problem and volunteer to assist in remedying it, pointing out to the learner what might be done differently to get a better result. What is learned is of immediate practical relevance and usefulness. This instrumental value of musical knowledge also drives motivation in providing a reason for teaching and learning. Keeping alive the tradition is an important reason for teaching and learning and, as in the rule model, musicians need to understand the principles and procedures that undergird this practice. Still, unlike the rule-oriented curriculum, rather than organizing a rational program of musical instruction, in the informal curriculum students master the rules somewhat idiosyncratically and haphazardly, according to when either they or teachers sense a need to learn them. The fact that the knowledge to be learned is often specialized and partial rather than intentionally comprehensive allows students to pursue the aspects of music that interest them. Since their knowledge is likely to be partial and selective and may require the participation of groups of musicians, the resultant musical community or "band" permits those with relatively limited skills an opportunity to play and sing together and thereby multiplies the musical talents of each musician. Serendipity in the specific musical knowledge taught and learned and the manner of its presentation and engagement allows for opportunities along the way that might be missed in formally designed programs of musical study. Sometimes, students and teachers may pursue various musical interests without the necessity of conforming to what others do.

Among the potential flaws of an informal curriculum, however, the focus on practice may render it insufficiently theoretical and reflective. It is possible that a curriculum contextualized in terms of a particular musical practice may be de-contextualized when looked at in the larger and even global world of music curricula. For example, a home-schooled girl growing up in Appalachia may pick up the fiddle and learn this tradition in a contextualized way; that is, in the midst of family rehearsals and performances that are often social occasions. This musical tradition, however, is quite removed from other classical and vernacular traditions that some of the young people in her high school know. While she has learned her own tradition contextually, her knowledge is not contextualized against the wider backdrop of contemporary classical and popular musics. Focusing on traditional practice may leave her insufficiently able to engage her tradition critically or contribute to others. The practical nature of her program of instruction may bypass theoretical understandings, and in the absence of independent judgment and the tools for imaginative thought and practice, she is unprepared to forge new musical traditions or criticize the one she has inherited. Without a systematic approach, the transmission of musical knowledge may be too serendipitous and idiosyncratic. In a pervasively functional music, there may be less attention to music for its own sake. Given that teaching is only as good as what this teacher says and does, and realistically, not all teachers are expert practitioners, this approach to curriculum may help to create "a cult of amateurism."[49] The serendipitous and idiosyncratic ways in which music is engaged by learners may not provide a sufficiently robust means of ensuring the transmission of shared beliefs, values, and practices across the tradition's practitioners. The resulting musical understandings may be too narrow, especially in a multicultural society in which multiple musical traditions coexist.

Regarding administration, this model presents several advantages. Informality does not require large scale organizations but can take place in small groups and privately. It may necessitate general but not specific administrative planning.[50] Involving families and other societal institutions in music education broadens its reach and raises the possibility for institutional cooperation, so that the musical environments that surround young and old alike are consistent throughout society. It suggests a happy and familial atmosphere grounded in love, tact, respect, and duty. Its reliance, for example, on duty underscores the need for steadfastness and commitment on the part of all those involved in the work of music education. Quite apart from inclination, even in instructional circumstances that are less than the "best fit" of teachers and students, duty obliges teachers and students alike to transcend their personal inclinations.

But administration is also problematic in this model. When music education is conducted in the private sphere and is not necessarily a matter of public policy, it may not happen naturally as expected. Relying on informality as a principal means of transmitting a musical tradition from one generation to another may not suffice; expecting it to bubble up informally may be insufficiently robust an approach to music education, which may also require top-down administrative organization. Defining informality outside the arena of public policy accords less importance to music education than if it is a part of publicly organized general education. Not only is it unsystematic and possibly of differing quality, but this model does not ensure that music education is available to all members of society as a matter of public policy.[51] Being out of the public eye, it may also be less accountable than formal music education and more difficult to monitor and regulate. This public invisibility may also render it subject to abuse and insufficiently transparent in determining the presence or nature of abuse. When it is more or less invisible to the public, it is an easy step to take a "laissez-faire" approach to music education and leave it up to private initiative to ensure public music education in society at large. Also, the sometimes romanticized visions of informal music education may be far from the mark and less effective than its proponents might imagine. Without formality and systematic instruction by experts, valuable aspects of musical culture may be lost. Restraint, dignity, intellectual engagement, and virtuosity and exponent know-how may disappear in an emerging amateurism forwarded by those with limited musical expertise. There is also a danger in applying the metaphor of home literally to think of a school as home. Such an approach can be simplistic in failing to distinguish between schools and homes. Unduly romanticizing homes may be off-putting to those whose home lives were or are dysfunctional and whose memories of or feelings about home are unhappy ones.

SUMMARY

It is clear that these pictures evoke sometimes tender and humane images of home and informality. Still there are advantages and disadvantages. Among the advantages are a humane approach to music education based on such values as love, caring, tact, and duty, the role of informality as a means of much music education around the world, and the emphasis on receptive aspects of learning. There are also the often conversational character of teacher and student interaction, the importance of conserving tradition, the practical thrust of the curriculum, and the often spontaneous ways in which informality arises in the midst of activities in which interest centers on other aspects than music education. On the other hand, among its disadvantages is the fact that, when taken alone, music education construed as informality may not constitute a sufficient basis for transmitting musical traditions and may conjure up negative pictures of abuse and unhappiness. It may be too rhapsodic, idiosyncratic, and insufficiently systematic an approach to teaching; it may rely too heavily on student interest and insight, privilege some teachers and students at the expense of others, and constitute too narrow a curriculum and organizational framework for music education in the public sphere. As with the healing model, there are also dangers in construing the metaphor of home literally when it is intended figuratively, thus conflating metaphor and model. So it is clear that while informality can contribute importantly to music education, considerable care needs to be taken in applying it as the principal or sole picture of music education.

12
GUIDE AND PEDAGOGY

We turn now to pictures of *guide* and *pedagogy* that have been a part of music education since antiquity. Presently they are especially important, because the teaching of music performance and pedagogy courses is often offered in conservatories and schools of music as means of preparing musicians as teachers of music.[1] I draw upon the metaphor of a guide, in the sense of one who "advises or shows the way to others," the "directing principle or standard," or a "structure or marking which directs the motion or positioning of something."[2] Children may also think of their parents as guides. In his poem "Father and Son," Stanley Kunitz writes of his anguish at the death of his stepfather, "'Father!' I cried, 'Return! You know / The way . . .'"[3] This ambiguity among persons, principles, and structures is useful, since it suggests that these pictures can be viewed in various ways that shed light on music education.

GUIDE

I think of our extended tour of Spain and Portugal one summer. Always independent travelers, we had little time to plan ahead this particular year. We had not been to these countries, our knowledge of the Spanish language was limited, and English is not widely spoken in parts of Spain. After studying our guide books, it seemed a good move to take a guided tour of these countries. There are places that we had wanted to see and UNESCO world heritage sites that caught our interest. We did not have the luxury of months and years, only weeks at our disposal to explore these countries. How to see something of them while also being able to get into some depth in at least a few places? Among the Spanish cities on our list were the university cities of Spain—Salamanca, Grenada, and Seville. There were smaller gems, such as Toledo, Segovia, Córdoba, and Avila. The major cities of Madrid and Barcelona were tempting, as was the Costa del Sol. I had read of Lisbon and the Portuguese countryside, and seeing this part of the Atlantic coast was also intriguing. We could not see everything; choices needed to be made.

Those who have traveled on tours know that one's first introduction to the tour is usually a glossy catalog with pictures (mainly on sunny days) that tempt the traveler with various budgets and interests in mind. We selected our tour pragmatically, with a view to finding a fit between our interests and the time we had available. Three tours might have fitted the bill, but only the one at the top of our list was available for us to join. Our visit to Spain would focus on the provinces of Old Castille and Léon and Andalusia; we would not be able to visit Barcelona, but we could see the university cities, three of the four gems, and we would get to know parts of Madrid quite well. There was the bonus of Gibraltar, Costa del Sol, and Lisbon.[4] The fit of our objectives and the time available with what this tour offered seemed good. Now, would it be as the brochures seemed to promise?

We arrived in Madrid a few days before the tour began with time to acclimate to the new time zone. Finding ourselves in a hotel in the heart of an upscale residential area with lots of shopping and other activities nearby and taking a taxi down to the old part of the city, we began to adjust to the language, culture (especially the very late meals that had us eating dinner at night at least two or three hours later than we were used to doing), and taking in the sights of the city on our own. The day before the tour began in earnest, we were on our way to Segovia on the first of the side trips additional to the base tour. The small group assembled was awestruck by this magnificent little Roman city with its viaduct, twelfth-century El Alcázar, and narrow, winding streets bordered by ancient buildings. The El Alcázar, going back to the Moors, was everything a picture-book version of a castle should be. Our local guide was a mine of information as she led us through the city streets, brought us out to its central square, thence to the castle, and down a hillside to our waiting coach. We returned to Madrid thankful for all that we had seen and photographed, the delicious pastries we had consumed, and the unexpected grandeur and age of this wonderfully preserved city. We had begun to know the international group with whom we would travel for the next two weeks. We had already come to the view that should the rest of the tour measure up to this one day, we would be very fortunate.

The tour began officially the next morning. We were to board a coach that would carry us a thousand miles around Spain and Portugal. Felix, our tour guide, met us at the coach door and checked us off against his master list to ensure that all those who were supposed to be on the tour were present, and at the appointed hour we left our hotel. This is Felix's living. Having taken a course as a tour guide, he accompanies travelers from around the world who may not know his country, its language, or its customs. It is his responsibility to ensure that all of the hotel arrangements are made, luggage is ferried to and from the hotel rooms where tour members are staying, meals included in the tour are arranged for, and entrance tickets to various cultural sites are secured so that group members need not wait in the sometimes long lines outside these attractions. Felix works with other specialist guides who lead tours of the various cities and towns visited. So, for example, a tour of Córdoba might be led by a guide who lives and works in the city and knows it intimately, takes us over territory that we might not otherwise find, and enables us to see what we might not in other ways be able to see. As we approach the place where lunch will be served, Felix calls to confirm that the group will soon be there, and he telephones ahead to the hotel at which the group will stay to ensure that the staff are ready to receive us. His function is to ensure that our travel is smooth and we can focus on experiencing what is to be known in these countries. The contractual relationship between the tourists and the company that hires Felix requires that he deliver what is promised in the tour brochures.

What qualities does the guide possess? Since Felix accompanies the tourists, rather than simply sending us unescorted, he is, in fact, a group leader. He needs to keep the group together so that some do not stray off or get lost. On a long journey such as this, he enjoys working with people and getting along with the various personalities, ethnic backgrounds, customs, and needs of the members of his group. Someone may get sick, and he finds medical help and helps to make travel arrangements for any who cannot complete the tour. He consults with the tourists and tempts us with extra side trips that meet our specific interests. He is not only a salesman but a first-rate communicator who is able to explain himself well in response to our often unexpected questions. He wins the trust of those on the tour, since we are often dependent on him. It is easy in these old Spanish cities to get lost in a virtual maze of narrow streets, and without a knowledge of the language it could be difficult to find the group again. So he is like a shepherd, constantly checking on his little flock, counting and recounting tour members in order to ensure that everyone is there. He is patient and persistent in insisting that the group keeps on schedule and that some do not needlessly waste the time of others by wandering off on their own.

Travelers led by a guide become a group or "family" at least for a short time. Felix's task is to motivate his band and build bonds between those who begin the tour as strangers and become friends during the journey. One way that he accomplishes this is with his fund of songs that might appeal to this international group of travelers. It has been years since I have sung on the bus, but sing we do as we work our way through quite an extensive song repertoire that most of the group already know. Americans, Australians, Canadians, and South Africans are on this tour, and the songs include vernacular songs from these countries. Felix also has a sense of humor in order to handle sometimes difficult and sensitive matters and foster an *esprit de corps* among the tour members. His fund of jokes seems endless, his timing immaculate, and he knows how and when to tell the right joke or story. Should a group member be late, he employs strategies so that the offenders are not late again. He also leads games that are "mixers," bringing together the various travelers and passing the time on a long journey. Some people would seek to sit in the best seats in the bus, so he employs a rotational system that mixes different people together and rotates seating positions around the bus. Stopping to greet this one or that, he keeps relationships among the travelers egalitarian and avoids preferring some over others. Eating, drinking, and traveling together forges bonds between the travelers and sometimes creates frictions. Toward the end of the trip, members of the group have begun making friendships and preferring the company of some over others. By this time, Felix has won the affection of his group members, and when the group stops for photographs at a particularly picturesque spot, members of the group pose with him with arms around each other. This band of travelers has become a community as we travel together on the same road and in the same direction for a time. We are sad when we must part at the end of our journey.

The guide is in a position of trust. Felix has been entrusted to lead the group according to commitments already made to the travelers. As travelers, we trust that he knows where he is going and will protect us from danger. The tour company and Felix decide which places are safe for travel and what travelers should see. For example, the bullfight symbolizes the machismo of Spanish culture, and in Spain, the bull must be killed in the ring. Felix does not take his group to see a bullfight. Why would Felix not take this group of travelers to see an event so central to Spanish myth and other aspects of its culture? The answer, according to Felix, lies in his and the tour company's belief that this violence can be deeply offensive and upsetting to travelers, so much so that tourists who attend a bullfight sometimes faint and have to be carried out ill after observing the spectacle. Accordingly, entrusted with our health and well-being, the designers of this tour of Spain and Portugal exclude the bullfight from our itinerary. Those who wish to see a bullfight can encounter one, and Felix is willing to make the arrangements for those of his tour group who desire this experience.

Along the way, Felix surprises us with the unexpected. In Granada, for example, we visit Gypsy caves and see a performance of their dance and music. In Seville, he arranges for us to see a breathtaking late-night performance of flamenco music and dance. The weather being cool on the Costa del Sol, Felix arranges for us to visit Morocco. Visiting this country even briefly gives many in our group the opportunity to visit a North African country and city for the first time. Some places on the tour turn out to be gems that are surprising in their appeal. I cannot forget our visit to the Mezquita, a mosque-turned-cathedral in Córdoba—one of the most moving spiritual experiences I have ever had. Or visiting the Jewish quarters in the cities of Toledo, Córdoba, and Seville that were once teeming centers of cultural life. Coming upon a statue of Moses Maimonides, a noted Jewish philosopher, in a square in Córdoba and visiting the Jewish synagogues that once were thriving cores of learning is serendipitous and unexpected. To view the whitewashed villages of southern Spain, with bougainvillea cascading over high walls and potted plants in profusion on wrought iron balconies, is to be entranced with unexpected beauty, especially for one who has not traveled in Spain. In Portugal, Felix wants us to see the Algarve, experience something of the city of Lisbon and the nearby towns of Cascais, Sintra, and Estoril, and visit the Shrine of Fatima. For Felix, these are not surprises; he has been this way many times before. Still, discovering these things is delightful for the travelers, and Felix knows the sorts of experiences calculated to evoke this delight and wonder.

Along the way, one destination becomes the means to another end. Sometimes our way takes us through olive groves, orchards, vineyards, and pastures, other times through rugged mountains and rocky and arid terrain, and still others through forests or beside lakes and oceans. Always, Felix keeps us savoring the moment but looking forward to where we are going next. Some in his company have their own destinations in mind. For me, it is to take in the old city of Salamanca where Isadore taught music at the University. I have long wanted to see this important seat of Renaissance musical learning, one of the first places where music entered the university curriculum. I also want to see for myself the mellow stones, to which writers have referred, that glowed golden in the sunshine. To visit the beautifully preserved walled city of Avila, where Teresa labored in her convent and fostered musical study in her community of women, is to imagine a world far removed from the present. Few on the tour may have cared for Salamanca and Avila, yet for me they are places where music history comes alive in living color. I am indebted to Felix for taking us this way when we might have gone another.

When visiting a city or town, Felix can be counted on for advice as to where we might find refreshments, souvenirs, local arts and crafts, and other places not to miss when we have time on our own. Serendipity means that we sometimes find delightful places without his aid. Still, having someone with us who knows this place well helps us make informed and wise choices about how we can use the time we have most effectively. Felix can break down a new place into manageable, bite-size units, so that we are not overwhelmed by the new but are able to focus on the things of most interest to us. Moving around the lovely, gracious city of Seville, memorialized in Mozart opera and by other European classical musicians, we have Felix there to help us find the addresses we seek and enjoy the richness that the city offers. Looking back, I am amazed at the sheer intensity of the experience. We accessed far more than we might have seen alone and unaccompanied, even had we had more time to prepare for our visit. So we feel well advised and well helped in making this tour fit as closely as possible to our various interests. Photographing landscapes, we might fall behind others without this compunction to capture moments on film. Yet our experience is enriched as Felix tells us where particularly interesting vistas are to be found. To sit near a grotto high on a mountain overlooking the deep-blue of the Mediterranean is to capture on film and in memory's eye a wondrous scene.

PEDAGOGY

Pedagogy refers variously to "a place of instruction," "instruction, discipline, training," "a system of introductory training," a means of guidance," the "art, occupation, or practice of teaching," "theory or principles of education," and "a method of teaching based on such a theory."[5] Vestiges of its origins in servitude remain, and music education supports musical practice by ensuring the transmission of its beliefs, values, and practices to the next generation.[6] Well-traveled territory in music education, pedagogical materials include musical treatises from the Renaissance to the present day and methods of class instruction in schools.[7] Philosophical writings on music and music education by Francis Sparshott, David Elliott, Vernon Howard, Donald Schön, and Frede Nielsen also examine aspects of musical pedagogy.[8]

Music. Pedagogy focuses on musical practice and music is construed as beliefs that are enacted practically by a tradition's exponents and public.[9] Music is viewed as comprising social as well as psychological and acoustic phenomena, in which context shapes what is done musically and how its musicians and public interpret what is done. This focus on the notion of music as what musicians do (and believe as it fosters and is reinforced or impacted by practice) emphasizes the doing and undergoing of music, especially as seen in the phenomenal world. It highlights the experiential and performative nature of music and focuses on the verb "to music" as a way of thinking of music as process rather than just as product.[10] Although some may view music scientifically and systematically as a basis for music educational practice, and thereby seek universalistic perspectives that emphasize the shared properties of music *qua* music, the principal thrust of this model is relativistic in the sense that each musical tradition or practice needs to be regarded in the light of its particular assumptions, values, beliefs, mores, and expectations.[11] Rather than see one music in terms of another, or adjudicate, for example, one vernacular music according to the tenets of another classical music, this model holds that each musical practice has its own value as a means of human expression and merits attention as much as another. It is therefore incumbent on musicians and their publics to be respectful of this musical diversity as they cross from one music to another when opportunities present. Experiencing another's music enables people to understand the music that is their own heritage from others' perspectives and thereby more critically and broadmindedly engage music and its meaning. This mind-set leads to an internationalist and multicultural view of music and music education.[12] Without understanding the social context in which music is made, they may fail to grasp its meaning and relevance to those whose music it is.

Doing music is crucial, and traditional approaches are valued. In order to understand music, one must know how it is made.[13] Making and taking music, whether through composing, improvising, performing, or listening, provides a means of deep engagement with music that transforms people's lives and constitutes means whereby they can actively engage in and undergo the musical experience. Being inside the music allows the individual to grasp things that would otherwise be hidden from view and thereby gain an intimate understanding of how this music works.[14] Musicking is about things that are seen, heard, and otherwise felt. Each music's continuance as a tradition requires its transmission by expert musicians, because it is impossible for teachers to point out musical elements unless they are themselves exponents of this music. Knowing this musical practice intimately requires one to know it as those "inside" the tradition know it; knowing it as those "outside" the tradition know it also requires musicians to undertake "border crossings" and become skilled in more than one musical tradition.[15] This knowledge tends to blur the boundaries between performers, composers, improvisers, and music teachers. As in the informality model, music's traditional aspects are stressed and the wisdom passed on from one generation to the next is revered. Musical practices are oriented toward the past rather than toward effecting change, received wisdom is regarded as normative, and a music's chief exponents ensure that the practice persists into the future. This approach resists tendencies to homogenize music and fosters musical diversity as each practice is cultivated for its own sake. It cultivates spiritual values as the myths of the past are transmitted to each successive generation.[16]

Teaching. Teachers need leadership skills because individual students and groups of students look to them for guidance. Groups are involved, so teaching is construed socially and psychologically. Even in individual instruction, a solitary teacher and student comprise a dyad, the smallest social group. The teacher's social skills are also on display where large groups are involved. Leaders require the skills to motivate, encourage, and persuade others to follow them. Personal qualities such as organizational skills, the ability to explain and articulate ideas clearly, tact, resilience, a sense of humor, and the ability to motivate others are important characteristics for the teacher who serves as a guide. Organizational skills require the teacher to have a tidy mind and the aptitude and preparation to formulate appropriate procedures that enable those who follow to meet the goals that have been set. Exposition is the important skill of clarifying ideas and practices so that they are easily understood by others.[17] Tact requires a sense of diplomacy and the intuitive knowing what to do and say in a particular time, place, or situation.[18] Resilience conveys notions of "elasticity," acts of "recoiling" and "rebounding," of being able to "recover quickly from difficult conditions,"[19] and the strength of character, determination, and persistence to undertake a task successfully and meet the goals that have been set even when confronted with difficulties and unexpected problems along the way. A sense of humor is the ability to laugh and enjoy life, not take oneself too seriously, and raise the spirits of others one leads. The ability to motivate others speaks to an understanding of how to foster others' desire to pursue the goals that have been set. Thinking of these qualities in terms of the leadership of students and other colleagues, it is clear that such teachers enjoy working with people, especially young people but also those who are older, and have the kind of personalities that are attractive to students and other colleagues.

In this model, teachers are first and foremost musicians, expert in the musical traditions they teach, and cosmopolitan in their musical outlook. They possess an authority that comes from their expertise and is recognized by their students.[20] Guiding students and developing their theoretical and practical musical skills is comprehensive in its inclusion of the gamut of skills from habits and techniques to critical thinking skills from elementary to advanced levels; it also entails training and schooling.[21] Training is a matter of cultivating the skills and techniques required in a particular musical practice.[22] As in the apprenticeship and growth models, knowing how to do this music requires teachers to plan a program of work that allows their students to progress successfully and step by step from elementary to advanced levels of performance and understanding. Teachers need the ability to analyze sometimes complex matters into their constituent elements and systematically bring the students along. This ability is predicated partly on the principle of antecedence; that is, teachers teach what is needed before other things can be successfully undertaken at each successive stage of the process.[23] Schooling refers not only to the places where students gather to learn from teachers but to the process of learning the discipline of music; it is an ambiguous idea referring both to a set of beliefs and practices and to those places in, or ideas around which, like-minded people gather.[24]

Teaching in pedagogy mode proceeds formally and informally, and skills are systematically grounded and employed.[25] Formal teaching proceeds by means such as instruction, example, practice, and reflection.[26] Instruction refers to the teacher's ability to expound, explain, describe, define, and give direction to music students.[27] As in the rule model, teachers ensure that students grasp the practice's directing principles. Example denotes the teacher's demonstration of the tradition's practices through such means as exemplars, models, or scaled down instances, and even anti-examples or instances that are the opposite of desired attributes. Practice provides opportunities for students to work on their own to perfect their own skills and techniques toward the ideal of mastery that they have in mind.[28] Some teachers monitor their students' practice, while others develop routines that they require their students to follow when practicing.[29] Reflection ensures that students have the opportunity to think before, in the midst of, and after performances, evaluate what they have done, and make course corrections along the way. In respect of practice and reflection, as in conditions of informality, teachers provide their students with opportunities to teach themselves. Formal teaching is complemented by informal teaching by such means as osmosis, observation, participation, and sensibility.[30] Osmosis takes advantage of the absorptive tendency of human beings to be affected by their surroundings. Observation connotes the teacher's insistence on students noticing and copying salient features of their own performances. Participation refers to the teaching that goes on by virtue of being in a community and engaging in its rituals. Sensibility refers to teachers cultivating their students' sensitivity and openness to opportunities to learn and experience music directly. Contra the production mode, or the notion of impression in which teachers mold their students, teachers recognize that they can only do so much for them. The view of their task as one of leading their students to places where they must act for themselves, see for themselves, hear for themselves, and feel for themselves renders teachers somewhat helpless. This notion of teaching evokes the modes of growth, energy, and rule and casts teachers in the role of helpers of their students rather than as active agents in their learning. Just as a guide leads travelers to a monument and provides them opportunities to experience it, it is up to the travelers to make what they can of it; the guide can direct their attention to this aspect or that, but it is ultimately the travelers' responsibility to engage it in the ways they choose.

Learning. In the pedagogy model, students choose those with whom they wish to study.[31] They know their teachers' reputations as performers and teachers, and they hope that their teachers' reputations will "rub off," so that as a result of studying with them, they will likewise have an outstanding musical career. Following this logic, the most prestigious teachers attract the most students, probably more than they can possibly teach, and the least prestigious teachers attract the fewest students, teaching whoever is left after more prestigious teachers have selected their students. On the face of things, the most prestigious teachers have their pick of the students; the best students are likely to have their first choice of teachers, while the least qualified, talented, or apt students are least likely to have their first choice. Although things are more complicated than this (some students want particular qualities in their teachers and may opt for teachers on other bases than eminence), the less advanced and talented students are likely to have less choice than their more advanced and gifted colleagues.

Receptive learning is particularly important because students are dependent on their teachers, especially at early stages of music education, and committed to their own learning.[32] As in the apprenticeship and rule models, students learn the expectations, norms, and rules that undergird a musical practice; in order to ensure a systematic knowledge of music, learning is primarily formal, and informal learning is ancillary to formal learning. For the student, learning by means of instruction, example, practice, and reflection is emphasized more than by osmosis, imitation, participation, and sensibility. Acquiring procedural knowledge or "knowing how" is a sometimes challenging process that relies on students' imaginative and intuitive insight into what the teacher is up to.[33] By insight, I refer to the student's ability to "see into" or grasp what the teacher is saying and doing.[34] Imagination is perceptive, felt, intuitive, and reasoned and enables insight to occur.[35] Surprise and serendipity also surface along the way.[36] Students' discoveries are spiritual and sensuous as they encounter important existential questions on the road to musical wisdom, come to know themselves more deeply, better grasp their strengths and weaknesses, and understand the things that bring them joy.[37] Teachers also learn as they discover the particular approaches needed for each of their students.[38] The model's reliance on students' insight limits what teachers are able to do and places the onus on students whose learning is determined, mainly, by what they decide to do.[39] As in apprenticeship, learning is receptive, and it is up to the students to come to a knowledge of a particular musical practice and be able to do it. Receptivity is not passivity but, as in the energy model, necessitates students' commitment and effort, expressed in their intellectual focus and concentration in their lessons, diligence and care in attending to their teachers' words and actions, and practice between their lessons. Their commitment spills over into informal situations.[40]

Instruction. Thinking socially about music instruction also includes psychological and even physiological aspects. As in the community mode, pedagogy is both processual and product-oriented, so we may consider its dynamic as well as its static qualities. Understanding pedagogy as a dynamic endeavor requires including the study of social processes as means of grasping what is going on; these include goal-setting, motivation, socialization, personification, image preservation, communication, cooperation, competition, conflict resolution, segmentation, motive ascription, and time-space coordination.[41] Psychological issues of musicians' temperament, musical ability, identity, development, and cognition are important considerations in shaping the nature of teacher and student interaction; they also provide important evidence for the ways in which individuals and groups function in musical contexts.[42] Studies that classify different group activities in music also provide different perspectives on its work.[43] Such studies are like still pictures at particular moments of time rather than movies ongoing throughout time. Status studies that determine the state-of-affairs at specific times also illumine the nature of what is going on in the instructional situation.[44] Still, since the time-scales of social groups are very short, and minutes, hours, days, weeks, months, or years may make all the difference, the picture at a particular moment may be quite different from that at another.

Pedagogical instruction is goal-oriented. Rather than a journey for the journey's sake, teachers and students have particular ends in view. Teachers may have longer-term ends than the students' more immediate objectives, and there is a sense that teachers expect their students to accomplish such-and-such during a course of instruction. Whatever the specific objectives, teachers' expectations are clear and students are expected to meet them. Students are also invested in this instruction, and they have the sense that their teachers will deliver the promised guidance and help. Teachers and their students more or less have some choice in the matter, and there is an acceptable if sometimes less than optimal "fit" between what teachers and students expect. As distinct from the community model, goals are fairly unambiguous and closed rather than open-ended. Formal instruction receives more emphasis than informal instruction because teachers wish to lead their students systematically to particular traditional understandings and practices. Although the model fosters "communities of practice" and independence on the part of students, teachers wish to pass on to their students the tradition of which they are exponents.[45] The lesson becomes a primary time and place in which this instruction is carried on, sometimes with individual students and often with groups of students. Generally scheduled ahead of time and planned for by teachers and their students, the lesson formats followed include the lecture, discussion, demonstration, and tutorial (known, in the past, as a recitation), and these strategies significantly impact the nature of the teacher-student interaction. In the lecture, the teacher may expound on a topic with illustrative examples and then invite questions from students. Less formal lectures may allow for questions during the exposition. The discussion consists of a formal conversation between teacher and students in which the teacher may pose questions in Socratic vein and student responses lead to still further questions as the teacher guides the conversation to certain clear ends. Discussions are not intended as free explorations but are actively guided by the teacher in particular directions, while also inviting student input from time to time. Demonstrations enable teachers (and designated students) to show as well as tell, or to exemplify as well as explain the topic at hand.

Tutorials, often the basis for private or small group lessons, consist of students bringing certain prepared work to the lesson for the teacher's analysis, commentary, and advice. The onus is on the students to prepare ahead of the lesson, and a different sort of dialogue emerges than that in lecture, discussion, and demonstration.[46]

The communication in the pedagogy model is both directive on the teacher's part and conversational between teachers and their students. It is directive in the sense that teachers are set on reaching particular goals, and the teachers' goals are privileged over those of the students. This is so because, as for the apprenticeship and rule models, the onus is on students to come to a knowledge of a musical practice, not for teachers to guide instruction in the individualistic and idiosyncratic directions in which students might wish to travel. Unlike in the community and even the growth models, students have less input into the overall direction of instruction even though they may have some more limited input into specific aspects within the general instructional objectives.[47] Regarding the conversational character of communication, students are restricted in certain respects; but they also have some room to move within these restrictions.[48] Tutorials provide an instructional format that cultivates discovery on the student's part and constitutes an important means whereby reflective practitioners are developed.[49] Students' preparation ahead of the lesson revolves around problems they have already set out to address.[50] Lessons constitute an ongoing conversation between teacher and student, often directed by the teacher but sometimes generated through questions by the student. This conversation is not one between equals; the teacher holds the greater power and control, is the final arbiter of student work, and directs the student in ways deemed appropriate within the frame of this artistic tradition. The teacher's questions prompt the student to imagine things differently and to develop the critical insight into this particular problem. The student's preparation provides a basis for looking back at what has been accomplished prior to the lesson—a sort of "backward" instruction that nevertheless points toward what the student might accomplish in the future.

Curriculum. In the pedagogy model, music students work on music according to the scope and sequence of activities planned by the teacher. Such activities may, of course, take into account students' interests, but these are only starting points. The directions in which these activities go are not necessarily the result of a collaborative and dialogical exercise, as is more common in the community model, but are framed, as in the growth model, by the teacher's decisions. This action plan is definitive and unambiguous in its objectives and products.[51] Instructional objectives are clear, and the teacher provides certain frames of reference and a scope and sequence of activities that guide students as they undertake their musical study.[52] Students come with individual strengths and weaknesses, habits that need to be unlearned, and significant gaps in their musical understanding, and these deficiencies are remedied while building on students' strengths and interests in ways that make sense sequentially. The teacher leads a diverse group of students through a program of study that is progressive and systematic so that all benefit from common knowledge, skills, and techniques, move from elementary to advanced skills and understandings, and maintain their own musical interests.

This curriculum is performance-based, contextualized, and evaluated summatively. By performance-based, I mean that the curriculum is pervasively practical and theory is expected to relate to what musicians do.[53] Contextualization arises as the various aspects of the music curriculum are integrated, and the subject matter relates to the rest of lived life.[54] In asserting this requirement for practical experience, the teacher also follows a historical precedent akin to apprenticeship in that students are expected to gradually assume more musical responsibilities as their expertise and experience advance.[55] The importance of summative evaluation arises in the pedagogy model because teachers are particularly interested in whether or to what degree students have met or exceeded the stated criteria. The model therefore relies upon examinations as a means of student assessment. These take different forms. As with the rule model, the traditional approach in performance in the United States is for students to perform before a panel of judges referred to as a jury. This panel is charged with assessing the worth of the performance and communicating the strengths and weaknesses of the performance to the student. Such occasions are often "high stakes" performances from the students' perspective; they are held at the end of a term or course of study, and students' progress often depends on the degree to which their performances meet or exceed the mark.[56] These occasions are often marked by student nervousness and large social distance between examiners and students and may intimidate students rather than constitute friendly and convivial gatherings. Formative evaluation can also occur in the context of informal class meetings where critical comments are intended to assist students to improve their performance; but even here, each performance is a summative event in which students demonstrate what they have accomplished. Their efforts are adjudicated against the backdrop of what others, particularly skilled exponents, do.

Administration. In pedagogy mode, the administration of music education is clearly articulated and formal. As in the production model, an organizational flow chart manifests in clearly delineated roles and responsibilities, hierarchical lines of authority, and differences in power and agency. In the organization's power structure, administrators are situated at the top, teachers are squeezed in the middle, and students are at the bottom. Since the times and spaces requested by teachers according to their curricular and instructional plans are limited and some are more desirable than others, administrators are charged with negotiating these differing interests and needs. They assign spaces and times to be used by the organization and its teachers and their students, acting as referees and arbiters of time and space when conflicting interests and pressures arise.[57]

Administrators are responsible for providing the resources needed by teachers and students in teaching, learning, instruction, and curriculum. Given the practical and performance-based nature of pedagogy, the spaces where music is made and taken are of primary interest. One of the central spaces required by a music program is a performing space or concert hall, an acoustic space designed especially for making and listening to musical sounds. Within the Western classical tradition, such spaces are expected to have particular acoustic properties, and these may differ from those required by other traditions. Musicians also need access to halls akin to the modern concert hall, as well as other more intimate performance spaces designed for the rehearsal and performance of salon or chamber music. These spaces are crucial in allowing students to hear music in the acoustic environments for which it is designed; they also galvanize a music program by offering concert opportunities for other community organizations and attract professional musicians who want to perform in them. Other resources include musical instruments; associated technologies for teaching, composing, performing, producing, and recording music; library holdings of scores, recordings, and other published materials; teaching faculty and staff of appropriate caliber; students acceptable to the faculty; and fellowships to support student study and faculty creative and teaching activities. Today these resources are often expensive, and so administrators may need to raise private funds and endowments for the support of the music program, and to augment funds raised through student fees, university or institutional support, and other gifts and bequests. In elementary and secondary schools teachers sometimes take on these fundraising tasks, which are made easier by the public nature of musical performance, the fact that it can be adjudicated readily, and the clarity of performative results measured against the organization's objectives and purposes. The power of this "demonstration effect" is evident in "copycat" approaches by other organizations and institutions that may also seek to imitate this organization's successes.[58]

CRITIQUE

Among the musical benefits, this model's cosmopolitan view of music situates it within the culture in which it is found and regards music broadly and comparatively. Its practical emphasis tempers speculative approaches to music and helps to keep the tradition alive by focusing on what musicians do rather than just what they think. It also resurrects an old view of music as doing and undergoing and recaptures ancient views of music's meaning as a part of ordinary life and in regard to the practices of musicians.[59] As with apprenticeship, this emphasis on musical techniques focuses the attention of musician-teachers on the skills that aspiring musicians need to be able to demonstrate. By emphasizing practice, it subverts the hegemony of abstract thought that predominates in higher learning, at least in the West.

There are also musical disadvantages. The emphasis on musical practice may neglect the beliefs that undergird them. Music pedagogy may become fixated on training and schooling and on inculcating techniques and skills, losing sight of the humanistic aspects of music and the wider social and cultural realities that intersect with it. It is also possible that matters concerning music's social and cultural context may assume such prominence that they overshadow important specifically musical ideas, techniques, and skills.[60] Process does not equal product, knowledge of one does not presuppose knowledge of the other, and since these understandings differ, they both bring different insights. To focus exclusively on music practice is to understand only a part of music. Also, being preoccupied with the phenomenal attributes of music may neglect its important spiritual qualities. Given the ambiguity of musical practice, it is difficult to be precise about what it means and the scope of the pedagogy that depends on it.

Teaching in this model has several strengths. In the hands of a competent professional or exponent of a tradition, it is informed by a broad and deep knowledge of the subject matter and a systematic study of teaching practices. Its emphasis on leadership and the teacher's example provides a basis for students to be confident in their teachers and practical models for them to follow. As teachers intimately know the subject matter, students can receive a systematic preparation concerning knowledge about the subject matter and an ability to make music. The model also allows teachers to take advantage of and build upon student interests and impulses and to construct a program of experiential learning. Since teachers are also participants in a dialogical process, there are opportunities to learn from insights that students bring to the pedagogical situation.

Among the problems in teaching with this model, pedagogy may be excessively directive, seeking to funnel knowledge more or less exclusively through teachers to students and allowing students insufficient time and space to follow their own interests and proclivities. Pedagogy requires teachers to be exponents of the musics they teach; thus it becomes necessary for them to both know about and know how to do these musics. This is a tall order. The amount of time expended to become an exponent of even one musical tradition may make it difficult for teachers to be expert in several. Yet without this deep knowledge of more than one musical tradition, it is difficult to imagine how teachers can lead their students in border crossings from one musical tradition to another. The best that might be hoped for, practically, might be that teachers are exponents of one musical tradition with passing knowledge of another. Beyond this, it is necessary to call upon the expertise of exponents of other traditions.[61] The expectation that music teachers need to be exponents in at least one musical tradition and preferably more requires allocating much more time in teacher preparation to cultivating musicianship—a practical difficulty considering the already over-crowded nature of teacher preparation programs and the constraints imposed by governmental and other professional regulations. Although pedagogy relies on teachers not abusing their considerable power over students, some teachers regrettably misuse this power and abuse their students. There is the reality that empowering students, since they are so powerless in pedagogy, may be even more pressing than empowering teachers.

On the one hand, learning in this model has several strengths. Among them, students can exercise choice in who their teachers are, thereby helping to ensure that student and teacher are in more or less agreement about the objectives of learning. Pedagogy's emphasis on receptive learning enables students to benefit from their teachers' experiences and avoid needless mistakes along the way. The necessity for students committing to and investing in their own learning helps them strive to reach their potential (where their own choice is an important determinant in what they may achieve). Insight and discovery learning also allow for serendipity and surprise, highlighting the fact that not everything in learning can be pre-planned. Unexpected moments make it possible for students to experience wonder and awe, to know music spiritually and reverently, as they also grasp it intellectually, emotionally, and physically.

On the other hand, learning in this model suffers from certain disadvantages. Since teachers plan their curricula and instructional programs, students have limited choice in how they may proceed. A sinister reading of the teacher's professed concern for the student is to see students being manipulated by their teachers into believing that they have choice when in fact it is more apparent than real. Under these circumstances, it is difficult to imagine students "following their bliss" unless it so happens that what their teachers want to teach them is what they want to learn; their freedoms are definitely limited.[62] Teachers do not always act in the best interests of their students, and it is hard to see how students will have much freedom to diverge from what and how their teachers have planned for them to learn. Limiting and directing student learning can breed dependence on the teacher, student apathy, and reluctance to commit to the projects at hand, thus undermining the model's assumptions of student engagement and commitment.

Instruction in pedagogy mode also has benefits. This dynamic and social view of teacher and student interaction highlights process as well as product. As in the energy model, the possibilities for teacher and student choice allow for positive vibes between teacher and student, making it more likely that their interaction in this situation will be pleasant and suggesting that they are more likely to agree on the objectives and means of musical instruction. The clear and goal-directed nature of teacher and student interaction also implies that instructional objectives will be achieved. As with the production model, music education is not left to chance but is planned for by policy makers. The mix of directive and conversational interaction between teachers and their students is pragmatic in its acknowledgment of the teacher's superior expertise and the student's desire to have some input into the instructional process. This asymmetry in power between teacher and student, wherein the student needs to trust the teacher and the teacher needs to use this greater power wisely, is a practical strategy for dealing with a practical reality. Emphasizing tutorials as a means of delivering instruction allows students to develop as much as they are able before submitting their work to their teachers' examination. When this engagement between teachers and their students is mutually respectful, it allows students to develop the kinds of thinking and doing that they need as accomplished exponents of a musical practice even before they are able to do so entirely on their own.

Among the limitations of instruction in this model are its assumptions regarding teacher and student choice and the asymmetrical power relations between them. Although pedagogy depends on teacher and student choice for more or less the best fit of teachers and students, the reality is less benign. As with apprenticeship instruction, the most prestigious teachers and the most gifted and devoted students are likely to have more choice than less prestigious teachers and less gifted and devoted students. In such a situation, inequities arise in which those with greater talent and skill are preferred over those with less. For public systems of education, such instructional situations are not in the best interests of fostering democracies, since they may be unjust and inhumane. Although they may contribute to the well-being and happiness of some, these benefits come at the price of the well-being and happiness of others. The asymmetrical power of teachers and students is paternalistic and patronizing in its assumption that teachers know better than their students what these students need and always act in their students' best interests. Things can go wrong in the pedagogical conversation: students may have insufficient confidence in their own ability, or teachers may fail to see their students' predicaments or exploit them when their own self-interests conflict with those of their students. When students and teachers do not see eye to eye, students may resent their teachers or teachers may be exasperated with their students. The relative and real powerlessness of students works against their self-confidence, emerging authority, and accomplishment required in this model. Also the social distance between teachers and students is exacerbated, and the model's hope that teachers may be trusted guides for and helpers of their students is undermined when teachers must pass summative judgments on their students' work.

Curriculum also enjoys important benefits in the model. The scope and sequence of activities make good use of teacher expertise and experience and have the advantage of being relatively unambiguous. This clarity makes it easier for students to know what to do and how to do it. Ironically, teachers' framing of activities in ways that limit student choice may facilitate the development of student creativity. The limits and boundaries on student choice not only can reduce anxiety when confronting a multitude of creative options but can focus student attention on the particular skills needed to develop in specific ways. As teachers set progressively more complicated and difficult musical challenges for their students, it is possible to construct a progressive path whereby they can be successful at every stage in the process. Regarding a music within its social and cultural context enables students to grasp the integrated and holistic nature of knowledge and see its relevance to the rest of their lives. Seeing music as practical, through a focus on what musicians do, also contributes to students' growing cosmopolitan sense of music and their valuing of practice as well as theory. As in the rule model, emphasizing summative evaluation provides a measure of objectivity in assessing the degree to which students are progressing and aids teachers in making the judgments needed to treat all their students respectfully, carefully, tactfully, fairly, and dispassionately.

Among the detractions of this curriculum, since the teacher often plans the program in advance of instruction, students may not be interested in or committed to the teacher's approach to the subject matter. They may find it irrelevant, uninteresting, or irksome, and it may be difficult for them to construct their own independent approaches to music. Learning a tradition and a practice requires that students meet or exceed the expectations of the music's exponents, and those who cannot accomplish what is asked of them are sometimes punished severely. The "high stakes" summative evaluation, often in the form of public examinations in which the students' failures are there for all to see and hear (and talk about) only exacerbate the situation. Student failure in respect of the musical subject matter is compounded by social failure, a sense of shame, or cynicism that may be felt by those who are unsuccessful. Given that any musical practice's exponents constitute a minority of the population, even in vernacular musics, most people cannot be expected to attain the musical virtuosity of skilled exponents and are liable to experience feelings of failure and embarrassment if they are expected to become virtuosi. So pedagogy cannot form the sole basis for systems of music education intended to provide most people with a sense of musical success and the possibility to go on to enjoy and learn music.

There are several advantages of administration in pedagogy mode. This is a "can do," businesslike, and professional approach that gets things accomplished; it requires a no-nonsense, top-down, systematic organization that clarifies the roles and responsibilities of all those within the system. Administrators are expected to provide the resources for teachers and students to do their work effectively, and as in the growth model, administrators and teachers work collaboratively to ensure that all of the requirements are in place to enable to teachers and their students to accomplish the tasks at hand. Unlike in the mode of informality, administrators plan in advance for formal instruction in order to systematically meet the organization's objectives. This systematic approach thinks through what needs to be accomplished and how; it seeks to implement the planned strategies practically and successfully. In planning for success, this approach is more likely to achieve it than just leaving it to happenstance. One demonstration of success is likely to spawn another, and so pedagogy takes advantage of the "demonstration effect," in which instructional successes spread from person to person, place to place, and time to time.

Nevertheless, problems come to mind. Among them, the top-down hierarchical organization renders students as among the most powerless of those involved in music education rather than the focus of the organization's attention and interest. Things in the phenomenal world are often messier than theoretical propositions suggest and, although educational philosophers seek to clarify ideas, ambiguity is evident in much educational practice and discourse.[63] Clarity of organizational purposes and procedures can stultify creative expression that might "bubble up" from its base, especially when clarity is confused with dogmatism and inflexibility, brooking no alteration of purposes and procedures and insufficiently assisting those on the margins or between the cracks of the organization's commitments. There is a danger that those who work on behalf of music education may emphasize clarity for clarity's sake without realizing the possibilities and potentialities of ambiguity and fuzziness. Nor do musician educators possess perfect foresight or omniscience. Administrative decisions are often undertaken in the context of incomplete information and imperfect understanding. Unexpected consequences flow from administrative policies, and it is likely that the plans made will need to be adjusted as they are applied practically. Whereas an administrator may have anticipated these or those resources and secured them, personnel changes or social and cultural developments may require that this plan be reworked in the midst of action. Flatter and more collegial organizations may be in a better position to respond to change than those that are hierarchical and directive. The "copycat" phenomenon or "demonstration effect" to which I have referred may also prompt some to think too uncritically about the things they see others doing in their haste to jump on the latest fad or "bandwagon."

SUMMARY

It is clear that the guide and pedagogy pictures provide important and helpful insights into music education. Their cosmopolitan, comparative, and practical view of music, emphasis on personal and social characteristics of teachers, investment of students in their own education, dynamic social view of instruction, systematic approach to curriculum, and goal-oriented administration are among the benefits noted. Detractions include their emphasis on practical and contextual rather than theoretical and musical aspects, potential for misuse of teacher power, limitations to student freedom, inequity of choice in instructional situations, high-stakes evaluation of students, and top-down directive approach to administration. Their possibilities are impeded by the practical realities of human nature and the specific circumstances of music education. Taken alone, these pictures cannot suffice as a basis for music education. Yet it is important not to lose the best they have to offer. So, the challenge becomes one of determining how to apply them in ways that, insofar as possible, capture their ideals and avoid their pitfalls.

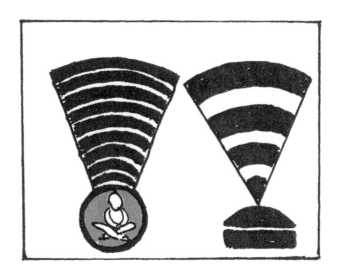

13
WEB AND CONNECTIVITY

At first glance, the *web* and *connectivity* pictures seem to be of recent vintage, but a closer look at them suggests that they may be older that we thought. These pictures impact education and music education in important ways. Ivan Illich is among the mid-twentieth-century writers to propose educational webs as a means of revolutionizing general education.[1] He envisages informally organized and operated networks or communities facilitated by the technologies already in place in his day. These would enable people with common interests to be matched, gain access to the knowledge they seek, and share their skills with others. Music teachers are often among the first to harness new technologies, whether instrumental innovations, publishing and distribution of music, or mass media. Early in the twentieth century, music teachers created music curricula based on new music recording technologies and developed approaches to make use of the player piano, music recordings, and the radio as means of music education.[2] In the present century, writers have reflected on and proposed approaches to the use of new technologies in music and music education.[3]

WEB

By web, I mean "a complex system of interconnected elements," such as a spider might construct to catch its prey. Walking in the woods, our path takes us beneath a spider's web. The threads are sticky; the web is a neatly woven, symmetrical, and artistically wrought trap. I wonder at the instinct and effort expended in order to spin this deadly device. Rather than a seemingly chaotic result of playful action, the spider's web has the more sinister if also essential purpose of entrapment and destruction. After all, this is the spider's means of finding its food, and without food, it cannot live. The web may be multiplied in networks of webs that spread across large areas and are destructive in their power.[4]

Even more compelling in today's technologically oriented world is the World Wide Web. In this web, technological advances enable the creation of interconnected information systems that permit communication from one part to another. At the beginning of the twentieth-first century, the internet was "a combination of library, gallery, recording studio, cinema, billboard, postal system, shopping arcade, timetable, bank, classroom, newspaper, and club bulletin" multiplied "by an indefinitely large number" over an "unlimited spread," and other possibilities as well.[5] Notwithstanding that this communication is grounded in physical linkages of one sort or another and enabled by scientific, mathematical, and technological principles, it constitutes a virtual or abstract world apart from the phenomenal world. This world seems not altogether unlike the cave in Plato's allegory—one that is separate from the world of ordinary appearances grasped by the senses of sight, smell, hearing, taste, and touch.[6] So compelling is this web that it seems as fully present as the physical world, even though it is distinct from it in another, separate realm of existence. Were Plato alive today, he might well use the internet and its related web—the "killer application" for the internet—as a means to illustrate the distinction between ordinary existence and the abstract and virtual reality of the mind and all that lies beyond the phenomenal world.[7]

In contrast to the chaos of a tangle, we think of the web as a system that is specifically designed for its purpose. In differentiating between a web and a tangle, I think of Snugglepot and Cuddlepie, twin sister tortoiseshell cats who have spent the evening transforming a neat ball of wool into a confused mass that stretches down the hallway.[8] Those who are familiar with young cats will understand the work involved in sorting out this tangle and returning the wool to anything approaching its original state. Since one strand is connected to all of the other parts, some shaking out of the mess may help. Knots have appeared and painstaking work is required to untangle the thread, follow it back to its source, and roll the wool back into a ball—so much work, in fact, that we may be tempted to simply provide this wool as a toy for these kitties and not bother trying to undo their play.

This resulting chaotic and confused tangle differs from the orderly way in which the spider spins its web and the architects of the World Wide Web construct a systematic means of communication. Even though the web may appear chaotic on first glance, as we look deeper, we discover purpose and order at work.

The independence of the web is evident in the languages and names invented to serve it, protocols constructed to facilitate communication among those who use it, systems of rules and laws devised by the individuals, groups, institutions, and societies that develop around it and are identified with and constrained by it. Virtual communities of people who may never have met face to face emerge, develop, mature, regress, and cease to be.[9] These social and cultural systems develop their own norms, expectations, beliefs, values, attitudes, and practices.

When the web first appeared in the West, spawned mainly in the military and the academy, it seemed to embody the ideal of a free-wheeling democratic society whose purpose was to develop and share information immediately and widely without the intervention of external agencies or controls. Cracks in this democratic culture quickly appeared as corporate power and control over the web grew and governments sought to block access to particular sites that were not, as they saw it, in the national interest. Its rapid growth necessitated the development of search engines, which became the means of filtering information and controlling access to it. The rise of advertisement and censorship on the part of commercial and political interests manipulated what had been designed as a free system of information exchange and began a process of mediamorphosis that transformed the web into a part of a mass-mediated information and entertainment industry including print publications, television, radio, phone and cable, film, and computer-generated media.[10] The entertainment and information industry became heavily centralized, controlled largely by a relatively few multinational corporations and distribution networks, licenses, and the like, as the largest and most powerful companies muscled out or absorbed the smaller enterprises that populated the web at outset.

From its inception, several values undergirded the web: internationalism, populism, communitarianism, virtuality, individualism, and technophilia.[11] Briefly stated, internationalism in the sense of "the principle of community of interests or action between different nations" stands for its tendency to foster cooperation between nation-states, even though in its global reach, such action may limit the prerogatives and even subvert the boundaries of nation-states.[12] Its technological means and ends permit participants to connect with like-minded others and form communities around the world beyond the power of nation-states to control. Populism, in the sense of representing "the interests of ordinary people," underscores the power of the people and a universalistic belief in the importance of wide access to education as to other aspects of culture, among other things, for all earthlings.[13] The system's many nodes and networks are designed to empower all of its members to directly communicate to others their ideas and practices.[14] Communitarianism, or the belief in the centrality of collective and egalitarian human association, belief, and action, is especially potent in the web's design and operation.[15] The web's interconnections permit groups of people to interact and it fosters, as it also reflects, collective action. These communities, or "milieu cultures," are predicated on the values of human interaction and association.[16] Virtuality refers to the value of a life lived beyond the physically observed world of ordinary existence that looks, as technology advances, more and more like the ordinary world.[17] Webophiles deem virtuality a good, because interactive media effectively interconnect people around the world in vital ways. Although individualism may seem antithetical to community, a closer examination reveals a dialectical, ironical, or even paradoxical situation. The web may alienate people from traditional communities in which they historically dwelt and empower them to form communities of their own choosing based on such factors as particular interests and geographical locations, thereby potentially subverting, fracturing, and fragmenting social affiliations in lived life. These networks are forged as instances of individual thought and action rather than, as often happens in ordinary life, by physical proximity, religious persuasion, or familial ties. Technophilia refers to the positive engagement with technology that depends on embracing the values of technological change and obsolescence.[18] As the virtual world of the web comes ever closer to ordinary lived experience, and appears ready to transcend it, the technical means of achieving these ends require constant replacement as better and more engaging interactions are found. Denizens of the web embrace these new developments and the power that they provide, even if there are not significant problems that these inventions are meant to remedy.[19]

The web works in virtual time and space, apart from and independent of the phenomenal world. We refer to "cyberspace"—in which we "*exist* and *act*" rather than simply "*observe.*"[20] This time and space is virtual, or psychologically apprehended, and is vital and distinct from the phenomenal world.[21] For example, educational applications of video-conferencing through cameras and microphones connected to computers allow people to see and hear each other even though they are located in different places and time zones. Websites have the aura of places that we may "visit" and access information, and "chat rooms" or "cafes" allow us to discuss matters of interest synchronously (either voice or text discussions in real time) or asynchronously (by posting messages that may be read by others and responded to at a later time). Some websites are set up to enable the disclosure of personal or confidential information as well as that intended for public consumption. Layers of security control access to these environments. The technology that allows, facilitates, and constricts this access is all but invisible in a virtual world that is visually and aurally appealing and accessed through such senses as touch, sight, and sound.

This world's ease of access, effortlessness, and speed are among its most seductive features. As time has gone by, the web has become more "user friendly," intuitive in its operation, and even affective in its use of symbols of human sensitivity and friendliness. Websites welcome us by name, presenting lists of things that we might find useful in the future; and should we require assistance, helpful people stand ready to guide us and respond to our questions. That these people may be virtual rather than real, and this seeming friendliness technologically derived and automatically generated, may escape our notice. We also expect instantaneous gratification of our wishes and that our questions will be answered immediately and satisfactorily.

All of this communication seems vital because it takes on aspects of face-to-face communication in the phenomenal world—so compelling and seemingly safe that some may disclose more information about themselves in their web conversations than they might divulge in face-to-face conversations with people in their ordinary lived lives. This reality is not an unmixed blessing. Although it can facilitate the forming of personal relationships, it also renders the internet a particularly potent weapon for those who prey on others by hiding behind masks, fraudulently misrepresenting themselves, tricking others into self-disclosures that can be used against them, and stealing their personal information. The rapidly increasing amounts of information stored on the web and growing numbers of people using and dependent on it render the web an important center of criminal activity and a source of surveillance by representatives of societal institutions.

The pervasive surveillance is almost invisible to many people on the web who unwittingly leave behind permanent electronic trails. Buried sometimes deep beneath the surface, a record may be kept of one's every move on the web. This trail can be mined for personal information that can then be used by powerful others. Surveillance also renders web participants' actions public and accountable rather than private and confidential and provides a clear record that can be employed by others for invasive and sometimes sinister purposes.

The web relies upon communication, information exchange, and connections between individuals and groups. The social character of these networks is facilitated by mathematical algorithms. Rather than offering a direct, unfiltered interaction between people in the phenomenal world, technology serves as a filter or buffer between people. The algorithms by which communication proceeds determine the character of possible interactions. Participating in these virtual communities can also impact the nature of the interactions between people in the physical world. Particular forms of discourse and information are available by virtue of the web's influence. For example, certain means of musical experience beyond "live" music making and taking are available by virtue of thinking of music in terms of downloadable electronic files that can be accessed free of charge or for a fee. In this environment, people may be rendered more isolated from others, without the demands, expectations, and constraints of ordinary physical human interaction in the lived world.

The sheer amount of information available with such apparent ease and speed can evoke a sense of wonder and awe. To be able to see and hear things, even virtually, that otherwise would lie beyond ordinary lived experience can engender reverence for the power of this technology, the possibilities that it offers, and the widespread availability of information heretofore restricted to face-to-face human communication. For musicians, to see, hear, and participate in musical performances with those who are remote from us, in the remarkable clarity that is now possible, is to wonder at the power of the human intellect to devise such things (and yet this is quickly taken for granted). There are many possibilities for the good that these technologies might do, notwithstanding the dangers they also pose.

The web builds on, as it also transforms, the nature of the human impulse to communicate with others and form friendship groups, organizations, and societal institutions. From antiquity, whether it be extended family groups, clans, tribes, towns, cities, or states, humans have created communication networks or webs of information exchange. Gossip, rumor, and news have passed through these connections from time immemorial. While today's web has a special character that is influenced and mediated by technology, it is also rooted in the perennial human information exchange.

In thinking about the web, I want to avoid the extremes of "neo-Luddism"—the tendency to repudiate technology and its influence—on the one hand, and "technophilism"—or an enthusiastic and uncritical belief in the advantages of technology—on the other.[22] Steering such a middle course allows us to see benefits and detractions of this metaphor and its associated model for music education. As I write, such is the importance of these pictures that they may well constitute an important means whereby "spheres of musical validity" are formed. By spheres of validity, I mean that musical groups coalesce around particular beliefs and practices under the aegis of such societal institutions such as the family, religion, music profession, and politics.[23]

Whether it be the spider's web or the World Wide Web, the notion of *web* is construed ambiguously, both literally in the phenomenal world and figuratively in psychologically perceived time and space. It can be seen from a variety of perspectives and in many different particular ways; it is rooted in the past while also forward-looking. As with other pictures in this gallery, there are various possibilities for music education. We now turn to a description of a model spawned by this metaphor to see what we can see.

CONNECTIVITY

By connectivity, I refer to "the state or extent of being connected," "conjoined; fastened or linked together," in the technological sense of the intersection of computing "platforms, systems, and applications" and the dynamic process of connection and interconnection.[24] Connection refers to "a personal relation of intercourse, intimacy, common interest, or action" or "a body, or circle of persons connected together, or with whom one is connected, by political or religious ties, or by commercial relations." For example, there is "a body of fellow-worshippers, of political sympathizers, a circle of clients, customers, who share common ties."[25] Whether contacts between people, or the points of contacts, meeting points between two systems—for example, transportation nodes and networks or the virtual connections possible in the web—intersections, interrelationships, and contacts are central to this model and the means whereby it operates. It is construed ambiguously: statically as product or state of being, and dynamically as a process of becoming, literally and figuratively. The possibilities of the web for music education are evident in such things as electronic journals, online research communities, the use of interactive technologies in music teaching, distance learning initiatives, and web-based programs of music education.[26] Although the pace of technological change may quickly render present realities obsolete, enough is known to imagine how this model may work at least for the foreseeable future.[27]

Music. New types of musical experiences and musical communities form through technological means. Music is now envisaged virtually, as video and sonic recordings that are electronically and digitally mediated and downloaded as files on a variety of technological devices. The sights and sounds so communicated are experienced intuitively, subjectively, sensually, and immanently. Rather than transcendent and spiritual realities that are known intellectually, music is immanent, or heard "within" oneself as subject rather than "without" as object. The experience of listening through earpieces brings the music close to the self rather than keeping it at a psychic distance. Sound is self-selectively intense in that listeners, composers, or performers can set its volume at whatever level suits their individual preferences. Pitches, timbres, and visual images are among the aspects that can be manipulated to personalize the experience. Digitizing music potentially changes recorded musical sounds, rendering them different from analog recordings and live performances. This manipulation of sounds thereby potentially transforms live music making, as it also permits new forms of musical experience reliant on these technologies.[28] Audiovisual recordings broaden musical experience beyond the purely sonic to encompass its visual and other sensory aspects as well.[29] These technologies help to forge new musical identities and communities comprising musicians and their publics who may be physically separated in time and space.[30] Collaborations between musicians or between teachers and students can broaden, alter the musical communities in which musicians live and work, and render them less time- or place-bound. The ontological status of music metamorphoses from a social event with live musicians making music in a particular time and place to electronic files that may be listened to quite apart from the presence of live acoustic musicians, instruments, and audiences.

Musicians are also empowered to directly control musical production, transmission, and consumption and to compose, perform, and produce music of their own choice. This possibility challenges the power of patrons, impresarios, managers, and others who may seek to control all aspects of the production and distribution of music. In modern times, multinational corporations have come to control much of the "music industry" through an array of means such as corporate power structures, interlocking directorships, distribution arrangements, and marketing and advertising strategies that diminish the control musicians have over the music that they perform and the financial returns they receive for their work.[31] Connectivity allows musicians to bypass this system and take their work directly to their public, creating milieu cultures that enable them to have more control over what they perform and how.[32] Even though increasing corporate and political among other interests are intent on curbing their independence, and connections with the most powerful corporate interests in the musical world may be advantageous, still, musicians are enabled to bypass these traditional agencies in important ways.

Teaching in connectivity mode broadens beyond instructional situations that require teachers' physical presence to those in which students in other places can access their instruction through technological means. Its purpose is often expressly intellectual. The virtuality of this experience renders the situation engaging and "like the real thing" in terms of being physically present with a teacher or student. From the teacher's point of view, one may clearly see and hear one's students in real time or asynchronously, directly or through audiovisual recordings; one may hear their compositions, improvisations, or performances, and treat them as if they were here in this particular place. Teaching is conceived in the more limited terms of doing the work of instruction than the more ambiguous and broad terms of living a life that is shared more fully with one's students. Teachers show as well as tell the student what to do in communicating propositional and procedural knowledge about music. Teaching techniques such as synchronous discussions with students or live teaching segments in real time often emphasize formal instruction, although these approaches can also be complemented by asynchronous conversations or demonstrations across times in which teacher and student need not be present simultaneously but may post messages or files for the other to see later.[33] When teaching is entirely virtual, it is also necessary to maintain regular contact with students who (like the teacher) can be distracted by the immediate and pressing claims of ordinary life.

The roles that teachers take on in the learning webs are more like "custodians, museum guides, or reference librarians" who point to where information may be found.[34] The openness of the web to multitudinous, not necessarily authoritative, and often uncensored postings allows the spread of misinformation, propaganda, and even violence just as it also can purvey information and even wisdom. Like the guide, teachers formally and informally help students to negotiate cyberspace safely and successfully, think critically, and evaluate the value of the available information.[35] Teachers and students come together informally or are brought together formally around shared interests. Rather than based on credentialing of knowledge learned in the midst of certified institutionally approved and accredited programs, teachers' qualifications are principally defined by what they know and can do. As a result they are expected to provide "skill models," and their skills matter more than their educational pedigrees.[36] Their competence is assessed in terms of their ability to "create and operate" the kinds of "educational exchanges and networks"; to "guide students and parents in the use of these networks"; and to "act as *primus inter pares* in undertaking difficult intellectual exploratory journeys."[37] The formal "master–disciple relationship" is "priceless" in helping students to master skills.[38] It can be found alongside informal education, in which teacher and student may be peers, the roles of teacher and student may be interchangeable, and the teacher is defined as the one in possession of knowledge of skills that another, the student, seeks to possess.

Learning relies on virtual interpersonal connections between teachers and students. Students can learn from teachers formally, and access information through technical means informally, that would be unavailable were they restricted to learning from a particular teacher in a particular time and place. As information can also be accessed hypertextually, that is, one can enter or leave the material at differing points, learning can be individualized, serendipitous, and intrinsically motivating.[39] This learning also results in disparate outcomes as learners pursue material of most immediate interest. Although it may occur in the midst of interaction with others in the lived world, proponents of connectivity see learning as ultimately an individual and solitary experience that is cognitive, affective, and psychomotor. Students' engagement with subject matter in the process of coming to know it is what is at most issue in connectivity learning. True, ideas and practices may suggest themselves to a person in the midst of conversations with others, but without this individual engagement, learning would not necessarily occur. There may be more risk-taking by learners in dealing with others in virtual classrooms than in face-to-face instructional situations. When people do not expect to physically meet or relate with others in a virtual classroom on an extended basis, they may be blunter in their comments and less concerned about what others may think of them. They may be more apt to try out difficult things because their classmates are not part of their ordinary social circle, and thus their social standing is less impacted by what these others think about and how they act toward them. Inhibitions created by social pressures in ordinary life may be less constricting in the virtual classroom. Written words sometimes have a more powerful impact and cut more deeply, provoking more extreme reactions, than words spoken in face-to-face communication.

Aside from formal learning that is planned and undertaken systematically, informal learning, unplanned, serendipitous, and sometimes within the context of activities that are not intentionally pedagogical, is also important.[40] The student's desire for knowledge constitutes the principal impetus for learning. In "publicly prescribed learning," there is an exploitative "attempt to produce specified behavioral changes which can be measured and for which the processor can be held accountable"; this results in "the pacification of the new generation within specifically engineered enclaves which will seduce them into the dream world of their elders."[41] In contrast to this approach, students in the connectivity model are liberated to follow their own interests and talents. Such learning is primarily casual, often a "by-product of some other activity," and "even most intentional learning is not the result of programmed instruction."[42] Still, formal learning has a crucial role to play in the new educational institutions that would be created to foster lifelong learning for everyone whether informal or formal.

The "virtual" nature of learning in connectivity means that students learn what such-and-such is like.[43] This is learning "of a sort" that cannot be equated with physical experience of the thing in question. To watch a picture of a musical instrument with which one is unfamiliar is not to hold it in one's hands, feel the weight of it, pluck its strings, grasp a mallet to hit a percussion instrument, finger its valves, press one's fingers in its holes, or create a sound by blowing into it. One may come close to these realities and possess propositional knowledge about what it is like to do these things, but there is nothing like feeling this viscerally through actually physically engaging with the instrument.[44] Such learning may have other values. When experience is virtual or "as if" it were lived experience in the phenomenal world, learners gain insights into matters that would otherwise be outside their horizons of understanding. They may never be able to travel physically to a particular place or meet these musicians face to face, but they can understand more clearly what those musics may be like. Learners are able to empathize more readily with different others, and new modes of knowing or literacies are potentially opened that require interrogation.[45] Viewing technologically mediated learning as deficient in some ways and only ever approaching learning in the context of normative face-to-face instruction fails to grasp the different qualities of virtual and face-to-face learning and the possibilities that in certain respects, at least, this learning may transcend that in face-to-face situations. Virtual learning, or coming to know what something is like, may be a vivid, intense, and utterly engrossing experience that transcends ordinary existence and prompts learning that might not otherwise take place without technological mediation.[46]

Instruction is enabled through an array of technologies that permit vivid audio-visual and interactive experiences of subject matter by teachers and students who choose to engage with each other virtually in cyberspace. Personal interaction is mediated technologically rather than directly experienced as in lived life.[47] The authenticity, trust, and selflessness that undergirds community-style instruction cannot be relied upon in the mode of connectivity. Rather, participants may need to rely on more limited and unverifiable verbal and nonverbal cues and gestures than those commonly evident in face-to-face interaction. Although technology increasingly approaches the vibrancy and emotional valence of face-to-face engagement of teachers and students, it may be employed to attractively prepackage material for presentation to students in standardized ways and thereby effectively silence teacher and student interaction. If created by "experts" in the field, such packages may limit teacher interactions with students to assessments of student work rather than designing and implementing the whole interactive process. Since assessment is facilitated by the public and the electronically verifiable nature of online interaction between teachers and their students, it may be tempting to use these tools to gather a wide array of information, whether or not such information is essential to instruction. Teachers' ability to exercise professional judgments in matters of instructional design and evaluation, or students' willingness to take risks in an atmosphere of continuing surveillance, may be restricted. The use of prepackaged presentations and reliance on "teacher-proof" instructional approaches seem akin to the production or consumption models in restricting a two-way dialogue between teacher and student.

The construction of webs that bring together teacher and student around common interests and proclivities impacts the nature of personal experiences and social interactions. Shared interests and the student's desire to master particular skills or access certain knowledge create an instructional situation where both teacher and student have choice.[48] I have hypothesized that matching teachers and students affords some of the most productive teaching and learning and is possibly optimal for music education. In informal situations of peer-to-peer instruction, the personal interrelationship is bound to be fairly egalitarian of a sort encountered in community, whereas in formal instruction involving, say, a skilled exponent and neophyte, the personal engagement of teacher and student may take on a character not unlike that in pedagogy instruction.

Although mediated technologically, the interaction between teachers and students need be no less compelling than in face-to-face situations. Formal and informal instruction may be transformative as participants are prompted to think, act, and be in new or different ways through an array of conversations, presentations, and performances. It is also possible that a sense of community may emerge, permitting extended dialogues among teachers and their students to spill over beyond formal instruction into other times, between individual and group lessons, and profoundly impact their lived lives. The extended conversations that are possible in "times between" formal instruction can help to solidify personal bonds between participants as they become better acquainted with each other; they can also help to develop a collective sense of shared purposes and interests, an *esprit de corps* among the participants, and a sense of group identity.[49]

Curriculum is also mediated technologically and virtually; teachers and students can access people, instruments, instructional materials, information, and interactive experiences that appeal vitally to the imagination and take advantage of individual teacher and student interests.[50] The design of the curriculum is crucially important and the particular limitations inbuilt in the technologies determine how teachers and learners access the material of instruction. It is likely that teams of teachers and technologists design the curriculum, although crucial decision-making is delegated to technological specialists who gain increased power in the process by virtue of the central role technology plays. Those teachers who possess technological expertise may be intimately involved in the design process, while those without this expertise may be relegated to the role of technicians, using pre-packaged material they are provided by others. Alternately, they may serve as consultants or moderators of the activities generated within the strictures of already designed and inflexible programs. Whereas a teacher in a face-to-face situation may improvise freely and change course midway through the instruction in an organic and thoughtful process, technologically mediated curricula need to be designed before instruction begins, set up, tested, and debugged over time. They can, at present writing, only approach the nimbleness and facility of teacher's ongoing judgments and decisions about how to engage these students in music making and taking.[51] In hypertextual and other dynamic curricular approaches, the freedom of teachers and learners to engage subject matter differently and on their own terms is somewhat illusory, because mathematical algorithms and other technological assumptions constrict these possibilities and are planned for ahead of time.

This curriculum may also be particularly suited to the development of specific skills. Its openness and open-endedness with regard to the individual backgrounds and interests of lifelong learners and their different educational objectives necessitate that students have the tools to navigate a plethora of possibilities and are in the position to be able to take advantage of them fully. To this end, networks offer reference services to particular educational objects and people, skill exchanges, and peer matching opportunities. People are able to find and access information and skills unhindered by their past educational backgrounds.[52] Procedural knowledge has a central role in the curriculum as a means whereby learners can traverse these networks. More than memorizing or regurgitating prescribed information, students learn where knowledge may be found and pursue those things that are of interest to them. Self-designed programs of study are particularly appropriate for, and mediated by, technologies that foster learners' independence and cater to their particular interests and proclivities. Connectivity permits individually tailored programs of study that are constructed by learners around their previous experiences.[53] The ready availability of information removes some of the drudgery involved in simply locating and procuring it, freeing teachers and students to focus on more substantive matters. Certain musical skills, such as ear training and sight singing, can be developed effectively through technologically mediated drills. Relegating repetitive exercises and drills to technologically mediated instruction can allow teachers and students to focus on more complex and advanced thought and action.

Administration in the connectivity model is no longer place-bound, but it requires particular organizational arrangements that operate in cyberspace as well as in the phenomenal world. Virtual entities foster collaborations between people in different places and institutions, and challenge the predominance of face-to-face educational organizations.[54] In a visionary statement of connectivity and a radical departure from traditional schooling, Illich advocates the end of obligatory schooling and public support for the "huge professional apparatus of education," the dismantling of traditional schools, and their replacement with new educational institutions based on "learning" webs, "opportunity" webs, or "networks" that might promote access to knowledge for everyone who seeks it.[55] Illich sees these new educational institutions as a "formal" means of education and the "inverse" of schooling as carried on in his day that might seem, on the face of things, to be antithetical to public education.[56] For him, technology offers a means to make "free speech, free assembly, and free press truly universal and fully educational," and develop "independence and learning or bureaucracy and teaching."[57] It can be harnessed as a means of liberating learning and providing the learner "with new links to the world instead of continuing to funnel all educational programs through the teacher."[58] These educational webs can take advantage of learners' desires to learn at every stage of life, democratize and humanize education, and "heighten the opportunity for each one to transform each moment of his [or her] living into one of living, sharing, and caring."[59]

Among the administrative skills required in the connectivity model, Illich notes that it is necessary to build and maintain the "roads providing access to resources," which can be taken figuratively and literally to describe a smooth and accessible network permitting the free flow of information all across it. Leaders with such skills demonstrate "genius at keeping themselves out of people's way" and "facilitating encounters among students, skill models, educational leaders, and educational objects."[60] When the system does not work well, a special class of administrators responsible for technical design, maintenance, and repair is required to unclog the roadblocks, build new roads, or repair those worn out with constant use. Laws and policies enacted to forbid discrimination against all those within and without the educational system require that administrators attend not only to the particulars of their own networks but to the wider societal and political realities in which they operate. To this end, their work is devoted to liberatory ends.[61] Cultivating group morale and a sense of *esprit de corps* are especially important in heterogeneous and fluid organizations where participants may work independently and alone rather than face-to-face, and where they need to feel valued and a part of the organization's work.[62] Given the public nature of technologically mediated education and the availability of tools already at hand, administrators may monitor teachers, students, and staff, if for no other reason than these tools are available. The digitizing of information puts a plethora of data at administrators' fingertips, and quantifying it is likewise a tempting option, especially when driven by fiscal imperatives.[63] Interpreting these data is an important challenge in an environment in which so much information is available.

The claims of change and obsolescence challenge traditional ideas and foster a forward-looking approach throughout the organization. Flexibility, nimbleness, creativity, technical savvy, self-reliance, cooperativeness, and independent-mindedness are among the qualities required by administrators and policy makers if they are to survive and thrive in uncertain and changing environments. Although change may be a constant at the present time, this may not always be the case; transformative inventions have a way of settling into more stable circumstances as beliefs and practices become standardized and expectations more solidified. Still, it is in the nature of technological invention to create new ideas and practices and to spawn unexpected consequences. It is unclear if or when the present change in today's world will result in a less frenetic pattern of change in the future.

CRITIQUE

What are the musical advantages and disadvantages of connectivity? Among the advantages of technologically mediated music, it is possible for musicians to collaborate who might otherwise not be able to meet or work together. The potentially international perspectives on music possible through the web widen musical horizons and make possible changes in musical traditions as one comes in contact with another. Beyond the limitations of live performance in a particular place, people in different places can participate in these musics as composers, improvisers, performers, listeners, and producers, and these intersections may speed up the pace of change in musical traditions. Such changes can enliven traditions that might otherwise become stultified or fossilized by ensuring that they bump up against other, different traditions. Technological innovations also remove some of the barriers to featuring new compositions, improvisations, and performances, especially in those traditions in which a wealth of already composed music might otherwise squeeze out the possibilities to make and take new repertoire. Audiovisual technologies make music that can be both seen and heard more widely accessible, and the lifelike quality of some technologies allow those who cannot otherwise be present when this music is made to feel as if they are there. Music is released from its time-boundedness in order to be seen and heard in other times, beyond those of the musicians who make it and the audiences who take it. Recordings preserve musical traditions for future generations to study, even if the artists themselves are unable to pass them on, and these realities reduce the fragility of otherwise oral traditions, enable them to become more robust, and alter the nature of musical authority.[64] As the musical horizons of those who participate in and hear them are broadened, cosmopolitan musical understandings are cultivated.

Nevertheless, among its disadvantages, conceiving music as electronically generated sights and sounds may undermine live acoustic music making and taking and decontextualize music from the particular circumstances of its creation. Immortalizing musicians by playing video and audio recordings of their compositions and performances long after their death brings the past to life, but in the process can blur the passage of time, mythologizing people and their music that might otherwise grow more obscure. Cluttering today's music making and taking with the music of the past potentially makes less space and time for today's musical creations. Thinking of music virtually rather than actually and emphasizing mediated rather than direct musical experience, or what music is like rather than what it is, can leave people one remove from immediate apprehension. The indirectness or mediation of the virtual experience, while approaching the phenomenal world, may be impoverished at least in certain respects. The prevalence of recorded music may contribute to repeating, devaluing, objectifying, and commodifying music, robbing it of its immediacy, freshness, and vitality and altering the performance practice of a tradition.[65]

Teaching is potentially enriched by such things as the collaborations of teachers with technological experts who can broaden the teacher's reach beyond face-to-face experiences. In the best circumstances, these experts can provide vivid experiences that can complement if also replace aspects of a teacher's work. Recorded examples in vivid color and sound can enhance the teacher's explanations, bringing alive things that would otherwise be beyond a student's understanding and demonstrating how things should or could be done. Web-based drills and exercises can relieve teachers of much of the more mundane and repetitive work in order to focus on aspects that can motivate students and provide greater depth of understanding. Interactive devices can provide ways of allowing teachers to take advantage of student interests and individualize instruction even when teaching groups of students. Increasing the number of teachers by involving others in instruction may also broaden any one teacher's appeal and reveal different points of view and approaches among which students may choose.

Among its flaws, where teachers do not possess the requisite technological skills or are excluded from the process of curriculum design by corporate control of technological resources, it is possible that teachers may be marginalized and disempowered, restricted to a limited array of instructional responsibilities. When teachers must teach curricula developed by others, instead of being able to exercise their professional judgments over the entire process of curriculum design and its implementation, they are only able to impact how particular subject matter is dealt with within stringent guidelines; they can serve only consultative and mentoring roles or as technicians who employ the devices of others. In such circumstances, teachers do not have the same range of choices as they might have in face-to-face and unmediated instructional situations. Rather than being close to their students or living with them over an extended time, and thereby conveying a way of life as well as information and wisdom, teachers are envisaged merely as conduits of information within the context of limited instructional contexts. When the teacher's range of instructional decision making is severely limited, there is potentially less personal satisfaction from doing one's work and exercising one's professional judgments.

On the bright side, learning what something is like can help access a broader array of experiences than those possible in face-to-face "live" instruction. This sort of virtual learning can transcend humdrum or ordinary lived learning. Since it exists in cyberspace, it may appeal especially to those people who might otherwise be ostracized or marginalized in the lived world.[66] This learning may be particularly attractive to adult learners with family and work obligations who are unable or unwilling to study at brick-and-mortar institutions. Since learning can be individualized, students are able to learn at their own pace, in their own ways, and at times of their own choosing, thereby contributing to their intrinsic motivation. Through taking account of their interests, dispositions, desires, and needs, this learning can also be humane. Virtual learning enables people to try out something without actually impacting the lived world and can provide a useful stage in learning before performing in the phenomenal, world where actions may be more consequential and effects more lasting.

On the dark side, learning may be circumscribed. Since much of the instructional program needs to be preplanned, there is less freedom to accommodate student input into the process, even when individualized learning is ostensibly the objective. So much information is available that learners may be afflicted by information overload, and they may have insufficient time and energy to absorb the plethora of available information. Freedom of choice on the learner's part may also be illusory, especially when learning is mediated and constricted by the prior choices of technologists who ultimately control the parameters and the avenues whereby learning is fostered. Technologies open many potential if also seductive avenues for learners to explore, and teachers and their students may become distracted by these possibilities. The sheer plethora of possibilities may cause them to be become uncertain, confused, frustrated, and immobilized into inaction. Those learners who are more comfortable with directive and restricted approaches may also find this open and rhapsodic learning to be counterproductive. Also, the focus on individual learning may overlook the opportunities for social interactions with other teachers and students and the imperatives of socializing learners for the lived world in which face-to-face relationships are important. When used in conjunction with face-to-face instruction, learners may be distracted by the technology and pay less attention to the class instruction as they multitask.

The positive possibilities of instruction are compelling. Providing opportunities for student-teacher interaction that transcend a particular time and place potentially broaden and enrich instructional means and ends. Carefully preplanning and designing instruction beforehand enables consideration of possibilities and choices of strategies that directly meet the needs and interests of teachers and their students. Where teachers and students are intimately involved in instructional design, technologies can be developed that may intensify their interaction and make it more enjoyable and meaningful. Recognizing the limitations and fallibility of any individual teacher or student, technologies can help diminish errors or mistakes that might otherwise be made. If a teacher errs in providing incorrect information or does not know the answer to a particular question, help is immediately available through means of search engines and databases. The availability of technologically mediated resources allows teachers and students to focus on important questions for which answers may not be immediately available. The technologically generated interactive possibilities for teachers and students permit lively exchanges that help to bring alive the subject under study. Virtual and potentially transformative communities emerge from the interaction of teachers and students in cyberspace.

Among the detractions of instruction in conditions of connectivity, the technological mediation of personal interactions between teachers and students may militate against authentic relationships, and the public nature of the communication may cause them to be wary and unwilling to participate fully in the process. When participants may be masked and not fully present to others, it is difficult to imagine how it would be possible to create transformative communities in the lived world. Trust, mutual respect, and regard can only be built up among all of the participants in the instructional situation when participants are authentically and fully present to one another.[67] The formal and constricted scope of instruction can limit the extent to which teachers and students spend time together and the range of activities in which they can participate. Where instruction is entirely virtual, something of the urgency of ongoing personal interaction may be lost; it is easy to become preoccupied with other pressing aspects of lived life and lose touch with the instruction at hand. Even in face-to-face settings, participants can be so distracted by technology that they interact less with others in the class.[68]

Curriculum in connectivity mode has several advantages. The scope of study is broadened to foster international understandings that go beyond those gained from a particular person in a place or time. Instructional materials may be constantly updated and made relevant to students while also presented in compelling and dynamic ways. Approaches to the subject matter can be individualized and carefully interrogated ahead of instruction to take advantage of a wider array of expertise than any one teacher might possess. Teachers and students can enter into or leave the subject matter in their own ways and at their own times. The curriculum's results are potentially divergent as students follow their own interests and construct their own understandings.

Among its disadvantages, where the acquisition of information for information's sake constitutes the centerpiece of curriculum, the wisdom that comes from prioritizing and integrating knowledge is bypassed, and the curriculum can focus on trivial matters and the acquisition of technical skills. Failing to employ sufficiently the evident possibilities of learner-constructed knowledge, and failing to see the curriculum as a dynamic process whereby learners interact with others and with the subject matter, can produce a traditional top-down "banking" education. This approach emphasizes traditional knowledge determined by experts and passed on to students who receive knowledge as passive vessels. The constant press for change and development of new technologies whereby new experiences are fostered may also devalue the traditions of the past. Failing to see the important distinctions between the virtual world of cyberspace and the ordinary lived world, and confusing the learning of what something is like with direct experience of it, may leave students in the predicament of Plato's cave. They may imagine that they are experiencing all that there is while failing to grasp the limitations of this world or understanding the value of other rich experiences in the phenomenal world. In confusing fact and fancy, teachers and their students may overlook the value of carefully distinguishing virtual and lived experience.

Administration has the potential benefits of nimble, flexible, and virtual organizational systems and procedures designed expressly for cyberspace. Since these structures may be flatter and more egalitarian, they can foster the active participation of all those involved in the process, thereby giving them a voice in what should be said and done. This empowerment of all participants can lead to higher morale and happiness within the educational process than is the case when people feel powerless to affect the circumstances in which they teach and learn. In a lived world in which assessment and evaluation are particularly important, the ready accessibility of a wide array of data and procedures for their interpretation can be a boon to policy makers charged with determining and justifying the course of music educational policy and practice.

Still, administration in this model has a dark side. Connectivity potentially widens the gap between those who have access to technologies and are educated regarding them and those who do not. Technological access is often a matter of education and wealth, and so those who are literate and economically favored may be advantaged over those who are illiterate and poor. Without social policies directed toward ameliorating these problems, it seems likely that a technologically mediated music education would exacerbate these gaps and fissures and thereby contribute to even greater inequities of the technology gap. Having the tools to monitor and evaluate the activities of teachers and their students in cyberspace may foster a preoccupation with evaluation that detracts from teaching, learning, and instruction. Evaluation may become so important as to drive music educational policy making, causing it to become inhumane and lose focus on the people involved. Where corporate values and top-down, bottom-line, and fiscally driven thought and practice dominate technologically mediated music education, organizations may become excessively hierarchical, authoritarian, and unresponsive to changes in their environments, tending to exclude the ideas and practices of different others. As in the production and consumption models, administration may brook little dissent or freedom of expression, monitor the organization's members, and fail to protect personal privacy. Thus, hoped-for democratic means and ends may not prevail.

SUMMARY

The pictures of web-connectivity offer a rich array of possibilities that are ambiguous, literal and figurative, and suggestive of particular ways of thinking, doing, and being in music education as in other aspects of lived life. Beyond the evocative metaphor of the web, aspects of music, teaching, learning, instruction, curriculum, and administration have bright and dark sides. On the bright side, there are possibilities for widening and changing musics that are less time- and space-bound, collaborative teaching, virtual and life long learning, intensified instruction, broader curricula, and administrative flexibility. On the dark side, acoustic and live musical experience may be undermined, teachers' freedom restricted, learning stultified, instruction rendered inauthentic, and information acquisition and assessment overemphasized. Given these possibilities, should we wish to rescue the best aspects while avoiding the worst, it is important to weigh the possibilities of these pictures for our individual lived situations and determine how we should move forward in the future. This may be simple in principle but it is not necessarily easy to do in practice.[69]

14

PICTURE AND PRACTICE

We come, now, to all-important questions concerning how these pictures of music education relate to its theory and practice. Unpacking these questions entails examining the implications for music educational theory of the metaphors and models, respectively, which in turn invites discussing the qualities of thought that are required in applying this approach to music educational practice and listing several questions that remain for the future. Stepping back from the individual pictures in order to view the gallery as a whole reveals how comparative approaches of this sort address persistent and important questions in music education and raise others for our contemplation. They provide openings that enrich our view of music education and are helpful practically, as we work through challenges in our lived lives as music teachers, students, and those interested in music education. They also disturb or unsettle matters that are taken for granted, and suggest rethinking and reconstructing music educational thought and practice.

It is tempting to leave these pictures be, ambiguous as they are, and simply plump for an indeterminate solution that requires teachers to individually examine them and act according to their best lights. The variety of pictures, with their differing strengths and weaknesses, complicates the task of music education and suggests a multiplicity of possible ends and means in its work. Their subjective appeal implies ambiguity and indeterminacy in the sense that no one set of pictures suffices; music education is ongoing within the frame of various pictures—metaphors and models. The selectivity of these pictures also suggests the possibility of others that are not described and examined here. This open system suggests incompleteness and fallibility, so that we cannot expect to find a single and final answer to the questions posed.

Nevertheless, music education is carried on in the phenomenal world and is often a matter of public policy. A practitioner (or theorist for that matter) rightly wants to know how such a nebulous and complicated view can be helpful to music educational practice. We arrive at something approaching wisdom at the place where the one and the many comprise a unity, at least for certain tenuous and practical purposes, and it is this broad grasp of these pictures that I now seek.[1] There is no happy reconciliation of all differences, no resolution of all ambiguities, or the requirement that we then know all that we need to know. Rather, working our way through the evident paradoxes, ironies, tensions, conflicts, surprises, resonances, and possibilities in this gallery, we have at least some answers to some of the questions, further questions to ask for the future, and suggestions of practical ways in which we may go about addressing them. So we now examine the gallery as a whole, first regarding the metaphors and then the models.

IMPLICATIONS OF THE METAPHORS

The pictures I have discussed fall into various categories. There are the most obvious categories of places and people. Eight metaphors concern places: the boutique, village, factory, garden, court, seashore, home, and web; four depict persons and their respective roles: the artist, revolutionary, therapist, and guide. They also represent a variety of institutions and natural environments, although these overlap one with another and their institutional affiliations or associations are not always clear-cut.[2] What is particularly interesting about this gallery is the breadth and variety of instances of music education expressed in and encompassed not only by publicly supported music education but by lifelong music education in other societal institutions and natural settings.

Examining the values that are implicated in the metaphors and that underlie practices in each of these pictures, it is interesting to group these metaphors institutionally. Here, it is clear how institutional values are reflected in music educational ideas and practices. To begin with commerce, we see two different pictures portrayed, in the boutique and the factory. The boutique features such values as specialization, service, efficiency, competition, commodification, differentiation, and fashion or sensuous appeal to clients or customers. The factory values standardization, objectification, commodification, competition, predictability, efficiency, functionality, and mechanization. Notice the similarities in such values as commodification, competition, and efficiency. Still, whereas the boutique values differentiation, the factory values standardization and predictability. These values are not of equal worth, and some drive others. Thus, for example, efficiency is the most compelling value because the objective of companies is to make a profit, and if not a profit (in the case of not-for-profit corporations), at least to break even and be accountable and transparent to shareholders in the enterprise.

Metaphors that are rooted particularly in the family are seen in the home and the garden. In the case of the home, particularity in being time- and place-bound, domesticity, informality, love, idealism, spirituality, caring, happiness, play, work, and fidelity are of especial importance, while in the garden, values of naturalism, formality, informality, caring, experience, growth, and particularity play out both similarly to and differently from those in the family. Caring and informality are evident in both metaphors, although their tenor, application, and influence are quite different when combined with other values. There are the evident tensions among some values—for example, in the garden's formality and informality.

Differing professional interests in music education in this gallery are found in the metaphors of the artist and guide. Of all the metaphors, these are probably the most obvious and least surprising, and the most likely to have been frozen or literalized in music education. I seek to infuse new life into considerations of the artist and distinguish it from its corresponding model of apprenticeship, just as I wish to rethink the guide in distinction to its corresponding model of pedagogy—a model that I want to reinvigorate. For the artist, aesthetic and artistic values are complemented by those of inspiration, discipline, practice, self-expression, idealization, canonization, esotericism, elitism, caring, and virtuosity. For the guide, a different array of values is implicated, including pluralism, practicality, pleasure, specialization, clarity, innovation, communication, serendipity, dialogue, and sensation. The one is more focused on music making and taking, and the other on the process whereby musicians are formed; the one is more focused on specified ends in view and the other on the open-ended construction and discovery of knowledge for oneself.

Two contrasting instances of politics reveal themselves in the village and the revolutionary metaphors. In the village we see such values as caring, exclusivity, inclusivity, dialogue, equality, freedom, romanticism, nostalgia, tradition, simplicity, and identity, whereas the revolutionary represents values of violence, dislocation, transformation, utilitarianism, holism, dialogue, heroism, evangelicalism, freedom, resistance, and praxis (construed as theory and practice or arousing conscience to action).[3] Here the differences between the two images are quite striking—the one embracing tradition, and the other resistance to and transformation of it. Despite these differences, common values of freedom and dialogue are evident in both metaphors. Again, tensions between values are evident, for example in the inclusivity and exclusivity of the village—inclusivity in the sense that different others within the village may be included while at the same time excluding others outside its boundaries in order to preserve its identity.

Other social institutions representing areas of health, law, technology, and environmental policy are also represented in the gallery. Here, I cite the metaphors of the therapist, courtroom, web, and seashore, respectively. The therapist exemplifies such values as healing and well-being, holism, ritual, caring, spirituality, expertise, observation, scientific and technical skill, humanitarianism, informality, and process—values that are consonant with the practice of medicine in all of its forms. By contrast, the courtroom exemplifies formality, gravitas, rule, justice, reason, judgment, equality, tradition, and ritual—consonant with the theory and practice of law and evocative, also, of religion. The web exemplifies contrasting values of internationalism, populism, communitarianism, virtuality, individualism, and technophilism. The sole natural example, although sharing features with the garden and sometimes under the control of families, governments, and/or commercial interests, is the metaphor of the seashore. Here, values of naturalism, elementalism, dynamism, romanticism, simplicity, profundity, play, pleasure, holism, sensation, vitality, fragility, and change are evident and reflect the role of nature and environmental policy considerations.

These various value-sets and their respective implications for music education prompt the question as to which and whose values should prevail. At stake is the philosophical justification for the means and ends of music education and its wider role in public policy and cultural affairs. Where possibilities exist for good or evil, questions arise about how to forge policies that take advantage of the best and avoid the worst of the possibilities that flow from these pictures. Matters of value are interconnected with questions of institutional involvement in music education and the particular roles they do and should play. Whether or to what extent music education ought to be conducted in the private or public sphere or both—whether under the aegis of families and/or communities, publicly supported schools, music professional organizations, religions, commercial enterprises, and/or other societal institutions—these are crucially important questions. Likewise, how these sometimes conflicting institutional interests can be accommodated in various ways and to differing degrees is also a significant matter. Where these sometimes very different value-sets conflict, finding ways to forge a rapprochement between them, negotiate between them, or resolve disputes that can inevitably be expected to arise in adjudicating them is a central concern.

IMPLICATIONS OF THE MODELS

Drawing on an earlier published classification of general aims of music education, I briefly sketch the aims and methods of these models.[4] The aims of consumption (drawing on the boutique) are various: to enrich culture; to benefit the well-being of people, responding to their perceived needs and wants by presenting attractive and appealing experiences that are also seen as useful to people; and to democratize culture by enabling those more esoteric and less accessible musics to be known by as many people as possible, irrespective of their social class, language, gender, age, or whatever barriers that might otherwise stand between them and this understanding. The methods whereby these aims are accomplished include attractive packaging and marketing of musical materials; strategies to motivate students to want to know these musics; treating music as a product to be consumed by selling access to this experience; treating music curricula as products to be marketed and sold; and emphasizing summative forms of evaluation to quantify or otherwise measure the extent to which objectives are realized.

Community (from the village) features such aims as developing communities of musicians and learners; enriching culture by sharing musical knowledge across the boundaries of different musical and cultural traditions; ennobling people through emphasizing that education is about people rather than subject matter and through cultivating diversity, plurality, mutuality, and civility; fostering humane societies; transforming musical traditions through dialogue and enculturation; and forging individual and collective identity and an enhanced sense of and respect for one's self and others. These aims are accomplished primarily through dialogical means such as developing imagination as a way of knowing self, world, and what lies beyond; fostering the arts as a means of humane education; employing collaborative and cooperative learning strategies; emphasizing reason, critical thinking, and the development of judgment; and utilizing formative evaluation in order to assist with, and foster improvement in, all aspects of music education.

Apprenticeship (based on the artist) fosters particular aims including transmitting and transforming musical traditions, cultivating musical skills, and ensuring a continuing supply of skilled professional musicians in particular musical practices, especially those that are esoteric or out of the musical mainstream. To these ends, the means employed include musical training, whereby teachers teach by precept and example; formal and informal means of musical learning; the exercise of choice, allowing students and teachers to select their teachers and students, respectively; individual and small group instruction tailored to student abilities; summative evaluation to ensure that professional standards are attained and maintained; and institutions such as conservatories established to ensure formal instruction and the provision of resources needed to accomplish this task.

Transgression (evoked by the revolutionary) is committed to the objective of transforming musical and music educational traditions in the hope of benefiting and ennobling people and enriching culture. This involves unmasking traditions that need to be changed and building better ones in their stead. Methods employed to achieve these aims include introducing new musical ideas and practices; cultivating approaches to teaching and learning that make people aware of things that need to be changed and motivating and energizing them toward making this change; employing action-oriented and dialogical instructional methods; fostering constructivist approaches to curriculum and critical thinking among all participants in music education; designing and implementing opportunities for border crossings among musical traditions; and organizing music education in ways that are cellular and permit the wide exercise of choice in all aspects of music education.

Production (from the factory) aims to create musicians and audiences, thereby benefiting people by providing a steady stream of musicians who can have a means to earn a livelihood, and developing audiences for whom music is entertaining and pleasurable. In seeking to produce things that will be useful to society, it aims to ensure and expand the opportunities for self-expression and cultural enrichment. It achieves these aims through teaching musical skills and developing the technical means for music making and taking; employing standardized teaching methods that impress knowledge into students; emphasizing learning approaches that are efficient, standardized, and scientific and that prompt receptive learning; operating instruction in a hierarchical fashion in which a one-way, formal, rational, and didactic transmission of information to students prevails; regarding and treating curriculum as a standardized and rationalized system in which predictable outcomes can be expected; making use of summative evaluation as a means of assessing outcomes and efficiency in the process; and operating efficiency-driven and data-driven management systems to organize music education.

Growth (drawing on the garden) aims to benefit people through facilitating the natural development of their musical self-expression and musical aptitude and potential, and, through accomplishing these aims, enrich culture. It also seeks to transform musical traditions and those who make and take music and develop musical communities through creating rich musical environments and nurturing people individually and collectively. It accomplishes these aims through emphasizing aesthetic and artistic values and transforming musical traditions by fostering new and divergent musical expressions. Teaching focuses on cultivating a musical environment in which learning takes place holistically, naturally, and pleasurably and in ways appropriate to maturation. Instruction is dialogical, individualized, and democratic; curriculum is processual, cyclical, experiential, and evaluated formatively and summatively; and administration creates conditions that facilitate freedom while also fostering social control.

Healing (based on the therapist) aims to benefit people and foster civil societies through promoting personal health and well-being and social cohesiveness. It also seeks to develop musical communities comprising groups of caring people who relate to each other authentically, respectfully, and sympathetically. It accomplishes these aims by such approaches as emphasizing the utilitarian and ritualistic purposes of music; holistic, spiritual, and caring approaches to teaching; individualized approaches to learning that promote self-understanding; contextualized, integrated, accessible, and choice-based approaches to curriculum; and flat administrative structures that are dialogical, humane, and civil.

Rule (from the courtroom) aims to cultivate knowledge of musical traditions, including their beliefs and practices, and thereby benefit and ennoble people and enrich culture. It seeks to realize these aims through such methods as conserving musical traditions, especially the systems underlying them; fostering reasoned, intellectual, expository, and formal approaches to teaching, particularly through schooling and training; emphasizing systematic, rationalized, and receptive ways of learning; taking a one-sided, unidirectional approach to instruction in which communication goes from teacher to student; emphasizing a stock-of-knowledge approach to curriculum that comprehensively covers material and employs summative evaluation as a means of ensuring that expectations are met; and employing administrative procedures and policies that organize instruction in systematic ways.

Energy (based on the seashore) seeks to benefit people through motivating them to be "wide awake" to their own situations and those of others with whom they are affiliated, enriching culture through making musicking a vital activity and a continuing part of human society, and transforming musical traditions through introducing new musics and practices and ensuring that they continue to flourish. It also fosters musical communities as individuals work together for the common good musically and in other ways. These objectives are realized through such means as attending to new musical practices and energizing old ones out of the limelight; relying on charismatic and personable teachers to motivate students; learning in informal and experiential ways through such means as osmosis, participation, observation, and sensibility; employing choice-based approaches to instruction that seek situations of reciprocal empathy between teachers and students; employing curricula that are constructivist, playful, pleasurable, and evaluated formatively; and organizing administrative procedures that are nimble and change-oriented.

Informality (from the home) seeks to benefit people through cultivating musical self-expression and enjoyment of music making and taking. It also aims to develop musical communities in which participants share musical beliefs and practices, thereby ensuring that musical traditions are passed from one generation to the next. It accomplishes these aims through such means as emphasizing and nurturing traditional musical practices; using informal approaches to instruction in which teachers assume particular teaching roles by virtue of their superior expertise and experience; and emphasizing informal learning through osmosis, observation, participation, and sensibility in circumstances that are often serendipitous, rhapsodic, and incidental to other activities. Instruction is often given by example and is occasionally didactic; the curriculum is canonical, traditional, and practical; and administration is largely informal and rhapsodic, and generally organized by older family members or more experienced musicians.

Pedagogy (from the guide) seeks to develop musical communities by preparing performers and listeners with the skills and knowledge of particular traditions to discover new knowledge or reclaim old knowledge that has been forgotten in order to enrich musical traditions and cultures. On the assumption that such knowledge and wisdom is presumed to tend toward the good or to constitute a means of ethical and moral development, it aims to benefit and ennoble people. These ends are accomplished through such means as focusing on music as a practice that involves doing, as well as understanding what to do; teaching through qualities of leadership, personal charisma, and the use of such techniques as the tutorial; learning through the exercise of choice, receiving the teacher's instruction, and acquiring practical skills through practice; conceiving of instruction as a social activity that takes place formally and informally and can be standardized and planned for in advance; treating curriculum as a scope and sequence activity that is planned for scrupulously by the teacher; and administering its work through clear organizational structures and mandates that are accountable and transparent to its participants and public.

Connectivity (from the web) seeks to benefit people by contributing to individual understanding of self and others, developing virtual communities and enhancing connections between people, enriching culture through shared musical and cultural knowledge internationally, and transforming musical traditions by means of border crossings and the mediation of various technologies. These ends are achieved through creating new means of musical expression; fostering formal and informal teaching; stressing virtual, individualized, intensive, serendipitous, and constructivist learning; relying on technologically mediated instruction; constructing hypertextual and technologically mediated curriculum; and undertaking flexible, nimble, and assessment-driven and even surveillance-preoccupied administration.

Generally speaking, there is more disparity in the aims and methods than in the values that underlie them. Although certain aims reappear throughout (for example, developing musical communities, transforming musical traditions, enriching culture, benefiting and ennobling people) in different combinations and to different degrees, the means whereby these aims are realized are diverse. Although musicians and educators may agree generally with particular principles, the manner in which these are carried out may be quite different, leading to disagreements about the particulars of the aims and methods. The particular mix of specific attributes colors the interpretation of the generalities that undergird them. This particularistic and divergent character of music education means that nuances can be as important as its principal features, and judgments of its work are appropriately based as much on specific as on general characteristics. The particular character of institutional aims and methods also colors the specific ways in which values play out in music education and complicates and problematizes grand narratives, or theories of everything in the world, of music education. So we focus as much on the particularities as the general characteristics of music education.[5]

Breaking out the aims, the models also have distinctive profiles. Consumption and production share the aims of benefiting people and enriching culture; transgression, healing, and rule share the aims of benefiting and ennobling people and enriching culture; and all of the others have different profiles of aims. Some, such as community and connectivity, have wide-ranging aims, while others, like consumption, production, and informality, are narrower in scope. Of those that share aims—for example, production and consumption—we see them as mirror images of a sort, in the sense that consumption focuses on the taking of music and production on its making. The enrichment of culture and the benefit of people are two of the most common aims, shared by community, transgression, healing, rule, pedagogy, and connectivity. Consumption, production, informality, growth, apprenticeship, energy, and connectivity hope to benefit people but do not necessarily hope to ennoble them. Informality, apprenticeship, and connectivity are more concerned with the development of musical communities than with the enrichment of culture. Regarding cultural transformation and transmission, growth, community, energy, and connectivity focus on transformation while rule, apprenticeship, and pedagogy focus on transmission. These various profiles of aims reveal how the specific combinations affect the character of the model, and in the cases where the general aims are similar, the specifics of the model play out quite differently in each case. All of these models share at least two general aims, and some feature most of them. Music education, insofar as it is pictured above, draws on a variety of aims, and these aims differ in their salience and potency.

Of course, in every general discussion such as this one, caveats and exceptions come immediately to mind. For example, although the growth model may not necessarily seek to ennoble people, it may do so indirectly by fostering the musical development of as many people as possible. Connectivity may hope to bring people together in virtual communities or milieu cultures but may contribute to individualizing them and separating them from one another in their lived lives. These realities raise the possibility of primary and secondary aims, or those aims that drive a model and those that may follow as a consequence of other aims or are parasitic on them. Although my present focus is necessarily limited to those aims that seem to be central or primary rather than peripheral or secondary and are construed generally rather than specifically, these matters also warrant attention.

Generally speaking, two groups of models emerge in regard to the methods employed: the first includes consumption, apprenticeship, rule, informality, and pedagogy; the second includes community, transgression, growth, healing, energy, informality, and connectivity. The first group fosters traditional views of music that are conservative in their emphasis on the past, while the second emphasizes new music in ways that challenge musical traditions; the first takes a didactic approach to teaching, while the second is more conversational or dialogical; the first emphasizes receptive learning and the second, constructivist learning; the first features a hierarchical interaction between teacher and student, while the second is egalitarian; the first features pre-set, subject-centered, product-oriented, and convergent curricula, and the second, rhapsodic, serendipitous, divergent, people-centered, and process-oriented curricula; the first is administered tightly and formally, while the second is administered loosely and informally.

On the face of things, these groups look like examples of Dewey's "traditional" and "progressive" education, or Freire's "banking" and "liberatory" education, respectively.[6] Nevertheless, things are not this simple. I have shown that the values underlying these various pictures (both metaphors and models) have advantages and disadvantages, and that once we look more specifically at the emergent models, there is greater diversity and complexity than might at first appear. I see the situation as dialectical and either/or thinking as too simplistic, and I want to rescue the useful aspects of each model and avoid the worst.[7] Rather than ascribing ethical valences to each of these groups and suggesting that those methods in the second are inherently "better" than those in the first, the crucial test becomes one of seeing the extent to which they are liberatory and transformative in their particular applications.[8]

Matters become more complex when one thinks more specifically about the approaches to music, teaching, learning, instruction, curriculum, and administration in these models. As with their aims, there is a rich variety in their specific methods and approaches. Consider the traditional attitudes toward music manifest in the first group. Regarding music in the consumption model as a thing or a product to be sold to consumers or clients is very different from apprenticeship, where music is regarded as a distinguished tradition with beliefs and practices to be preserved; the production model, which systematically creates supplies of musicians and listeners needed in order to ensure the survival and flourishing of musical traditions; the rule model, where normative theories and practices are conveyed to this music's practitioners and publics; or pedagogy, which systematically attends to the reclamation or discovery of knowledge. Contrast these with the second group, in which more open and change-oriented approaches to music prevail. This more open perspective on music in community is of a very different character than in transgression mode, where musicians and others set out to change traditions and develop new ones; the growth model, in which a processual approach takes especial account of maturation and other natural aspects; the energy model, which emphasizes new traditions and music in a constructive rather than critical fashion as it searches for ways to keep musical traditions alive; and connectivity in which technologically mediated musics challenge traditional acoustic and live music making. Examined more specifically, then, these models are nuanced regarding their musical perspectives and practices—differences and similarities that reflect their respective aims. We may be more sympathetic to some approaches than others but unwilling to jettison one group or the other.

The same is true in regard to teaching. Among the didactic approaches in the first group, we can distinguish the consumption model, in which teachers employ technical means to make music known to their students and entice them to receive what they have to give; apprenticeship, which relies on teachers as the recipients of a musical heritage of great worth to train and school their students to know about and be able to do this music; the production model, which relies on teachers as technicians who employ standardized methods to achieve predetermined ends; the rule model, in which teachers convey the principles that lie beneath the practices; and pedagogy, in which teachers lead their students to new understandings. A similar variety shows up in the dialogical teaching approaches in the second group. In conditions of community, teachers engage in conversations that develop imagination, civility, humanity, and social cohesiveness; in transgression mode, teacher conversations with students subvert the status quo even at the price of challenging the present social order; in the growth model, teachers focus on developing environments for conversations that foster individual development; in teaching modeled on healing, teachers' conversations with students are predicated on the belief that some things are amiss and need to be rectified; in energy mode, teacher charisma and energy are vital to finding the best social and psychological matches for teacher and student interaction; in the state of informality, teaching roles differ in the conversation and shift between teacher and student; and in teaching through connectivity, teachers communicate virtually in ways that are mediated technologically. Examined more specifically, what might at first appear to be two types turns out to be more complex, and each of the models in both groups may be valuable or problematic.

Also, regarding learning, we might break out the two groups in terms of their emphasis on receptive and constructive learning, respectively. In the first group, learning in consumption is receptive in the sense that students take the passive role of recipients of attractively packaged information; in learning through apprentice-ship, students receive knowledge from teachers but are also actively engaged in mastering the beliefs and practices bequeathed to them; in rule-oriented learning, students' focus is on grasping the underlying rationality of particular musical ideas and practices and gradually applying these principles less slavishly and more cre-atively; and in pedagogy, the learners' focus is on discovering how to do music and know about it. Likewise, in the second group, in community, learning is viewed processually as a means whereby reason and critical thinking in social as well as individual settings are applied to music; in the transgression model, learning is action-oriented or praxial in the sense that theory comes together with practice; in learning through growth, the focus is upon the natural processes whereby under-standing evolves over time; in energy mode, learning is a matter of the social and psychological impact of teacher-student interaction; in conditions of informal-ity, learning often occurs serendipitously and unintentionally, and teaching and learning roles may be interchangeable; and in the connectivity model, learning is idiosyncratic and virtual, often a matter of grasping what something is like. We see, again, an array of specific and distinctive qualities of learning within both of the groups that may be seen to be of differing value.

In terms of instruction, the two groups, while generally similar in terms of their contrasting foci on hierarchical and formal approaches on the one hand (the first group) and egalitarian and informal approaches on the other (the second group), likewise manifest important differences between and among them. In the first group, the consumption model relies on the teacher having an attractive product to peddle to the student and seems client-oriented in the necessity of satisfying the student; apprenticeship features a wide social distance between teacher and stu-dent in which the student is clearly subordinate to, and must satisfy, the teacher; instruction as production insists on standardized, predictable, and efficient means of teacher and student interaction in the context of music practices; the rule model dictates that the teacher show and tell the student principles that are both theoretical and practical; and pedagogy takes a social view of the interaction between teacher and student such that the teacher is the leader and the student the follower. In the second group, community involves respectful, humane, collaborative, and egali-tarian interactions between teacher and student in ways that promote group cohe-sion; instruction as transgression involves critical discourse and interaction in ways that unsettle, surprise, and subvert the status quo and that may pose danger; in the growth model instruction is inherently individualistic, particularistic, and diver-gent and necessitates teacher and student taking advantage of moments when stu-dents are ready to learn; the healing mode likewise envisions an individual endeav-or that requires spiritual as well as physical readiness on the teacher's and student's part; the energy model is grounded on the holistic interaction of those involved in instruction and their attraction one to another; instruction in informality is especially egalitarian in that the roles of teacher and student may be interchangeable and interaction takes place in the midst of activities that are not intentionally pedagogical; and instruction though connectivity implies technologically mediated, free-wheeling, and sometimes blunt interrelationships between teacher and student. When the models are examined more specifically, instruction, too, while falling out generally into two different groups, is nuanced, varied, and value-laden.

Curriculum also falls into two groups, the first group featuring a set, predetermined, and subject-centered plan of work that fosters convergent ends and is product-oriented, and the second group being a rhapsodic, serendipitous, person-centered, and evolving process with divergent ends as it is constructed by teachers and students along the way. Notwithstanding these generalizations, there is considerable curricular diversity within both groups. In the first group, consumption prepackages attractive subject matter for students to know; apprenticeship features a long-term program of practical study that students gradually master; production seeks to make practitioners and theorists who will be music makers rather than takers by standardized, rationalized, and efficient means; rule focuses on underlying principles of the ideas and practices of particular traditions in a rational manner; and pedagogy employs systematic techniques in order to lead students to grasp the subject matter. By contrast, in the second group, community takes an often group-oriented approach to music that benefits those within the group; transgression employs conversations as means of understanding self, others, and whatever lies beyond to enable change; growth attends to the development of people systematically, cyclically, and experientially; healing seeks to holistically and experientially engage ideas and practices in ways that remedy human suffering, pain, angst, and ennui; energy is playful and holistic in its emphasis on motivating and inspiring teachers and learners; informality focuses on the need to know such-and-such in the midst of other aspects of lived life; and connectivity makes possible the intensity of a wide array of attractively prepared materials and experiences that are arranged hypertextually so that they can be accessed in various ways and to differing degrees. We see some interesting nuances, notwithstanding the evident general similarities within each group, and these complicate the curricular models that emerge.

Administration likewise breaks out into two groups, the first organized hierarchically and formally and the second more egalitarian, with flatter, more informal administrative structures. In the first group, the consumption model requires a formal system of administration, heavily reliant on advertising and summative evaluation; administration of apprenticeship is more elitist and specialized and is typically organized into schools or traditions; the rule model relies on the formulation of policies, procedures, regulations, and laws; and administration as pedagogy features clear organizational purposes and methods. In the second group, community may emerge spontaneously out of friendship groups, requiring no formal organization; transgression relies for administration on cellular models to effect change; the growth model requires a collegial and dialogical administrative style in order to ensure that individual interests and abilities are paramount so as to secure orderly development of these interests and abilities; the healing mode requires a flat organizational structure in which civility, humanity, and caring are paramount; the energy model likewise suggests a flat and versatile organizational structure allowing small, self-directed groups to flourish from time to time; informality is distinguished by a flexible and open system that is not necessarily coordinated but may arise serendipitously and rhapsodically from time to time; and connectivity requires an adroit and nimble administrative structure that can thrive in an environment in which change is the norm. Once more, these administrative attributes not only reveal generally construed commonalities but important specific nuances and differences as well. These approaches may be attractive or repellent to varying degrees.

Analyzing the methods employed within each of the theories of music education, then, reveals two different groups of models that seem more or less consistent across the range of their musical commitments—teaching, learning, instruction, curriculum, and administration—yet suggest support for still other, more specific categories of methods that remain to be systematically described and that interrelate or overlap one with another. As in the case of values and aims, it becomes clear why overlaps, similarities, and differences emerge among these models and why it is important to cast pictures of music education at different levels of generality and specificity. The analysis also clarifies why and how disagreements and misunderstandings can emerge when music educators approach the task of mapping the field conceptually at different levels of generality. The more specific the analysis, the more complex and problematic the situation appears to be, and the more difficult it is to apply metaphors and models, conceived generally, to the specific situations in which all those involved in music educational work. It is clear that ambiguity and fallibility are distinguishing features of music educational thought and practice; rather than pretending that it is possible to overcome them, and a philosopher might wish to clarify matters insofar as possible, it is useful to recognize these qualities as characteristic features of music education in the phenomenal world and devise approaches to its work that take them into account.[9]

PRACTICAL APPLICATIONS

In discussing how these pictures can be helpful practically, I want to emphasize the sorts of thinking that this gallery of pictures requires, since thinking is at the root of doing and being. My point is to show that the ways in which we envisage our tasks as music teachers affect our actions and our decisions about how to live our lives. At a time in which anti-intellectualism is rife, and appeals to emotion and sensation are too frequently seen in public discourse, this gallery of pictures reminds us of our obligations to think carefully about our work and to act in ways that are astute, reasonable, civil, sympathetic, and humane. Given the multiplicities and pluralities, ambiguities, and gaps and fissures in our knowledge, it is tempting to retreat to dichotomous and either/or thinking rather than think more dialogically, dialectically, dynamically, and inclusively about the worlds of music education, or at least in a manner that grants the extent to which we are caught up in the midst of things in a vital sense of becoming. But how to think? What are some of the characteristics of the sorts of thinking and acting that are implied in the pictures before us? Here is a short list.

Thinking imaginatively is vital.[10] Seeing things differently than we might have envisaged them before is not just a matter of a rational exercise that tests our deductive, inductive, and analogical powers, although it may do that. Rather, we also need to be able to think holistically and immediately so that we can seize the moments that offer opportunities for coming to know music. Our perceptive powers are also important, especially as they apply to all the aspects of music, understanding others as well as self and interpreting the cues that are indicative of deeper and broader realities and are crucial in deciding what to do. There is also a sense of knowing that may not be effectively or fully articulated as speech or other discursive means and implicates the whole body in this thinking.[11] In short, imagination is cognitive and corporeal. Thought-action is enacted by human beings whose minds, bodies, and souls are inextricably interconnected.

Thinking critically involves the art of being able to construct ideas and practices and interrogate them.[12] Such thinking enables us to sort through the plethora of value systems, aims, and methods that these pictures represent, figure out which are most important, and determine what should be kept and what discarded. Beneath the superstructure of practices that they express, it is important to excavate the ideas that they represent. Many music educational practices have been implemented practically on the basis of beliefs that have yet to be criticized, and it is important to ask whether or not these ideas and the practices that draw from them have merit, especially in this time and place. These pictures show us that every way of thinking or doing things has its unexpected consequences and detractions; when we encounter them, it is important to try to ameliorate the detractions, limitations, and flaws wherever possible.[13] Clarifying the nature of our values, aims, and methods helps us to better grasp music educational beliefs and practices and understand self, other, and whatever lies beyond.

Thinking cyclically is an important function of mind and action. If we cannot do everything, we can at least do something; if we cannot do everything at once, we can do something now and something later. This seems to have been true for teachers in the past.[14] If it is not possible to think or to teach others to think intuitively, analytically, and synthetically all at once, it is possible to break out the learning process into phases in which these qualities may be emphasized at different points.[15] Similarly with these pictures. Some may be called upon at one time and others may be drawn on at another. For example, models that fall within the first group, stressing formal and teacher-directed instruction, may be employed when students need to gain a systematic knowledge of particular musical skills; those that are informal and dialogical may be drawn on when students desire knowledge of a particular sort or are exploring a new musical practice on their own. Different pictures may be useful in different phases, aspects, or particular situations of music education; over the whole educational process, they can be used for specific purposes at one time or another. It might not be possible to combine them all together at once, but over the long term, they can be used at different times. The practical challenge for teachers is to arrange and order these pictures in the most effective ways. This notion is complicated by the fact that some pictures resonate with the zeitgeist of a particular time or place. In a conservative time, pictures in the first group may be in the ascendancy, although it may be important to counteract these conservative influences with more progressive ones in the second group. Finding this balance is difficult, especially when music education is conducted in the public sphere. Even so, we are further ahead when we can name our realities and work through them systematically than when they remain mysterious or unnamed.

Thinking open-mindedly suggests that present decisions are not taken for all time; if other, better options emerge along the way, it is important to continue to think and rethink our plans in the future. Of course, precedents are important, and we need to be thoughtful about the future implications of present particular actions. Still, a plan for today's situation does not mean that we are necessarily stuck with it forever, especially if it turns out to be ill-considered or if other, better positions are found. Admitting that we are wrong or that the unexpected consequences of our actions have brought about deleterious effects is a good thing; it allows us to make course corrections when necessary. Revisiting our ideas and practices when they are contested affords opportunities to challenge received wisdom and ask if better alternatives are available. Fallibility necessitates thoughtful reflection on our actions and their effects going forward; this is so because we act in the midst of incomplete information, and unexpected results (both good and bad) are bound to flow from what we say and do. We would be well served by frankly and quickly admitting our errors, attempting to remedy them insofar as possible, and making course corrections where needed. Ideas and practices have a time, are contested, and may pass away as others take their place. The dispositions of contesting ideas and practices and giving ground graciously when better ideas and practices arise are sure signs of professionalism in music education and indicate that we are thinking open-mindedly.

Thinking practically suggests a particular interest in the ways ideas play out in the phenomenal world. Ideas do not suffice; they are tested by practice and in the nature of their consequences. This reality necessitates strategic planning that situates ideas in the midst of action, explores the ways in which they might be applied, and decides which plans are the most appropriate for these particular situations. Compromises are necessary because music education takes place within institutions; some people disagree and will not give way, and change must sometimes await their departure, retirement, death, or the ascendancy of a different institutional or societal milieu. Taking into account these practical and political realities requires working effectively with others to try to accomplish the necessary ends. I know of no more effective framework for coming to agreement about particular music educational ends and means than through liberal and democratic ideals and procedures. Still, we need to be on guard against the tyranny of the majority, or attempts to squelch opposition by exercising the trappings of democracy without its heart.

Thinking dialogically is crucial, because if we are alone, we may not discover how things might be different or better.[16] These pictures suggest that it is especially important to look and listen, to receive and undergo rather than constantly act and do. The sort of transformative thinking that I have in mind welcomes other, different, and even conflicting perspectives; through engaging them civilly and humanely, and opening oneself to them, it offers "hospitality" or the welcoming honoring of differences, or "cosmopolitanism," or the art of being able to appreciate different others.[17] This is not a Pollyannaesque world in which everyone is always happy and contented. Rather, these conversations need to be conducted within certain legal and political frames that provide a supportive context for them.[18] I admit that institutional settings may affect the ease with which authentic, respectful, and sympathetic conversations of the sort I have in mind can be conducted. Still, democratic institutions offer the most hope for these conversations; without hope, I cannot see any point to educational discourse of any sort. Notions of "life, liberty, and the pursuit of happiness" as ideals (if not always demonstrated in practice) foster dialogical thinking and conversations, just as they are strengthened by them.[19] Dialogical thought is an appropriate starting place in improving the situation.

Thinking systematically is vital for a broad and long-term view of music education. Its breadth offers opportunities to think expansively about the many aspects of music education and view them as parts of a multifaceted enterprise that might be coordinated more effectively for the benefit of humankind. Efforts to transcend national borders by creating international conversations, or to transcend institutional borders by creating mechanisms to coordinate activities across several institutions have the effect of going beyond the borders of music to influence the wider culture. As a musician, one wants to see societies in which the arts are valued for their contributions to human well-being and happiness, where the lives of all people are enriched by music making and taking, and in which people live together in harmony and peace, treating each other humanely and civilly. These are noble aims worth aspiring to even if they remain forever out of reach. Such cultural aims require a broad vision that includes all of the societal institutions involved in musical and artistic education, in which all parts of society are seen as interconnected, and where we attend to the entire system rather than a part of it. Not only does this perspective need to be broad and global, but it also needs to take the long view, in which patience and determination are evident over the long haul. When music educators take this long view and keep in mind those qualities that are worth preserving, even if this stance leaves us out of fashion for a while, we can avoid throwing out the best of the old along with the worst. Thinking historically, and remembering the stories of the past, enable us to take the long view and avoid the unnecessary mistakes that bedeviled our predecessors.

Thinking sympathetically is an important practice of thought and action. Qualities such as compassion, generosity, and tact need to characterize the interpretations of these pictures and the ways in which they are applied in the phenomenal world. In dealing with those who share our commitments or differ in the ways they see the world and propose to act in it, it is important to seek to grasp how others see things, be generous in our interpretations of others' beliefs and practices, and then act as carefully and discreetly as possible.[20] Perfection is not evident in the phenomenal world, and compassion is required if we are to rescue the best of what is there while also standing against the worst. Kant's image of the "crooked timber of humanity" suggests the wisdom of working with rather than against that grain, in the hope that the beauty that lies in the tangles and knots can emerge in the process of polishing and shaping.[21]

These and other dispositions of thought clearly impact our actions in the phenomenal world. They offer ways in which we may interrogate the pictures before us, assess their worth, and determine how and to what extent they can be applied to our lived situations. Rather than using them to prescribe a single specific course of action, music education policy makers are invited to think through these pictures, posit others, and work out strategies that are appropriate to particular situations. Instead of expecting any one philosopher to dictate music educational policy, all music educators need to reflect on what needs to be done in practice and participate in making its plans.

QUESTIONS RAISED

The questions raised in these pages are of as much interest as the answers provided. We do see some answers. Still, this gallery of pictures opens different ways of philosophizing and applying these ideas, none of which suffices. We seem to be beset on every hand by questions that take us in different directions. These multiplicities and diversities, ambiguities and uncertainties, inconsistencies and opportunities suggest the importance of thinking and rethinking our work broadly and deeply. Not all of the directions are complete or clear; still, there are possibilities galore, territories yet to be explored, and a myriad of openings and opportunities to reconceptualize and transform music education.

Among these, my sketches of various metaphors and models provide instances of a wider universe of possibilities that might be developed. Expanding those that I have already suggested and adding others that are not included in this present writing can enrich our understanding of music educational thought and practice around the world. Multiple models could flow from an expanded array of metaphors and offer a more detailed and systematic description than is possible here. The values, aims, and methods I have briefly sketched need to be mapped more exhaustively, and their particulars described systematically and specifically. Such undertakings and extensions afford fertile soil for related research and open numerous possible ways to conceptualize and practice music education.

My emphasis on the importance of particularities as well as generalities raises questions about what ought to be the purpose of theory-building in music education. If theories are not intended solely to be prescriptive or the basis for refutation, what are their purposes? Should they also serve to illumine situations, prompt systematic and symptomatic thought about practical situations, and inspire music educators to act in particular ways? How shall theories and practices construed at different levels of generality be developed, integrated, and interrogated? To this point, our research enterprise in music education has yet to take sufficient account of the impact of various levels of generality and the discontinuities, tensions, and misunderstandings created when findings at one level of generality are applied uncritically to others. Anthropological, sociological, psychological, physiological, and physical insights need to be thought of not only in their own terms but in terms of how they relate to findings at other levels of generality. Obviously, a careful examination of these questions lies outside the scope of the present study. Still, answers are needed to them. They clarify the necessity of thinking about the whole cloth of music education rather than just the specific pieces that comprise it, and undertaking broad and extensive theoretical as well as empirical research. These questions may be so broad as to necessitate teams of researchers with varying expertise.

Philosophical questions related to the values that ought to guide music education and their related aims and methods are particularly important. For me, matters of value are among the most pressing facing music educational philosophers today. Rather than seeking the Tolkien ring of power, the "one philosophy to rule them all," these pictures of music education open the prospect of a gallery of pictures, rich in possibilities and potentialities, and representing a wide array of music educational practices around the world and throughout history.[22] Thinking of openings rather than closings offers various metaphors and related models that suggest still others, prompting us to think and act imaginatively, critically, cyclically, open-mindedly, practically, dialogically, systematically, and compassionately.

I love the possibilities and the hope in these pictures. Although we may never think as well as we wish we might, or achieve all that for which we hope, and notwithstanding the flaws in our being, these pictures remind us that as music educators and those interested in its work, we are engaged in an artful, humane, and hopeful undertaking. The pictures prompt and sometimes prod us to integrity, to be and act in ways that are consonant with our thinking, and through our influence, make the worlds in which we have a hand better for our being in them. They inspire us to be, think, and do better than we have done in the past. And this suffices for now.

NOTES

PREFACE

1. See Virginia Richardson, "Stewards of a Field, Stewards of an Enterprise: The Doctorate in Education," in Chris Golde and George Walker, eds., *Envisioning the Future of Doctoral Education: Preparing Stewards of the Discipline—Carnegie Essays on the Doctorate* (San Francisco: Jossey-Bass, 2006), 251–267. A version of this paper was presented under the aegis of the Committee of Institutional Cooperation (CIC) and hosted by the Bienen School of Music, Northwestern University, Evanston, Ill., in October 2004.

2. Iris M. Yob, "The Symbols of Religion: An Analysis of the Ideas of Paul Tillich, Mircea Eliade and Janet Soskice for Religious Education," doctoral diss., Harvard Graduate School of Education, 1990, and her "Thinking Constructively with Metaphors: A Review of Barbara J. Thayer-Bacon, *Transforming Critical Thinking: Thinking Constructively,*" *Studies in Philosophy and Education* 22.2 (2003): 127–138.

3. For example, see "Symposium *Music and Philosophy: Emotion and Reason,*" *Musiikkikasvatus/The Finnish Journal of Music Education* 11.1–2 (2008): 60–84, contributed to by Estelle R. Jorgensen, Marja Heimonen, and Heidi Westerlund and Lauri Väkevä.

4. Philip Pullman, *His Dark Materials,* 3 vols.: *The Golden Compass* (rev. ed., New York: Alfred A. Knopf, 2002); *The Subtle Knife* (rev. ed., New York: Alfred A. Knopf, 2002); *The Amber Spyglass* (New York: Dell Laurel-Leaf, 2003).

5. For a biographical sketch on Millicent Hodson as one of the Patten Lecturers at Indiana University in 2003, see http://patten.indiana.edu/formerLecturers (accessed July 12, 2010).

6. Estelle R. Jorgensen, "The Revolutionary, Transgression, and Music Education," invited address to *Musica ficta*/Lived Realities: A Conference on Exclusions and Engagements in Music, Education and the Arts, University of Toronto, Canada, Jan. 24–27, 2008.

1. METAPHOR AND MODEL

1. For example, Percy Scholes explains musical forms narratively; Andrea Boyea describes Native American music in terms of stories; Deanne Bogdan thinks of music performance dialogically; Randall Everett Allsup and Heidi Westerlund mine the garage band as a metaphor and model of music education, respectively; Elizabeth Gould regards women's experience of instrumental conducting nomadically; and Allsup invokes Darwinian views of evolution in addressing change in music education. See Percy A. Scholes, *Music, the Child and the Masterpiece: A Comprehensive Handbook of Aims and Methods in All That Is Usually Called "Musical Appreciation"* (London: Oxford University Press; Humphrey Milford, 1935), 88–89; Andrea Boyea, "Teaching Native American Music with Story for Multicultural Ends," *Philosophy of Music Education Review* 8.1 (Spring 2000): 14–23;

Deanne Bogdan, "Musical Listening and Performance as Embodied Dialogism," *Philosophy of Music Education Review* 9.1 (Spring 2001): 3–22; Randall Everett Allsup, "Mutual Learning and Democratic Action in Instrumental Music Education," *Journal of Research in Music Education* 51.1 (Spring 2003): 24–37; Heidi Westerlund, "Garage Bands: A Future Model for Developing Musical Expertise?" *International Journal of Music Education* 24.2 (2006): 119–125; Elizabeth Gould, "Nomadic Turns: Epistemology, Experience, and Women University Band Directors," *Philosophy of Music Education Review* 13.2 (Fall 2005): 147–164; and Randall Everett Allsup, "Species Counterpoint: Darwin and the Evolution of Forms," *Philosophy of Music Education Review* 14.2 (Fall 2006): 159–174.

    2. Vernon A. Howard, *Learning By All Means: Lessons from the Arts: A Study in the Philosophy of Education* (New York: Peter Lang, 1992), 49.

    3. Immanuel Kant (*The Critique of Judgement,* trans. James Creed Meredith [1952; repr., Oxford: Oxford University Press, 1957], p. 58) refers to the *"free play* of the cognitive faculties," while Friedrich Schiller (*On the Aesthetic Education of Man in a Series of Letters,* ed. and trans. Elizabeth M. Wilkinson and L. A. Willoughby [Oxford: Clarendon Press, 1967], Letter 27) describes the aesthetic experience as one of play—a notion expressing the sense of imagination and free enjoyment of the work of art rather than trivializing the aesthetic and artistic experience. It is important to distinguish between the concept of the mind "at play" in the midst of the experience of art, and the purpose of the aesthetic experience as one of play.

    Other writers such as Johan Huizinga, David Baily Harned, and Ernst Cassirer variously characterize the aesthetic experience as one of play. Johan Huizinga (*Homo Ludens: A Study of the Play Element in Culture* [1950; repr., Boston: Beacon, 1955], ch. 10) suggests that "culture arises in the form of play, that it is played from the beginning," and that this is especially true of music. David Baily Harned (*Theology and the Arts* [Philadelphia: Westminster Press, 1966], 46) follows Huizinga, with the qualification that art is a "kind of play, endowed with its own autonomy and independence. But it is an impure expression of the play impulse, because it is integrally related to our ordinary lives." Ernst Cassirer (*An Essay on Man: An Introduction to a Philosophy of Human Culture* [New Haven, Conn.: Yale University Press, 1944], 163–170) argues that art understood as "symbolic language" involves the discovery of knowledge rather than simply play, purposive rather than non-purposive behavior, concentration or "the intensification of our energies" rather than simply a "relaxing process." In the present context, the imagination "at play" refers more to the activity of mind in the midst of musical experience than to the characterization of musical experience as a species of play. The two notions should not be equated.

    Likewise, R. G. [Robin George] Collingwood and Susanne Langer agree on the importance of imagination for the arts and music, respectively. In his discussion of the imagination in the aesthetic experience, R. G. Collingwood (*The Principles of Art* [Oxford: Oxford University Press, 1938], 151) notes that a work of art "is something imagined" and a "total activity which the person enjoying it apprehends, or is conscious of, by the use of his [or her] imagination." Susanne K. Langer (*Feeling and Form: A Theory of Art Developed from Philosophy in a New Key* [London: Routledge and Kegan Paul, 1953], 123) comments that in the act of composition "A perfectly free imagination suffers from very lack of pressure . . ." and the making of aesthetic forms is governed by "laws of imagination" (p. 234) so that a work of art "comes to the percipient as an experience" (p. 241). In *Philosophy in a New Key: A Study in the Symbolism of Reason, Rite, and Art* (3rd ed., Cambridge, Mass.: Harvard

University Press, 1982), she adds that it is "the imagination that responds to music" (p. 244) and "We see significance *in* things long before we know what we are seeing" (p. 251). She explains that the "aesthetic emotion" felt in the experience of works of art springs from the intellectual "triumph" of "achieving insight into literally 'unspeakable' realities" (p. 262).

4. Mary J. Reichling, "Images of Imagination," *Journal of Research in Music Education* 38.4 (Winter 1990): 284–293.

5. For example, see Donald N. Ferguson, *Music as Metaphor: The Elements of Expression* (Minneapolis: University of Minnesota Press, 1960). For Langer (*Feeling and Form*, 27), music bears "a close logical similarity to the forms of human feeling—forms of growth, attenuation, flowing and stowing, conflict and resolution, speed, arrest, terrific excitement, calm . . ." suggesting that music is figurative of inner felt life. In describing the experience of a work of art, Langer (*Philosophy in a New Key*, 262) goes further than "'secondary imagination' that sees metaphorically" to invoke the "tertiary imagination" (borrowed from L. A. [Louis Arnaud] Reid [*Knowledge and Truth*, London: Macmillan, 1923], 132), denoting "subject-matter imaginatively experienced *in* the work of art . . . , theoretically distinguishable from its expressiveness."

6. Langer, *Feeling and Form*, 32.

7. See Frede V. Nielsen, "Didactology as a Field of Theory and Research in Music Education," *Philosophy of Music Education Review* 13.1 (Spring 2005): 5–19.

8. See, e.g., David J. Elliott, *Music Matters: A New Philosophy of Music Education* (New York: Oxford University Press, 1995); David J. Elliott, "Music and Affect: The Praxial View," *Philosophy of Music Education Review* 8.2 (Fall 2000): 79–88; Thomas A. Regelski, "The Aristotelian Bases of Praxis for Music and Music Education as Praxis," *Philosophy of Music Education Review* 6.1 (Spring 1998): 22–59; Bennett Reimer, *A Philosophy of Music Education* (Englewood Cliffs, N.J.: Prentice-Hall, 1970).

9. On this point, see Max van Manen, *The Tact of Teaching: The Meaning of Pedagogical Thoughtfulness* (Albany: State University of New York Press, 1991), esp. ch. 6.

10. On "multiplicities and pluralities," see Maxine Greene, *The Dialectic of Freedom* New York: Teachers College Press, 1988), esp. ch. 4.

11. John Dewey, *Experience and Education* ([1938]; repr., New York: Collier Books, 1963), 17, criticizes either/or approaches to education that unnecessarily polarize alternatives and fail to see the transformative possibilities of their synthesis.

12. Nelson Goodman, *Languages of Art: An Approach to a Theory of Symbols* (Indianapolis: Hackett, 1976), 69.

13. Max Black, *Models and Metaphors: Studies in Language and Philosophy* (Ithaca, N.Y.: Cornell University Press, 1962), ch. 3, and "More about Metaphor," in *Metaphor and Thought*, ed. Andrew Ortony (Cambridge: Cambridge University Press, 1979), 19–43; Goodman, *Languages of Art*, 71–73, 80.

14. Goodman, *Languages of Art*, 69–70, 73. Also see Mary Schaaldenbrand, "Metaphoric Imagination: Kinship through Conflict," in *Studies in the Philosophy of Paul Ricoeur*, ed. Charles E. Reagan (Athens: Ohio University Press, 1979).

15. Black, *Models and Metaphors*, 39, 44.

16. Ibid., 219, 230, 231, 239.

17. Ibid., 239.

18. See, e.g., the models discussed in Bruce Joyce and Marsha Weil, *Models of Teaching*, 3rd ed. (Englewood Cliffs, N.J.: Prentice-Hall, 1986), that might once have been figurative

but gradually come to be taken literally. I am reminded of Nelson Goodman's argument on the difference between a forgery and the authentic picture in his *Languages of Art,* 99–112.

19. Iris M. Yob, "Thinking Constructively with Metaphors: A Review of Barbara Thayer-Bacon's *Transforming Critical Thinking*," *Studies in Philosophy and Education* 22 (2003): 127–138.

20. Edward A. Tiryakian, "Sociology and Existential Phenomenology," in *Phenomenology and the Social Sciences,* vol. 1, ed. Maurice Natanson (Evanston, Ill.: Northwestern University Press, 1973), 187–222. Tiryakian defines an assumptive frame of reference (AFR) as "a general orientation to the world within which human subjects act and react toward others, make projects, and evaluate events." It is "multifaceted and multidimensional," composed in part of "ideas and representations we make of the world on the basis of empirical knowledge," "generalized feelings and sentiments about the world or parts of the world, including groups of others," and it includes imagery and moral expectations of others (199–201).

21. Thomas Luckmann, ed., *Phenomenology and Sociology: Selected Readings* (Harmondsworth: Penguin, 1978).

22. Iris M. Yob, "The Cognitive Emotions and Emotional Cognitions," *Studies in Philosophy and Education* 16 (1997): 43–57.

23. Iris M. Yob, chapter titled About Symbols in "Religious Education and the Role of Symbolism," doctoral diss., Harvard University, 1990. See also Israel Scheffler, "In Praise of Cognitive Emotions," in *Inquiries: Philosophical Studies of Language, Science, and Learning,* pt. 3 (Indianapolis: Hackett, 1986). For a discussion of exemplification among other functions of symbols, see Goodman, *Languages of Art,* 52–57.

24. Zoltán Kodály, *The Selected Writings of Zoltán Kodály,* ed. Ferenc Bónis, trans. Lili Halápy and Fred Macnicol (London: Boosey and Hawkes, 1974), 140.

25. On Kodály's ideas, see Micheal Houlahan and Philip Tacka, *Kodaly Today: A Cognitive Approach to Music* (New York: Oxford University Press, 2007).

26. On ambiguity, see Israel Scheffler, *Beyond the Letter: A Philosophical Inquiry into Ambiguity, Vagueness and Metaphor in Language* (London: Routledge and Kegan Paul, 1979).

27. This commissioned drawing was completed by the artist in 2004. Millicent Hodson is known for her historical reconstructions of ballets, including Nijinksy's choreography of Stravinsky's *Le Sacre du printemps.* See her *Nijinsky's Crime Against Grace: Reconstruction Score of the Original Choreography for Le Sacre du printemps* (Stuyvesant, N.Y.: Pendragon, 1996).

28. On dance as a metaphor for the arts, see Susanne K. Langer, *Problems of Art: Ten Philosophical Lectures* (New York: Charles Scribner's Sons, 1957), ch. 1.

29. See Edward Slingerland, "Conceptual Metaphor Theory as Methodology for Comparative Religion," *Journal of the American Academy of Religion* 72.1 (Mar. 2004): 1–31; George Lakoff, "The Contemporary Theory of Metaphor," in *Metaphor and Thought,* 2nd ed., ed. Andrew Ortony (Cambridge: Cambridge University Press, 1993), 202–251; George Lakoff and Mark Johnson, *Metaphors We Live By* (Chicago: Chicago University Press, 1980).

30. Slingerland, "Conceptual Metaphor Theory as Methodology for Comparative Religion," 12, 13.

31. Susanne K. Langer, *Philosophy in a New Key,* esp. chs. 4, 6, 7, 8.

32. Estelle R. Jorgensen, "On the Development of a Theory of Music Instruction," *Psychology of Music* 8 (1980): 25–30.

33. Estelle R. Jorgensen, *In Search of Music Education* (Urbana: University of Illinois Press, 1997), ch. 2.

34. On instruction, see Howard, *Learning By All Means,* ch. 5.

35. Even in the case of an independently operated studio, a teacher works within the frame of an institution or professional association, be it a system of graded examinations or performances, competitions arranged by a professional association or organization, or expectations of musician colleagues and family members.

36. On the steward and conservation and on the pilgrim and quest, see Estelle R. Jorgensen, "Seeing Double: A Comparative Approach to Music Education," *Musiikkikasvatus/The Finnish Journal of Music Education* 11.1–2 (2008): 60–84.

37. I think, e.g., of the twentieth-century civil rights activist Rosa Parks, among other American women of color who subverted racism by her act of transgression in sitting in the front of the bus rather than at its rear where the law decreed that she should sit as a person of color.

38. For example, Donald Arnstine, *Democracy and the Arts of Schooling* (Albany: State University of New York Press, 1995) provides "real life" fictional stories meant to approximate lived situations.

39. Paulo Freire, *Pedagogy of Hope: Reliving Pedagogy of the Oppressed,* trans. Robert R. Barr (New York: Continuum, 1994), observes that hope is at the center of education.

40. For an analysis of the various images of music see Estelle R. Jorgensen, *Transforming Music Education* (Bloomington: Indiana University Press, 2003), ch. 4.

2. BOUTIQUE AND CONSUMPTION

1. *OED Online,* s.v. "boutique," http://dictionary.oed.com (accessed July 14, 2010).

2. As Immanuel Kant, *The Critique of Judgement,* §7, p. 52, explains, aesthetic judgment entails the assumption that others ought to agree with us.

3. Arthur G. Powell, Eleanor Farrar, and David K. Cohen's *The Shopping Mall High School: Winners and Losers in the Educational Marketplace* (Boston: Houghton Mifflin, 1985), esp. ch. 3, titled "Specialty Shops."

4. Julia Eklund Koza, *Stepping Across: Four Interdisciplinary Studies of Education and Cultural Politics* (New York: Peter Lang, 2003), esp. ch. 1, "No Hero of Mine: Disney, Popular Culture, and Education," and her "A Realm Without Angels: MENC's Partnership with Disney and Other Major Corporations," *Philosophy of Music Education Review* 10.2 (Fall 2002): 72–79.

5. This emphasis on the economic sense of consumption, that is, what the customers, clients, or beneficiaries of music education think and do, differs from its physiological sense of consuming food and drink or its archaic medical sense of a disease.

6. Theodor Adorno, *Introduction to the Sociology of Music,* trans. E. B. Ashton (New York: Seabury, 1976), 6–8, 14–17, describes the "culture consumer" as a "copious, sometimes a voracious listener, well-informed," "collector of records" who is joined by the "entertainment listener," a lowly although prolific listener for whom "*music is entertainment* and no more." These listeners are in a similar predicament to those described by Jacques Attali, *Noise: The Political Economy of Music,* trans. Brian Massumi (Minneapolis: University of Minnesota Press, 1985), ch. 4, where repetitions of recorded performances gradually

lose their spiritual power. Also, see Tia DeNora, *After Adorno: Rethinking Music Sociology* (Cambridge: Cambridge University Press, 2003), passim.

7. For a classic study of musical taste, see Paul Randolph Farnsworth, *Musical Taste: Its Measurement and Cultural Nature* (Stanford, Calif.: Stanford University Press, 1950).

8. In his study of musical innovation and market conditions, Michael Christianen, "Cycles in Symbol Production? A New Model to Explain Concentration, Diversity and Innovation in the Music Industry," *Popular Music* 14.1 (Jan. 1995): 55–93, found that "in the long term," there was a "strong correlation between trend in concentration, and trends in diversity and innovation" and that these were inversely correlated (84).

9. Dewey, *Experience and Education*, 70, 71, moves from students' impulses, inclinations, interests, and passions through a dialogical approach toward long-term growth until the student's understanding eventually approximates that of an exponent's understanding.

10. Friedrich Schiller, *On the Aesthetic Education of Man in a Series of Letters*, letter 9, pp. 60, 61, urges artists to give people what they need and not want they want.

11. In North America, the public supports fashionable music programs; highly visible musical performances by ensembles, chamber musicians, and soloists who win competitions and in other ways prove their preeminence; a preponderance of popular music; little emphasis on the history and theory of music; emotional support and counseling services in private lessons; and opportunities for student relaxation in the midst of other onerous or "heavy" academic courses in general education.

12. On Orff's philosophy of primitivism, see Andreas Liess, *Carl Orff*, trans. Adelheid and Herbert Parkin (London: Calder and Boyars, 1966), 38, 39.

13. For example, the barred instruments in the Instrumentarium have removable bars; old instruments such as viols, recorders, portative organs, and the like can be played at various levels of complexity; and the use of pentatonic whole-tone scales and neighboring chords before tonic-dominant relationships add to the ease of access to these instruments. See Carl Orff and Gunild Keetman, *Orff-Schulwerk: Musik für Kinder*, 5 vols. (Mainz: Schott, 1954).

14. This implicit belief in free market forces and laissez-faire economics as appropriate ways to organize education is supported in Milton and Rose Friedman, *Free to Choose: A Personal Statement* (San Diego, Calif.: Harcourt Brace, 1990).

15. On choice-based instructional types in music, see Estelle R. Jorgensen, "On a Choice-based Instructional Typology in Music," *Journal of Research in Music Education* 29 (1981): 97–102, and "An Analysis of Aspects of Type IV Music Instruction in a Teacher-student Dyad," *Quarterly Journal of Music Teaching and Learning* 6.1 (Spring 1995): 16–31.

16. This approach is akin to Paulo Freire's view of "banking education" or Dewey's idea of "traditional" education, wherein the learner is the vessel into which knowledge is "poured" by the teacher. On banking education, see Paulo Freire, *Pedagogy of the Oppressed*, trans. Myra Bergman Ramos (rev. ed., New York: Continuum, 1993), ch. 2; on traditional education, see Dewey, *Experience and Education*, ch. 1.

17. On the "stock" of cultural knowledge, see Jane Roland Martin, *Cultural Miseducation: In Search of a Democratic Solution* (New York: Teachers College Press, 2002).

18. Alfred North Whitehead, *The Aims of Education and Other Essays* ([1929]; repr., New York: Free Press, 1967), 1, criticizes "inert" knowledge that lacks vitality.

19. Jorgensen, "On a Choice-based Instructional Typology in Music."

20. This intersection of physical, emotional, and intellectual responses to learning is supported philosophically by Israel Scheffler, *In Praise of the Cognitive Emotions and Other Essays in the Philosophy of Education* (New York: Routledge, 1991), ch. 1, and Iris M. Yob, "The Cognitive Emotions and Emotional Cognitions," 43–57, respectively, who write concerning the cognitive emotions (emotion centered on thought, such as surprise or the joy of verification) and the emotional cognitions (thought centered on emotion, such as that evident in ritual, myth, and the arts).

21. Estelle R. Jorgensen, "On a Choice-based Instructional Typology in Music" and "An Analysis of Aspects of Type IV Music Instruction in a Teacher-student Dyad."

22. In the United States, e.g., music basal-series textbooks or graded texts for school use are prepackaged for teacher delivery and student consumption. New school music texts are tested mainly in the largest markets such as California and Texas, and more sparsely populated and smaller states have less influence in shaping music textbooks. Although texts are customized to some degree, this customization takes place within the framework of profitability considerations.

23. For example, Thomas A. Regelski's approach to general music is predicated on a robust theoretical basis. See his *Teaching General Music in Grades 4–8: A Musicianship Approach* (New York: Oxford University Press, 2004), and his "action learning paradigm for curriculum development" in appendix A, 250–257. Regelski believes that his reader "must understand this theory in order to effect" its related practical strategies. Thomas A. Regelski, personal correspondence, Feb. 9, 2009. His is among a few modern approaches to rival the integration of theory with practice evidenced in the work of Émile Jaques-Dalcroze. See, e.g., Émile Jaques-Dalcroze, *Rhythm, Music and Education,* trans., Harold F. Rubinstein ([1921]; repr., New York: Arno Press, 1976).

24. Regelski, personal correspondence, Feb. 7, 2009, comments that he was encouraged by his reviewers to "shorten" the amount of space accorded to his discussion of theoretical issues in order to focus on practical matters and thereby please the market to which he and his publisher wished to appeal.

25. The longevity of textbooks such as Boethius's *De institutione musica* in print and in use for hundreds of years is foreign to the present reality of publishers bringing out a stream of new editions and licensing arrangements to promote the flow of money into the corporation. Standard music educational texts at the elementary, secondary, and tertiary level are commonly released in multiple editions, each one of which brings authors and publishers additional royalties and profits, and must be purchased by those who want to keep up to date with sometimes modest changes evident in them. Prices of music textbooks are set at whatever the market will bear in order to contribute to corporate profitability. Authors also labor to bring their textbooks up to date with new and attractive materials that reflect current concerns.

26. Among twentieth-century justifications for music and the arts, see James Mursell, *Human Values in Music Education* (New York: Silver, Burdett, 1934); Bennett Reimer, *A Philosophy of Music Education*, his *A Philosophy of Music Education,* 2nd ed. (Englewood Cliffs, N.J.: Prentice-Hall, 1989); and his *A Philosophy of Music Education: Advancing the Vision*, 3rd ed. (Englewood Cliffs, N.J.: Prentice-Hall, 2003); Harry S. Broudy, *Enlightened*

Cherishing: An Essay on Aesthetic Education (Urbana: Published for Kappa Delta Pi by University of Illinois Press, 1972); Elliot W. Eisner, *Cognition and Curriculum Reconsidered*, 2nd ed. (New York: Teachers College Press, 1994), passim, and his *The Arts and the Creation of Mind* (New Haven, Conn.: Yale University Press, 2002).

27. This preoccupation with fashion and the latest mediated craze and hype may serve to confirm Zoltán Kodály's fear that if not unchecked, it destroys what is indigenous and esoteric, it is unhealthful, and "bad taste in art is a veritable sickness of the soul." See Zoltán Kodály, *The Selected Writings*, 120. In like vein, James MacMillan, "God, Theology and Music," *New Blackfriars* 81.947 (Jan. 2000), DOI: 10.1111/j.1741-2005.2000.tb07819.x, http://www3.interscience.wiley.com/journal/119036977/, prods musicians and educators to recapture in music education what people need spiritually from music rather than just what they want sensually.

28. Percy A. Scholes, *Music, the Child and the Masterpiece*, 100–105, criticizes the American preoccupation with presentation, plugging instead for a curricular focus on substance, on the spiritual rather than sensory aspects of music. Looking back over music texts of the past allows us to see how much more visually and presentationally oriented our present society is when compared to earlier times.

3. VILLAGE AND COMMUNITY

1. See, e.g., John Dewey, *Democracy and Education: An Introduction to the Philosophy of Education* ([1916]; repr., New York: Free Press, 1966); Maria Montessori, *The Discovery of the Child,* trans. M. Joseph Costelloe (New York: Ballantine Books, 1967), and her *The Absorbent Mind,* trans. Claude A. Claremont (New York: Dell, 1967); Maxine Greene, *The Dialectic of Freedom*, and her *Releasing the Imagination: Essays on Education, the Arts, and Social Change* (San Francisco: Jossey-Bass, 1995); Jane Roland Martin, *The Schoolhome: Rethinking Schools for Changing Families* (Cambridge, Mass.: Harvard University Press, 1992); Parker J. Palmer, *The Courage to Teach: Exploring the Inner Landscape of a Teacher's Life* (San Francisco: Jossey-Bass, 1998); Raymond Gaita, *A Common Humanity: Thinking about Love and Truth and Justice,* 2nd ed. (London: Routledge, 2000); Nel Noddings, *Caring: A Feminine Approach to Ethics and Moral Education* (Berkeley: University of California Press, 1984), and *Happiness and Education* (Cambridge: Cambridge University Press, 2003); Paul G. Woodford, *Democracy and Music Education: Liberalism, Ethics, and the Politics of Practice* (Bloomington: Indiana University Press, 2005).

2. John Dewey, *The Public and its Problems* ([1927]; repr., Denver, Colo.: Alan Swallow, 1954?), 40–41. Looking closer to home may have tempered his romantic view of the village.

3. Dewey, *Democracy and Education*, 99, 358, 360.

4. J. R. Martin, *The Schoolhome,* esp. ch. 1, follows Maria Montessori's notion of the *casa di bambini* or the home of the young children; see Maria Montessori, *The Montessori Method,* trans. Anne E. George (New York: Schocken Books, 1988); Montessori, *The Discovery of the Child*, ch. 3. Also see Greene, *The Dialectic of Freedom*, esp. ch. 4; Noddings, *Happiness and Education*, esp. 220–224.

5. For Abraham H. Maslow, *Toward a Psychology of Being,* 2nd ed. (New York: D. Van Nostrand, 1968), esp. pts. 2 and 3, and his "Music, Education, and Peak Experiences," in *Documentary Report of the Tanglewood Symposium,* ed. Robert A. Choate (Washington,

D.C.: Music Educators National Conference, 1968), 70–73, developing toward self-actualization is predicated on meeting such basic needs as safety in food and shelter, which, if not met, would cause illness. Noddings, *Happiness and Education,* ch. 3, complicates notions of what constitute "basic" needs to include others such as the need for "home."

6. See Christopher Small, *Music-Society-Education: A Radical Examination of the Prophetic Function of Music in Western, Eastern and African Cultures with its Impact on Society and its Use in Education,* 2nd ed. (London: John Calder, 1980), and his *Musicking: The Meanings of Performing and Listening* (Hanover, N.H.: University Press of New England, 1998).

7. See, e.g., Charles Keil and Steven Feld, *Music Grooves: Essays and Dialogues,* 2nd ed. (Tucson, Ariz.: Fenestra Books, 2005); Patricia Shehan Campbell, *Tunes and Grooves for Music Education: Music for Classroom Use* (Upper Saddle River, N.J.: Pearson Prentice Hall, 2008).

8. On "spheres of musical validity," see Estelle R. Jorgensen, *In Search of Music Education*, ch. 2.

9. See Lucy Green, *Music on Deaf Ears: Musical Meaning, Ideology and Education* (Manchester, UK: Manchester University Press, 1988), chs. 2, 3. Also see John Shepherd, *Music as Social Text* (Cambridge, UK: Polity Press, 1991).

10. For example, through a multi-media presentation, Anthony Palmer, "Exploring American Culture Through Its Folk Music: A New Approach to Integration of Subject Matter," presentation to Walden University, San Diego, Calif., Mar. 11, 2005, available from the author at ajpalmer@bu.edu, demonstrates how songs of the American Depression of the 1930s relate intimately to their place and time and to our present realities.

11. Estelle R. Jorgensen, "Myth, Song, and Music Education: The Case of Tolkien's *The Lord of the Rings* and Swann's *The Road Goes Ever On,*" *Journal of Aesthetic Education* 40.3 (Fall 2006): 1–21, and "Music, Myth, and Education: The Case of *The Lord of the Rings* Film Trilogy," *Journal of Aesthetic Education* 44.1 (Spring 2010): 44–57.

12. On Zentner's processes and my application of them to music education, see Henry Zentner, *Prelude to Administrative Theory: Essays in Social Structure and Social Process* (Calgary: Strayer Publications, 1973), esp. ch. 7; Estelle R. Jorgensen, "On the Recruitment Process in Amateur Ensembles," *Canadian University Music Review* no. 6 (1985): 293–318, and "Developmental Phases in Selected British Choirs," *Canadian University Music Review* no. 7 (1986): 188–225. For example, personification or identity construction alerts teachers to music's function as an identity marker and to every social group's need for symbols of group identity, be they flags, names, or uniforms. Image preservation, or the need for each group to continue to expand and preserve its collective reputation, prompts teachers to care about the musical reputations of the groups they may be called upon to organize, foster, maintain, and if necessary, resuscitate. As a means of information exchange, communication plays a central role in the community in shaping the interactions of individual members. Since communication is formal and informal, music teachers need to be cognizant of and skilled in ways to facilitate the construction and exchange of knowledge that benefits the musical community.

13. Even those, such as Palmer, *The Courage to Teach,* passim, who focus on the teacher's "inner life" and subjective psychological experience, admit to the importance of group action and group evaluation.

14. In his discussion of social control, Dewey, *Education and Experience,* esp. ch. 4, views the teacher's role as that of umpire or coach, applying agreed-upon rules to particular situations. Here, discipline is exerted by the group as much as by the teacher's dictates.

15. On various sorts of artistic rules, see Vernon Howard, *Artistry: The Work of Artists* (Indianapolis: Hackett, 1982), esp. ch. 4. For example, choral directors provide choir members with an understanding of the rules and the skills needed in following them, including the conduct of rehearsals and performances, sight reading and singing skills, and stylistic practices. These theoretical and practical rules provide a basis upon which the various aspects of musical learning may be systematically grounded.

16. See, e.g., Dewey, *Democracy and Education,* 6, 360; Greene, *Releasing the Imagination,* 198.

17. See van Manen, *The Tact of Teaching,* esp. chs. 6–8.

18. Teachers may accomplish this in various practical ways. Instruments for music making, equipment for generating, recording, and playing recorded sounds, video equipment to illustrate how things look, technology to permit access to the mass media, musical scores, books, music stands, risers, pictures, and models are among the sorts of things that music rooms are equipped with in order to properly serve as a music home in which the music community can meet and learn. Field trips beyond the studio, classroom, and rehearsal area to hear live music, see art exhibits, attend plays, and visit museums are among the wide array of practical activities in which this active learning community engages. For Maxine Greene, *Variations on a Blue Guitar: The Lincoln Center Institute Lectures on Aesthetic Education* (New York: Teachers College Press, 2001), teachers come to Lincoln Center where, as well as hearing and seeing performances of various sorts, they converse together and reflect on these experiences.

19. Jane Roland Martin, *Reclaiming a Conversation: The Ideal of the Educated Woman* (New Haven, Conn.: Yale University Press, 1985), argues that extending the reach of education to informal and private life is essential in better preparing boys and girls and men and women to live happy and productive lives. Also, Thomas Henry Collinson, *Diary of an Organist's Apprentice at Durham Cathedral 1871–1875,* ed. Francis Collinson (Aberdeen, UK: Aberdeen University Press, 1982), describes a way of life learned as he lived with a group of fellow organist apprentices in Victorian England. Watching and listening to his teacher and older students, he became an organist and church musician at an early age. Since the students lived together, Collinson and his fellows came to know the teacher and their fellow apprentices intimately and in a far wider range of ways than would have been possible otherwise.

20. For example, in a newspaper account of the way of life of a Midwestern Evangelical Christian family (*The Boston Globe,* 267 [88] [Mar. 29, 2005]: A1, A6), this family's political, familial, economic, and musical way of life is shaped compellingly by its religious commitments as its way of life centers around the church. A music teacher at the school these children attend would need to advocate a way of life that is consonant with this family's religious commitments and sensibilities and those of different others in this school. In a multicultural milieu, difficulties and conflicts in various conceptions of possible and desirable ways of life are likely. Although open-mindedness and resourcefulness on the part of the community are required if it is to resolve these challenges and thrive, it is difficult to imagine how this particular family will tolerate ways of life that go counter to its religious commitments.

21. This is the case, e.g., in Celebration, Florida, designed by the Walt Disney Company as a perfect town in which the residents are supposed to be "happy ever after." On Celebration, Florida, see http://www.celebrationtowncenter.com/ (accessed June 9, 2010).

22. For Jerome Bruner, *Acts of Meaning* (Cambridge, Mass.: Harvard University Press, 1990), students construct knowledge, or an understanding of a field's ideas, and build the array of skills for its practices in differing ways. Also, see John Dewey, *The Child and the Curriculum* (1902) in *The Child and the Curriculum, and The School and Society,* combined ed. (Chicago: University of Chicago Press, 1956).

23. Palmer, *Courage to Teach,* 102, 107, depicts teachers and students as fellow learners gathered around subjects of great worth. Israel Scheffler, *Reason and Teaching* ([1973]; repr., Indianapolis: Bobbs-Merrill, 1973), ch. 9, posits that subject matter is best chosen with reference to its validity and generalizability to a wide range of ideas and practices.

24. See, e.g., Greene, *The Dialectic of Freedom,* xi, 11, 16, 17.

25. See Jorgensen, *Transforming Music Education,* 101–108.

26. These may be the moments that Maslow, in *Toward a Psychology of Being* (70–73), terms "peak experiences," times when a group of people is utterly taken up and preoccupied with this music, experiencing a sense of what Mihály Csikszentmihályi calls "flow," an effortlessness and pleasure that comes when they are "in" this music and absorbed in it. Also see Mihály Csikszentmihályi, *Flow: The Psychology of Optimal Experience* (New York: HarperPerennial, 1991).

27. For a description of the ways in which place impacts curriculum, see Joe L. Kincheloe and William F. Pinar, eds., *Curriculum as Social Psychoanalysis: The Significance of Place* (Albany: State University of New York Press, 1991). The impact of place on artists and their work is evident, e.g., on Cape Cod, which for centuries has been fertile ground for writers who have reflected on and portrayed various aspects of life on this peninsula. See Robert Finch, ed., *A Place Apart: A Cape Cod Reader* (New York: W. W. Norton, 1993).

28. A classification of social processes provided by Zentner, *Prelude to Administrative Theory,* ch. 7, identifies goal-setting, time-space allocation, communication, competition, segmentation, specialization, loyalty-maintenance, personification, image preservation, recruitment, and socialization as among the processes common to all social groups. Each process is driven by norm-sets that define the group's expectations about the ways in which it should operate.

29. Douglas McGregor, "Theory X and Theory Y," in *Organization Theory: Selected Readings,* 2nd ed., ed. D. S. Pugh (Harmondsworth, UK: Penguin, 1984), 317–333.

30. In counterpoint with McGregor's influential theories X and Y, William G. Ouchi, *Theory Z: How American Business can Meet the Japanese Challenge* (Reading, Mass.: Addison-Wesley, 1981), offers what Abraham H. Maslow, *The Farther Reaches of Human Nature* ([1971]; repr., Harmondsworth, UK: Penguin Books, 1972), ch. 22, terms "Theory Z." See, e.g., the differing pictures of organizations in Gareth Morgan, *Images of Organization* (Beverly Hills, Calif.: Sage, 1986).

31. Among the educational proponents of this approach, see Paulo Freire, *Pedagogy of the Oppressed,* esp. ch. 4; Palmer, *The Courage to Teach,* esp. ch. 7.

32. James Mursell's mid-twentieth-century advocacy of the social values of music and William Channing Woodbridge's nineteenth-century claim that vocal music instruction would improve school discipline and cultivate "habits of order, obedience, and union" that would transfer to other areas of life still resonate today. See William Channing Woodbridge,

A Lecture on Vocal Music as a Branch of Common Education. Delivered in the Representatives' Hall, Boston, August 24, 1830, Before the American Institute of Instruction (Boston: Hilliard, Gray, Little and Wilkins, 1831); James L. Mursell, *Human Values in Music Education,* and his *Education for American Democracy* (New York: W. W. Norton, 1943), and his *Principles of Democratic Education* (New York: Norton, 1955).

33. See Martin, *Reclaiming a Conversation,* esp. ch. 7.

34. See Seyla Benhabib, *The Claims of Culture: Equality and Diversity in the Global Era* (Princeton, N.J.: Princeton University Press, 2002), 19, 20.

35. Freire, *Pedagogy of the Oppressed,* 29.

36. Dewey, *The Public and Its Problems,* 40–41.

37. For a discussion of the dark and bright sides of community, see Estelle R. Jorgensen, "Music Education as Community," *Journal of Aesthetic Education* 29.3 (Fall 1995): 71–84.

38. On this point, see Small, *Music-Society-Education,* and his *Musicking.*

39. Wayne Booth, *For the Love of It: Amateuring and its Rivals* (Chicago: University of Chicago Press, 1999).

40. James H. Stone, "Mid-Nineteenth-Century American Beliefs in the Social Values of Music," *The Musical Quarterly* 43.1 (Jan. 1957): 38–49, argues that a cult of musical amateurism that grew up around the rise of publicly supported music education in the United States retarded the development of professional music making in the nineteenth century. In his view, the fixation with amateur music making downplayed acquiring advanced musical skills and suggested that all might participate musically irrespective of their natural or cultivated musical proclivities.

41. See Dewey, *Democracy and Education,* esp. ch. 7; Woodford, *Music Education and Democracy.*

42. For example, Gilbert Highet, *The Art of Teaching* ([1950]; repr., New York: Vintage Books, 1989), 89–107, and Percy A. Scholes, *Music, the Child and the Masterpiece,* 100–116, defend old-fashioned lecturing and exposition as principal teaching approaches. They are unconcerned about building community and much more interested in ensuring that students grasp the subject matter of classics and music, respectively.

43. This may be the case for women teachers and academics, e.g., Madeleine R. Grumet, *Bitter Milk: Women and Teaching* (Amherst: University of Massachusetts Press, 1988) and Jane Roland Martin, *Coming of Age in Academe: Rekindling Women's Hopes and Reforming the Academy* (New York: Routledge, 2000).

44. For example, as a member of a small class of pianists studying in Germany in the mid-nineteenth century, Amy Fay, *Music-Study in Germany in the Nineteenth Century from the Home Correspondence of Amy Fay* ([1880]; repr., New York: Dover, 1965), took group lessons with such well-known pianist-teachers as Tausig and Liszt. Her lessons took on the aura of performances; students' playing was subject to public scrutiny by the teacher and other students. The necessity of performing publicly while also learning required students to practice and prepare for their lessons. The group lessons were intense, moving, and inspiring experiences that, according to Fay's account, sometimes consumed hours at a stretch. The students often socialized together, attending concerts and other cultural events as they studied to become professional pianists. Doubtless studying in this way provoked insights for Fay that she might never have discovered otherwise.

45. On this point, see Greene, *Dialectic of Freedom,* 17.

46. Fay comments that she and her colleagues would place the music they had prepared on the piano and Liszt would choose which pieces he wanted to hear. She would be called upon and others might not, especially if they incurred Liszt's displeasure. On her time with Liszt, see Fay, *Music-Study in Germany,* 205–247.

47. See Whitehead, *The Aims of Education,* ch. 2. For a cyclical approach to music education, see the model developed by June Boyce-Tillman and Keith Swanwick in Keith Swanwick, *Music, Mind, and Education* (London: Routledge, 1988), ch. 5; and Keith Swanwick and June Tillman, "The Sequence of Musical Development," *British Journal of Music Education* 3.3 (1986): 305–339. Also, see Estelle R. Jorgensen, "Philosophical Issues in Curriculum," in *The New Handbook of Research on Music Teaching and Learning,* ed. Richard Colwell and Carol Richardson (Oxford: Oxford University Press, 2002), 48–62.

48. In the wake of Bruner's cyclical theories, efforts such as the Manhattanville Music Curriculum Project (MMCP) have found limited success. On the MMCP, see Ronald B. Thomas, ed., *MMCP Synthesis: A Structure for Music Education* (Elnora, N.Y.: Media Inc., n.d. [1971).

49. In my own application of MMCP ideas in the Milton Williams Junior High School Project in Calgary, Canada, I found it difficult to mesh all of the various aspects of musical experience within the suggested developmental concepts. The study of music theory tended to take over the junior high school curriculum. See Estelle R. Jorgensen, "A Case Study in Two Divergent Research Methodologies in Music Education," *CAUSM Journal* 8.1 (1979): 33–72.

50. Charlene Morton, "Response to Bennett Reimer, 'Once More With Feeling: Reconciling Discrepant Accounts of Musical Affect,'" *Philosophy of Music Education Review* 12.1 (Spring 2004): 55–59, argues for musical cosmopolitanism in a multicultural society.

4. ARTIST AND APPRENTICESHIP

1. See John Dewey, *Democracy and Education,* 258.

2. See V. [Vernon] A. Howard, *Artistry,* and his *Learning By All Means*; David J. Elliott, *Music Matters.*

3. On art and craft, see Howard, *Artistry,* ch. 1.

4. For a discussion of significant and vital import, see Susanne K. Langer, *Philosophy in a New Key,* ch. 7, her *Feeling and Form,* passim, and her *Problems of Art,* esp. ch. 4.

5. Even Immanuel Kant, *The Critique of Judgment,* §53, pp. 195–196, for whom music was among the lowliest of the arts, acknowledges its sentimental appeal and the judgments that are made on the basis of perceived sonic phenomena.

6. See Goodman, *Languages of Art,* 252–255.

7. Howard, *Artistry,* 158–160.

8. On creativity and exceptionality, see, e.g., Brewster Ghiselin, ed., *The Creative Process: A Symposium* ([1952]; repr., New York and Scarborough Ontario: New American Library, Mentor Book, 1952); Frank Brown, Alfonso Montuori, and Anthea Barron, *Creators on Creating: Awakening and Cultivating the Imaginative Mind* (New York: G. P. Putnam's Sons, 1997); Howard Gardner, *Extraordinary Minds: Portraits of Exceptional Individuals and an Examination of our Extraordinariness* (New York: Basic Books, 1997); Robert J. Sternbook, ed.,

Handbook of Creativity (Cambridge: Cambridge University Press, 1999); Robert J. Sternberg, Elena L. Grigorenko, and Jerome L. Singer, eds., *Creativity: From Potential to Realization* (Washington, D.C.: American Psychological Association, 2004); Howard Gardner, *Five Minds for the Future* (Boston: Harvard Business School Press, 2006).

9. See Howard, *Artistry*, ch. 6.

10. Although encouraged as a performer by her father Friedrich Wieck, Clara Schumann seems to have had less confidence in her abilities as a composer. See Nancy B. Reich, "Clara Schumann," in *Women Making Music: The Western Art Tradition, 1150–1950*, ed. Jane Bowers and Judith Tick (Urbana: University of Illinois Press, 1986), 249–281. Lucy Green, *Music, Gender, Education* (Cambridge: Cambridge University Press, 1997), suggests that women composing and improvising threatens femininity.

11. When Plato, *Republic*, trans., Robin Waterfield (Oxford: Oxford University Press, 1993), §401d, p. 100, said that music "sinks deep into the recesses of the soul," he may have been referring to this process of internalizing ways of thinking and acting that impact not only intellectually but also emotionally and physically.

12. I think of this metaphor as masculine since the word *mistress* has another connotation and the historical record reveals comparatively few women who have served the role of musical master. Although this situation has begun to change as more women have assumed the role, being a master is still often considered to be a manly role.

13. For example, as an apprentice is able, a church organist might begin to assign services to play, and in this manner, little by little, by successive approximation, the apprentice becomes an accomplished musician. See, e.g., Collinson, *The Diary of an Organist's Apprentice*.

14. See *Grove Music Online, Oxford Music Online*, s.v. "Guilds" (by Heinrich W. Schwab), http://www.oxfordmusiconline.com (accessed July 13, 2010). Also see Howard, *Artistry*, and his *Learning by All Means*, esp. pt. 2 (where he describes how, through instruction, practice, example, and reflection, the student gradually comes closer to imagined ideals embodied, expressed, exemplified, and embraced by the teacher); and Donald A. Schön, *Educating the Reflective Practitioner: Toward a New Design for Teaching and Learning in the Professions* (San Francisco: Jossey-Bass, 1987).

15. Jay Parini, "A Portrait of the Artist as Apprentice," *Chronicle of Higher Education* 47 no. 36, B24, May 18, 2004.

16. See Dan Schultz, "Hans-Jørgen Holman, 1925–1986," (2009) http://www.iamaonline .com/Bio/HOLMAN.htm (accessed July 23, 2010).

17. See Jorgensen, *In Search of Music Education*, ch. 1.

18. Music is not a free-for-all musical self-exposure but an expression of one's inner life musically. John Dewey, *Art as Experience* ([1934]; repr., New York: G. P. Putnam's Sons, 1979), 82, uses the metaphor of wine expressed from grapes for the artist's task of self-expression as different from merely letting off emotional steam in a musical fashion as in self-exposure.

19. On the difficulties in the student's way, see Howard, *Artistry*, esp. chs. 3, 4. This is a daunting process, since the student is not always clear what needs to be learned and why, and is dependent upon the teacher who is "in the know."

20. See Dewey, *Art as Experience*, ch. 4, esp. 59–60.

21. For example, an emergent jazz classical tradition, like its European counterpart, is also progressively more literate, academic, cerebral, and elitist. See, e.g., Paul F. Berliner, *Thinking in Jazz: The Infinite Art of Improvisation* (Chicago: Chicago University Press, 1994).

According to Daniel M. Neuman, *The Life of Music in North India: The Organization of an Artistic Tradition* (Detroit: Wayne State University Press, 1980), the ustads of the North Indian classical tradition traditionally prided themselves on protecting and preserving their tradition against intrusions by the unworthy and insufficiently musical.

22. For example, a left-handed apprentice conductor whom we shall call Janice may desire to conduct the beat patterns with her left hand. However, the master insists that she use her right hand, because this is a right-handed world and this is the convention, even though such a move may leave Janice at a disadvantage when she has less flexibility in her right hand than her left.

23. See Schön, *Educating the Reflective Practitioner,* passim. Gilbert Highet, *The Art of Teaching,* 107–116, would probably think of this approach as a form of "tutoring."

24. Marie may have done the best she could with the piece in the time she has put in on practice. Since she has been busy this week, she may have practiced insufficiently in the hope that inspiration will strike in the midst of the lesson, as it did last week. There may be passages she has not quite mastered and stumbles over. She may have used bowings or fingerings that need to be remediated in order to give the music a smoother flow. She may have practiced by starting at the first measure, playing until she breaks down, starting again at the first measure, and playing until she breaks down, and so on, rather than effectively analyzing the score, remedying the most problematic passages, and then learning the other sections part by part in a more analytic way. Since she is impatient, she may have failed to listen carefully to the notes she plays and attempted to play the piece at tempo before she is ready technically.

25. Sometimes what the teacher says (or plays in demonstration to Marie) may make a dramatic difference to her playing, and there may be a significant breakthrough on her part. At other times, little by little, part by part, the teacher works with what Marie has prepared, assigns exercises and repertoire for further practice, and helps her to understand what she is doing.

26. See Howard, *Artistry,* chs. 3, 4, and his *Learning by All Means,* 5, 7.

27. On this "rule" model of teaching, see Israel Scheffler, *Reason and Teaching,* 76–80.

28. Howard's analysis of this language reveals the power of metaphors in shaping the master's direction for the student in non-technical ways that might enable an immediacy of instruction and make it more possible for the student to do what the teacher requires. Howard's example of the way in which a technical description of the singing process can disrupt the student's learning of how to sing is a case in point. Instead, he notes, a teacher may use a metaphor to enable the student to imagine what is being called for in the hope that this picture will provide the spark to prompt the desired action.

29. For example, there is the vocal *passaggio,* as the student moves from one *fache* or part of the range to the next, the overtone series in brass instruments, and the various parts of woodwind ranges in which various fingerings come into play. Making the entire range of an instrument smooth and homogeneous is challenging for musicians to learn, and teachers may find metaphors useful in helping students unify the sound produced over the entire range of their instruments.

30. See Estelle R. Jorgensen, *The Art of Teaching Music* (Bloomington: Indiana University Press, 2008), 155, 221.

31. For example, even if string teachers were to agree that certain general bowing approaches should be followed by all students, the particular emphasis of apprenticeship

teaching is on finding the right challenges that enable students to successfully play their in-struments in specific pieces. What might begin as a generally strategic approach to bowing rapidly becomes individualized. Even in a string class in which approaches to bowing have been more or less standardized, teachers need to attend individually to every student. For this reason, the best teachers in the Suzuki tradition employ assistants to help them meet the individual needs of their students. For example, Mimi Zweig and Brenda Brenner have a fleet of assistants who are, themselves, apprentices of their particular string teaching meth-ods, and who help provide individual attention for students. They are right to be critical of approaches to string teaching that pay insufficient attention to the individual differences of students. On Mimi Zweig's approach to string pedagogy, see http://www.stringpedagogy. com/ (accessed July 21, 2010). See also Brenda Brenner, "Reflecting on the Rationales for String Study in Schools," *Philosophy of Music Education Review* 18.1 (Spring 2010): 45–64.

32. On the "apprentice's sorcery," see Howard, *Artistry*, 75–76.

33. See Howard, *Learning by all Means*, esp. pt. 2 (where he describes how, through in-struction, practice, example, and reflection, the student gradually comes closer to imagined ideals embodied, expressed, exemplified, and embraced by the teacher).

34. Jaques-Dalcroze, *Rhythm, Music and Education*, 128, makes use of anti-example to foster what he calls "dissociation" or musical separation of mind and body as a means of learning music. For example, he might ask that a rising musical line be rendered physically by bending and crouching lower and lower, thereby ironically highlighting the upwardly moving musical line in the student's mind and enabling separation between a heard and imaginary musical line.

35. See Howard, *Artistry*, ch. 6. Peter Miksza, "Relationships among Impulsiveness, Locus of Control, Sex, and Music Practice," *Journal of Research in Music Education* 54.4 (Winter 2006): 308–323, refers to practice as the musician's intentional efforts to improve performance. José Antonio Lopez, "Pedagogical Principles for the College Classical Guitar Teacher," doctoral diss., Indiana University, 2004, esp. ch. 3, is after this intellectual engage-ment; he wants to call such practice *study*, since he connects the word *practice* with the sort of mindless and time-consuming repetition and development of physical skills that may re-sult in muscle memory but do not necessarily benefit intellectual understanding. My sense, though, is that since practice is a commonly understood term among musicians, it may be better to reconceptualize it, as do Howard and Miksza, than to abandon it, as does Lopez.

36. On "reflection in the midst of action"—the immediate thinking that the artist does while actually doing that art, see Schön, *Educating the Reflective Practitioner*, esp. ch. 2.

37. See Jorgensen, *Transforming Music Education*, 102–107.

38. The musician seems to be working at a somewhat instinctual level, and apprentices need to cultivate these musical instincts, intuitions, and imaginings that are not always carefully or systematically thought through propositionally. On the instinctual engage-ment with music, see Aaron Copland, *Music and Imagination* (Cambridge, Mass.: Harvard University Press, 1952), 13; Roger Sessions, *The Musical Experience of Composer, Performer, Listener* ([1950]; repr., New York: Atheneum, 1962). 20. Neither writer would be satisfied with instinct but would insist on the education of musical imagination.

39. On artistic undergoing, see Dewey, *Art as Experience*, 44, 132.

40. On "getting a nose" for something, see Howard, *Artistry*, 75.

41. Among the sorts of teacher-directed learning, cf. Paulo Freire's concept of "banking" education, Dewey's notion of "traditional" education, and John Locke's *tabula rasa* theory.

See Paulo Freire, *Pedagogy of the Oppressed*, ch. 2; John Dewey, *Education and Experience* ([1938]; repr., New York: Collier Books, 1963), ch. 1; John Locke, *An Essay Concerning Human Understanding*, abridged and ed. A. D. Woozley (New York: Penguin Books, 1974); John Locke, *An Essay Concerning Humane Understanding*, 2 vols. (Project Gutenberg, 2004) http://www.gutenberg.org/etext/10615, and http://www.gutenberg.org/etext/10616 (accessed July 24, 2010).

42. Scheffler, *Reason and Teaching*, 71–76, refers to this as the "insight" model of teaching.

43. For example, in Ernesto Bitetti's guitar studio at Indiana University Jacobs School of Music, his most senior students teach beginners or those more junior in the program. On Ernesto Bitetti, see *Grove Music Online, Oxford Music Online*, s.v. "Bitetti, Ernesto" (by Peter Sensier and Graham Wade), http://www.oxfordmusiconline.com (accessed July 13, 2010).

44. For example, in the Western classical tradition, performers often publicly acknowledge their teachers in their biographies and return to their teachers in later life for further coaching. Such was the case, e.g., with Josef Gingold, whose many violin students continued to pay him respect into old age. At the memorial concert in his honor, the stage of the Musical Arts Center at Indiana University was filled to overflowing with hundreds of his students and former students, including professional violinists, who returned to express their allegiance to and love for their teacher. On Josef Gingold, see *Grove Music Online, Oxford Music Online*, s.v. "Gingold, Josef" (by Boris Schwarz and Margaret Campbell), http://www.oxfordmusiconline.com (accessed July 13, 2010).

45. Jason Edwards, "Schools of Oboe Playing: Formation, Transmission, and Evolution," doctoral diss., Indiana University, 2004, and Svet A. Atanasov, "A Description of Selected Aspects of Three Approaches to College-level Bassoon Instruction," doctoral diss., Indiana University, 2004, provide insight into the various European and American schools of oboe and bassoon teaching, respectively, whereby performers trace their lineage back through musical generations.

46. See Karl Geiringer, *The Bach Family: Seven Generations of Creative Genius* (New York: Oxford University Press, 1954); George Martin, *The Damrosch Dynasty: America's First Family of Music* (Boston: Houghton Mifflin, 1983); Neuman, *The Life of Music in North India*, ch. 5.

47. For example, the different character of oboe and bassoon reeds, bores of the instruments, playing positions, repertoire, and pedagogies continue to impact the sounds of these instruments and their performance practices.

48. Curzon was one of the leading exponents of Mozart's music of his day, see *Grove Music Online, Oxford Music Online*, s.v. "Curzon, Sir Clifford" (by Max Loppert), http://www.oxfordmusiconline.com (accessed July 13, 2010).

49. This has been true from ancient times. For example, liturgists in ancient Mesopotamia knew complex rituals that might take days to perform. See Henry George Farmer, "The Music of Ancient Mesopotamia," in *New Oxford History of Music*, vol. 1: *Ancient and Oriental Music* (London: Oxford University Press, 1957): 228–254. Also see *Grove Music Online, Oxford Music Online*, s.v. "Mesopotamia" (by Anne Kilmer), http://www.oxfordmusiconline.com (accessed July 13, 2010). On ancient Babylonian liturgies, see, e.g., Stephen Langdon, *Tammuz and Ishtar: A Monograph upon Babylonian Religion and Theology, Containing Extensive Extracts from the Tammuz Liturgies and All of the Arbela Oracles* (Oxford: Clarendon Press, 1914).

50. Nor is this something confined to the Western classical tradition. In popular musics emanating from the West but now internationalized, many musicians count themselves as artists and regard the traditions they represent as of great value. As a result, they sometimes find themselves at odds with merchants who would purvey their music as merely a commodity. Nor is it unusual to encounter popular musicians who, disenchanted with commercial attitudes to their music, strike out independently to perform and record music that speaks artistically irrespective of its commercial viability.

51. For example, an aspiring operatic soprano needs a rich knowledge of languages, opportunities to sing in amateur, semi-professional, and professional settings as she prepares herself for this way of life. She may be advised to travel, hear leading opera singers, see a wealth of opera performed, and learn how to conduct herself as an opera singer. There are certain expectations of operatic sopranos, especially those who aspire to be divas or to sing regularly at a professional level, and this soprano needs to understand what will be required of her. A singing teacher may set up informal opportunities for her to sing and act roles in more nurturing environments such as master classes and opera workshops. When she is ready, her teacher may advise her to audition for particular roles with amateur, semi-professional, or professional companies. As she begins to take on these roles, her repertoire grows, her confidence and poise develop, and she gradually meets progressively greater challenges. So, as the teacher assesses this soprano, she is thinking through a series of increasingly more challenging activities that cover not only learning the opera repertoire, but more broadly, preparing her to succeed in the world of opera after her initial study is complete. Some things will be learned simply by singing opera and being in situations that are not intentionally pedagogical but end up being so. Socialization and enculturation are at work as the teacher ensures that these experiences our soprano has and undergoes are within the frame of a community of others and that her preparation is very broad so that she may also sing more intelligently as she grasps the wider culture of which this repertoire is a part.

52. See Bernarr Rainbow and Gordon Cox, *Music in Educational Thought and Practice: A Survey from 800 BC* (Woodbridge, UK: Boydell, 2007); *Grove Music Online, Oxford Music Online*, s.v. "Conservatories" (by William Weber et al.), http://www.oxfordmusiconline.com (accessed July 13, 2010).

53. Herman B Wells, *Being Lucky: Reminiscences and Reflections* (Bloomington: Indiana University Press, 1980), was a visionary mid-twentieth-century president of Indiana University who envisaged a world-class school of music and gave it all the resources needed to implement an apprenticeship model. For a history of the Indiana University Jacobs School of Music, see George M. Logan, *The Indiana University School of Music: A History* (Bloomington: Indiana University Press, 2000). The result was the astonishing development of a music school that is, today, one of the great centers of musical instruction.

54. See Henry Kingsbury, *Music, Talent, and Performance: A Conservatory Cultural System* (Philadelphia: Temple University Press, 1988); Bruno Nettl, *Heartland Excursions: Ethnomusicological Reflections on Schools of Music* (Urbana: University of Illinois Press, 1995).

55. Over the years, the Royal Conservatory of Music in Toronto has had ties with the University of Toronto and its students are prepared to continue their musical study at this or other universities. In Australia, students are examined in various locations across the

country by musicians representing the Australian Music Examinations Board. The Board's work is supported by conservatories such as the Sydney Conservatorium of Music, affiliated with the University of Sydney. Although most music schools in the United States are affiliated with a university or college, independent music schools such as the Juilliard School also cater to the advanced preparation of musicians. Despite these differing arrangements for musical study, all share many of the self-same attributes of apprenticeship music education. They are more or less independently operating institutions serving musical rather than other ends, in the particular musical traditions they represent, and with the express purpose of preparing practitioners of those traditions. Musical considerations are their principal *raison d'être*.

56. Jaques-Dalcroze, *Rhythm, Music and Education*, 16, describes the need to protect against those who would "clutter" music with their "ridiculous pretensions." While he writes specifically about school-age music education, he might just as well refer to music education at more advanced levels as well.

57. For example, some music departments, schools, and conservatories in the United States refuse to join or have opted out of the National Association of Schools of Music because of concerns that what they wish to do musically is constrained by other institutions with different interests.

5. REVOLUTIONARY AND TRANSGRESSION

1. Cervantes's Don Quixote tilts at windmills. He passionately seeks to realize a seemingly impossible dream, is willing to die in the attempt, and becomes, in the process, a tragic figure in the Spanish revolutionary history of shaking off foreign domination and achieving national identity and independence. See Miguel de Cervantes Saavedra, *Don Quixote: Fourth-centenary Translation*, trans. Tom Lathrop (Newark, Del.: Cervantes and Co., 2005).

2. See, e.g., J. R. R. [John Ronald Reuel] Tolkien's pictures, including those for *The Lord of the Rings*, and Jacques Attali's discussion of Brueghel's *Carnival's Quarrel with Lent*. See J. [John] R. R. Tolkien, *Pictures by J. R. R. Tolkien* (London: G. Allen & Unwin, 1979); Attali, *Noise: The Political Economy of Music*, 21–24.

3. American revolutionaries were not only against the British but for an independent republic. They drew up a Declaration of Independence, a manifesto of their beliefs and commitments that enshrined the ideals and principles for which they stood. This declaration was no mean, timid, or limited statement of intent, but a grand vision for a small group of colonies committed to an independent republic. Their resistance to British rule was an obvious element of the revolution, but it also drew from their commitments to certain other principles. Their hopes for what they might achieve and convictions of the rightness of their cause held the revolution together and fueled the ensuing resistance to British power.

4. See "Music in the Public Schools," *Dwight's Journal of Music* 10 (1857): 178; Seminar on Music Education, Music in our Schools (1963), *A Search for Improvement; Report of the Yale Seminar on Music Education*, prepared by Claude V. Palisca ([Washington] U.S. Dept. of Health, Education, and Welfare, Office of Education [1962]); *Documentary Report of the Tanglewood Symposium*, ed. Robert A. Choate (Washington, D.C.: Music Educators

National Conference, 1968), 138, 139. Also, the original MAYDAY "manifesto" was softened to a set of "regulative ideals" and later to "action ideals," published on the MAYDAY group's website at http://www.maydaygroup.org/ (accessed July 13, 2010).

5. See Nell Porter Brown, "Chords of Revolution: A Jazz Musician Thrives in Brooklyn," *Harvard Magazine* 107.5 (May–June 2005): 75–78.

6. See Ron Sakolsky and Fred Wei-Han Ho, eds., *Sounding Off: Music as Subversion/Resistance/Revolution* (Brooklyn, N.Y.: Autonomedia, 1995).

7. Brown, "Chords of Revolution," 75.

8. Ibid., 76.

9. For example, freedom and solidarity in community are themes in the work of Maxine Greene, *Dialectic of Freedom*, and bell hooks, *Teaching to Transgress: Education as the Practice of Freedom* (New York: Routledge, 1994), who observe that some people may not think of how things might be different unless they are in the midst of such a group.

10. Standing at the bridge over the Alabama River where they began this now famous trek, I imagined their solidarity in confronting those who sought to prevent them from passing over the bridge—how they must have gained courage as they stood together, determined to complete the task they had undertaken. Visitors can trace this march in March 1965 at the Selma to Montgomery National Historic Trail; see http://www.nps.gov/semo/ (accessed July 19, 2010).

11. See Greene, *Dialectic of Freedom*; hooks, *Teaching to Transgress*.

12. See "Three Crosses Burned in Durham," *Boston Globe,* Friday, May 27, 2005, A20.

13. See Martin Luther King Jr., *The Words of Martin Luther King, Jr.,* sel., Coretta Scott King, 2nd ed. (New York: Newmarket Press, 2001); Malcolm X with Alex Haley, *The Autobiography of Malcolm X* (New York: Ballantine Books, 1999).

14. For example, this was the case with Mahatma Gandhi, who endured years of exile, hardship, and imprisonment for his ideas and practices before eventually being acclaimed for his efforts to bring about Indian independence. See Mahatma Gandhi, *An Autobiography, or, The Story of my Experiments with Truth* [electronic resource] (Ahmedabad: Navajivan Pub. House, 1996); Mahatma Gandhi, *Vows and Observances* (Berkeley, Calif.: Berkeley Hills Books, 1999); Richard L. Johnson, *Gandhi's Experiments with Truth: Essential Writings By and About Mahatma Gandhi* (Lanham, Md.: Lexington Books, 2006).

15. See Neil Postman and Charles Weingartner, *Teaching as a Subversive Activity* (New York: Dell, 1969); Illich, *Deschooling Society;* Freire, *Pedagogy of the Oppressed;* Maxine Greene, *Dialectic of Freedom* and *Releasing the Imagination: Essays on Education, the Arts, and Social Change* (San Francisco: Jossey-Bass, 1995); J. R. Martin, *Reclaiming a Conversation, The Schoolhome,* and *Cultural Miseducation;* hooks, *Teaching to Transgress;* Noddings, *Happiness and Education.*

16. See, e.g., Thomas A. Regelski, "Scientism in Experimental Music Research," *Philosophy of Music Education Review* 4.1 (Spring 1996): 3–19; Elizabeth S. Gould, "Getting the Whole Picture: The View from Here," *Philosophy of Music Education Review* 2.2: (Fall 1994): 92–98, and her "Nomadic Turns"; Patricia O'Toole, "Threatening Behaviors: Transgressive Acts in Music Education," *Philosophy of Music Education Review* 10.1 (Spring 2002): 3–17; Julia Eklund Koza, *Stepping Across*; Randall Everett Allsup, "Hard Times: Philosophy and the Fundamentalist Imagination," *Philosophy of Music Education Review* 13.2 (Fall 2005): 139–142; Cathy Benedict, "Naming our Reality: Negotiating and Creating Meaning in

the Margin," *Philosophy of Music Education Review* 15.1 (Spring 2007): 23–35; Randall Everett Allsup and Cathy Benedict, "The Problems of Band: An Inquiry into the Future of Instrumental Music," *Philosophy of Music Education Review* 16.2 (Fall 2008): 156–173.

17. On conscientization, see Freire, *Pedagogy of the Oppressed*, 17, 18, and *Pedagogy of Hope*, 101–103.

18. See, e.g., Greene, *Dialectic of Freedom*; Randall Everett Allsup, "Activating Self-Transformation through Improvisation in Instrumental Music Teaching," *Philosophy of Music Education Review* 5.2 (Fall 1997): 80–85.

19. Ivan Illich, *Deschooling Society* (London: Marion Boyars, 1970), 73, 75.

20. See Illich, *Deschooling Society,* esp. chs. 6, 7.

21. For the etymology of transgression in the Latin, *transgredī*, see *OED Online*, s.v. "transgression," http://dictionary.oed.com (accessed July 14, 2010).

22. See Koza, *Stepping Across.*

23. For example, Galileo Galilei stepped beyond the accepted religious dogma of his time to espouse a heretical notion that the world moved around the sun. With other scientists, Galileo confronted the power of the Roman Church and, while reluctant to be out of communion with it, set out ideas and observations that led to dramatic astronomical and theological discoveries in the succeeding centuries. Galileo Galilei, "Letter to the Grand Duchess of Toscany," in *Three Thousand Years of Educational Wisdom: Selections from Great Documents,* ed. Robert Ulich, 2nd ed. (Cambridge, Mass.: Harvard University Press, 1954), 323–336.

24. When music serves utilitarian purposes, it is expected to be accessible to a wide range of people. For example, Hans Werner Henze, *Music and Politics: Collected Writings 1953–81,* trans. Peter Labanyi (London: Faber and Faber, 1982), writes about how political principles guided his composition of revolutionary music. The music used for propaganda and political purposes is often simple, accessible, and conservative, since those who partake in these revolutions are ordinary people with unsophisticated musical tastes. See, e.g., Arnold Perris, *Music as Propaganda: Art to Persuade, Art to Control* (Westport, Conn.: Greenwood, 1985); Rebecca Wagner Oettinger, *Music as Propaganda in the German Reformation* (Aldershot; Burlington, Vt.: Ashgate, 2001); Richard A. Etlin, *Art, Culture, and Media under the Third Reich* (Chicago: University of Chicago Press, 2002); Neil Edmunds, *Soviet Music and Society Under Lenin and Stalin: The Baton and Sickle* (New York: RoutledgeCurzon, 2004); Tibet Information Network, *Unity and Discord: Music and Politics in Contemporary Tibet* (London: Tibet Information Network, 2004). On the music of the Depression and worker songs, see the soundtrack of the television documentary, "The Great Depression": *The Great Depression* [sound recording]: *American Music in the 30's* (New York, N.Y.: Columbia, p1993), 1 sound disc, CK 57589 Columbia; Terese M. Volk, "Little Red Songbooks: Songs for the Labor Force in America," *Journal of Research in Music Education* 49 (Spring 2001): 33–48; Bill C. Malone and David Stricklin, *Southern Music/ American Music,* rev. ed. (Lexington: University of Kentucky Press, 2003); William H. Young and Nancy K. Young, *Music of the Great Depression* (Westport, Conn.: Greenwood, 2005).

25. See, e.g., Hildegard von Bingen, *Ordo virtutum* [sound recording] (Freiburg: Deutsche Harmonia Mundi, [1991], p1982), 2 compact discs; *Hildegard of Bingen's Book of Divine Works with Letters and Songs,* Santa Fe, N.M.: Bear and Co., 1987); Matthew Fox, ed., *Hildegard of Bingen's Scivias,* trans. Bruce Hozeski (Santa Fe, N.M.: Bear and Co.,

1986); Harold C. Schonberg, *The Great Pianists from Mozart to the Present* (New York: Simon and Schuster, 1963), ch. 5; Reginald R. Gerig, *Famous Pianists and Their Technique* (Bloomington: Indiana University Press, 2007), ch. 6; Igor Stravinsky, *Poetics of Music in the Form of Six Lessons,* trans. Arthur Knodel and Ingolf Dahl (Cambridge, Mass.: Harvard University Press, 1942); Arnold Schoenberg, *The Musical Idea and the Logic, Technique, and Art of Its Presentation,* ed. and trans. Patricia Carpenter and Severine Neff ([1995]; repr., Bloomington: Indiana University Press, 2006); Duke Ellington, *The Essential Duke Ellington* [sound recording] (New York: Sony BMG Music Entertainment, 2005), 2 compact discs, originally released 1927–1960; Billie Holiday, *God Bless the Child* (New York]: HarperCollins/Amistad, 2004) and her *Lady Day* [sound recording]: *The Best of Billie Holiday* ([New York]: Columbia/Legacy, p2001), 2 sound discs, C2K 85979 Columbia/ Legacy; *The Beatles Anthology* [videorecording] [Los Angeles, Calif.: Capitol Records, 2003), 5 videodiscs; Paul Simon, *Graceland* [videorecording] ([New York]: Eagle Rock Entertainment, 2005), 1 videodisc; Carole King, *Her Greatest Hits* [sound recording]: *Songs of Long Ago* (New York: Ode, 1999), 1 compact disc, EK 65846, and *Tapestry* [sound recording] (New York: Ode/Epic/Legacy, p1999), 1 compact disc, EK 65850 Ode/Epic/Legacy; for a list of John Williams' film scores, see http://jwexperience.jw-music.net/filmscores.html (accessed Mar. 12, 2008), e.g., his film score for *Harry Potter and the Sorcerer's Stone* [videorecording] (Burbank, Calif.: Distributed by Warner Home Video, [2007]), 1 videodisc; for Marin Alsop, "She's at the Top of her Field, and Coming to Tanglewood," *Boston Sunday Globe* June 5, 2005, N9; for Butch Morris, "When He Conducts, The Electricity Flows: Butch Morris Blazes Trails with his Distinctive Improvisational Technique," *Boston Sunday Globe,* June 12, 2005, N3.

26. Philip may transgress by performing the piece at a significantly slower or faster tempo than that called for in the score, or by employing various interpretative gestures such as *rubato,* phrasing, and articulation differently than might be expected. He may gain something of a reputation for giving more romantic or individualistic readings than the more classical and conservative readings of other pianists. His inclusion on his recital program of the Clara Schumann piece rather than the more canonical music of her husband, Robert, may also constitute a transgressive act in its deliberate move to widen the canon. When performing, Philip is generally expected to dress in "concert attire"—a remnant of the servant uniforms worn in earlier times. Should he arrive to play his concert with shirtsleeves rolled up, or in a T-shirt, shorts, and sandals, or an excessively flamboyant and heavily laced shirt, or heavy goth makeup, or a skin-tight Batman outfit, or in drag, he risks a critic's comment or ridicule—or he may be sent home to change. Although musicians in some places have begun to talk informally to their concert audiences, it is still often considered inappropriate in some settings for Philip to explain the piece he is playing; he is expected to make music only and not to speak unless it is called for in the musical score. Should he address the audience before or after his performance, he may also transgress the taken-for-granted expectations of his silence. Humor, unless it is written into the musical score, may also be considered unacceptable, and Philip would transgress if he cracks jokes as he sits at the piano just before playing his recital or hums and sings along with his playing as did Glenn Gould. See Jonathan Cott, *Conversations with Glenn Gould* ([1984]; repr., Chicago: University of Chicago Press, 2005); Glenn Gould, *The Complete Toccatas and Inventions* [sound recording]/ Johann Sebastian Bach (New York: CBS Masterworks, [1987] 2 sound

discs). Previously released on MS 6622, D3S 754, MP 38768, M 35144, M 353831 (1963–1964, 1979–1980).

27. This was the case, e.g., in Dmitry Shostakovich's transgression of the musical sensibilities of Soviet Realism. On Shostakovich, see, e.g., *Grove Music Online, Oxford Music Online,* s.v. "Shostakovich, Dmitry" (by David Fanning and Laurel Fay), http://www.oxfordmusiconline.com (accessed July 15, 2010); Mikuláš Bek, Geoffrey Chew, and Petr Macek, *Socialist Realism and Music* (Brno, Czech Republic: Institute of Musicology, Masaryk University, 2004); Brian Morton, *Shostakovich: His Life and Music* (London: Haus, 2006).

28. See Michael Chanan, *Musica practica: The Social Practice of Western Music from Gregorian Chant to Postmodernism* (London: Verso, 1994).

29. As hooks, *Teaching to Transgress,* passim, notes, transgressive teaching is an important site of resistance to the establishment's power and a means whereby teachers express their pedagogical care for their students and the subjects they teach. See, e.g., R. [Richard] S. Peters, *Ethics and Education* (London: George Allen and Unwin, 1970); Israel Scheffler, *Reason and Education* ([1973]; repr., Indianapolis: Bobbs-Merrill, 1973); David Carr, *Educating the Virtues: An Essay on the Philosophical Psychology of Moral Development and Education* (London: Routledge, 1991); David Carr, "The Significance of Music for the Promotion of Moral and Spiritual Virtue," *Philosophy of Music Education Review* 14.2 (Fall 2006): 103–117.

30. Koza argues against the power of corporate interests in music education and for the importance of music teachers resisting and repudiating capitalistic interests and power; against the role of racism and militarism in American music education in favor of an inclusive, humane, and joyful music education. Gould challenges the gender disparities particularly in instrumental music teaching and learning and suggests that instrumental music teaching become genuinely inclusive and affirming of females as well as males, and the entire range of sexualities. O'Toole prods music teachers to approach choral conducting in democratic ways that appeal to the hearts and minds of singers. Green advocates that teachers genuinely and respectfully embrace the popular music of our time. Allsup urges music teachers to dialogue with students in transformative ways and invokes garage bands as a metaphor for a different approach to instrumental music education in schools.

31. See Jorgensen, *In Search of Music Education,* esp. ch. 3.

32. See Jorgensen, *Transforming Music Education,* 101–108.

33. See Palmer, *The Courage to Teach,* esp. chs. 4 and 5.

34. In the United States, the success of the New Horizon band and Sweet Adelines and SPBSA barbershop quartet movements, and amateur and professional choirs, bands, and orchestras that cater to seniors and adults or are multigenerational in character, illustrates the power of envisioning music education as lifelong learning. On the New Horizons bands, see Roy E. Ernst and Scott Emmons, "New Horizons for Senior Adults," *Music Educators Journal* 79 (Dec. 1992): 30–34; Don D. Coffman and Katherine M. Levy, "Senior Adult Bands: Music's New Horizon," *Music Educators Journal* 84 (Nov. 1997): 17–22; Don D. Coffman and Mary S. Adamek, "Perceived Social Support of New Horizons Band Participants," *Contributions to Music Education* 28.1 (2001): 27–40. For a case study of a band devoted to lifelong learning, see C. C. Wilhjelm Jr., "A Case Study of the Ridgewood Concert Band, A New Jersey Community Band Dedicated to Life-long Learning," doctoral

diss., Columbia Univ. Teachers College, 1998, *Dissertation Abstracts International*, 59 Jan 1999 p2413A. For a recording of the Society for the Preservation and Encouragement of Barber Shop Quartet Singing in America (SPEBSQSA) 1998 international competition in Atlanta, see *Can't Stop Singing!* [sound recording] (Burbank, Calif.: PBS Records, p1999 ([s.l.]: manufactured and distributed by Warner Bros. Records), 1 sound disc, 9 47396-2 Warner Bros. Records, with tracks by Michigan Jake, Turning Point, Revival, BSQ, Standing Room Only, and FRED.

35. For Greene and J. R. Martin, this possibility is empowering for students and teachers, since it enables learners to place their own interpretations on the subject matter and conceptualize it in ways that are most meaningful to them. On the power of naming one's reality, especially in the case of those who have been disenfranchised in the past, see Greene, *The Dialectic of Freedom*, and J. R. Martin, *Reclaiming a Conversation* and *Coming of Age in Academe*.

36. For example, rather than accepting that the student receives from the music teacher the appropriate nomenclature and rules for musical notation, R. Murray Schafer, *The Thinking Ear: Complete Writings on Music Education* (Toronto: Arcana Editions, 1986, 1988), transgresses by encouraging students to invent their own notational systems as they come to understand music. At first, and even later, their schemes may be graphic and suggestive rather than traditionally scored and prescriptive, but as learning proceeds, students gradually grasp how notation both limits and enhances musical performance, the various ways musical notation has worked historically and functions presently, and the differences between musical traditions in which notation plays a significant or minor role, if any.

37. See Allsup, "Activating Self-Transformation through Improvisation in Instrumental Music Teaching."

38. As Donald Arnstine, *Democracy and the Arts of Schooling*, chs. 3, 4, explains, dispositions are tendencies to act in particular ways. The purpose of education is to cultivate democratic thought and practice so that students are disposed to act with reference to these democratic purposes. Aesthetic experience has a role to play in the development of these dispositions.

39. Martin Buber, *I and Thou*, trans. Walter A. Kaufmann (New York: Scribner, 1970) refers to this interrelationship as *I and thou* in the sense that participants regard this knowledge with wonder, mystery, and even awe, and honor this subject as they also honor each other.

40. Passions are restrained so that this can be a place free of predatory behavior and exploitative conduct, and in order to foster self-expression rather than unbridled self-exposure. See Dewey, *Art as Experience*, 62.

41. See Jorgensen, *In Search of Music Education*, passim.

42. For example, Lucy Green, *How Popular Musicians Learn: A Way Ahead for Music Education* (Aldershot, UK: Ashgate, 2002), and her *Music, Informal Learning and the School: A New Classroom Pedagogy* (Aldershot, UK: Ashgate, 2008), advocates enculturation and informal music education of a sort exemplified in British rock bands as a way forward for school music. Also see Ivan Illich, *Celebration of Awareness: A Call for Institutional Revolution* (Garden City, N.Y.: Doubleday, 1970); Illich, *Deschooling Society*; Freire, *Pedagogy of the Oppressed* and his *Pedagogy of Hope*. Illich's assertion of the importance of institutional revolution and lifelong learning unfettered by formal schooling and Freire's

argument for adult literacy training underscore the importance of continuing and informal education into adulthood as means of transforming society.

43. By way of a problem-posing curriculum, John Dewey, *Education and Experience* ([1938]; repr., New York: Collier Books, 1963), 86–89, urges the scientific method as the principal approach to the study of subject matter. This approach privileges rational means of investigation whereby propositions are systematically tested and is most suited to subjects in which propositional knowledge is central. In music, as in the other arts, other considerations come into play. Dewey, *Art as Experience*, 44, 132, 155, requires the productive as well as the receptive aspects of direct individual engagement with the arts. Although he suggests that school music curricula need to focus on affording a direct cultural knowledge about music and the other arts rather than on acquiring musical skills, his writings can be read to suggest that students need to do and undergo music as well as learn about it.

44. Keith Swanwick makes this point in his *Teaching Music Musically* (New York: Routledge, 1999).

45. For example, the music of Hapsburg Spain might be integrated into a broad and integrated study of Spanish culture, history, language, politics, and Spain's relations with its colonies in the Americas. Playing a contemporary recording of the Escorial choir school, along with showing pictures of this monastery, might help to bring alive the traditional role of music in the Roman Church liturgy, the *schola cantorum* tradition, the intersection of this monastic and liturgical music with the Jewish and Moorish musical heritage of Toledo and Córdoba, and such vernacular musics as the Gypsy music of Grenada and the flamenco musicians and dancers of Seville. These intersections of religious and vernacular traditions could readily be compared to present-day American realities, and the sounds and sights of Gregorian chant as sung by Spanish boy choirs might be compared with present-day choir schools such as that in the National Cathedral in Washington, D.C. As students come to better understand this music that might otherwise seem strange to their ears, they might also attempt a chant from the collection in the *Juilliard Repertory*. They could also begin to catalog the similarities and differences of this music from their various religious traditions. See Escolanía del Real Monasterio San Lorenzo del Escorial, *In paradisum* [sound recording] (Dies, 2004): Dies 200407, compact disc. For a study of the education of the boy choir at the Washington National Cathedral, see Steven Edward Hendricks, "The Washington National Cathedral Boy Choir: Musical, Spiritual, and Academic Training of the Choristers through the Twentieth Century," doctoral diss., Ball State Univ., 2003, *Dissertation Abstracts International*, 64 (Nov. 2003): 1575. For a recording of the Cathedral Boy Choristers, among others, see *PBS presents Denyce Graves* [sound recording]: *A Cathedral Christmas* ([s.l.]: PBS, 1997, 1 compact disc. Also see the Juilliard Repertory Project, *Juilliard Repertory Library,* reference/library ed. (Cincinnati: Canyon Press, 1970) 20–23, including "Ut queant laxis, Hymn to St. John the Baptist," which was used as a basis for teaching the gamut, *ut, re, mi, fa, sol,* and *la* (23).

46. For Illich and Freire, knowledge is politicized and a means of excluding some people from the centers of power. Students can explore the subjects in which they are interested and their lived realities from a political and economic perspective. As they grasp how the state of affairs in which they are situated has come about, they can come to know what they need to do politically in order to change it. Woodford proposes a critical pedagogy that likewise situates music education as an agent for democracy. See Illich, *Deschooling Society*

and *Celebration of Awareness;* Freire, *Pedagogy of the Oppressed* and *Pedagogy of Hope;* and Woodford, *Democracy and Music Education.*

47. See Austin B. Caswell, "Canonicity in Academe: A Music Historian's View," in *Philosopher, Teacher, Musician: Perspectives on Music Education,* ed. Estelle R. Jorgensen (Urbana: University of Illinois Press, 1993), 129–145. For a critical examination of the lives of professional musicians, see Lise Vaugeois, "Examining the Political: Materiality, Ideology, and Power in the Lives of Professional Musicians," *Philosophy of Music Education Review* 15.1 (Spring 2007): 23–21.

48. On "border crossings," see Henry A. Giroux, *Border Crossings: Cultural Workers and the Politics of Education* ([1992]; repr., New York; London: Routledge, 1993). On musical cosmopolitanism, see Morton, "Response to Bennett Reimer," 55–59.

49. Traveling in Morocco with an Arab guide, I began to see my Western ideas more critically from the perspective of one for whom they are alien and even repugnant. The traditional musics I heard were also those of very different others for whom the music with which I have grown up and lived may be strange. This particular border crossing caused me to see the musical culture in which I had been steeped more critically, as if from the perspective of an "outsider" looking in.

50. June Boyce-Tillman, "Towards an Ecology of Music Education," *Philosophy of Music Education Review* 12.2 (Fall 2004): 102–125, argues that Western culture is disposed to value particular qualities and reject or ignore others. This reality leaves people out of balance and harmony as they are forced to repudiate certain characteristics and develop others—a selective development that negatively impacts their health and well-being. Likewise, Nodding's argument in her *Happiness and Education,* that education should be pleasurable, is at odds with a political culture bent on educational work, assessment, and accountability.

51. For example, Freire, *Pedagogy of the Oppressed,* ch. 4, advocates the construction of grassroots, informally constructed groups as a means for liberatory education. Palmer, *Courage to Teach,* ch. 7, advises teachers to form cells or groups that exercise political pressure progressively more widely as a means of educational transformation.

52. For example, in place of schools, Illich, *Deschooling Education,* ch. 6, promotes the establishment of educational networks or "learning webs" whereby liberatory education can be forwarded informally as well as formally.

53. This may be seen in the efforts of Horace Mann to establish common schools in Massachusetts. It is also evident in legislation regarding public education that mandates particular transformative actions, e.g., prohibitions against the exclusion of people by virtue of their color, race, religion, ethnicity, language, or sexual identity.

54. For example, a distance-learning university providing advanced education for mid-career adults was established as a means of meeting the needs of students who wished to improve the world. Before it became a publicly held company, it was important to see how the change occurred through the lives and work of its graduates and its effects rippled out into society. The university's relatively flat and collegial structure and student-centered program was designed to facilitate an action-oriented education for its students. Its profit motive, as a means of rewarding private investors who underwrote its expenses, seemed consonant with their intrinsic commitment to the betterment of society and interest in demonstrating the reality of the change attributable to its influence. After it was sold from private ownership to a for-profit publicly held company and subsequently taken private, a dramatic change

occurred. As a participant in the process, I observed that when the interests of transgression and consumption collided, consumption carried the day.

55. From ancient times, exemplified in Plato's approval of only two modes for use in the schools of his imagined Republican ideal, we see examples of revolutionary music that may be overly restrictive and utilitarian. See Plato, *Republic,* §399a, p. 96..

56. Palmer, *Courage to Teach,* esp. ch. 2.

57. In Communist Hungary after World War II, for example, Zoltán Kodály's system of sight-singing training, designed to cultivate a knowledge and love of Hungarian culture, left little room for divergence. Among the North American interpreters of Zoltán Kodály's ideas, see Lois Choksy, *The Kodály Context: Creating an Environment for Musical Learning* (Englewood Cliffs N.J.: Prentice-Hall, 1981) and her *The Kodály Method: Comprehensive Music Education from Infant to Adult,* 2nd ed. (Englewood Cliffs N.J.: Prentice-Hall, 1988); Jean Sinor, "Zoltan Kodaly's Folk Tradition," *Music Educators Journal* 69 (Dec. 1982): 33–34; Micheál Houlahan and Philip Tacka, *Zoltán Kodály: A Guide to Research* (New York: Garland, 1998); Philip Tacka and Micheál Houlahan, *Sound Thinking: Developing Musical Literacy* ([New York]: Boosey & Hawkes, 1995).

58. For example, Antioch College was founded in Yellow Springs, Ohio, in 1852 with Horace Mann as its first president. Its motto read: "Be ashamed to die until you win some victory for humanity." See its website at http://www.antioch-college.edu/ (accessed July 15, 2010).

59. *Documentary Report of the Tanglewood Symposium,* 139.

60. Patricia Shehan Campbell, private communication, 1990.

6. FACTORY AND PRODUCTION

1. Modifications in old-style assembly-line facilities of the sort invented by Henry Ford in the United States for the manufacture of automobiles also reflect subsequent changes in the ways in which employees interact with each other and the machinery they operate. These changes include the decline in the power of worker unions in American factories, the removal of many factories to lower-cost environments, and the increased emphasis on manufacturing teams as opposed to individual workers working entirely alone.

2. The word *factory* has its origins in the Latin factōrium, a "place or instrument of making" ("recorded in [the] sense of an 'oil press'") from *facēre* to make." See *OED Online,* s.v. "factory," http://dictionary.oed.com (accessed July 14, 2010). I suppose that *factōria* existed because some farmers could not afford or did not have the time to press the olives they grew. The larger the scale of operation and the more expensive the machinery, the more likely that specialized *factōria* would develop.

3. See, e.g., William Henry Hill, Arthur F. Hill, and Alfred Ebsworth Hill, *The Violinmakers of the Guarneri Family, 1626–1762, Their Life and Work* (London: Holland Press Ltd. [1965]); Tony Faber, *Stradivari's Genius: Five Violins, One Cello, and Three Centuries of Enduring Perfection* (New York: Random House, 2004); Carlo Bonetti, *A Genealogy of the Amati Family of Violin Makers, 1500–1740* ([Iowa City, Iowa]: Maecenas Press, 1989); George Hart, *The Violin: Its Famous Makers and their Imitators* (London: Dulau, 1875); A. Mason Clarke, *The Violin and Old Violin Makers Being a Historical and Biographical Account*

of the Violin with Facsimiles of Labels of the Old Makers (New York: Somerset Publishers, n.d. [1979]); *Grove Music Online, Oxford Music Online,* s.v. "Stradivari" (by Charles Beare, Carlo Chiesa, and Duane Rosengard), http://www.oxfordmusiconline.com (accessed July 15, 2010); *Grove Music Online, Oxford Music Online,* s.v. "Guarneri" (by Charles Beare, Carlo Chiesa, and Duane Rosengard), http://www.oxfordmusiconline.com (accessed July 15, 2010); *Grove Music Online, Oxford Music Online,* s.v. "Amati" (by Charles Beare, Carlo Chiesa, and Philip J. Kass), http://www.oxfordmusiconline.com (accessed July 15, 2010).

4. The technology used as a means of production also contributes to this dehumanization; see Jerold J. Abrams, "A Technological Galaxy: Heidegger and the Philosophy of Technology in *Star Wars,*" in *Star Wars and Philosophy: More Powerful than You can Possibly Imagine,* ed. Kevin S. Decker and Jason T. Eberl (Chicago: Open Court, 2005), 107–119. For Abrams, following Heidegger, technology creates "ontological amnesia" that renders people deeply forgetful of their own existence and causes them to despair. The only way to escape this ennui and despair is through supernatural intervention. Seen within the perspective of Heideggerian philosophy, Darth Vader has "forgotten the man he used to be" and he is ultimately saved "by the semi-divine power of the Force and through the actions of Luke." As Abrams notes, "Vader begins to remember. He returns to himself and becomes Anakin Skywalker once again" and then destroys the Emperor and repudiates the Dark Side of the Force. This unmasking is complete when, before he dies, his "body/machine" being broken, in an act full of symbolic meaning when read from a Heideggerian perspective, he asks Luke "to take off his horrible mask and 'uncover' his true being from the shroud of artifice" (119).

5. The emergence of the "weekend" as a time away from work for which many Americans work to live symbolizes workers' need to escape their working conditions and find more natural and spiritually satisfying environments in which to recreate. Retail businesses are sometimes housed in factory-like warehouse environments, churches and public schools are designed like factories, sports arenas and movie theaters feature industrial architecture and stadium seating, and homes are built like factory lofts.

6. By contrast, I think of a factory situated in a beautiful garden where workers can gather, lunch, and stroll during breaks throughout the day. This garden somehow humanizes the factory, its workers take pride in it, and its presence helps to balance what would otherwise be a dull place in which to spend one's working hours. At this time, the Sanitarium Gardens are among some of the outstanding private gardens in Christchurch, New Zealand.

7. For a historical sketch of the rise of European conservatories, see Bernarr Rainbow and Gordon Cox, *Music in Educational Thought and Practice.*

8. Among his writings concerning efficiency and the school curriculum, see Franklin Bobbitt, "The Elimination of Waste in Education," *Elementary School Teacher* 12 (6) (Feb. 1912): 259–271, and his *The Curriculum* (New York: Houghton Mifflin, 1918).

9. Competency-based education uses instructional objectives and breaks down musical instruction into the self-same sorts of atomistic and measurable objectives and behaviors that earlier writers such as Bobbitt had proposed. See Clifford K. Madsen and Cornelia Yarbrough, *Competency-Based Music Education* (Englewood Cliffs, N.J.: Prentice-Hall, 1980).

10. See, e.g., Zoltán Kodály, *333 Elementary Exercises in Sightsinging,* ed. Percy M. Young (New York: Boosey and Hawkes, 1963); Shinichi Suzuki, *Suzuki Violin School,* international ed., 10 vols. (Evanston, Ill.: Summy-Birchard, 1978–).

11. See websites for the Associated Board of the Royal Schools of Music, at http://www.abrsm.org (accessed July 15, 2010); the Australian Music Examinations Board, http://www.ameb.edu.au/ (accessed July 15, 2010); the Royal Conservatory of Music, Toronto, Canada, at http://www.rcmusic.ca/ (accessed July 15, 2010).

12. In a similar vein to Susanne K. Langer, *Mind: An Essay on Human Feeling*, vol. 1 (Baltimore, Md.: Johns Hopkins University Press, 1967), ch. 2, titled "Idols of the Laboratory"; Thomas A. Regelski, "On 'Methodolatry' and Music Teaching as Critical and Reflective Praxis," *Philosophy of Music Education Review* 10 (2) (Fall 2002): 102–123, criticizes the "methodolatry" or over-valuing of instructional and research methods in music.

13. Roger Sessions, *The Musical Experience of Composer, Performer, Listener*, 27, comments that music is a language that "communicates" in a manner that is "perfectly clear." Such communication depends on commonly held assumptions that make this communication possible. For example, Sessions sees musical notation as an achievement over the past centuries, providing a means whereby composers can set out their musical ideas clearly in ways that can be grasped by performers (68). Without agreements on such things as scale temperaments, concert pitches, and the meaning of symbols employed in musical notation, this communication, at least among Western classically trained musicians and their audiences, could not exist. As musical traditions become larger-scale and more widespread, increasing standardization is to be expected. As Zentner, *Prelude to Administrative Theory*, ch. 7, argues, standardization is characteristic of all social institutions.

14. For a classic social history of the orchestra in the Euroclassical tradition, see Henry Raynor, *The Orchestra: A History* (New York: Charles Scribner's Sons, 1978). John H. Mueller, *The American Symphony Orchestra: A Social History of Musical Taste* (Bloomington: Indiana University Press, 1951), also details some of these social changes in orchestras and the changing musical taste that they both reflected and spawned in the United States up to the mid-twentieth century. For a more recent sociological reflection on the changing face of the orchestra and the role of the conductor, see Christopher Small, *Musicking: The Meanings of Performing and Listening* (Hanover, N.H.: University Press of New England for Wesleyan University Press, 1998), esp. chs. 4, 5.

15. See Robert Philip, *Performing Music in the Age of Recording* (New Haven, Conn.: Yale University Press, 2004); *Grove Music Online, Oxford Music Online,* s.v. "Electro-acoustic Music" (by Simon Emmerson and Denis Smalley), http://www.oxfordmusiconline.com (accessed July 15, 2010); *The Oxford Dictionary of Music, Oxford Music Online,* s.v. "Electronic Music," http://www.oxfordmusiconline.com (accessed July 15, 2010); Hans-Joachim Braun, ed., *"I Sing the Body Electric": Music and Technology in the 20th Century* ([Hofheim]: Wolke, 2000); Gerry Bloustien, Margaret Peters, and Susan Luckman, eds., *Sonic Synergies: Music Technology, Community, Identity* (Aldershot, UK: Ashgate, 2008).

16. See *The Oxford Companion to Music, Oxford Music Online,* s.v. "Societies" (by John Borwick), http://www.oxfordmusiconline.com (accessed July 15, 2010).

17. As Anthony E. Kemp, *The Musical Temperament: Psychology and Personality of Musicians* ([1996]; repr., Oxford: Oxford University Press, 2000), notes, these differences may have a psychological as well as social basis.

18. Richard Dyer, "As POPSearch '05 Moves Forward, So Does a Tenor from '04," *The Boston Globe,* Friday, June 10, 2005, C20, reports that Renee Fleming's Decca recording "Haunted Heart" features "a tone quality few would connect with an opera singer's. Fleming almost always sings in the lowest part of her voice, an octave or more below her money

notes, with an intimate, sultry sound that would require amplification to be heard in live performance . . ."

19. Kurt Blaukopf, *Musical Life in a Changing Society: Aspects of Music Sociology*, rev. ed., trans. David Marinelli (Portland, Ore.: Amadeus Press, 1992), chs. 20, 29, labels these technologically based musical mutations as "mediamorphosis," whereby the media transform acoustic musical sound.

20. Musicians' guilds were forged at a time when a merchant class developed and music became an important part of the political economy. On guilds, see *Grove Music Online, Oxford Music Online*, s.v. "Guilds" (by Heinrich W. Schwab), http://www.oxfordmusiconline.com (accessed July 15, 2010).

21. These agencies include the Associated Board of the Royal Colleges of Music in the United Kingdom, the National Association of Schools of Music in the United States, and governmental committees in the various European continental countries. For a history and description of the Associated Board of the Royal Schools of Music (founded 1889), see the Board's website, http://www.abrsm.org/ (accessed July 15, 2010); *Grove Music Online, Oxford Music Online*, s.v. "Associated Board of the Royal Schools of Music" (by David Allinson), http://www.oxfordmusiconline.com (accessed July 15. 2010); *The Oxford Companion to Music, Oxford Music Online*, s.v. "Associated Board of the Royal Schools of Music" (by Piers Spencer), http://www.oxfordmusiconline.com (accessed July 24, 2010).

On the National Association of Schools of Music (founded 1924), see the Association's website at http://nasm.arts-accredit.org/ (accessed July 15, 2010).

The Bologna Declaration of June 19, 1999, was a joint statement by European Ministers of Education geared toward standardizing European higher education. See http://www. magna-charta.org/pdf/BOLOGNA_DECLARATION.pdf (accessed July 21, 2010). This declaration has been the guiding document for the Bologna Process. The impact of this process on higher music education in Nordic countries, for example, is addressed by Marja Heimonen in a report titled "Nordic Higher Music Education: The Member Institutions of the Nordic Council of Conservatories" (Nordiska Konservatorierådet, 2004), p. 5. She writes: "The original document of the Bologna Declaration was signed by 29 European countries including Denmark, Finland, Iceland, Norway and Sweden. This Declaration is said to be a binding commitment to an action programme. The common goal is to create a European space for higher education." The aims included the "adoption of a system based on two main cycles," "adoption of a Bachelor–Master structure," and "establishment of a system of credits (ECTS system)."

As she notes: "The aim is to promote mobility of students, teachers and researchers and to increase co-operation within the European context. The Bologna Declaration will have implications also in the field of higher music education in the Nordic countries especially on the following issues: (a) duration of study, (b) use of the structure of two cycles, (c) titles of qualifications and degrees, (d) use of a system of ECTS credits."

22. In the United States, teachers might consult *The National Standards for Arts Education: What Every Young American Should Know and Be Able to Do in the Arts*, ed. Michael Blakeslee (Reston, Va.: Music Educators National Conference, 1994) and state-mandated musical objectives in order to determine what to teach and how to teach it. These standards are often defined broadly. Approved textbooks, musical materials, and instruments also channel teacher decisions about what subject matter will be taught and how.

Alternatively, Canadian piano teachers preparing students to take the examinations of the Royal Conservatory of Music in Toronto need to consult the syllabi at the grade levels at which their students are working. They are then in a position to determine their studio programs so that all their students can complete the requirements and successfully pass the examinations for at least one grade level each year. Reports on these examinations alert them to particular things for which examiners are looking and impact the ways in which they teach the piano. Also, choral, band, and orchestra teachers wishing to place their students in competitions and festivals need to prepare their ensembles to perform specified repertoire successfully at their appropriate grade level. Adjudicators' comments on their ensembles' performances likewise provide guidance in meeting the specified performance standards.

23. When their supervisors insist on entering their students in music competitions, music teachers must prepare their students for these competitions if they wish to keep their positions. If the school administration insists that the instrumental teacher leads the school's marching band in providing music for athletic events, he or she is obliged to do so or seek another position. Specific national or statewide standards may also render teachers relatively powerless in determining what to teach. When methodological norms are also in place and administrators decree that music is to be taught in particular ways, teachers are left with little they can do to tailor their curricula to the specific interests and needs of their students or reshape their programs in other ways. If the musical repertoire is more or less specified, teachers' freedom to choose music to be studied with their students disappears, and they need to focus on satisfying these others and carrying out orders that do not always meet their wishes.

24. The term "impression model" was coined by Israel Scheffler, *Reason and Teaching*, ch. 6, titled: "Philosophical Models of Teaching (1964)."

25. Emphasizing convergent thinking and normative performance also plays out in music performance, e.g., as musicians imitate recordings of authoritative performances, interpret music in ways that are likely to appeal to the judges of musical competitions, and perform repertoire that is considered most canonical. Philip, *Performing Music in the Age of Recording*, esp. chs. 3 and 4, addresses the loss of freedom on the part of musicians that results from the power of recorded performances to define and shape musical expectations.

26. By mastery learning, I take them to mean that learners must surmount challenges all along the way of their education. That is, as progressively more difficult tasks are assigned to them, at each point, they must successfully demonstrate the requisite knowledge and skill before proceeding to the next level. Interestingly, June Boyce-Tillman and Keith Swanwick place mastery at the bottom level of their music curriculum spiral, since without the requisite skills, they argue, students are unable to progress to other aspects of musicality. See Swanwick and Tillman, "The Sequence of Musical Development"; Swanwick, *Music, Mind, and Education*, 43, 44, 64, 65, 68, 76. Their use of the word *mastery* seems to differ from ordinary English usage, in which mastery connotes "power," "control," "superiority," or a "comprehensive knowledge or command of a subject or skill." See *OED Online,* s.v. "mastery, *n.,*" http://dictionary.oed.com (accessed July 14, 2010); the word also connotes such ideas as "superiority or ascendancy in battle or competition, or in a struggle of any kind; victory resulting in domination or subjugation," "superior force or power," "the state or condition of being master, controller, or ruler; authority, dominion, control; an instance of this," and "an action demonstrating or involving great skill or power." This is hardly what

Tillman and Swanwick mean, since they intend to build on the "mastery" of certain core understandings and skills. So they must consider mastery relativistically with reference to the learner's particular stage of development and achievement.

27. For example, pieces of music are examined in statistically quantifiable and formulaic ways. The application of set theory and mathematical analysis to music theory is a case in point. These data then become bases upon which to drive decision-making. For example, the receipt of one mathematically computed grade rather than another may determine whether a student is permitted or encouraged to continue musical study.

28. Buber, *I and Thou*, advocates a subjective interaction as each partner in the dialogue regards the other, and is regarded by the other, with sensitivity, respect, and empathy.

29. For example, I may keep a precious stone in a safety deposit box or another safe place, but I am not so concerned about keeping a less valuable piece of jewelry in an easily accessible place. I treat these objects differently because they are of different "worth."

30. For example, the Samuel Barber Cello Concerto may be considered more worthwhile than the John Williams film score to *Star Wars: Episode III—Revenge of the Sith* because the Barber concerto is abstract and the Williams score is representational or programmatic. See Richard Dyer, "Latest 'Star Wars' Score is an Emotional Adventure," *The Boston Globe*, Monday, June 6, 2005, B7.

31. Kevin S. Decker, "By Any Means Necessary: Tyranny, Democracy, Republic, and Empire," in *Star Wars and Philosophy*, ed. Decker and Eberl, 168–180, quotes George Lucas's speech by Palpatine accepting "radical 'emergency powers' in order to combat the political Separatists": "It is with great reluctance that I have agreed to this calling. I love democracy. I love the Republic. The power you give me I will lay down when this crisis has abated. And as my first act with this new authority, I will create a Grand Army of the Republic to counter the increasing threats of the Separatists" (174).

32. Ralph W. Tyler, *Basic Principles of Curriculum and Instruction* (Chicago: University of Chicago Press, 1949), formalized these questions systematically in what is known as the "Tyler Rationale."

33. See Jorgensen, "Philosophical Issues in Curriculum."

34. Yarbrough and Madsen, *Competency-Based Music Education,* outline one such approach based on a comprehensive model of music teaching. For example, the specific competencies required for efficient classroom management, ensemble conducting, historical and theoretical knowledge of music, ear-training and sight singing skills, instrumental and vocal skills, knowledge of educational history and law, and state educational regulations are analyzed into mutually exclusive categories.

35. Having been prepared in this manner, it would be reasonable for teachers, in turn, to analyze the national standards for music education, state-approved requirements for music curricula, and local mandates and expectations into their constituent elements and operationalize them as objectives that can be assessed as behaviors in the phenomenal world. They might then render these objectives into instructional programs and rationally evaluate the results according to pre-specified criteria. This systematic approach then feeds into the next instructional cycle.

36. See Estelle R. Jorgensen, "From Cloister to Corporation: Music Education and the Changing Face of the Academy," in *The Sociology of Music Education II: Papers from the Music Education Symposium at the University of Oklahoma,* ed. Roger A. Rideout and Stephen P. Paul (Amherst, Mass.: Rideout and Paul, 2000), 19–30.

37. The United Nations Convention on the Rights of the Child was adopted in the United Nations General Assembly, November 20, 1989, and ratified by all nations except the United States and Somalia, at http://www.unicef.org/crc/ (accessed July 15, 2010).

38. At a concert by the Simon Symphonietta, June 4, 2005, at Falmouth Academy, Massachusetts, I was struck by what is lost by the insistence in much nineteenth- and twentieth-century classical music on writing out music in full. The program consisted of Antonio Vivaldi's Concerto in F Major (RV 569), Guiseppe Tartini's Violin Concerto in G Minor, and George Frideric Handel's complete Water Music (heard as the Suite I and a second grouping of Suites II and III reordered by the conductor), and the musicians had substantial opportunities to ornament. These improvisations seemed, to my ear, to be freely and musically rendered so as to make them at one with the composers' musical sketch. Musicians and conductor seemed to enjoy this collaborative musical undertaking, and their demeanor contrasted with orchestras where players have less freedom in improvisation and sometimes seem bored, listless, or irritated at repeating overplayed pieces written out in full.

39. On "traditional education" and "banking education," respectively, see John Dewey, *Experience and Education*, ch. 1; Paulo Freire, *Pedagogy of the Oppressed*, esp. chs. 2, 3.

40. Dissertation studies of off/on-task behavior in music education during the past decade include: Melissa Katia Madsen, "The Effect of Accurate/Inaccurate Teacher Instruction, High/Low Teacher Delivery, and On-/Off-Task Student Behavior on Musicians' Evaluation of Teacher Effectiveness," doctoral diss. (Louisiana State University and Agricultural and Mechanical College, 1999), *Dissertation Abstracts International,* vol. 61 (Sept. 2000), p. 926A, with a published article based on this work in Katia Madsen, "The Effect of Accuracy of Instruction, Teacher Delivery, and Student Attentiveness on Musicians' Evaluation of Teacher Effectiveness," *Journal of Research in Music Education* 51.1 (Spring 2003): 38–50; Geoffrey Artie Reynolds, "Effects of a Tangible Goal on Students' Perceptions and Off-task Behaviors," doctoral diss. (University of Arizona, 2000), *Dissertation Abstracts International,* vol. 61 (Apr. 2001), p. 3935A.

41. See Thomas, ed., *MMCP Synthesis,* passim.

42. On "inert" knowledge, see Whitehead, *The Aims of Education,* 1.

7. GARDEN AND GROWTH

1. See Gen. 1: 26–2:10. I think, e.g., of the courtyard of the Mosque of Córdoba (*Mezquita de Córdoba*), Spain.

2. In the United States gardens are often looked upon as part of a landscaping plan that will enhance a building's appeal. Not trusting their own judgment, some people call in consultants to help them landscape their properties. These are often the sorts of gardens featured in architectural magazines and on television programs in which landscape architects "make over" properties so that they will be appealing to others.

3. Walking through the Botanical Gardens of Hamburg in the latter part of May, e.g., we encountered masses of flowering rhododendron bushes in pinks, yellows, whites, maroons, reds, and apricots set amid waterfalls, pools, and hillocks. This garden would be impossible to see other than by following its winding pathways.

4. The word *garden* as a noun refers to "an enclosed piece of ground devoted to the cultivation of flowers, fruit, or vegetables, often preceded by some defining word, as

flower-, fruit-, kitchen-, market-, strawberry-garden, etc.," and as a verb means "to cultivate a garden; to work in a garden as a gardener." See *OED Online,* s.v. "garden, *n.*" and "garden, *v.*," http://dictionary.oed.com (accessed July 14, 2010). This word comes more immediately from the French "gardin" and "jardin," with its roots in the Latin word "gardinum" and the Old French "gardum."

5. For example, Moya L. Andrews and her illustrator, Gillian Harris, *Perennials Short and Tall: A Seasonal Progression of Flowers for Your Garden* (Bloomington: Indiana University Press, 2008), offer an illustrated guide to plants suited to gardens in the Midwestern United States.

6. In coming to Indiana, we loved the old-fashioned hollyhocks, often growing alongside limestone buildings. One particular color—a very dark maroon, almost black—caught my fancy. These very dark-colored hollyhocks were planted alongside other hollyhocks of various shades of pink. Every year they came up on the sunny side of the cottage, in different places. Sometimes these dark hollyhocks were in profusion, and other times not. The germination of these hollyhocks is governed by scientific and genetic laws in which gradual change takes place from one generation to the next. Should we not interfere in this natural process, those hollyhocks possessing the characteristics most suited to this particular place will naturally predominate. If we undertake the science of selecting those hollyhock characteristics we most desire, the change over time may be even more marked.

7. See Scott Russell Sanders, *Staying Put: Making a Home in a Restless World* (Boston: Beacon Press, 1993).

8. John Dewey, *A Common Faith* (New Haven, Conn.: Yale University Press, 1943), 86, notes that knowledge is "a product of the cooperative and communicative operations of human beings living together." One's sense of possibility and desire is rooted in an imagination shaped by the particular communities of which one is a part, and the places and times in which one lives.

9. Sometimes, as with the Mytoi Gardens on Chappaquiddick Island, Martha's Vineyard, or the Polly Hill Arboretum in West Tisbury, Martha's Vineyard, Massachusetts, gardens are so beautiful that people want them to be kept in perpetuity, and they are willed to foundations to be preserved and developed for generations to come. See C. L. Fornari, "The Perfect Nature Weekend," *Cape Cod Life* (Special 2009 Annual Guide): 94–98.

10. Plato, *Republic,* §401d, p. 100.

11. On the natural world, see Aristotle, *Politics,* trans. H. Rackham (Cambridge, Mass.: Harvard University Press, 1932), book 1. For his educational ideas, see books 7 and 8.

12. See Jean-Jacques Rousseau, *Émile,* trans. Barbara Foxley (New York: Dutton, 1911).

13. For a brief discussion of the problems raised by the ambiguity of the relationship between the arts and artistic education, morality, and human nature, see Reginald Snell, "Introduction," in *On the Aesthetic Education of Man In a Series of Letters,* trans. Reginald Snell ([1954]; repr., New York: Frederick Ungar, 1965), 14–16. Also, see Friedrich Schiller, *On the Aesthetic Education of Man,* passim.

14. See Johann Heinrich Pestalozzi, *Leonard and Gertrude,* trans. and abridged by Eva Channing (Boston: D. C. Heath, 1901).

15. See John Dewey, *Democracy and Education,* ch. 4, and his *Experience and Nature* (New York: Dover, 1958), passim; Greene, *The Dialectic of Freedom*; Noddings, *Caring,* and her *Happiness and Education.*

16. See Chanan, *Musica Practica;* Shinichi Suzuki, *Nurtured by Love: A New Approach to Education,* trans. Waltraud Suzuki (New York: Exposition Press, 1969); and Allsup, "Species Counterpoint."

17. See Chanan, *Musica Practica.*

18. See Blaukopf, *Musical Life in a Changing Society;* Theodor W. Adorno, *Aesthetic Theory,* trans. C. Lenhardt (London: Routledge and Kegan Paul, 1984) and Adorno's *Introduction to the Sociology of Music;* Tia DeNora, *After Adorno: Rethinking Music Sociology.*

19. See Martin, *Cultural Miseducation.*

20. See Jorgensen, "Developmental Phases in Selected British Choirs" and *In Search of Music Education,* ch. 2.

21. For a discussion of musical schooling and training, see Jorgensen, *In Search of Music Education,* 4–13. School music methods include those outlined by Jaques-Dalcroze, *Rhythm, Music and Education;* Kodály, *The Selected Writings;* Suzuki, *Nurtured by Love.*

22. The increasing internationalization of schools of instrumental pedagogy is evident in Jason Edwards, "Schools of Oboe Playing"; Svet A. Atanasov, "A Description of Selected Aspects of Three Approaches to College-Level Bassoon Instruction."

23. In an effort to widen the classical canon to include the works of composers from the Americas, Maya Frieman Hoover, ed., *A Guide to the Latin American Art Song Repertoire: An Annotated Catalog of Twentieth-Century Art Songs for Voice and Piano* (Bloomington: Indiana University Press, 2010), catalogues Spanish-language songs from South American countries. Marin Alsop champions Samuel Barber's orchestral music. Among the recordings conducted by Marin Alsop are Samuel Barber, *Capricorn Concerto* [sound recording] ([Hong Kong]: Naxos, 2004, 8.559135 Naxos Music Library), compact disc; Samuel Barber, *Orchestral Works,* v. 1, including Symphonies 1 and 2; Essay for Orchestra, Overture to The School for Scandal ([Hong Kong]: Naxos, 2004, 8.559024 Naxos Music Library), compact disc; Samuel Barber, *Orchestral Works,* v. 2, including the Cello concerto, op. 22; Medea: suite, op. 23; Adagio for strings, op. 11 ([Hong Kong]: Naxos, 2004, 8.559088 Naxos Music Library), compact disc. Projects such as these follow efforts of others in the past, e.g., Felix Mendelssohn's efforts to bring J. S. Bach's music out of obscurity. For a discussion of aspects of the 1829 performances of Bach's *St. Matthew Passion* by the Berlin-Singakademie led by Mendelssohn, see Michael Marissen, "Religious Aims in Mendelsohn's Berlin-Singakademie Performances of Bach's *St. Matthew Passion,*" *The Musical Quarterly* 77.4 (Winter, 1993) doi:10.1093/mq/77.4.718 http://www.jstor.org/stable/724355. Marissen notes that the fact that the Berlin-Singakademie already owned a great deal of Bach's choral music may have factored into Mendelssohn's choice of this piece. National organizations such as the American Music Center provide a forum for new American composers and compositions to be forwarded. See the American Music Center's website http://www.amc .net/ (accessed July 15, 2010).

24. Among writers who espouse these views, Susanne K. Langer, *The Practice of Philosophy* (New York: Henry Holt, 1930), 162, 163, refers to the arts, myths, and religions as "intensive" symbols rather than her later term "presentational" symbols. Dewey, *Art as Experience,* passim, esp. chs. 3, 4, and 8, likewise views the arts as means whereby ordinary human experience is intensified and rendered captivating to those who do and undergo them. In her argument for recapturing classical ideals in contemporary education and culture, Martha Nussbaum, *Cultivating Humanity: A Classical Defense of Reform in*

Liberal Education (Cambridge, Mass.: Harvard University Press, 1997), takes a humanistic approach that values human beings and sees culture as a vital expression of that humanity. Her arguments for multicultural approaches to education draw on those of ancient Greek philosophers and respect the many different ways in which people are, live in, and see the world. These values serve as ideals that inspire people to seek to live by them.

25. For John Dewey, *Education as Experience* ([1938]; repr., New York: Collier Books, 1963), 42, this involves relating what is being done in the classroom to other subjects and the rest of the students' lived lives, while also integrating present activities with those in the past.

26. Dewey, ibid., esp., 47–50, believes that every situation or interaction between the student and the environment leaves "deposits" or memories of felt responses to them that may either help or hinder future development.

27. While the teacher's responsibility, in Dewey's view, is to help students make the sorts of connections and constructions that promote their long-term development of intellectual, emotional, and physical powers, Scholes, *Music, The Child and the Masterpiece*, 81, sees this task differently, as a matter of removing roadblocks that clutter students' paths to understanding music so that they can more clearly grasp its meaning.

28. Dewey, *Experience and Education*, esp. ch. 1, is at pains to break down artificial dichotomies and think holistically and dialectically about how to bring together such things as theory and practice. On the cultivation of dispositions to act in particular ways, that is, treat ideas in ways that students are inclined to live by them, see Arnstine, *Democracy and the Arts of Schooling*, esp. ch. 3.

29. Writing earlier, Rousseau, *Émile*, passim, believes that Émile and Sophie will grow up naturally good because they are brought up in tune with the natural world (Émile more so than Sophie, who seems more housebound).

30. See Jorgensen, *In Search of Music Education*, ch. 1.

31. For example, an expert singing teacher gives instruction to a boy whose natural singing voice is thereby enhanced; because his voice is more effectively produced, it may become richer and more beautiful than before.

32. For example, Jaques-Dalcroze designs a sequential program for the development of "inner hearing," just as Kodály composes pieces in the *Choral Method* as means of systematically developing sight-singing skills. Jaques-Dalcroze, *Rhythm, Music and Education*; Kodály, *The Selected Writings*.

33. See Dewey, *Experience and Education*, 58.

34. Such naturalistic and ethnographic research is evident, e.g., in Patricia Shehan Campbell, *Songs in Their Heads: Music and Its Meaning in Children's Lives* (New York: Oxford University Press, 1998); Green, *How Popular Musicians Learn* and *Music, Informal Learning and the School*. For discussions of research on musical development as applied to music education, see, e.g., Heiner Gembris, "The Development of Musical Abilities," in Colwell and Richardson, eds., *The New Handbook of Research on Music Teaching and Learning*, 487–508; Bruce Torff, "A Comparative Review of Human Ability Theory: Context, Structure, Development," in Colwell and Richardson, eds., *The New Handbook of Research on Music Teaching and Learning*, 509–521; David J. Hargreaves and Adrian North, eds., *Musical Development and Learning: The International Perspective* (London: Continuum, 2001 [2002 printing]).

35. Dewey, *Democracy and Education,* ch. 11; Dewey, *Experience and Education,* chs. 7, 8, makes a case for the importance of scientific research in music education.

36. For Dewey, *Democracy and Education,* ch. 7, and Dewey, *Experience and Education,* ch. 4, this approach provides young people with experience in making democracies work.

37. Howard, *Artistry,* 94–99, notes that at first students slavishly follow the rules, while later they are governed by (and sometimes transgress) them. These rules cover both propositional and procedural knowledge of music and take time to develop. Only experts or competent practitioners possess the maturity required to fully grasp the rule systems in their respective musical traditions.

38. For Suzuki, *Nurtured by Love,* 9–11, 23–25, 27, 29, 31, musical talent is largely determined by environmental factors. Since Japanese children learn to speak Japanese, he reasons, children ought to be able to learn music if instruction is carried out by the "mother tongue" method, that is, in the same way that children learn to speak their language. Beginning musical instruction at a very early age, ensuring parental support and attendance at children's lessons, listening to outstanding musical performances and repeated playing of the same pieces, tackling progressively more difficult repertoire and technique, and participating in continuous and humane instruction are among the requisite characteristics Suzuki advances. Suzuki sees the home as an important educational agent and utilizes it in surrounding children with exemplary music at home and enlisting parents' assistance in the young child's musical education. Contra those who view musical ability is a rare gift, Suzuki regards it as widespread; he believes that many children are capable of becoming musicians if their musicality is cultivated in a carefully structured environment.

39. This occurs much as Howard's "apprentice's sorcery" in which the neophyte singer comes to know how to sing. See Howard, *Artistry,* 75–80.

40. For a revision of Bloom's taxonomy of educational objectives, see Robert J. Marzano and John S. Kendall, *The New Taxonomy of Educational Objectives,* 2nd ed. (Thousand Oaks, Calif.: Corwin Press, 2007). For a discussion of how this redrawn taxonomy relates to cognitive, affective, and psychomotor knowledge domains, see ch. 4.

41. Dewey, *Democracy and Education,* 258, criticizes the emphasis on training in school music because he also sees music as a field within the humanities and an aspect of enculturation, and its place in general education is often defended for these reasons. For Kodály, however, a systematic program of study is needed to cultivate an ability to read and sing music at sight—central skills in the performance of a musically literate tradition. Without these abilities, much of the musical repertoire of the Western classical tradition is out of the reach of ordinary people. Kodály wishes all children to have the capacity to access music that would otherwise be reserved for the musically elite, and so he builds a curriculum around skill development and its expression in vocal music. Dewey seems not to grasp the power that such skill development may have on music making and taking for ordinary people. So he is inclined to urge music teachers to treat music as a field of study in the humanities rather than a skills-oriented subject—an approach that suggests, practically speaking, a listening-oriented program of musical study.

42. References to Piaget's ideas in music educational research are reported by authors in Richard Colwell, ed., *Handbook of Research on Music Teaching and Learning* (New York: Schirmer Books, 1992), passim, and Colwell and Richardson, eds., *The New Handbook of Research on Music Teaching and Learning,* passim.

43. For example, as a girl begins her study of the trombone, her teacher can rejoice in the apparent latency and possibility of what she might achieve in the future. As she gains greater competence as a musician, latency becomes actuality, and her teacher can be pleased with her progress and playing at an intermediate level. When she wins a professional orchestra position, her teacher may now be happy for her command of the instrument and her musical knowledge as an exponent of the trombone and its literature.

44. Nel Noddings, *Happiness and Education*, argues that happiness needs to be both a means and end of education.

45. See Jorgensen, *In Search of Music Education*, 87–90. Watching and listening to the Cape Cod Chorale in a performance of choral and vocal music and arrangements of music by George Gershwin and Leonard Bernstein, I was struck by the sheer joy performing this concert elicited in singers and audience alike. I saw many singers whose faces were lit up with joy. Audience members who were on hand to support their friends and family members and celebrate the choir's achievement likewise smiled proudly and waved to choir members. These singers obviously enjoyed making music under the direction of Chris Roberts, a high school music teacher, with the help of their accompanist Cathy Bonnett, a church musician and music theater director. For this group of amateur musicians, this concert, an end of their endeavors of previous months, can inspire them to remain in this choir and develop their musicianship and their singing voices in the future. On the Cape Cod Chorale, its director, Chris Roberts, and accompanist, Cathy Bonnett, see the Chorale's website, http://capecodchorale.org/ (accessed July 15, 2010).

46. On living knowledge and avoiding "inert knowledge," see Whitehead, *The Aims of Education*, 1, 2; on music's "vital import," see Langer, *Philosophy in a New Key*, ch. 8, and *Feeling and Form*, 31, 32.

47. Dewey, *Experience and Education*, 59.

48. On rule-governed behavior as a basis for social control, see ibid., 52, 53. This responsibility removes the teacher to a more socially distant position than Parker J. Palmer, *The Courage to Teach*, ch. 5, would prefer.

49. On fostering civil public spaces in which democratic education can proceed, see Dewey, *Experience and Education*, ch. 4; Greene, *The Dialectic of Freedom*, esp. chs. 1, 4.

50. The "reciprocal empathy" between teachers and students is beneficial for music teaching and learning. By reciprocal empathy, I mean that teacher and student are able to imagine the other's predicament, feel at one with it, and respond positively to the other. See Jorgensen, "On a Choice-Based Instructional Typology in Music."

51. Noddings, *Caring*, construes this disposition as caring and invests it with a dispassionate quality of sympathy, compassion, and affection with the other's best interests in mind. J. R. Martin, *The Schoolhome*, thinks in terms of the nurturing home as a metaphor for the genuine love, understanding, and consideration that needs to obtain in schools. Van Manen, *The Tact of Teaching*, 5–7, regards tact as the capacity to effectively interact with the student *in loco parentis*.

52. Dewey, *Experience and Education*, 29, acknowledges that this approach to education is more difficult to accomplish than the "old" or "traditional" approaches typical of production or consumption.

53. By all accounts, even Dewey probably did not meet the interests of all of his students equally well; as a professor, he was "modest and retiring," considered "one of the most

popular, most satisfactory classroom lecturers in the University," and also regarded by his detractors as "[c]old, impersonal, psychological, sphinx-like, anomalous, and petrifying to flunkers." See Brian A. Williams, "Thought and Action: John Dewey at the University of Michigan" (Ann Arbor, Mich.: Bentley Historical Library, University of Michigan, Bulletin Bentley Historical Library No. 44, July 1998), 22, 23. Available online at http://www.soe .umich.edu/dewey/ (accessed July 25, 2010). His lecturing style would never have suited another teacher, such as Austin Caswell, who preferred to question his students closely. While some students might opt for a lecture of the sort Dewey might give, others might choose a Socratic conversation of the kind Caswell would lead. Caswell served on the musicology faculty of the Indiana University Jacobs School of Music (1966–1996) and taught a popular undergraduate course for the Hutton Honors College at Indiana University (1973–2006). See "Obituary of Austin B. Caswell," *Herald Times*, Bloomington, Ind., March 3, 2006. I am indebted to Malcolm H. Brown for bringing this to my attention.

54. See Greene, *The Dialectic of Freedom*, ch. 5.

55. See William Pinar, "*Currere*: Toward Reconceptualization," in William Pinar, ed., *Curriculum Theorizing: The Reconceptualists* (Berkeley, Calif.: McCutchan, 1975), 396–414.

56. See John Dewey, *The Child and the Curriculum, and The School and Society*, 3–31.

57. For example, the child comes to school music with a background of familial, religious, and other prior musical experiences. Especially for those who have not had earlier musical training, music needs to be approached from the child's perspective rather than the exponent's. Gradually, the child comes to construct music in a more musically informed way. The teacher's challenge is to move the child from initially intuitive to more systematic constructions of music.

58. This idea initially grounded American music education and was attributed by Hans Georg Nägeli, Michael Traugott Pfeiffer, William Channing Woodbridge, and Lowell Mason to Johann Heinrich Pestalozzi, who took a similar approach to the study of school subject matter. Although they were mistaken in this attribution, the spirit of Pestalozzi's teaching of "sound before sight," or experience before conceptualizing music, stuck. For a critical analysis of the rationale advanced for the introduction of vocal music into publicly supported schools, see Estelle R. Jorgensen, "William Channing Woodbridge's Lecture 'On Vocal Music as a Branch of Common Education' Revisited," *Studies in Music* (University of Western Australia) no. 18 (1984): 1–32. This approach is exemplified today in the singing games used by teachers in the Kodály as well as other approaches. On singing games in music education, see Jorgensen, *The Art of Teaching Music*, 118.

59. For a discussion of these "rhythms" and the seamless cyclical approach to everything that is studied, see Whitehead, *The Aims of Education*, ch. 3.

60. Among the instances in which these ideas play out in music education, Heidi Westerlund, *Bridging Experience, Action, and Culture in Music Education* (Helsinki: Studia Musica 16, Sibelius Academy, 2002), lays out ways in which Dewey's developmental and experiential plan are likely to unfold in the study of music. She attends especially to its naturalistic and humane aspects and the importance of the links between music and other aspects of lived life that are pregnant in Dewey's writings. This holistic and experiential approach shares much in common with the "life world" approaches to music education proposed by Eva Alerby and Cecilia Ferm, "Learning Music: Embodied Experience in the Life-World," *Philosophy of Music Education Review* 13 (2) (Fall 2005): 177–185; it ensures

that students approach the study of music from the perspective of their lived experiences. In this approach, students map their musical worlds and document, describe, express, and name them. They record such things as family and religious musical events of which they are a part, e.g., a grandmother singing a folk or popular song from an earlier era, a hymn or chant being sung, a sampling of their favorite recordings, and a collection of pictures of their musical heroes. They describe concerts they attend, field trips to a musical museum the class takes, and interviews with musicians who visit the classroom. In these and other ways, the curriculum starts with validating their musical personae. They go on to make music in groups such as garage bands, choirs, wind ensembles, jazz combos, steel drum bands, Orff instrumentaria, guitar and piano classes, singing and playing alone and together in all sorts of ways with the purpose of acquiring the requisite musical techniques, vocabulary, and broader cultural understandings of the musics they make and take. During this process, they may become skilled guitarists, pianists, steel drum performers, handbell ringers, fiddlers, violinists, saxophonists, flutists, trumpeters, singers, recording engineers, producers, and sight readers and singers of music. They also know this music's famous people and exemplary works, its history and theoretical underpinnings. Students also go on not only to see how music integrates with their lived experiences and the wider culture of which they are a part, but to understand that the musical traditions and civilizations to which they are heirs form a part of the world's musics and cultures. The romance is still alive, but it is now overlaid with a musician's systematic grasp of this music and its intersections and dissonances with others. From an unsystematic and idiosyncratic view of music, students have moved to the musician's more systematic and generalized understandings. They not only know about music but they can also make it. They possess an array of skills from habits and physical skills to critical thinking skills and cultural understandings.

61. Among those to interrogate the knowledge claims of the establishment, see, e.g., Michael W. Apple, *Official Knowledge: Democratic Education in a Conservative Age*, 2nd ed. (New York: Routledge, 2000).

62. Dewey, *Art as Experience*, 266–269, 272–274, anticipates this ambiguity of musical meaning when he suggests the crucial role of imagination in apprehending music.

63. Think, e.g., of the impact that school music teachers have had on the study of music in the academy over the past four decades as they have embraced popular music as a major vehicle of music education. Gradually, the stance of university and college music study has changed to adopt a pluralist view of music that includes popular music study within a previously and almost exclusively classical curriculum. It has taken the better part of a working lifetime for this change to become institutionalized (although this is a drop in the bucket of musical history, it represents a rapid change when viewed within the frame of millennia).

64. See Aristotle, *Nicomachean Ethics*, trans. and ed. Roger Crisp (Cambridge: Cambridge University Press, 2000), esp. §§1106b, 1107a, 1109a, pp. 29–31, 34–35.

65. Some teachers, such as Jaques-Dalcroze, *Rhythm, Music and Education*, 16, 29, 38, would have teachers make summative evaluations that impact whether or not children will continue their musical studies after a comparatively short period of musical instruction. Many more seem comfortable with a more extended period of instruction covering elementary and at least the early years of secondary schooling before taking such a summative view.

66. See Scheffler, *In Praise of the Cognitive Emotions*, 3–17; Yob, "The Cognitive Emotions and Emotional Cognitions."

67. Martin Luther insists, e.g., that all classroom teachers, regardless of their specialty, be musicians; if they cannot sing and play instruments, he does not consider them fit to

be teachers. For a discussion of Martin Luther's music educational philosophy, see Joe E. Tarry, "Music in the Educational Philosophy of Martin Luther," *Journal of Research in Music Education* 21.4 (Winter 1973): 355–365.

68. As I write, the Oxford University dons have rejected an administrative reorganization modeled on corporate principles. They argue that the relatively flat and collegial governance structure in place for centuries, with tutors who meet with students individually and in small groups, permits them to focus on the individual development of their students. Decision-making is pervasively dialogical, and conversations between administrators, dons, and students ensure that the needs, interests, and development of students are among the foremost considerations in the various colleges that comprise the university. To reorganize Oxford corporately in order to appease donors and create a more nimble organization would, in their view, enforce a more production-oriented and top-down approach. Rather than teach students, they believe that they would be expected to produce research and be seen to be "transparent" in ways typical of business. They see this dramatic change as abandoning their own and the university's primary mission. See "Oxford Dons Reject Corporate Structure," *Boston Sunday Globe,* June 12, 2005, A13.

69. Oxford's long-standing success in cultivating scholars for centuries rests partly on this combination of lectures to larger groups with small group and individual tutoring of students where teachers know their students and help them progress through their degree programs. Just as large ensemble and class instruction are regularly combined with chamber music ensembles and other small class or individual instrumental instruction in academic music programs, one would expect to find the same combination in elementary and secondary school music programs. This expectation is implied in the American music educational profession's recommendations that students ought to play and sing alone and with others. I am unsure that the implications of such seemingly simple statements have been thought through fully, but these expectations would further necessitate large and small group and individual musical instruction in elementary and secondary schools. See *The National Standards for Arts Education.*

70. For example, the long time scales of the natural world contrast with short time scales of social events, where the passage of moments, minutes, hours, days, weeks, and even years can mean that realities change from time to time and place to place. For a discussion of time scales in music educational research, see Jorgensen, "A Case Study in Two Divergent Research Methodologies in Music Education." Likewise, the species of the natural world and species counterpoint in music, while figuratively similar, are literally distinct, and Darwinian notions of incremental change, mutations, and the survival of the fittest observed in the natural world do not apply necessarily and literally to musics. See Allsup, "Species Counterpoint."

71. See Suzuki, *Nurtured by Love,* 90, 94, 96.

72. See van Manen, *The Tact of Teaching,* esp. chs. 6–8.

73. Highet, *The Art of Teaching,* 176, 179, 180, 185, cites the case of Judas Iscariot, who studied with Jesus, an excellent teacher who cared about him, but nevertheless betrayed him. Martin, *Reclaiming a Conversation,* ch. 3, also criticizes Rousseau's project of educating Émile naturally as misguided and short-sighted, especially in respect of how he could be expected to relate to Sophie.

74. See Scheffler, *Reason and Teaching,* 71–76.

75. See ibid., 79, 80.

76. Buber, *I and Thou,* envisages a respectful and reciprocal dialogue.

77. Lewis Rowell, *Thinking about Music: An Introduction to the Philosophy of Music* (Amherst: University of Massachusetts Press, 1983), 175–176, lists endings among the musical values that characterize Western classical music.

78. A boy may not play the violin because he (or his guardian) chooses not to do so; he may prefer the piano over the violin. Putting him in a violin class with other tiny tots may not be in his best interest; it might be better for him to play games out-of-doors until later, when he can take up the piano. Even if parents surround their children with certain musics, as they grow older, they may go in very different directions musically. For a philosophical discussion of human potential in education, see Scheffler, *In Praise of the Cognitive Emotions*, ch. 2.

79. I recall transformations in lives of students when they realized, sometimes for the first time, that they were up against something that they could not yet do but must be able to do. Sometimes, the realization of unmet challenges that they walked away from comes back to haunt them in later life. I think, for example, of adults who lament that they should have stuck with their piano lessons in their youth. The going was sometimes difficult, but now they recognize what their teachers wanted for them, and some belatedly take up the study of the piano as adults. Did these early musical experiences impact them negatively? Yes. Still, they also learned something of great value from the experience, and in their adulthood, they contemplate what they have missed but what they might still gain in study now. Those who teach the piano to adults know that these sorts of students are some of the most rewarding to teach; they take their study most seriously and derive great pleasure from the success they achieve. Sometimes the opportunity has passed them by, and it is no longer possible for them to play; this is as it sometimes is in life. See Susan Laird, "Musical Hunger: A Philosophical Testimonial of Miseducation," *Philosophy of Music Education Review* 17.1 (Spring 2009): 4–21.

80. For example, Robert Shaw was beloved by his singers and referred to them as his "dear people." See Joseph A. Mussulman, *Dear People . . . Robert Shaw* (Bloomington: Indiana University Press, 1979).

81. For example, some of the musicians I meet are aghast at Christopher Small's portrayal, in *Musicking: The Meanings of Performing and Listening* (Hanover, N.H.: University Press of New England for Wesleyan University Press, 1998), of the concert hall in political, social, and, economic terms that, in their view, misconstrue what is actually going on.

8. THERAPIST AND HEALING

1. Diana Schmück and Bonnie Campbell, professional musicians and studio teachers in Evanston, Illinois, urged me to write on these pictures that are, in their view, among the most important for individual performance instruction of the sort typical in the United States.

2. For the etymology of "therapy," or the "medical treatment of disease," from the Latin word *therapia* and the Greek, *therapeia*, see *OED Online*, s.v. "therapy," http://dictionary.oed.com (accessed July 16, 2010).

3. See *OED Online*, s.v. "therapist," http://dictionary.oed.com (accessed July 16, 2010).

4. See *OED Online*, s.v. "healing, *vbl n*¹," http://dictionary.oed.com (accessed July 16, 2010); *OED Online*, s.v. "healing, *ppl. a.*," http://dictionary.oed.com (accessed July 16, 2010).

5. I subsequently discovered a resonance in her beliefs about the human body with those of Moshe Feldenkrais, *Awareness through Movement: Health Exercises for Personal Growth* (San Francisco: HarperSanFrancisco, 1990).

6. Nel Noddings, *Caring,* esp. chs. 2, 3, would refer to her as the "one-caring."

7. For an analysis of the distinctions between propositional and procedural knowledge, see Scheffler, *In Praise of the Cognitive Emotions*, ch. 3.

8. William Shakespeare's warrior Coriolanus says: "[I]t is no little thing to make / Mine eyes to sweat compassion." Shakespeare, *The Tragedy of Coriolanus*, act 5, scene 3 (Project Gutenberg, 1998) http://www.gutenberg.org/etext/1535 (accessed July 24, 2010). Nancy Sherman, "When Johnny Comes Home," *The Boston Globe,* Monday June 20, 2005, A11, observes, in commenting on Coriolanus's statement, that "this is a lesson doctors and therapists at military hospitals know well." As a warrior, Coriolanus is trained as a stoic to bear suffering, and it is hard to hear and see the other with depth of feeling. Shakespeare may be on to this tension in his depiction of the warrior's difficulty experiencing what would bring one to "sweat compassion." Although Katina differs from Coriolanus in that he is trained to destroy life and she seeks to save it, the needs of others and their sometimes distressing conditions may necessitate her being in a similar place to Coriolanus's compassion on the battlefield.

9. Among her remedies, Katina urges her patients to sing and chant. She is like music therapists who employ music in the service of health and well-being. For example, Gertrud Orff, *The Orff Music Therapy: Active Furthering of the Development of the Child,* trans. Margaret Murray (London: Schott, 1980), advocates the use of the Orff approach to music therapy in treating children with various incapacities including Down syndrome. Also see Paul Nordoff and Clive Robbins, *Therapy in Music for Handicapped Children* (London: Victor Gollancz, 1971). Elizabeth Anne Bauer, "What is an Appropriate Approach to Piano Instruction for Students with Down Syndrome?" doctoral diss., Indiana University, Bloomington, May 2003, notes that music therapy may be particularly effective with Down Syndrome children. For recent texts in music therapy, see Simon Gilbertson, *Music Therapy and Traumatic Brain Injury: A Light on a Dark Night* (London: Jessica Kingsley, 2008); Amelia Oldfield, *Music Therapy with Children and their Families* (London: Jessica Kingsley, 2008); Mary Butterton, *Listening to Music in Psychotherapy* (Oxford: Radcliffe, 2008).

10. See June Boyce-Tillman, *Constructing Musical Healing: The Wounds that Sing* (London: Jessica Kingsley, 2000).

11. See June Boyce-Tillman, "Towards an Ecology of Music Education."

12. See Maslow, "Music, Education, and Peak Experiences."

13. See Noddings, *Happiness and Education;* Anthony J. Palmer, "Music Education and Spirituality: A Philosophical Exploration," *Philosophy of Music Education Review* 3.2 (Fall 1995): 91–106, and his "Music Education and Spirituality: A Philosophical Exploration II," *Philosophy of Music Education Review* 14.2 (Fall 2006): 143–158; Deanne Bogdan, "Musical Spirituality: Reflections on Identity and the Ethics of Embodied Aesthetic Experience in/ and the Academy," *Journal of Aesthetic Education* 37.2 (Summer 2003): 80–98; Iris M. Yob, "The School as Sacred Space," unpublished paper presented to Presented to *Reasons of the Heart: Myth, Meaning, and Education,* an international conference, University of Edinburgh, Sept. 9–12, 2004, available from the author at iris.yob@waldenu.edu; Bennett Reimer, "The Experience of Profundity in Music," *Journal of Aesthetic Education* 29.4 (Winter 1995):

1–21; Estelle R. Jorgensen, "Religious Music in Education," *Philosophy of Music Education Review* 1.2 (Fall 1993): 103–114.

14. For example, David's music calmed King Saul just as musicians accompanied soldiers to battle. See 1. Samuel 16: 23; Joshua 15: 16.

15. See Iris M. Yob, "The Cognitive Emotions and Emotional Cognitions," *Studies in Philosophy and Education* 16 (1997): 43–57. Susanne K. Langer, *Philosophy in a New Key: A Study in the Symbolism of Reason, Rite, and Art,* 3rd ed. (Cambridge, Mass.: Harvard University Press, 1957), especially ch. 8, stresses that the arts, religions, myths, and rituals widen and deepen the many ways in which people are able to give voice to what she calls "feeling." For her, feeling is all that cannot be expressed propositionally in words, mathematical symbols, and scientific formulae, yet is thought, emoted, and physically sensed. Langer's holistic and subjective account of musical meaning also resonates with John Dewey's dialectical view of music as the process of doing and undergoing in specifically musical and artistic ways that differ from those of the sciences and intensify ordinary experience. See his *Art as Experience,* esp. ch. 3. Dewey's metaphor of expressing grapes into wine connotes this intensity and difficulty of articulating felt thought enacted as thought-emotion-sensation, a process different from the sciences yet having things in common with them (ibid., 64).

16. For a sampling of more recent writing on the scientific underpinnings of music and its relationship to the philosophy of music, see, e.g., Robin Maconie, *The Science of Music* (Oxford: Oxford University Press, 1997); Robert J. Zatorre, *The Biological Foundations of Music* (New York: New York Academy of Sciences, 2001); G. Avanzini, *The Neurosciences and Music II: From Perception to Performance* (New York: New York Academy of Sciences, 2005); Daniel J. Schneck, *The Music Effect: Music Physiology and Clinical Applications* (London: Jessica Kingsley, 2006); Richard Colwell, ed., *MENC Handbook of Musical Cognition and Development* (New York: Oxford University Press, 2006); Gary McPherson, *The Child as Musician: A Handbook of Musical Development* (Oxford: Oxford University Press, 2006); Peter Kivy, *Music, Language, and Cognition: and Other Essays in the Aesthetics of Music* (Oxford: Oxford University Press, 2007); Marc Leman, *Embodied Music Cognition and Mediation Technology* (Cambridge, Mass.: MIT Press, 2008); Benjamin D. Koen, with Jacqueline Lloyd, Gregory Barz, and Karen Brummel-Smith, associate eds., *The Oxford Handbook of Medical Ethnomusicology* (Oxford: Oxford University Press, 2008).

17. Plato's endorsement of only the Dorian and Phrygian modes in general education was grounded in their presumed positive impact on character development and the negative impact of other modes. For Glaucon's comments to Socrates on the desirability of the Dorian and Phrygian modes in general education, see Plato, *Republic,* §399a, p. 96. Since prolonged listening to high-decibel music has been demonstrated to contribute to deafness, healing requires that musical amplification is at acceptable levels and only musics that are demonstrably healthful are fostered in general education. For a discussion of acoustically unsafe environments in music instruction see Jorgensen, *Art of Teaching Music,* 192, and Randall D. Royer, "Sound Pressure Levels and Frequencies Generated in Secondary Public School Band Rooms," doctoral diss., University of Utah, 1996. I am indebted for Charles P. Schmidt for bringing this reference to my attention.

18. Some instruments lend themselves to potential injuries. Consider the trunk twisted in order to play the violin, the slouching posture manifested by some players to encompass the double bass, the high pressure on facial muscles in forming an embouchure in perform-

ing wind instruments, and the stress caused by some vocal techniques employed in singing with microphones. Some musicians find such approaches as the Alexander Technique to be helpful in assuming a more relaxed and natural posture and thereby preventing injury. For an experimental study on the use of the Alexander Technique by music performers, see Elizabeth R. Valentine, David F. P. Fitzgerald, Tessa L. Gorton, Jennifer A. Hudson, and Elizabeth R. C. Symonds, "The Effect of Lessons in the Alexander Technique on Music Performance in High and Low Stress Situations," *Psychology of Music* 23.2 (1995): 129–141. For information on the Alexander Technique for music performers, see "The Complete Guide to the Alexander Technique," at http://www.alexandertechnique.com/ (accessed July 19, 2010).

19. For example, therapeutic, mystical, and trance states are associated with musics around the world. On musical healing, see Penelope Gouk, ed., *Musical Healing in Cultural Contexts* (Aldershot: Ashgate, 2000). On mysticism and music see, e.g., Joscelyn Godwin, *Harmonies of Heaven and Earth: Mysticism in Music from Antiquity to the Avant-Garde* (Rochester, Vt.: Inner Traditions International, 1995); Maxwell Steer, *Music and Mysticism* (Amsterdam: Harwood Academic Publishers, 1996). On music and trance states, see, e.g., Gilbert Rouget, *Music and Trance: A Theory of the Relations Between Music and Possession* (Chicago: University of Chicago Press, 1985); Judith O. Becker, *Deep Listeners: Music, Emotion, and Trancing* (Bloomington: Indiana University Press, 2004); David Aldridge, *Music and Altered States: Consciousness, Transcendence, Therapy and Addiction* (London: Jennifer Kingsley Publishers, 2006).

20. John Blacking, *How Musical is Man?* (London: Faber and Faber, 1976), 44, 45, reports that his attempt to perform Venda music engendered complaints by a performer preparing to go into a trance because his contributions disrupted the music's flow and impeded her concentration.

21. See Judith Vander, *Songprints: The Musical Experience of Five Shoshone Women* (Urbana: University of Illinois Press), 293.

22. On music therapy methods, see, e.g., Denise Erdonmez Grocke, *Receptive Methods in Music Therapy: Techniques and Clinical Applications for Music Therapy Clinicians, Educators, and Students* (London: Jessica Kingsley Publishers, 2007).

23. This view goes contrary to Jean-Jacques Rousseau's argument in *Émile*, 5, that human nature is inherently good.

24. Witness those teachers who establish residential schools for deprived children, provide school food programs for hungry children, work with parents to assist them in locating clean and affordable housing, join with law enforcement officials in reporting child abuse, root out violence to children, coach sport teams, lead service and other clubs for boys and girls, spend time with students in order to win their trust and confidence, and treat them with affection and respect.

25. Neil Postman, *Teaching as a Conserving Activity* (New York: Dell, 1979), ch. 1, refers to this educational remediation of the things lacking in society as an *isomorphic* or *thermostatic* approach to teaching.

26. Such activities as lining up outside the classroom to go together quietly to their desks, sit down, prepare class materials, participate in daily opening exercises in standing and greeting the teacher, singing a song of welcome, reciting a pledge of loyalty, moving into the classroom activities smoothly because all of the things needed are in place, receiving teachers' instructions quietly and obeying them, asking and answering questions with hands

raised, singing a good-bye song at class's end, lining up to go out of the classroom quietly in an orderly manner can indicate that everything has a place and everything is in its place.

27. By empathetic, I mean that teachers are able to put themselves in their students' position and imaginatively see the subject matter as their students might see it. Compassion goes further to act sympathetically toward students irrespective of how lovable they are.

28. For example, a rigid, tense, and flat-fingered approach to the piano keyboard indicates specific technical problems that require solution. This student needs to adopt a different hand position at the keyboard and play in ways that are more relaxed and less taut and stressful. Equally problematic is how the teacher plans to bring the student from this currently tight hand position to a more relaxed style of playing that will leave the student less likely to suffer injury in the future. Disorders such as tendinitis and repetitive stress disorder are likely outcomes of poor technique and practice routines, and remedying this student's technique and practice schedule opens the possibility for the pianist's health and well-being.

29. Abraham H. Maslow, "A Theory of Human Motivation," *Psychological Review* 50 (1943): 370–396; Abraham H. Maslow, *Motivation and Personality,* 3rd ed., rev. by Robert Frager et al. (New York: Addison Wesley Longman, 1987), passim, places peak experiences of transcendence at the pinnacle of his hierarchy of needs and insists that all of the lower-order needs, including safety and affection, must be met before peak experiences are possible. Figuring out those things that are impeding the students' musical growth and designing ways to remedy them evokes Percy Scholes's notion of musical appreciation teaching as the process of removing roadblocks to students' musical understanding. See Scholes, *Music, the Child and the Masterpiece,* 81–96. This focus on removing impediments or roadblocks differs from Dewey's conception of eduction, whereby teachers begin with the natural capacities and interests of their students, and teaching seems more a matter of building onto what is already there. On educational growth, see John Dewey, *Democracy and Education,* 41–53, 54–55, 56, 321–322. For a discussion of eduction in music education, see Jorgensen, *In Search of Music Education,* 13–18.

30. See Abraham H. Maslow, "Music, Education, and Peak Experiences," 70–73; Abraham H. Maslow, *The Farther Reaches of Human Nature,* esp. chs. 12, 21, 22. Also see Mihály Csikszentmihályi, *Flow: The Psychology of Optimal Experience* (New York: Harper and Row, 1990).

31. As I write, this program has reached nearly 400,000 children over the past thirty years. Venezuela's population is about 25 million; this program has directly impacted a small proportion of young people. Its annual budget is $29 million—a modest cultural investment. See Indira A. R. Lakshmanan, "For Venezuela's Poor, Music Opens Doors," *The Boston Globe,* Wednesday, June 22, 2005, A1, A9. For information on el Sistema in the United States, see http://elsistemausa.org (accessed October 1, 2010).

32. Roger Sessions, *The Musical Experience of Composer, Performer, Listener,* sketches how the musical ideas in the classical composer's mind are notated in a score, interpreted by the performer, and imaginatively heard by the listener. Musical ideas, felt life, and sensuality are communicated from one to another, and Sessions notes the almost "instinctual" level at which musicians seem to be operating.

33. David J. Elliott, *Music Matters: A New Philosophy of Music Education* (New York: Oxford University Press, 1995), emphasizes this point in his performance-oriented plan for musical study.

34. Reimer, *A Philosophy of Music Education: Advancing the Vision,* also advocates performance as an important component of music education.

35. What is this inner felt life? Langer tells us what she thinks it is, and although the answer she gives gets her into a lot of philosophical trouble, her account, at least from a performing musician's point of view, seems near to the mark. See Langer, *Philosophy in a New Key,* 228, 235, 238, 245. Langer expands on the idea of the arts as expressions of human feeling in Langer, *Feeling and Form.* In a similar vein, Bogdan, "Musical Listening and Performance as Embodied Dialogism," describes philosophically what she is thinking, feeling, and doing as she prepares to perform and plays a piece of music on the piano.

36. See Reichling, "Images of Imagination."

37. See Buber, *I and Thou.*

38. See Bogdan, "Musical Listening and Performance as Embodied Dialogism."

39. See Jorgensen, *Transforming Music Education.*

40. For example, a jazz teacher who coaches his combo at school by day prepares it to play gigs in clubs by night; he brings to his class visiting jazz musicians who jam with the students; he books his musicians for jazz performances; and he helps them record their performances for class playback and analysis. Such a teacher melds formal and informal instruction; is students see their school jazz instruction merging seamlessly with their professional playing and the other parts of their lived lives. See J. [James] B. Dyas, "A Description, Comparison, and Interpretation of Two Exemplary Performing Arts High School Jazz Programs," doctoral diss., Indiana University Bloomington, December 2006.

41. For example, the music teacher might also be found visiting a history class or preparing songs and dances of the particular times the history class is investigating, helping the poetry teacher by setting a poem to music or leading a class in an already composed song setting of the poem, showing students how musical ideas spread from one country or city to another as they prepare maps for a social studies class, using musical examples to teach fractions or teaching fractions in the music class as the class learns metrical concepts, or testing scientific theories of wave motion and the harmonic series with various musical instruments.

42. This approach is well established in instrumental pedagogies. Here, teachers tailor repertoire to student needs and interests. Some instruments with large literatures, such as the piano and violin, may entail considerable solo and small ensemble playing. Other instruments with more limited solo repertoires may require considerable ensemble playing.

43. Carl Orff and Gunild Keetman's solution to this problem is to design simple classroom instruments that can easily and successfully be played by children with little musical experience so as to immediately produce a pleasant sound. Their program's accessibility also affords opportunities for teachers to use the approach with special needs students and may be a factor in its therapeutic use. Likewise, R. Murray Schafer's dialogical approach to music curriculum through the use of classroom sounds in composing is integrated with students' lived experiences. Its simplicity enables neophyte musicians to compose music from the very beginning of their musical education without the need for sophisticated musical knowledge, skills, and instrumental techniques. See Carl Orff, *The Schulwerk,* vol. 3 of *Carl Orff/Documentation, His Life and Works,* trans. Margaret Murray (New York: Schott, 1978), passim; Carl Orff and Gunild Keetman, *Musik für Kinder,* 5 vols. (Mainz: Schott, 1950). See Schafer, *The Thinking Ear.*

44. The success of el Sistema stems, in part, from the fact that students study music every day throughout the entire year, without significant breaks of time in between their lessons and practice sessions.

45. This is the case with el Sistema, which is now studied by musicians, educators, and politicians internationally as a model for musical, public, and social policy. Notice that the Venezuelan plan was forwarded by an influential classical musician with the political skills to set in motion a governmentally funded program of musical instruction, even in a political environment in which dissent was curtailed. This twentieth-century initiative is evocative of the impact of William Woodbridge and Lowell Mason in spearheading a grassroots movement for school music instruction in the nineteenth century. See Estelle R. Jorgensen, "Engineering Change in Music Education: A Model of the Political Process Underlying the Boston School Music Movement (1829–1838)," *Journal of Research in Music Education* 31.1 (Spring 1983): 67–75.

46. See Contemporary Music Project for Creativity in Music Education, *Comprehensive Musicianship: An Anthology of Evolving Thought; A Discussion of the First Ten Years (1959–1969) of the Contemporary Music Project, Particularly as They Relate to the Development of the Theory of Comprehensive Musicianship, as Reported in Articles and Speeches by Those Closely Associated with the Project* (Washington, D.C.: Music Educators National Conference, 1971).

47. For example, such an approach might also suggest team-taught courses so that a group of specialists bring various points of view to bear on any particular class. In this way, studio teachers might teach history, theory, and pedagogy, just as historians could conduct ensembles and teach instrumental or vocal lessons.

48. See, e.g., Laird, "Musical Hunger"; Estelle R. Jorgensen, "A Response to Susan Laird, 'Musical Hunger: A Philosophical Testimonial of Miseducation,'" *Philosophy of Music Education Review* 17.1 (Spring 2009): 75–80.

49. Illich, *Deschooling Society,* 31, notes that if "the *teacher-as-therapist* feels authorized to delve into the life of his [or her] pupil in order to help him [or her] grow as a person," students may be persuaded to "submit to a domestication" of their "vision of truth" or "sense of what is right." When the *teacher-as-therapist* is combined with the *teacher-as-custodian* and *teacher-as-moralist,* "The child must confront a man who wears an invisible triple crown, like the papal tiara, the symbol of triple authority combined in one person. For the child, the teacher pontificates as pastor, prophet, and priest . . ." (31).

50. See Scheffler, *Reason and Teaching,* ch. 6.

51. Imagine what an impact this program might have if the same approach were open to many more, and the range of musical, dance, artistic, and theatrical opportunities were broadened. Were such an enlarged program to feature the same student-centeredness and integrity of artistic instruction by musicians and artists proficient in their crafts and arts, the lives of millions of young people might be transformed and made whole. Some young people would likely excel as musicians and dancers, others would be more interested in teaching music and dance, composing, improvising, or producing music, and still others might go on to excel in other fields of study beyond music.

9. COURT AND RULE

1. See Charles Dickens, *Oliver Twist* (Mineola, N.Y.: Dover, 2002). On discipline, see Jorgensen, *The Art of Teaching Music,* 89–93.

2. See Scheffler, *Reason and Teaching*, 76–79; Ralph A. Smith, ed., *Discipline-Based Art Education: Origins, Meaning, and Development* (Urbana: University of Illinois Press, 1989); Charles Fowler, *Discipline-Based Music Education: A Conceptual Framework for the Teaching of Music*, A Report of the Proceedings of an Invitational Conference Based on Discipline-Based Music Education, Aug. 1994 (Chattanooga: University of Tennessee at Chattanooga, 1994).

3. In the United States, this use of the term "bench" is figurative as plaintiffs, defendants, counsel, and prosecution normally sit at chairs and tables.

4. In American law, the lawyers for the defense do not have to "prove" the defendant's innocence; they just need to show that there is reasonable doubt of the defendant's guilt, and the defendant must then be acquitted.

5. Her identity unbeknown to her husband, Portia musters powerful arguments that move her jury and rebut Shylock's demand that her husband pay his pound of flesh; the ship on which his wealth is staked is reputed to have sunk in a storm and Shylock insists that his bond be literally met. As her husband's life hangs in the balance, Portia argues that Shylock's demands are unjust and unmerciful. Not only does she win the case, but the ship reappears and her husband's fortune is restored. See William Shakespeare, *The Merchant of Venice*, act 4, scene 1 (Project Gutenberg, 2004), http://www.gutenberg.org/etext/1114 (accessed July 16, 2010). For a discussion of the various phases of Luther's trial and its verdict, including Luther's appearance before Cardinal Cajetan at the Diet of Augsburg, the Leipzig Debate between Luther and Johannes Meier von Eck, the Pope's condemnation, the trial, and the verdict, see James Atkinson, *The Trial of Luther* (London: Batsford, 1971), passim. Also see Michael A. Mullett, *Martin Luther* (London: Routledge, 2004), esp. chs. 4, 5, 6.

6. In the American legal system, lawyers may seek to stack the jury in favor of their case, and consultants are regularly called to assist in jury selection. After the trial, jury members are often willing to turn their experiences into lucrative speaking appointments and book contracts.

7. See *OED Online*, s.v. "just, a.," http://dictionary.oed.com (accessed July 14, 2010). The etymological roots of justice are from the Old French "justise, -ice (jostise) uprightness, equity, vindication of right, administration of law, jurisdiction, court of justice . . . ," see *OED Online*, s.v. "justice, n.," http://dictionary.oed.com (accessed July 14, 2010).

8. Intellect and emotion are interrelated in cognitive emotions and emotional cognitions. Scheffler, *In Praise of the Cognitive Emotions*, 9–15, identifies emotions that are parasitic on ideas, such as the joy of verification and surprise, and Yob, "The Cognitive Emotions and Emotional Cognitions," notices cognitions that are parasitic on emotions, such as music, religion, myth, and ritual.

9. For the etymology of the word *rule*, construed as a noun, see *OED Online*, s.v. "rule, n.," http://dictionary.oed.com (accessed July 14, 2010), from the Old French, "riule, reule, ruile, rule, etc.," and the Latin "*rēgula* straight stick, bar, ruler, pattern."

10. See *WordPerfect X4 Dictionary*, s.v. "ruler" (Corel Corporation, Oxford University Press, 2008).

11. See Dewey, *Democracy and Education*; Peters, *Ethics and Education*; Scheffler, *Reason and Teaching*.

12. See Fowler, *Discipline-Based Music Education*; Howard, *Artistry*, esp. chs. 3, 4; Bennett Reimer, "Would Discipline-based Music Education Make Sense?" *Music Educators Journal* 77 (May 1991): 21–28; Smith, ed., *Discipline-based Art Education*; Woodford, *Democracy and Music Education*; Marja Heimonen, "Music Education and Law: Regulation

as an Instrument," *Philosophy of Music Education Review* 11.2 (Fall 2003): 170–184, and "Justifying the Right to Music Education," *Philosophy of Music Education Review* 14.2 (Fall 2006): 119–141.

13. For a discussion of legal rights to music education, see Heimonen, "Music Education and Law: Regulation as an Instrument" and "Justifying the Right to Music Education."

14. See Howard, *Artistry,* 94–99, 112, 117.

15. The rules for writing music in common practice are based on principles derived from what composers or performers already do or have done. For example, beginning students of music theory learn rules concerning avoiding parallel octaves and fifths in writing for four voices that are based on tradition and derived from the study of compositions written over the common practice period. Likewise, rules concerning the various sorts of ornamentation of baroque music are garnered from treatises and manuals of the time documenting what performers normally did that the authors considered to be in good taste. C. P. E. Bach's treatise is simply a compendium of what he regarded as the appropriate and normative practices of his time. He does not invent the ornamentation in advance of music so much as codify and systematize what excellent keyboard players of his time do. See Carl Philipp Emanuel Bach, *Essay on the True Art of Playing Keyboard Instruments,* trans. and ed. William J. Mitchell (New York: W. W. Norton, 1949).

16. Howard applies Max Black's theory of rules and their use in showing the various ways in which artists relate to rules. See Max Black, "Rules and Routines," in *The Concept of Education,* ed. R. S. [Richard Stanley] Peters (London: Routledge and Kegan Paul, 1967).

17. For example, whereas a beginning composition student learns not to write parallel fifths and octaves, the more advanced composition student learns of occasions in which parallel fifths and octaves allow the creation of particular characteristics of tonal ambiguity that can be exploited to good musical effect. This is not yet an active subversion or rejection of the rules so much as an interpretation of them. Later, a composer may reject notions of common practice and tonality, and set out to develop new scale systems such as those in the dodecaphonic writing or twelve-tone rows evident, e.g., in the music of Anton Webern. Although still governed by some of the rules of the Western classical music practice, e.g., the use of classical forms such as the sonata, the composer now breaks the old harmonic and voice-leading rules and develops new rule-sets. On Anton Friedrich Wilhelm von Webern, see *Grove Music Online, Oxford Music Online,* s.v. "Webern, Anton" (by Kathryn Bailey), http://www.oxfordmusiconline.com (accessed July 19, 2010).

18. See Copland, *Music and Imagination,* 51–55.

19. See Langer, *Feeling and Form,* 18, 318–319, 324, 341.

20. See Scheffler, *Reason and Teaching,* 76–79. This reasoning may be related to emotions such as surprise and the joy of verification; see Scheffler, *In Praise of the Cognitive Emotions,* 9–15.

21. Although teachers are not always wise, dispassionate, and just, and sometimes misinterpret the motives, words, and actions of their students, justice remains something to be aspired to by teachers who think of their work within the frame of rule.

22. For Scheffler, *Reason and Teaching,* ch. 9, teaching is philosophical at root; teachers' values are determined and justified philosophically, and empirical findings regarding education are examined critically for what they mean for educational practice. As Scheffler, *In*

Praise of the Cognitive Emotions, ch. 12, notes, common educational "sins" such as forget-
ting and procrastination can be beneficial under certain circumstances; notions of educational potential turn out to be complex and ambiguous constructions; and models of teaching including impression, insight, and rule are problematical in one respect or another.

23. For example, a piano teacher's judgment concerning John's potential to be a classical pianist requires a sense of detachment from John, in order to think objectively about
whether he has the physical and psychological makeup and drive to make a success of such
a career. If John is to be well advised, the teacher needs to keep the universe of young classical pianists in mind in making a dispassionate assessment of John's chances. See Scheffler,
In Praise of the Cognitive Emotions, 25.

24. See *OED Online,* s.v. "restraint, *n.,*" http://dictionary.oed.com (accessed July 14,
2010).

25. Fair-mindedness is also seen in the appropriateness of the rewards and punishments
that teachers mete out, so that these fit the deeds done. Such teachers also keep in mind the
precedents that their decisions create for the future; what a teacher decides, now, must set a
useful precedent for decisions down the road. Experienced teachers know that students are
sensitive and observant concerning rewards and punishments. The tour or party this year's
ensemble enjoys will doubtless be expected by next year's, just as allowing absenteeism in
the ensemble last year impacts a teacher's ability to curb it this year.

26. On schooling, see Jorgensen, *In Search of Music Education,* 4–8.

27. See *OED Online,* s.v. "discipline, *n.,*" http://dictionary.oed.com (accessed July 14,
2010); and *WordPerfect X4 Dictionary,* s.v. "discipline."

28. Examples of this teaching are to be found in the studio and orchestral rehearsal.
Amy Fay, *Music-Study in Germany from the Home Correspondence of Amy Fay* ([1880];
repr., New York: Dover, 1965), 205–262, describes her piano studies with Lizst. He would
enter the room where the students were gathered, having placed their music on the piano.
Leafing through the music, he would decide which pieces he wanted to hear played and call
students to perform one by one. After each playing, he would offer critical commentary and
demonstrate particular passages. Some of his comments would be merciless and cutting
as he gave an unvarnished assessment of a student's performance. Other times, he would
praise a student for a performance. When the lesson was over (often after several hours,
leaving students exhausted), the class adjourned at his pleasure. Should students wish to
study with him, they would apply and await his decision to include them in his class. As
a brilliant pianist, he constituted the ruler against which the performances of the students
were measured. He offered such instruction as he wished to give in the manner he determined; he was subject to students' assessment of his teaching only as they might decide to
study with someone else if they did not value his teaching or think it was doing them any
good. His word was law.

Similarly, a maestro arrives at the orchestra rehearsal to find all the members awaiting
him, having already warmed up and tuned their instruments. Mounting the podium, he
taps his baton on the music stand and signals for the rehearsal to begin. He names the
pieces to be played in turn, determines particular measure numbers to be rehearsed, stops
the ensemble to correct particular passages as he deems necessary, issues directives to the
musicians to attend to particular aspects during and after the rehearsal, and expects musi-

cians to do exactly as he says and gestures, when and how he wants and indicates. Working his way through the pieces to be rehearsed, he chastises players whose performances do not meet his expectations, sometimes indicates approval when a performer or section does especially well, and brooks no interference or interpretative suggestions from any member of the ensemble. When the time allotted for the rehearsal is up, he dismisses the orchestra and departs immediately, leaving the musicians to pack up their instruments and leave, and other lowly minions to collect scores and tidy up afterward.

29. For a discussion of the United Nations Convention on the Rights of the Child and its implications for music education, see Marja Heimonen, *Music Education and Law: Regulation as an Instrument*, doctoral diss., Studia Musica 17 (Helsinki, Finland: Sibelius Academy, 2002), 178–182.

30. House Concurrent Resolution 121, "Recognizing the importance of school-based music education, and for other purposes," was introduced in the House during in the 110th Congress, 1st session, by Rep. Jim Cooper from Tennessee on April 17, 2007. The resolution was passed in the House on April 25, 2007, and in the Senate on May 15, 2007, by unanimous consent.

31. This is the case, e.g., within Indiana. See Charles P. Schmidt, Rhonda Baker, Beth Hayes, and Eva Kwan, "A Descriptive Study of Public School Music Curricula in Indiana," *Bulletin of the Council for Research in Music Education* no. 169 (Summer 2006): 25–37.

32. Early-twenty-first-century music educational symposia devoted to matters of social justice include: "International Conference on Music Education, Equity, and Social Justice," Teachers College, Columbia University, Oct. 6–8. 2006; *Musica ficta*/Lived Realities: A Conference on Exclusions and Engagements in Music, Education and the Arts, University of Toronto, Canada, Jan. 24–27, 2008.

33. See Woodford, *Democracy and Music Education*, passim.

34. See Howard, *Artistry*, 183.

35. Ibid., 94–99. Also see ch. 6.

36. On the perceptive, intuitive, felt, and reasoned aspects of imagination, see Reichling, "Images of Imagination."

37. Students need to demonstrate some degree of worthiness to receive the wisdom that the teacher seeks to impart. In some musics, such as the North Indian classical tradition, teachers test their students to determine their readiness to be entrusted with particular knowledge. See Neuman, *The Life of Music in North India*, 47–49.

38. Dewey, *Democracy and Education*, 258, advocates that school students receive a general musical education focused on music as a branch of the humanities. In his view, the teaching of musical skills at advanced levels should be less emphasized in general musical education, and music teachers should offer a broader cultural education.

39. This scheme is not far from that proposed by Jaques-Dalcroze, *Rhythm, Music and Education*, 16, in the early twentieth century when he suggested that serious musical study be undertaken until a point at which students are tested, and only those musically apt and interested students continue with further instruction.

40. On human potential, see Scheffler, *In Praise of the Cognitive Emotions*, ch. 2.

41. On impression, see Scheffler, *Reason and Teaching*, 68–71. This differs from John Dewey's notion of "ex-pression," in *Art as Experience*, ch. 4.

42. The teacher controls the order in which the lesson unfolds and calls upon students in the manner in which Liszt called for his students to play the particular pieces that he chose

to hear or the maestro orders the rehearsal, as described in n. 28 of this chapter.

43. On social control, see Dewey, *Experience and Education,* ch. 4.

44. Some studio teachers who are first and foremost performers have not necessarily had the opportunity to reflect on what they are up to as teachers. Rather, they are focused on passing on their knowledge to the next generation of musicians and ensuring that their students come to internalize the rules undergirding the Western classical tradition, and they may see this approach as a moral imperative. As they can control the aspects of formal instruction, they worry less about informal means of instruction that can be relegated to others. Such teachers may be busy professional musicians, and they may agree to teach only on these terms. Also, they may be revered and loved by their students for their uncompromising focus on musical performance at the highest levels.

45. Influential in the latter part of the twentieth century, these approaches were forwarded by Ralph Smith among others in art education, and Charles Fowler among others in music education.

46. For example, John Dewey, *The Child and the Curriculum, and The School and Society,* 3–31, thinks in terms of the child's mind-set and construction of knowledge as beginning points for instruction. I suppose he might advocate first focusing on musical activities that children make sense of intuitively. He might agree, e.g., with Kodály, *The Selected Writings of Zoltán Kodály,* 14, that in teaching the young fifty-four well-chosen songs, a teacher might implant "the chief basic phenomena of music" in their souls. I do not read Kodály to be saying that these songs need necessarily to be for the purpose of illustrating musical concepts. Rather, it seems, from his remarks, that the songs themselves suffice.

47. See *The National Standards for Arts Education.* In his earlier work, and as a classically trained musician himself, Reimer, *A Philosophy of Music Education,* passim, seeks to establish music in the school curriculum firmly and for its own sake rather than for the other purposes it may serve. On Reimer's involvement with music curriculum in the 1970s, see Bennett Reimer, "Education for Aesthetic Awareness: The Cleveland Area Project," *Music Educators Journal* 64.6 (Feb. 1978): 66–69. Also, see the music curricular guidelines produced following the Texas Legislature's authorization of the Texas Essential Knowledge and Skills (TEKS) in Center for Educational Development in Fine Arts (CEDFA), "Music Curriculum Framework," at http://www.cedfa.org/teaching/curriculum/musicframework. pdf (accessed July 23, 2010).

48. In later writing, Reimer, *A Philosophy of Music Education: Advancing the Vision,* and Bennett Reimer, ed., *World Musics and Music Education: Facing the Issues* (Reston, Va.: MENC—The National Association for Music Education, 2002), forwards vernacular musical traditions, and recent musical textbooks expand the music curriculum's focus on an array of musical traditions. See Jane Beethoven et al., *Silver Burdett Making Music,* 9 vols. (Glenview, Ill.: Pearson Education, 2005); Judy Bond et al., *Spotlight on Music,* 9 vols. (New York: Macmillan/McGraw-Hill, 2005).

49. See Dewey, *Experience and Education,* 52, 53.

50. Thinking about organizations dynamically in terms of social processes enables a systematic and comprehensive view of the organization and reveals how these relationships are understood symbolically. See Zentner, *Prelude to Administrative Theory,* ch. 7, for a provisional list of social processes that can be applied to music education in thinking about the ways in which faculty, students, and staff are recruited and socialized; how the organization identifies itself and preserves its image; how it fosters morale and rewards or punishes

members for abiding (or not) by its rules; and in what ways the organization is specialized, segmented, and unified, among other aspects. For anthropological and ethnographic perspectives on music educational institutions, respectively, see Kingsbury, *Music, Talent, and Performance,* and Nettl, *Heartland Excursions.*

51. Studying communication rules in a music conservatory reveals a heavy reliance on informal means of communication and the lack of empowerment of students. Kingsbury *Music, Talent, and Performance,* 36, finds, e.g., that when studio teachers are ill or away on concert tours, they sometimes post notes to this effect on their doors and request their students to find alternative lesson times. These alternative times need to accord with teachers' schedules, and they may post sign-up sheets with available times at which students can have their "makeup" lessons. These procedures reveal the underlying power structures in the organization.

52. On training and schooling, see Jorgensen, *In Search of Music Education,* 4–13.

53. On "generative ideas," see Langer, *Philosophy in a New Key,* ch. 1.

54. Langer elaborates this idea of mind in her trilogy, *Mind: An Essay on Human Feeling,* 3 vols. (Baltimore, Md.: Johns Hopkins University Press, 1967, 1972, 1982).

55. For a discussion of tune books and the instructional methods used in singing schools, see James A. Keene, *A History of Music Education in the United States* (Hanover, N.H.: University Press of New England, 1982), esp. chs. 2, 3.

10. SEASHORE AND ENERGY

1. "A Lake Person at Sea," Editorial, *The Boston Globe,* July 9, 2005, A12.

2. For an overview of Greek theoretical ideas about music, see Andrew Barker, ed., *Greek Musical Writings,* vol. 2: *Harmonic and Acoustic Theory* (Cambridge: Cambridge University Press,1989); Andrew Barker, *The Science of Harmonics in Classical Greece* (Cambridge: Cambridge University Press, 2007). For medieval expositions on classical ideas, see, e.g., Anicius Manlius Severinus Boethius, *Fundamentals of Music* [De institutione musica], trans. Calvin M. Bower, ed. Claude V. Palisca (New Haven, Conn.: Yale University Press, 1989); Mariken Teeuwen, *Harmony and the Music of the Spheres: The Ars Musica in Ninth-century Commentaries on Martianus Capella* (Leiden: Brill, 2002).

3. See, e.g., Fabre D'Olivet, *Music Explained as Science and Art and Considered in its Analogical Relations to Religious Mysteries, Ancient Mythology, and the History of the World,* trans. Joscelyn Godwin ([1928]; repr., Rochester, Vt.: Inner Traditions, 1987); Joscelyn Godwin, *Harmonies of Heaven and Earth: The Spiritual Dimensions of Music from Antiquity to the Avant-Garde* (Rochester, Vt.: Inner Traditions International, 1987); Jamie James, *The Music of the Spheres: Music, Science, and the Natural Order of the Universe* ([1993]; repr., London: Abacus, 1995). On acoustics and the physical bases for music, see, e.g., David M. Howard and Jamie Angus, *Acoustics and Psychoacoustics,* 3rd ed. (Oxford: Focal Press, 2006). Also see D. Gareth Loy, *Musimathics: The Mathematical Foundations of Music,* 2 vols. (Cambridge, Mass.: MIT Press, 2006–2007).

4. See Dewey, *Art as Experience,* esp. chs. 2, 3; Susanne K. Langer, *Philosophy in a New Key: A Study in the Symbolism of Reason, Rite, and Art,* esp. ch. 8.

5. See Noddings, *Happiness and Education.*

6. William Shakespeare, *The Tragedy of Julius Caesar,* act 4, scene 3 (Project Gutenberg, 1997), http://www.gutenberg.org/etext/1120 (accessed July 25, 2010).

7. See Conor Berry, "Debate Over Evolution Shuts Down IMAX Film," *Cape Cod Times,* Tuesday, July 5, 2005, A1+.

8. Psalm 107: 23.

9. Brewster's *Memoirs of Newton,* vol. 2. ch. 27, reprinted in John Bartlett, *Familiar Quotations: A Collection of Passages, Phrases and Proverbs Traced to their Sources in Ancient and Modern Literature,* 13th ed. (Boston: Little, Brown, 1955), 288. I am indebted to Iris Yob for bringing this quotation to my attention.

10. On the work of the Woods Hole Oceanographic Institution at Woods Hole, Massachusetts, see its website at http://www.whoi.edu (accessed July 23, 2010). It was here that a meeting of scientists, scholars, and educators was convened in the mid-twentieth century under the auspices of the National Academy of Sciences to address issues of science and education. Its report, written by Jerome Bruner, *The Process of Education* ([1960]; repr., Cambridge, Mass.: Harvard University Press, 1977), is well known to music educators, especially in connection with the idea of the "spiral curriculum."

11. On these distinctions in ways of meaning between science, religions, and arts, see, e.g., Philip H. Phenix, *Realms of Meaning: A Philosophy of the Curriculum for General Education* ([1964]; repr., Ventura, Calif.: Ventura County Superintendent of Schools Office, 1986). On comparisons between religious and scientific ways of knowing, see Iris M. Yob, "Religious Metaphor and Scientific Model: Grounds for Comparisons," *Religious Studies* 28 (1992): 475–485.

12. See *WordPerfect X4 Dictionary,* s.v. "energy." For similar expressions, such as "exercise of power, actual working, operation, activity," the "capacity and habit of strenuous exertion," and "[p]ower actively and efficiently displayed or exerted," see *OED Online,* s.v. "energy," http://dictionary.oed.com (accessed July 14, 2010).

13. Ibid.

14. See Carl E. Seashore, *In Search of Beauty in Music: A Scientific Approach to Musical Esthetics* (New York: Ronald Press [1947]) and *Psychology of Music* ([1938]; repr., New York: Dover, 1967); Orff and Keetman, *Orff-Schulwerk;* Orff, *The Schulwerk;* Langer, *Philosophy in a New Key;* Edwin E. Gordon, *Tonal and Rhythm Patterns, An Objective Analysis: A Taxonomy of Tonal Patterns and Rhythm Patterns and Seminal Experimental Evidence of Their Difficulty and Growth Rate* (Albany: SUNY Press, 1976); *Learning Sequences in Music: Skill, Content, and Patterns: A Music Learning Theory* (Chicago: GIA Publications, 1997); and *A Music Learning Theory for Newborn and Young Children* (Chicago: GIA Publications, 2003); Palmer, "Music Education and Spirituality: A Philosophical Exploration" and "Music Education and Spirituality: A Philosophical Exploration II"; Anthony J. Palmer, "Consciousness Studies and a Philosophy of Music Education," *Philosophy of Music Education Review* 8.2 (Fall 2000): 99–110; Mary J. Reichling, "Music, Imagination, and Play," *Journal of Aesthetic Education* 31.1 (Spring 1997): 41–55; Eleanor V. Stubley, "Musical Performance, Play, and Constructive Knowledge: Experiences of Self and Culture," *Philosophy of Music Education Review* 1.2 (Fall 1993): 94–102; "Field Theory and the Play of Musical Performance," *British Journal of Music Education* 12.3 (1995): 273–283; and "Meditations on the Letter A: The Hand as Nexus between Music and Language," *Philosophy of Music Education Review* 14.1 (Spring 2006): 42–55; Krista Riggs, "Foundations for Flow: A Philosophical Model for Studio Instruction," *Philosophy of Music Education Review* 14.20 (Fall 2006): 175–191. Also, see June Boyce-Tillman, *Unconventional Wisdom* (London: Equinox, 2007); Deanne Bogdan, "Music, Spirituality, and the Emotions: The Shiver-

Shimmer Factor," *Philosophy of Music Education Review* 18.2 (Fall 2010): 111–129; David Carr, "Exploring the Spiritual and Moral Light and Dark Sides of Musical Experience and Appreciation," *Philosophy of Music Education Review* 18.2 (Fall 2010): 130–144; Iris M. Yob, "Why is Music a Language of Spirituality?" *Philosophy of Music Education Review* 18.2 (Fall 2010): 145–151.

15. As Kemp, *The Musical Temperament*, 179–180, shows, extroversion is commonly seen in conductors as their personal appeal has much to do with their capacity to attract audiences and musicians alike. Personality factors also feature in admission criteria to music educational programs. For summaries of research on personality factors in music teaching, see Kemp, *The Musical Temperament*, ch. 12; Randall Pembrook and Cheryl Craig, "Teaching as a Profession: Two Variations on a Theme," in *The New Handbook of Research on Music Teaching and Learning*, 796–797; Paul G. Woodford, "The Social Construction of Music Teacher Identity in Undergraduate Music Education Majors," in *The New Handbook of Research on Music Teaching and Learning*, 683–684, 688. Examples of published studies include: Clifford K. Madsen, "Teacher Intensity in Relationship to Music Education," *Bulletin of the Council for Research in Music Education* no. 104 (Spring 1990): 38–46; Charles P. Schmidt, Rhonda Baker, Beth Hayes, and Eva Kwan, "Relationships Between Teacher Personality and Ratings of Applied Music Teaching Behavior," *Contributions to Music Education* no. 18 (1991): 20–35; Martin J. Bergee, "Symposium on Measurement and Evaluation in Music Education: The Relationship between Music Education Majors' Personality Profiles, Other Education Majors' Profiles, and Selected Indicators of Music Teaching Success (Missouri Pre-Professional Teacher Interview [MPTI])," *Bulletin of the Council for Research in Music Education* no. 112 (Spring 1992): 5–15; Jane W. Davidson, Derek G. Moore, John A. Sloboda, and Michael J. A. Howe, "Characteristics of Music Teachers and the Progress of Young Instrumentalists," *Journal of Research in Music Education* 46 (Spring 1998): 141–160; David J. Teachout, "The Relationship between Personality and the Teaching Effectiveness of Music Student Teachers," *Psychology of Music* 29.2 (2001): 179–192.

16. Works include: Eunice Boardman, ed., *Dimensions of Musical Thinking* (Reston, Va.: Music Educators National Conference, 1989) and *Dimensions of Musical Learning and Teaching: A Different Kind of Classroom* (Reston, Va.: MENC, National Association for Music Education, 2002); Julia E. Crane, *Music Teacher's Manual*, 7th ed. (Potsdam, N.Y.: Elliot Fay and Sons, 1915); Frances Elliott Clark, *Music Appreciation for Children; Designed to Meet the Needs of the Child Mind During the Period of Development, from First to Sixth Grade, Inclusive. Learning to Listen, Listening to Learn* (Camden, N.J.: Educational Department, RCA Manufacturing Co., 1939); Mary Goetze, *Simply Sung: Folk Songs Arranged in Three Parts for Young Singers* (UK: Schott Music Corp., 1984) and her *Global Voices Interactive* series, at her website, http://www.mjpublishing.com/ (accessed July 16, 2010); Lowell Mason and George J. Webb, arr., *The Boston Glee Book: Consisting of an Extensive Collection of Glees, Madrigals, and Rounds/ Selected from the Works of the Most Admired Composers, Together With Many New Pieces from the German; Arranged Expressly for this Work* ([1838]; repr., New York: Da Capo, 1977); Mary Helen Richards, *The ETM Process* (Portola Valley, Calif.: [149 Corte Madera Rd., Portola Valley 94025]: The Institute, 1980) and *The Music Language* (Portola Valley, Calif.: Richards Institute of Music Education and Research 1973); Robert Shaw, *The Robert Shaw Reader*, ed. Robert Blocker (New Haven, Conn.: Yale University Press, 2004); Pamela Wade, "Eloquently Speaking: In Conversation with Jean Sinor," *Kodály*

Envoy 18.2 (Fall 1991): 10–12; Jean Sinor, "Who is a Good Music Teacher?" *Kodály Envoy* 19.2 (1992): 4–7; "Meeting the Challenge of Future Classrooms," *Music Educators Journal* 79 (Oct. 1992): 22–25; and "Musical Development of Children and Kodály Pedagogy," *Kodály Envoy* (Spring 1980), reprinted 25.4 (Summer 1999): 9–12. Also see Carolyn Livingston, "Women in Music Education in the United States: Names Mentioned in History Books," *Journal of Research in Music Education* 45.1 (Spring 1997): 130–144; Carol A. Pemberton, *Lowell Mason: His Life and Work* (Ann Arbor, Mich.: UMI Research Press, 1985).

17. Seashore, *Psychology of Music,* argued that music is best understood in terms of its underlying elements—pitch, rhythm, dynamics, and timbre—and that musical perception is a matter of grasping these elemental qualities of music. For him, music education necessitates perceptual training in discriminating these elements. The listener grasps particular sonic wave motions as specific pitches, dynamics, rhythms, meters, or timbres (at least as heard by the listener, if not in terms of their scientific or acoustic particulars), constituting crucial elements in understanding music's import. Accordingly, Seashore designed tests to measure "musical" perception as delineated by these particular atomistic musical elements. See [Don] Lewis and [Joseph] Saetveit, *The Seashore Measures of Musical Talents,* 1939 revision sound recording (Psychological Corporation H8-OP-4914—OP-4915. [1957]), 1 12-inch disk, 33 ⅓ rpm, 12; Joseph Gerhard Saetveit, *Revision of the Seashore Measures of Musical Talents* [1940] Iowa City: University of Iowa Press, [1940]. Following Seashore's lead, Edwin E. Gordon, *Musical Aptitude Profile, Manual* (Chicago: Riverside Publishing, 1988) developed an approach to music education and tests and measures of audiation similarly broken down into particular elements.

18. See James L. Mursell, *Human Values in Music Education* (New York: Silver, Burdett [1934]). The debate between James Mursell and Seashore during the first part of the twentieth century hinged on whether or not these musical elements comprised music. See Estelle R. Jorgensen, "The Seashore-Mursell Debate on the Psychology of Music Revisited," in *Advances in Social-Psychology and Music Education Research,* ed. Patrice Madura Ward-Steinman (Farnham, UK: Ashgate), forthcoming.

19. On "moving plastic," see Jaques-Dalcroze, *Rhythm, Music and Education,* ch. 12. On "living form," see Susanne K. Langer, *Problems of Art,* esp. chs. 1, 3, 4.

20. What Boethius, *Fundamentals of Music,* saw intuitively and imaginatively, and speculative theorists have reasoned about for centuries, concerning the pervasive role of vibration in the cosmos, now turns out to have some scientific basis, albeit with a new twist.

21. Even if we should misinterpret another's music, there is still a sense of these sounds being musical, even if that is not their primary purpose. Watching and listening to a performance by Sweet Honey in the Rock, and notwithstanding that this music is not my own musical tradition, the earthiness and spirituality of this music in the African American tradition conjures a vision of Mother Earth singing and evokes women's choral singing and music making from ancient times, described eloquently by Sophie Drinker, *Music and Women: The Story of Women in their Relation to Music* ([1948]; repr., New York: Feminist Press at the City of New York University, 1995). It seems that ancient and present are fused in their performance, and the audience is brought into communion and connection with the group as they sing, move, and speak of life and death. For them, music has no boundaries; their songs and stories are in the long tradition from antiquity of epic singers, balladeers, and troubadours, and present images of good and evil, justice and inequity, love and war, and betrayal and heroism. See Sweet Honey in the Rock, *Raise Your Voice* (Harriman,

N.Y.: Firelight Media in association with Thirteen/WNET, 2005), 1 videodisc. This video-recording was originally produced for PBS *American Masters* (television program). Also see Bernice Johnson Reagon and Sweet Honey in the Rock, *We Who Believe in Freedom: Sweet Honey in the Rock—Still on the Journey* (New York: Anchor Books, 1993).

22. See Langer, *Philosophy in a New Key*, 227–228, 244, 245; Langer, *Problems of Art*, 36–39. These qualities of movement and energy may also help to explain the interest of composers in the sea. Among the sea symphonies, one thinks of, e.g., Ralph Vaughan Williams's *Symphony No. 1* and Howard Hanson's *Symphony No. 7*. Stubley's, "Meditations on the Letter A," invokes the hand as a metaphor for bodily involvement in making sounds and feeling them, reveals the deeply physical and spiritual experience of sound waves.

23. Mary J. Reichling, "Images of Imagination," analyzes the ways in which we play with music in devising and constructing these sounds and their meanings perceptually, feeling-fully, intuitively, and rationally.

24. Iris M. Yob, "Response to David Carr, 'The Significance of Music for the Promotion of Moral and Spiritual Virtue,'" *Philosophy of Music Education Review* 14.2 (Fall 2006): 209–213, refers to "Amazing Grace" as an instance where music seems to give voice to deep experiences that are widely shared. Recalling the music and other songs that gave voice to national sorrow after September 11, 2001, she remembers the pathos evoked for her by a lone piper playing "Amazing Grace" at Peggy's Cove, in Nova Scotia, Canada, not far from the place where hundreds of lives were lost when a plane went down in the Atlantic Ocean. There is the well-known story of the sinking of the R.M.S. *Titanic* in the North Atlantic on April 15, 1912, and the musicians who played as the ship sank without enough life boats to save all aboard. See Walter Lord, *The Night Lives On* (New York: William Morrow, 1986), ch. 11. Bennett Reimer, "Once More With Feeling: Reconciling Discrepant Accounts of Musical Affect," *Philosophy of Music Education Review* 12.1 (Spring 2004): 4–16, also writes of his visit to China and hearing, in the indigenous music he listened to there, something deeply meaningful, moving, and profound. For me, Beethoven's slow movements are often more moving than his brilliant and fast movements; here, he seems to capture a poignancy and depth of feeling evocative of the pathos of lived life.

25. For example, in the Sacred Harp gatherings in Alabama, extended families sing together and members take turns leading the singing of Christian hymn tunes that have their roots in earlier centuries. The energy of the singers (helped along by midday potluck lunches, spread out in buffet and picnic style) is both absorbed from others as it is exuded by them. A singer might come in the morning troubled or tired, and after singing in the group, leave happy and energized. See *Sweet is the Day: A Sacred Harp Family Portrait* (Sand Mountain: Alabama Folklife Association, 2001), 1 videodisc.

26. See, e.g., Gordon, *Music Learning Theory for Newborn and Young Children*, ch. 3.

27. On "virtual time," see Langer, *Feeling and Form*, ch. 7.

28. See Dewey, *Art as Experience*, ch. 3; Abraham H. Maslow, *Religions, Values, and Peak Experiences* (New York: Viking, 1970); and Csikszentmihályi, *Flow*.

29. For its theological sense, see *OED Online*, s.v. "charisma," http://dictionary.oed.com (accessed July 14, 2010).

30. We speak of a concentrated chemical solution when the molecules of a particular substance are crowded together. Focusing on the subject matter and the students requires intense or powerful listening and gazing. This chemical analogy highlights the force of the teacher's engagement of the students in musical and instructional situations. It may be

tempting to let other circumstances interfere, either personal feelings of well-being, tensions with colleagues and students, or other aspects of domestic or public life. Still, this teacher lays aside these other matters and approaches this particular student or class with single-minded interest and engagement. On the senses of "keeping of the mental faculties fixed on one object or set of objects," "the state of being so brought or massed together"; or "bringing to or toward a common centre or focus," see *OED Online,* s.v. "concentration," http://dictionary.oed.com (accessed July 14, 2010).

31. On eduction, see Jorgensen, *In Search of Music,* 13–18.

32. For example, a choral conductor wins over basses and tenors to join the choir even if their friends may think it somewhat effeminate for men to sing. They are so drawn to this music and this teacher that they cannot resist joining the choir. When they are preoccupied with this music and see that it is anything but effeminate but also involves power and control, they give themselves up to singing.

33. It is common to rely on attitudinal and global characteristics and gut-instinctual assessments about whether applicants for music teacher education programs have what it takes to succeed as music teachers. For example, a bubbly, articulate, bright, healthy, and enthusiastic person seems intuitively more promising than a shy, retiring, inarticulate, sickly, and unenthusiastic person. Those who educate music teachers often seek these qualities of energy in those who aspire to the work of music instruction.

34. Ever the student of human nature, Shakespeare has Julius Caesar say of Cassius: "Yon Cassius has a lean and hungry look; / He thinks too much; such men are dangerous." See Shakespeare, *Julius Caesar,* act 1, scene 2.

35. Gender attitudes and prejudices are particularly important. For example, boys who have been taught at home and at the church, synagogue, or mosque not to respect women will likely become men who do not respect women. For these boys and men, female teachers are hard-pressed to make the same impact as their male colleagues. Likewise, girls who have been taught to value the opinions of men more than those of women are likely to become women who look constantly to men for instruction and guidance. These girls and women, likewise, may value their female teachers less than their male colleagues. Given the reality of this socialization and prejudice against women, it is not surprising that women teachers are consistently evaluated lower than their male counterparts. No matter what women do, we encounter prejudice, and we can name the prejudice and speak and act against it as we are able. See bell hooks, *Teaching to Transgress,* passim.

36. See Jorgensen, *Transforming Music Education,* 101–108.

37. On osmosis, see Jorgensen, *Transforming Music Education,* 103.

38. For example, the Australian aboriginal sings into the mouth of the one who learns a song, thereby breathing it literally and figuratively into the student, see A. P. Elkin, "Arnhem Land Music," *Oceania* 26.3 (1956): 213–230. Among the Shoshone people of North America, a song is the possession of the one who dreams and creates it. See, e.g., Vander, *Songprints,* 66–67, 224, 229–232.

39. In the Jewish creation story, God speaks and it is done. See Genesis 1. The Indian raga is likewise breathed, *tala* refers to breath, and this breath carries spiritual power appropriate to particular occasions and times of day and life. See *Grove Music Online. Oxford Music Online,* s.v. "India" (by Regula Qureshi et al.), http://www.oxfordmusiconline.com (accessed July 16, 2010). In Christian thought, these mystical connotations are evident in Hildegard of Bingen's belief that she is "like a feather which has no weight from its own strength and

lets itself be carried by the wind," and chant and song are means whereby one partakes of supernatural power. Hildegard, "Letter 39: Hildegard to Wibert of Gembloux," in *Hildegard of Bingen's Book of Divine Works with Letters and Songs*, ed. Matthew Fox (Santa Fe, N.M.: Bear and Co., 1987), 348. A nineteenth-century Christian hymn by Edwin Hatch, "Breathe on me, breath of God," *NetHymnal*, http://www.cyberhymnal.org/ (accessed July 20, 2010), also proclaims, "Breathe on me, breath of God / Fill me with life anew."

40. Such a stripped-down and simple approach to musical learning requires working out which aspects are essential for all students to know and be able to do, and which can be sacrificed in order to achieve what is of most importance. Taking such an approach requires the sorts of musical projects that allow students to get to the heart of music and provide an immediate and accessible way to achieve musical learning.

41. See Noddings, *Happiness and Education*, ch. 1.

42. This approach is seen, e.g., in the American singing schools of the eighteenth and nineteenth centuries that often involved young and old learning together. See James A. Keene, *A History of Music Education in the United States* (Hanover, N.H.: University Press of New England, 1982), ch. 2. It is still the case in the Sacred Harp singing societies in the southeastern United States, where families are energized as grandparents, parents, children, and their extended families unite in singing together.

43. This is not only true in the classical tradition but in vernacular traditions where older generational members teach the young to play instruments and their traditional songs. On the Bach family, see Karl Geiringer, *The Bach Family*; and *Grove Music Online. Oxford Music Online*, s.v. "Bach" (by Christoph Wolff, et al.), http://www.oxfordmusiconline.com (accessed July 16, 2010). As Campbell, *Songs in their Heads*, shows, this process is to be seen in the lives of North American children she studies.

44. See Jorgensen, "On a Choice-Based Instructional Typology in Music," and Estelle R. Jorgensen, "Modelling Aspects of Type IV Music Instructional Triads," *Bulletin of the Council for Research in Music Education*, no. 137 (Summer 1998): 43–56.

45. See Jorgensen, "On a Choice-Based Instructional Typology in Music."

46. Westerlund, *Bridging Experience, Action, and Culture*, mines Dewey's writing in her argument that music education should focus on the student's present use-value of music.

47. For example, these living connections are so important that the loss of a generation to war, famine, or disease may leave the next bereft.

48. Rather than reflecting about music instruction after the fact, what Donald A. Schön refers to as "reflection-after-action" (*Educating the Reflective Practitioner*, esp. ch. 2), instruction in energy mode is focused on "thought-in-the-midst-of-action."

49. Some teachers are less polarizing than others, and there is not the same strength of attraction and repulsion for students. This reality renders adjudicating teacher effectiveness very difficult. Some might value strength of attraction, which is liable to result in extremes of inordinately high levels of effort and time expended by some students and unduly low levels of effort and time expended by others. Others might value teachers who are less polarizing and may arouse less energy (positive or negative). In this model, it seems that teachers who engender more energy from students are valued more than those who do not, even if they are more polarizing people. This is so because it is presumed that high levels of energy and intensity are likely to result in more dramatic musical growth on the part of teachers and their students.

50. For a historical study of strategies used by music teachers in rural and one-room schools in the American Midwest, see Pamela Stover, "Teacher Preparation, Methods and

Materials for Music Education in Rural and One-Room Schools in Selected Areas of the Midwest (1890–1950)," doctoral diss., Indiana University, Bloomington, May 2003.

51. See Orff and Keetman, *Orff-Schulwerk*; Orff, *The Schulwerk*.

52. See Orff, *The Schulwerk*, especially the ca. 1932 ensemble that contained the widest array of instruments, 135–136. After 1934, early instruments, such as portative organ, spinet, fidels, and viols were included in the dance orchestra, nicely complementing the dynamics of the percussion instruments.

53. See Stubley, "Musical Performance, Play, and Constructive Knowledge," and her "Field Theory and the Play of Musical Performance"; Reichling, "Music, Imagination, and Play." This idea of the centrality of play has ancient roots in the West. For example, Plato thought that to make music and the other arts is to be like the gods. Plato, *Laws*, trans., Benjamin Jowett (Project Gutenberg, 2008), http://www.gutenberg.org/etext/1750 (accessed July 19, 2010), book 7, §§803c–04b, says: "But man is created to be the plaything of the Gods; and therefore the aim of every one should be to pass through life, not in grim earnest, but playing at the noblest of pastimes, in another spirit from that which now prevails. For the common opinion is, that work is for the sake of play, war of peace; whereas in war there is neither amusement nor instruction worth speaking of. The life of peace is that which men should chiefly desire to lengthen out and improve. They should live sacrificing, singing, and dancing, with the view of propitiating Gods and heroes." Almost two millennia later, play still forms an important element of aesthetic education—although Friedrich Schiller's letter 26, from *On the Aesthetic Education of Man*, can be read ambivalently to suggest both that play and work need to be in balance and that play is superior to work. Rousseau, *Émile*, and Johann Heinrich Pestalozzi, *The Evening Hour of the Hermit*, ch. 10, trans., Robert Ulich, in Robert Ulich, ed., *Three Thousand Years of Educational Wisdom: Selections from Great Documents* (Cambridge: Cambridge University Press, 1950), 492–494, want to see children able to play naturally rather than treated as miniature adults.

54. Elliott, *Music Matters*, passim, is also after this active engagement and enjoyment of musicking as a focus and means of music education.

55. For example, Westerlund's advocacy of present experience is clear in her essay "Garage Bands: A Future Model for Developing Musical Expertise?"

56. In our time, given the high level of expectations of teachers and students alike, such material needs to be professional in appearance and sonic quality, colorful, interactive, hypertextual so that students can approach it from different directions and manipulate it in differing ways and at various levels of musical sophistication, and relevant to the various vernacular and popular music cultures from which students come. Beyond singing, young people are fascinated by musical instruments and technology as they apply to electronic storage, retrieval, and manipulation of sounds and communication of information. This richness of resources requires special space considerations, music options for students to study, and an array of courses that attract students to different musics, to performing, composing and improvising, listening, producing, dancing, music theater, and integrated arts projects. Contra the approach in *National Standards for Arts Education: What Every Young American Should Know and Be Able to Do in the Arts*, rather than mandate that everyone should do everything, these teachers think in terms of activities that allow students choices, a variety of musics, and ways to access them.

57. Campbell's account (*Songs in their Heads*, passim) of these games and activities in the school ground, cafeteria, school bus, and classroom reveals how they serve to bring pleasure to young people.

58. For example, planning periods of quietness and reflection amid the other musical activities can provide opportunities for students to unwind. Mounting energy may also prompt growing anxiety and boisterous behavior. Keeping this in mind, the teacher may allow the class to "bubble" for a while before moving on to another activity that has a calming and introspective effect.

59. Michael W. Apple, *Official Knowledge: Democratic Education in a Conservative Age*, regards the turn of the twenty-first century in the United States as a "conservative age." This conservatism is driven especially by the influence of Christian fundamentalism and the desire of some to institute a Christian theocracy. It takes time for liberal ideas to generate a conservative backlash, just as it takes time for conservative ideas to play out fully, to take hold and prompt an equally forceful liberal response. Capitalism took centuries to develop into its present American form and for its contributions and detractions to be evident to all, just as did communism in Russia and now in China. The present swing from a theocratic government to a more secular one in Iran can also be expected to take time, as did the movement from the Holy Roman Empire (controlled largely, at least regarding things spiritual, from Rome) to today's secular European societies. Pitirim Sorokin, *Social and Cultural Dynamics*, vol. 1 (New York: Bedminster, 1937), posited that societies overshoot Aristotle's "golden mean" and move from one extreme to another, sometimes over centuries. People eventually come to dislike being dictated to by religion or state. Inevitably, the powerful (whoever they are) lose public support. Sometimes the movement away from that control occurs gradually, and at other times the response is dramatic in wars, revolutions, genocides, and foreign interventions.

60. On phases of organizational development, see Jorgensen, "On the Recruitment Process in Amateur Ensembles."

61. See Shakespeare, *Julius Caesar*, Act 4, Scene 3.

62. See *OED Online*, s.v. "simplicity," http://dictionary.oed.com (accessed July 14, 2010).

63. On myth and music education, see Jorgensen, "Myth, Song, and Music Education."

64. See Max Weber, *The Rational and Social Foundations of Music*, trans. and ed. Don Martindale, Johannes Riedel, and Gertrude Neuwirth (Carbondale: Southern Illinois University Press, 1958).

65. On the notion of "primitive music," see Bruno Nettl, *The Study of Ethnomusicology: Twenty-nine Issues and Concepts* (Urbana: University of Illinois Press, 1983), 204–205.

66. See Scheffler, *In Praise of the Cognitive Emotions*, ch. 2.

67. For example, in the elementary school music program forwarded by Jaques-Dalcroze, *Rhythm, Music and Education*, 16, 38, children receive a comparatively short but intensive musical instruction given by competent teachers, after which they are tested. Those who do not satisfy on these tests are removed from music classes, which are then focused on the musically "apt" students. "Late bloomers" in music are likely to miss out in such an educational scheme.

68. See Whitehead, *The Aims of Education and Other Essays*, 1, 2.

69. Robert Frost, "The Road Not Taken," in Robert Frost, *The Complete Poems of Robert Frost* (New York: Holt, Rinehart and Winston, 1949).

11. HOME AND INFORMALITY

1. See Drinker, *Music and Women*; Montessori, *The Discovery of the Child*; J. R. Martin, *The Schoolhome*; van Manen, *The Tact of Teaching*; Campbell, *Lessons from the World: A*

Cross-Cultural Guide to Music Teaching and Learning (New York: Schirmer, 1991), and *Songs in Their Heads;* Green, *How Popular Musicians Learn* and *Music, Informal Learning and the School;* Greene, *The Dialectic of Freedom, Releasing the Imagination,* and *Variations on a Blue Guitar;* Marie McCarthy, *Passing It On: The Transmission of Music in Irish Culture* (Cork: Cork University Press, 1999); Suzuki, *Nurtured by Love;* Iris M. Yob, "The School as Sacred Space."

2. See *OED Online,* "domestic, *a.* and *n.,*" http://dictionary.oed.com (July 14, 2010); *OED Online,* s.v. "home, *n.* and *a.,*" http://dictionary.oed.com (accessed July 14, 2010).

3. See Sanders, *Staying Put.*

4. See Raimond Gaita, *A Common Humanity: Thinking about Love and Truth and Justice,* 2nd ed. (London: Routledge, 2000).

5. See van Manen, *The Tact of Teaching,* esp. chs. 6, 7.

6. See *WordPerfect X4 Dictionary,* s.v. "informality."

7. See *OED Online,* s.v. "form, *n.* and *v¹,*" http://dictionary.oed.com (accessed July 20, 2010).

8. On the public, see Dewey, *The Public and its Problems,* ch. 1.

9. It is intended to reach everyone in the "tribe," conceived literally and figuratively. Just as tribes of people learn its rituals, so the members of the military learn its chants, shanties, and songs. For a discussion of the family as an agent of music education see Jorgensen, *In Search of Music Education,* 45–48.

10. Neuman, *The Life of Music in North India,* describes how family groups of North Indian musicians form *ghārānas,* or specific schools that differ one from another. In the European tradition, the Bach and Damrosch families made music together at home and in convivial settings. See classic studies such as: Geiringer, *The Bach Family;* G. Martin, *The Damrosch Dynasty.* Pianists also form schools of piano playing; e.g., see Robert Philip, *Performing Music in the Age of Recording,* ch. 6, titled "Questions of Authority: Schools of Playing," esp. pp. 183–191.

11. This is the case, e.g., in jazz. See Berliner, *Thinking in Jazz,* esp. chs. 1, 2.

12. For example, even in bluegrass traditions that were once the exclusive preserve of families, virtuosi fiddlers and dancers sometimes set the musical expectations so high that ordinary people are excluded from performing in prominent venues, thereby exacerbating the differences between amateur and professional musicians.

13. As Steven Feld reveals in *Sound and Sentiment: Birds, Weeping, Poetics, and Song in Kaluli Expression,* 2nd ed. (Philadelphia: University of Pennsylvania Press, 1990), the people of the Sepik River area of Papua New Guinea think about their traditional music and its role in their rituals in aesthetic terms. As such indigenous people come in contact with Christianity, their traditional music and culture may be looked upon as evil, and they may take on the trappings of Western Christian musical practices and repudiate their old practices.

14. For example, the garage bands described by Green, *How Popular Musicians Learn,* make music in the context of jam sessions and other gigs that the band plays as a part of their lives. Their rituals of jamming and gigging are specific to particular traditions of rock music and differ from those of others even within the rock genre. Likewise, the traditional extended family gatherings around Northern Indian classical music have their own rituals. Ragas are played at particular times of the day, in the specific styles of each ghārāna, and with the nuances each family brings to the tradition. For a classic study of ragas in the North Indian tradition, see Walter Kaufmann, *The Ragas of North India* (Bloomington:

Published for the International Affairs Center by Indiana University Press [1968]). Within the European classical tradition, the informal learning of church musicians as they grow up within the Cathedral close, or of instrumentalists whose study is often informally acquired by immersion in European culture, reveals the importance of the rituals in which musicians participate socially. An aspiring Austrian musician may reason that time spent at a Viennese beer garden talking with musician friends may be just as useful to a musician's education as formal study at the conservatory. Making music in social gatherings of musicians is another way in which a music largely destined for the opera house and concert hall spills out into ordinary life.

15. See *OED Online*, s.v. "mentor, *n.* and *v.,*" http://dictionary.oed.com (accessed July 19, 2010). The word *mentor* derives from the Greek *Menter,* "the name of a character in the *Odyssey,* in whose likeness Athena appears to Telemachus and acts as his guide and adviser."

16. Green, *How Popular Musicians Learn,* 76–83, describes how teaching is accomplished when band musicians encounter technical difficulties in playing a piece after having listened to a recording of it; those who know how to solve the problems instruct them.

17. Listening to definitive performances and recordings is especially important. For a discussion of the role of recordings as a source of authority for Western classical musicians, see Philip, *Performing Music in the Age of Recording,* passim. A mentor is akin to a sports coach who helps players perform more effectively. Students are presumed to have the ability already, and the mentor or coach simply takes advantage of that ability and helps the musician improve her or his skills. In musician families, those who are older help those who are younger. For example, the Bach and Damrosch families illustrate ways in which the young of each generation are mentored and coached by relatives over successive generations. See Geiringer, *The Bach Family;* G. Martin, *The Damrosch Dynasty.*

18. On the transmission process of traditional North Indian classical music, see Neuman, *The Life of Music in North India,* 50–58. C. P. E. Bach, *Essay on the True Art of Playing Keyboard Instruments,* writes his treatise for the benefit of students to teach themselves. He provides clear examples of his points on ornamentation, e.g., and then expects the student to go and do likewise. This model of teaching relies on the student's insight into what is happening, and the student is expected to attend closely to what the teacher says and does.

19. On enculturation, socialization, schooling, and training, see Jorgensen, *In Search of Music Education,* 4–29.

20. For example, Green, *How Popular Musicians Learn,* 59–76, describes how the band members listen to recordings, imitate them, practice certain skills, and criticize each others' playing.

21. See Attali, *Noise: The Political Economy of Music,* 12, 13.

22. For example, Fanny Hensel was discouraged by the Mendelssohn family from following her compositional proclivities because she was expected to be a wife and mother; her brother Felix, on the other hand, was encouraged and expected to develop his musical talent. Diane Peacock Jezic, *Women Composers: The Lost Tradition Found* (New York: Feminist Press of the City University of New York, 1988), esp. 74, 75, 76, notes the restricting influence of the family members on Fanny's compositional output.

23. On musical transmission, see Jorgensen, *Transforming Music Education,* 101–108.

24. Plato, *Republic,* §401d, p. 100, posits that "rhythm and harmony sink more deeply into the mind than anything else and affect it more powerfully than anything else."

25. Suzuki, *Nurtured by Love,* 9 asserts that "Japanese children can all speak Japanese!" By participating in Japanese society and hearing Japanese spoken, all Japanese young peo-

ple of normal intelligence learn to speak Japanese. This learning is repetitive in the sense that they hear the same words, begin to associate these words with meanings, and eventually come to comprehend and speak the language. For Suzuki, students need to learn music in the same way. The child needs to be surrounded by an environment in which this music is heard repeatedly, absorbed, participated in, imitated, and felt. In such circumstances, the young child's earliest memories are of this music. Imitation is grounded in the copying of examples, whether in play or ritual. As young children see older people in the family play the violin, Suzuki believes, it is natural that they will want to play the violin too.

26. A trumpeter such as Dizzy Gillespie may discover how to play in a quite idiosyncratic way that would normally be repudiated by classically trained trumpeters as poor trumpet technique. A trumpeter might pick up an embouchure off-center on the lips, or with cheeks puffed out, and, without reference to which particular technique is the best, may find out his or her own way to play the instrument. See *Grove Music Online, Oxford Music Online,* s.v. "Gillespie, Dizzy" (by Thomas Owens), http://www.oxfordmusiconline.com (accessed July 19, 2010). I notice this, e.g., with pianists who have taught themselves to play. They may adopt idiosyncratic positions such as a flat hand or keyboard stance that professional pianists would repudiate, yet it works for these people and they play in ways that are comfortable for them.

27. In the Bach family, parents, uncles, older siblings, and other extended family members supervised the education of the young. See Geiringer, *The Bach Family,* passim; *Grove Music Online, Oxford Music Online,* s.v. "Bach" (by Christoph Wolff et al.), http://www.oxfordmusiconline.com (accessed July 19, 2010).

28. The young Damrosches grew up in a home in which music was part of the fabric of daily life. See G. Martin, *The Damrosch Dynasty,* passim.

29. The musical "jokes" in musical traditions that are regarded as "serious" reveal how formal and informal instruction come together. The after-dinner fun for the Bach family was the singing of quodlibets in which music was treated humorously. See *Grove Music Online, Oxford Music Online,* s.v. "Quodlibet" (by Maria Rika Maniates, Peter Branscombe, and Richard Freedman), http://www.oxfordmusiconline.com (accessed July 19, 2010). This singing must have influenced the young J. S. Bach as he learned his musical craft. He draws on this learning in his *Coffee Cantata,* a humorous text regarding the new craze of coffee drinking, put to music in a serious manner that might otherwise be a setting for a sacred cantata or a formal occasion at court or in the city. J. S. Bach, Cantata no. 211, "Schweigt stille, plaudert nicht" (Kaffeekantate). Also see *Oxford Dictionary of Music, Oxford Music Online,* s.v. "Musical Joke, A," http://www.oxfordmusiconline.com (accessed July 19, 2010).

30. In ancient Greece, e.g., advanced musical training was the province of slaves, and the noble-born might be aficionados but not expected to become virtuoso performers. On ancient Greek music, see *Grove Music Online, Oxford Music Online,* s.v. "Greece, §1: Ancient Greece" (by Thomas J. Mathiesen), http://www.oxfordmusiconline.com (accessed July 19, 2010). On music education in ancient Greece, see Rainbow and Cox, *Music in Educational Thought and Practice.* Also, among the traditional Venda studied by Blacking, *How Musical is Man?* 46–48, after puberty boys were actively encouraged not to take music beyond a certain elementary level so that they might participate in activities considered more suitable for males, namely government and earning a livelihood.

31. For example, among bluegrass fiddlers and bands, people recognize the difference between outstanding fiddlers and those who are good enough to play at family gatherings or community events but would be regarded as inferior in comparison to the gifted profes-

sional fiddlers. On some of the leading bluegrass musicians historically, see Tom Warlick and Lucy Warlick, *The WBT Briarhoppers: Eight Decades of a Bluegrass Band Made for Radio* (Jefferson, N.C.: McFarland, 2008). Bands act as filtering agents to accept or reject musicians who are or are not "up to their standards." This is also true of jazz musicians whose improvisations are regularly understood by other musicians to have particular attributes of ease of flow, ingenuity, technique, style, and grasp of the tradition in which they work. The quality of their work is known by other jazz exponents, and opportunities to perform with other musicians and in particular venues follow from these assessments.

32. See Noddings, *Caring.*

33. See van Manen, *The Tact of Teaching,* 73.

34. See Donald Kennedy, *Academic Duty* (Cambridge, Mass.: Harvard University Press, 1997).

35. Discovery of musical talent such as Simon Cowell's sponsorship of *Il Divo* illustrates how a musical competition dedicated to the discovery of new music professionals and entertaining the public pits musicians against others and yet provides a vehicle to educate them. A case in point is the grooming and hyping of *Il Divo*, a group of singers spotted on *American Idol* and brought together, prepared for a musical career, produced in a debut recording, hyped in the media and on national television, and provided the opportunity to appear at important venues such as "A Capitol Fourth" (an Independence Day concert in Washington, D.C.), on the West Lawn of the U.S. Capitol, Washington, D.C., July 4, 2005. Although they might be charismatic and talented individuals, Cowell apparently hoped to create a quartet of tenors in the mode of the "Three Tenors," a popular consort in the 1990s and early 2000s comprised of Plácido Domingo, José Carreras, and Luciano Pavarotti. See *Encyclopedia of Popular Music, Oxford Music Online,* s.v. "Domingo, Placido," http://www.oxfordmusiconline.com (accessed July 25, 2010). For a critical perspective, see Daniel Ginsberg, "Il Divo: Simon Says Opera, but the Ear Says Awful," *The Washington Post,* Sunday, Feb. 5, 2006; D02. A jazz or bluegrass gig may also be an opportunity for musicians to compete with each other. As I write, a Live 8 concert in London provides an excellent opportunity for young bands to assert themselves and older and more well-established bands to demonstrate their superiority to others on the lineup. For young players or singers, this event provides an opportunity to hear live music of their parents' and grandparents' generations while also assessing all of the bands. Once they make these assessments, a competitive element enters as one particular band is judged against another. On the Live 8 Concert, 2 July, 2005, see http://www.live8live.com/theconcerts/ (accessed July 19, 2010).

36. For example, it does not challenge the patriarchy inherent in the primacy of male ensembles in United States society and rooted in gospel male quartet singing. On the trainers of an extended family of black gospel quartet singers in Memphis, Tennessee during the mid-twentieth century, see Kip Lornell, *"Happy in the Service of the Lord": Afro-American Gospel Quartets in Memphis* (Urbana: University of Illinois Press, 1988), ch. 4. For a history of black male gospel groups and quartets, see Robert Darden, *People Get Ready! A New History of Black Gospel Music* (New York: Continuum, 2004), esp. chs. 11, 14. For example, a garage band becomes competent and thinks about gigging on a regular basis. Members might invite a businessperson to meet with them in order to discuss what they should charge for their gigs, how they should organize themselves financially, what they should look for in a manager, how they might market themselves effectively, and how they should take care of the various aspects of their name, dress, and distinctive attributes of their music and band image. Although they meet and chat informally, this discussion is an important aspect of their education and they receive advice to ponder.

37. For example, Paul McCartney started out in a working-class boy band, ended up as an accomplished popular songwriter and performer in the genre he pioneered, and was knighted (symbolic of his country's recognition of his work) for his contributions to English popular culture. Most of his music education was informal, yet he has made his way successfully as a popular musician. See Christopher Sandford, *McCartney* (New York: Carroll and Graf, 2006).

38. In the United States, Leonard Bernstein developed concerts for young people, and the Side-by-Side program arranged by the Indianapolis Symphony Orchestra allows young musicians to play with members of the orchestra. See Brian David Rozen, "The Contributions of Leonard Bernstein to Music Education: An Analysis of his 53 Young People's Concerts," doctoral diss., Eastman School of Music, University of Rochester, 1997. On the Indianapolis Symphony Orchestra's Side-by-Side program, see http://www.indianapolissymphony.org/learningcommunity/high_school/side_by_side (accessed July 19, 2010).

Students attending Bernstein's concerts might think of themselves as going to hear a concert. Entering the concert hall away from their normal school building, they see this activity as a field trip to a prominent concert venue, and they might be excited about getting away from their routine activities to do something outside the realm of their normal experience. Seated in the audience, they see an orchestra assembled—something that they may never have seen live before—and they hear Bernstein speak in his inimitable way about the music the ensemble is playing and the various instruments of the orchestra. What they take away from this program may be very individual. Some may leave with a desire to play one of the instruments they hear played. Others may come to the view that this music does not measure up to the jazz they hear played at one of the apartments on their street; even if they do not like classical music they now know that they prefer jazz. Maybe their teacher will take them to meet, hear, and talk with the jazz group or one of the other popular groups that regularly play in their neighborhood. Something here may fire their interest. Even if they have never sung much at home, their teacher may persuade one of the singers in the neighborhood to meet with the class, possibly sing for them, and invite them to sing too, and they may discover their own singing voices.

This is the way of Sweet Honey in the Rock, who, in addition to their concerts, regularly do workshops with music teachers and visit classrooms to talk informally and sing with students. Just going to one of their concerts may open the mind of a white person who has no clue of the African American experience. See Sweet Honey in the Rock, *Raise Your Voice* (Harriman, N.Y.: Firelight Media in association with Thirteen/WNET, 2005), 1 videodisc. This videorecording was originally produced for PBS *American Masters* (Television program). Also see Bernice Johnson Reagon and Sweet Honey in the Rock, *We Who Believe in Freedom: Sweet Honey in the Rock—Still on the Journey* (New York: Anchor Books, 1993).

39. Coming upon a small chamber ensemble rehearsing in an unscheduled room, we may see a remarkable sight. The ensemble is preparing for a performance that they have arranged on their own. We see the musicians working together intently, criticizing their own performance, and sometimes making remarkable progress. They have no teacher with them and they might not think of themselves as being engaged in teaching and learning, so focused are they on performing this music. Still, as with the garage band, informal music education is ongoing.

40. In Montessori's *casa de bambini* or homes for the little children and Martin's "school-home," feminine as well as masculine values are evident in this caring and nurturing environment. See Montessori, *Discovery of the Child;* Martin, *Schoolhome.*

41. I have already mentioned Fanny Hensel's compositional talent being repressed by her family because of the roles they had earmarked for her to fill. George Gershwin's *Porgy and Bess* calls for roles to be sung only by African Americans, for whom they were expressly written. On Gershwin, see Howard Pollack, *George Gershwin: His Life and Work* (Berkeley: University of California Press, 2006); in *Grove Music Online, Oxford Music Online,* s.v. "Gershwin, George" (by Richard Crawford, et al.) http://www.oxfordmusiconline.com (accessed July 19, 2010).

42. This was the case in the singing schools in the United States. See James A. Keene, *A History of Music,* ch. 2. The uneven quality of music learning was one of the reasons given for introducing vocal music into the common schools of Boston in the nineteenth century. See Jorgensen, "William Channing Woodbridge's Lecture."

43. On the "undergoing" as opposed to "doing" aspect of experience, see Dewey, *Art as Experience,* 44, 132, 155.

44. On "understanding how to go on," see Howard, *Artistry,* 61–65. The neophyte singer's experience is akin to the "apprentice's sorcery" (75–80).

45. See Scheffler, *In Praise of the Cognitive Emotions,* ch. 1.

46. For example, the rock musicians in the garage bands Green examined rely almost exclusively on hearing music. While orality may be an important attribute, these musicians may be limited by an inability to read music, a skill that might expand their musical horizons and allow them to access a wider array of music. On the power of listening and copying, see Green, *How Popular Musicians Learn,* 60–76.

47. Choirs may sing challenging music that requires musical literacy as well as orality. Congregations may also sing hymns and responses in multiple parts a cappella and with instrumental accompaniment, so that the young learn to carry a part, harmonize with others, and sing in their natural vocal ranges.

48. In such congregations, there may be little attention to cultivating musical taste or broadening it beyond popular music styles. A musician may be struck by the lack of high female voices in, and the poor quality of, congregational singing.

49. For a recent polemic on the impact of the internet on a rise in amateurism in contemporary culture, see Andrew Keen, *The Cult of the Amateur: How Today's Internet is Killing Our Culture* (New York: Doubleday, 2007). For a discussion of music educational beliefs that fostered a rise in musical amateurism in the nineteenth century, see Stone, "Mid-Nineteenth-Century American Beliefs in the Social Values of Music."

50. As I have noted earlier, just as Japanese children learn to speak Japanese, so, Suzuki, *Nurtured by Love,* argues, the young may learn to sing and play music.

51. The United Nations charter of children's rights specifies the child's right to know her or his culture, suggesting that musical knowledge, as an important element of culture, ought to be available to every child. For the United Nations Convention on the Rights of the Child, see http://www.unicef.org/crc/ (accessed July 23, 2010).

12. GUIDE AND PEDAGOGY

1. Curiously, in the United States and Canada, at least, music education and pedagogy are often regarded as separate fields—music education having to do with school music instruction and pedagogy relating to the teaching of group and private lessons in music performance, history, theory, and composition, especially at the college or university level.

2. See *WordPerfect X4 Dictionary*, s.v. "guide"; *OED Online*, s.v. "guide, *n.* and *v.*" http://dictionary.oed.com (accessed July 14, 2010). The word has its etymological roots in the French word *guide*, a variant of the earlier Old French *guie* and also the Roman word *guida*.

3. "Stanley Kunitz at 100," editorial, *The Boston Globe*, Friday, July 29, 2005, A14.

4. I had encountered Gibraltar in Patrick O'Brian's nautical and historical novels featuring the characters Jack Aubrey and Stephen Maturin. The volumes in this series may be regarded as one sweeping novel in various parts. For the first, see Patrick O'Brian, *Master and Commander* (New York: W. W. Norton, 1970).

5. See *OED Online*, s.v. "pedagogy, *n.*," http://dictionary.oed.com (accessed July 14, 2010). Pedagogy also refers to the systematic means whereby students are inducted into knowledge, as reflected in the German *pädagogik* or *pädagogisch,* construed as noun and adjective respectively. See *OED Online*, s.v. "pedagogic, *a.* and *n.*," http://dictionary.oed.com (accessed July 14, 2010).

6. The etymological roots of the word *pedagogue* lie in the Greek *paidagogos* (παιδαγωγός) and Latin *paedagōgus,* the slave who was entrusted with taking children to and from school and, later, a teacher and schoolmaster. See *OED Online*. s.v., "pedagogue, *n.*," http://dictionary.oed.com (accessed July 14, 2010).

7. On pedagogical treatises in music see, e.g., Albert R. Rice, "A Selection of Instrumental Vocal Tutors and Treatises Entered at Stationers' Hall, from 1789 to 1818," *The Galpin Society Journal* 41 (Oct. 1988): 16–23; and Maurice W. Riley, "A Tentative Bibliography of Early Wind Instrument Tutors," *Journal of Research in Music Education* 6.1 (Spring 1958): 3–24. Among the bibliographies of tutors for particular instrumental groups, however, is Thomas E. Warner, *An Annotated Bibliography of Woodwind Instruction Books, 1600–1830,* Detroit Studies in Music Bibliography, no. 11 (Detroit: Information Coordinators, 1967). I am indebted to David Lasocki for his assistance in locating this source. Most if not all the orchestral instruments of the Western classical tradition have their treatises and methods, as does the voice. For examples of nineteenth-century treatises, see, in voice, Manuel Garcia II, *A Complete Treatise on the Art of Singing: Complete and Unabridged* [École de Garcia], ed. and trans. Donald V. Paschke (New York: Da Capo, 1975 [1984]); Berton Coffin, "Vocal Pedagogy Classics: Garcia's New Treatise on the Art of Singing," *The NATS Bulletin* 38.2 (1981): 38–40; in violin, see, e.g., Joseph Joachim and Andreas Moser, *Violin School* [Violinschule], trans. Alfred Moffat (Berlin: N. Simrock, 1905). There are also the pedagogical literatures in such areas as music theory. For discussions of pedagogical aspects of music theory, see the *Journal of Music Theory Pedagogy*. Also see Mary Wennerstrom, "Music Theory Pedagogy: Selected Bibliography," last updated Jan. 5, 2007, at http://www.music.indiana.edu/department/theory/resources/ped_bib.pdf (accessed July 19, 2010).

Music educational writings include Orff and Keetman, *Musiik für Kinder;* Zoltán Kodály, *33 Two-part Exercises,* ed. Percy M. Young, English ed. (London: Boosey and Hawkes, 1966, 1954) and his *55 Two-part Exercises,* ed. Percy M. Young, English ed. (London: Boosey and Hawkes, 1965, 1954); Émile Jaques-Dalcroze, *Eurhythmics, Art, and Education*, trans. Frederick Rothwell, ed. Cynthia Cox (New York: Arno Press, 1976) and his *Rhythm, Music, and Education*, trans. Harold F. Rubenstein, rev. ed. ([London]: Dalcroze Society, 1980); Regelski, *Teaching General Music in Grades 4–8; Schafer, The Thinking Ear;* Suzuki, *Suzuki Violin School* and *Nurtured by Love;* Patricia Shehan Campbell, *Teaching Music Globally: Experiencing Music, Expressing Culture* (New York: Oxford University Press, 2004) and *Tunes and Grooves for Music Education;* Mary Goetze, *Global Voices Interactive* series at her website, http://www.mjpublishing.com (accessed July 16, 2010); Terese M. Volk, *Music,*

Education, and Multiculturalism: Foundations and Principles (New York: Oxford University Press, 1998); Barbara A. Brinson, *Choral Music Methods and Materials: Developing Successful Choral Programs (Grades 5 to 12)* (New York: Schirmer Books, 1996); Walter Lamble, *A Handbook for Beginning Choral Educators* (Bloomington: Indiana University Press, 2004); Robert W. Smith, Susan L. Smith, et al., *Band Expressions: Teacher Resource Guide* (Miami, Fla.: Warner Bros., 2004); John O'Reilly and Mark Williams, *Accent on Achievement: A Comprehensive Band Method that Develops Creativity and Musicianship—Flute Book 1* (Alfred Publishing Co., 1997); Tim Lautzenheiser, John Higgins, Charles Menghini, Paul Lavender, Tom C. Rhodes, Don Bierschenk, *Essential Elements 2000: Comprehensive Band Method—Conductor Book 1* (Milwaukee: Hal Leonard, 1999); Bruce Pearson, *Standard of Excellence: Comprehensive Band Method—Book 1—Conductor Score* (San Diego, Calif.: Neil A. Kjos Music, 1993). I am indebted to Lissa Fleming May for bringing these instrumental music education references to my attention.

8. For writings on music as practice, music education as praxis, artistry, and reflective practice in music among other professions, see Francis E. Sparshott, *The Theory of the Arts* (Princeton, N.J.: Princeton University Press, 1982) and "Aesthetics of Music: Limits and Grounds," in *What is Music: An Introduction to the Philosophy of Music*, ed. Philip Alperson ([1987]; repr., University Park: Pennsylvania State University Press, 1994), 33–98; Elliott, *Music Matters;* Howard, *Artistry;* Schön, *Educating the Reflective Practitioner.* Related to pedagogy, the word *didactic* refers to notions of "having the character or manner of a teacher," and "having the giving of instruction as its aim or object"; its plural, *didactics,* meaning "the science and art of teaching," is mined for music education by Nielsen, "Didactology as a Field of Theory and Research in Music Education." Also see *OED Online,* s.v. "didactic, *a.* and *n.,*" http://dictionary.oed.com (accessed July 14, 2010) referring to "having the character or manner of a teacher," and "having the giving of instruction as its aim or object." The German words *didaktik* and *pädagogik* should not be confused; they evoke differing philosophical traditions in education.

9. For example, Sparshott, *Theory of the Arts* and "Aesthetics of Music: Limits and Grounds," lays out a philosophy of music concerning what a tradition's musicians and public do. Rather than construe music in terms of abstract or even psychologically perceived and imagined sonic phenomena, Sparshott, Alperson, and their colleagues focus on musical practices in the phenomenal world and the social rituals of which they are a part. See Alperson, ed., *What is Music?* This view accords with those of sociologists of music such as Theodor Adorno, Curt Blaukopf, Peter Martin, Tia DeNora, John Shepherd, among other writers who relate music to wider sociocultural phenomena. See Adorno, *Aesthetic Theory* and *Introduction to Sociology,* ed. Chistoph Gödde, trans. Edmund Jephcott (Stanford, Calif.: Stanford University Press, 2000); Blaukopf, *Musical Life in a Changing Society;* Martin Clayton, Trevor Herbert, and Richard Middleton, eds., *The Cultural Study of Music: A Critical Introduction* (New York: Routledge, 2003); Peter J. Martin, *Sounds and Society: Themes in the Sociology of Music* (Manchester: Manchester University Press, 1995); DeNora, *After Adorno: Rethinking Music Sociology;* Derek B. Scott, ed., *Music, Culture, and Society: A Reader* (Oxford: Oxford University Press, 2002); Shepherd, *Music as Social Text.* Anthropologists and ethnomusicologists such as Henry Kingsbury, Bruno Nettl, Ruth Stone, Thomas Torino, and Albrecht Schneider and his colleagues likewise describe music in terms of what is done in the context of musical rituals and events and seek to interpret their meaning. See Kingsbury, *Music, Talent, and Performance* and *The Truth of*

Music: Empire, Law and Secrecy (Kennebunk, Maine: Full Court Press, 2005); Nettl, *The Study of Ethnomusicology* and *Heartland Excursions;* Ruth M. Stone, *Music in West Africa: Experiencing Music, Expressing Culture* (New York: Oxford University Press, 2005) and her *Theory for Ethnomusicology* (Upper Saddle River, N.J.: Pearson Prentice Hall, 2008); Thomas Turino, *Music as Social Life: The Politics of Participation* (Chicago: University of Chicago Press, 2008); Albrecht Schneider, ed., *Systematic and Comparative Musicology: Concepts, Methods, Findings* (Frankfurt am Main: Peter Lang, 2008).

10. See Philip Alperson, "What Should One Expect from a Philosophy of Music Education," in *Philosopher, Teacher, Musician: Perspectives on Music Education,* ed. Estelle R. Jorgensen (Urbana: University of Illinois Press, 1993); Elliott, *Music Matters,* esp. ch. 3. Following Alperson's lead, Elliott names his approach to music education *praxial;* that is, focused on the notion of music as what musicians do (and belief as it fosters and is reinforced or impacted by practice). Philip Alperson, "Robust Praxialism and the Anti-Aesthetic Turn," *Philosophy of Music Education Review* 18.2 (Fall 2010): 171–193, criticizes the interpretation of his ideas by some music educators. Small, *Musicking,* also advocates a practical and processual view of music.

11. See Maconie, *The Science of Music;* Frede V. Nielsen, *The Didactology of General Music Education* [in Danish] (Copenhagen: Akademisk Forlag, 1998).

12. See David J. Elliott, "Key Concepts in Multicultural Music Education," *International Journal of Music Education,* no. 13 (1989): 11–18.

13. This point is underscored elsewhere by Keith Swanwick, *Musical Knowledge: Intuition, Analysis and Music Education* (London: Routledge, 1994), who distinguishes the various epistemological aspects of music and likewise emphasizes a performance-based approach to music education. Swanwick's account seems consonant with John Dewey's belief that it is vital that any subject of study be engaged personally, vitally, experientially, and performatively. See John Dewey, *Art as Experience* and *Experience and Education.*

14. Elliott, *Music Matters,* 40, describes at least four dimensions of musicking involving the doer, the kind of doing, what is done, and the context in which it is done. For him, this is an active sense of music making including "performing, improvising, composing, arranging, and listening." Also involved is a sense of consciousness and intentionality in what is done, both respecting the music that is made and one's self (see esp. chs. 3, 4, 5).

15. See Giroux, *Border Crossings;* Elliott, "Key Concepts in Multicultural Music Education."

16. For example, the myths of the "jazz masters," the pioneers of jazz in the early part of the 20th century, are invoked and their contributions recognized in telling and re-telling their stories in film, print media, and personal storytelling. These earlier musicians live on in legend and recording, and their histories are preserved in museums and music halls. See Paul F. Berliner, *Thinking in Jazz: The Infinite Art of Jazz Improvisation* (Chicago: University of Chicago Press, 1994).

17. On exposition, see Jorgensen, *The Art of Teaching Music,* 217–222.

18. See van Manen, *The Tact of Teaching,* esp. ch. 6.

19. See *OED Online,* s.v. "resilience," http://dictionary.oed.com (accessed July 14, 2010); see *WordPerfect X4 Dictionary,* s.v. "resilience."

20. On pedagogical authority, see Donald Phillip Verene, *The Art of Humane Education* (Ithaca, N.Y.: Cornell University Press, 2002), ch. 2.

21. See Howard, *Artistry,* 183.

22. See Jorgensen, *In Search of Music Education,* 8–13.

23. See Jorgensen, *Art of Music Teaching,* 155, 221.

24. See Jorgensen, *In Search of Music Education,* 4–8.

25. For Nielsen, "Didactology as a Field of Theory and Research in Music Education," these skills are grounded in research findings.

26. Howard, *Learning by all Means,* part 2, derives these as means of learning, but they apply to teaching as well.

27. On explanation, especially definition, see Scholes, *Music, the Child and the Masterpiece.*

28. Howard, *Artistry,* ch. 6.

29. On the teaching of William Adam who developed a well-known practice routine for the trumpet, see Kevin Kjos, "Reflections on the Teaching of William Adam," doctoral diss., Indiana University School of Music, Bloomington, Indiana, 1997.

30. Jorgensen, *Transforming Music Education,* 102–107.

31. Ivan Galamian and Dorothy Delay are noted violin teachers of their generation who have trained well-known professional violinists. Many students who aspired to concert careers were attracted to them by virtue of their international reputations. On Ivan Galamian, see Elizabeth A. H. Green, Judith Galamian, Josef Gingold, and Meadowmount musicians, *Miraculous Teacher: Ivan Galamian and the Meadowmount Experience* ([Ann Arbor, Mich.]: Elizabeth A. H. Green; [Bryn Mawr, Pa.: Selling agent, Theodore Presser], 1993); Ivan Galamian, *Principles of Violin Playing & Teaching,* 3rd ed. (Ann Arbor, Mich.: Shar Products Co., [1999]). On Dorothy Delay, also, a student of Galamian, and later his assistant at Juilliard and Meadowmount, see Barbara Lourie Sand, *Teaching Genius: Dorothy DeLay and the Making of a Musician* (Portland, Ore.: Amadeus Press, 2000).

32. Since the teacher is in possession of privileged information, students rely on their teachers to divulge it. In the North Indian tradition, teachers are reluctant to do so until their students are ready to receive it, able to transmit it faithfully, and sufficiently trustworthy. Neuman, *The Life of Music in North India,* 49, reports the case of a teacher with "at least one student who studied with him for twenty-six years" and yet "not one of his students has yet qualified—in his opinion—to learn the surbahar."

33. See Howard, *Artistry,* 75–80.

34. See Scheffler, *Reason and Teaching,* 71–76.

35. See Reichling, "Images of Imagination."

36. For example, a young man who takes up the flute discovers a repertoire in baroque flute, recorder, piccolo, and multiphonics and other techniques employed in more recent flute writing that he never expected to encounter when he undertook his study. He may find that he delights in playing early repertoire that he did not anticipate when he set out to learn to play the twentieth-century French flute repertoire that drew him to a study of flute in the first place. Or he may discover a yearning to conduct or to play with a chamber ensemble that he had not considered when he first decided to become a concert flautist. As he performs, he may also discover a love of teaching the flute that leads him to prepare for a life as a performer and teacher of flute based at a conservatory or university rather than as the orchestral flautist he first set out to become.

37. For example, a young woman studying the trumpet may eventually realize that she is more drawn to social interaction with others than to the extensive solitary practice required if she is to become an outstanding trumpeter. She may also lack confidence in reliably play-

ing difficult notes. Taking stock of her interests, strengths, and weaknesses, she may opt for a career as a high school instrumental teacher. Here she is able to bring her strong organizational and social abilities together with her love of music and the trumpet. While she may play well, she discovers that she does not want to spend the time required for practice and rely upon performance for her livelihood.

38. We imagine the flute and trumpet teachers in the examples in the foregoing notes providing opportunities for their students to discover for themselves what they most want to do as they also discover how best to steer their students into the musical lives for which they are best suited. They may do just as much good for their students by advising those unsuited to a musical livelihood to undertake other things as they advise them about the particular appropriate musical specialties.

39. This idea seems consistent with Scheffler's argument that human potential relies heavily on students' choices about what they bring to their studies and their commitment to learning. It buttresses a long-standing practice among instrumental and vocal teachers to reward students, at least partly, for the effort they expend. See Scheffler, *In Praise of the Cognitive Emotions,* ch. 2, and Israel Scheffler, *Of Human Potential: An Essay in the Philosophy of Education* (Boston: Routledge and Kegan Paul, 1985).

40. For example, a violin student might attend concerts, play chamber music, and give recitals not required on her program. She might take up her teacher's invitation to visit an art gallery and view some of the impressionistic paintings on display, or travel to another city to hear a performance by an up-and-coming young violinist. She might gain further experience by playing gigs in a regional orchestra. She might take courses in art history, aesthetics, or acoustics as ways to expand her musical knowledge. If she is classically trained, she might also take courses in jazz, thereby developing her improvisational skills. In these and other ways, she extends her own learning beyond the confines of her specialization and contributes importantly to her own learning.

41. See Zentner, *Prelude to Administrative Theory,* ch. 7; Estelle R. Jorgensen, "On Resource Allocation in School Music," *Proceedings of the McGill Symposium in School Music Administration and Supervision, 1979,* ed. Estelle R. Jorgensen (Montreal: Faculty of Music, McGill University, 1980); "On the Decision-making Process in Music Education," *Journal of Educational Thought* 19.3 (1985): 218–237; and "On the Recruitment Process in Amateur Ensembles." Zentner's social processes have informed the discussion of leadership in Jorgensen, *The Art of Teaching Music,* ch. 5.

42. I think, e.g., of Rosamund Shuter-Dyson and Clive Gabriel's work on musical ability, Anthony Kemp's research on musicians' temperaments, Borje Stålhammar's and Christer Bouij's longitudinal studies of the musical identities of Swedish young people and music teacher identities, respectively, and Sandra Trehub's work on the musical capacities of very young children, to name a few studies internationally. See Rosamund Shuter-Dyson and Clive Gabriel, *The Psychology of Musical Ability,* 2nd ed. (London: Methuen, 1981); Kemp, *The Musical Temperament;* Diana Deutsch, ed., *The Psychology of Music,* 2nd ed. (San Diego, Calif.: Academic Press, 1999); Christer Bouij, "Music Teacher Identity Meets Working Life: Results from a Longitudinal Project about Swedish Music," in *Music and Human Beings— Music and Identity,* ed. Börje Stålhammar (Örebro: Universitetsbiblioteket, 2006); Börje Stålhammar, *Musical Identities and Music Education,* ed. Helena Eriksson, trans. Malcolm Forbes (Aachen: Shaker Verlag and Örebro University, 2006); Sandra E. Trehub, "Infants as

Musical Connoisseurs," in *The Child as Musician: A Handbook of Musical Development,* ed. Gary E. McPherson (Oxford: Oxford University Press, 2006).

43. See a classic study in this vein by Alphons Silbermann, *The Sociology of Music,* trans. Corbet Stewart ([1963]; repr., Westport, Conn.: Greenwood, 1977).

44. See, e.g., Charles P. Schmidt, Rhonda Baker, Beth Hayes, and Eva Kwan, "A Descriptive Study of Public School Music Programs in Indiana," *Bulletin of the Council for Research in Music Education* no. 169 (Summer 2006): 25-37.

45. Jean Lave and Etienne Wenger coined the term "community of practice" in their *Situated Learning: Legitimate Peripheral Participation* (Cambridge: Cambridge University Press, 1991). Also see Palmer, *The Courage to Teach,* esp. chs. 4-6; Lee S. Shulman, *The Wisdom of Practice: Essays on Teaching, Learning, and Learning to Teach,* ed. Suzanne M. Wilson (San Francisco: Jossey-Bass, 2004), esp. ch. 20, titled "Communities of Learners and Communities of Teachers."

46. See Highet, *The Art of Teaching,* 107-116.

47. For example, a piano teacher may want her students to come to a knowledge of all of the historical periods represented in the piano repertoire and additional literature originally written for other keyboard instruments. She may also expect her students to play not only the solo piano repertoire but chamber music and concerti. These are general objectives that the students cannot escape. Even if a pianist wants to play only the music of the romantic period, the teacher insists on a much more extensive and systematic coverage of the repertoire. Although students may choose to play particular pieces in this repertoire, the teacher's general frame significantly limits their freedom of choice.

48. This freedom necessitates a conversation between student pianist and teacher about which specific pieces might be learned and played. The student might ask her what she thinks of a particular combination of pieces for a recital program, and together the two may agree on those the student will learn and perform.

49. Schön, *Educating the Reflective Practitioner,* ch. 8, describes instructional situations in which architecture students are working with their teachers on siting and designing buildings and music master classes in which teachers are working with students on the performance of particular pieces.

50. See ibid., part 2. Architecture students face the problem of what to design within an array of particular sites, and music students confront the problem of how to perform these pieces. Before the students arrive at the lesson, they are already invested in their projects and have formed particular solutions to their respective architectural and musical problems. The architecture students have drawn drawings in preparation for their meetings with their teacher, and the music students have practiced what they are to play for their teacher. Experienced master teachers approach their students with a view to criticizing what their students have done and prompting their students to think about alternative constructions and possibilities.

51. For example, after a basic study of organ technique, an organ teacher then moves the student through the organ repertoire in a systematic way. All students are expected to practice for at least a certain minimum numbers of hours per day, and to play services in order to gain experience in performing on different organs, improvising, accompanying choirs and congregational singing. They may be taken on "organ crawls" by their teacher, field trips in which they visit different organs, learn the possibilities of various types and makers of organs in different styles, and attend recitals given by organists in the area. These

more informal activities are nevertheless understood to be mandatory by organ students in this studio. In group lessons, students hear each other play and learn from the teacher's comments to their fellows as well as on their own playing. Every student is expected to reach particular levels of performance on recitals that they are required to give during their program of study. Since students are expected to attend recitals given by their colleagues in the organ studio, these expectations are well known by all. There are also the required classes that they must attend and pass in such subjects as music history, theory, ear training, church music, organ literature, organ pedagogy, conducting, and choral ensembles. They may also need to take courses in the arts, humanities, and sciences to give them a broader preparation. It is presumably clear to them what they need to do, how they need to do it, and what results are to be expected by the end of their course of study.

52. For example, a teacher may have figured out a logical program of work to cover the study of percussion instruments for the duration of the diploma or degree program. He may have determined the repertoire, exercises, études, and ensemble activities to be required of all his students at each level of development. Since he is concerned that his students know all of the instruments comprising the orchestral percussion family and have expertise in some of them, he may have worked out in sequential order how this study is to progress. The keyboard instruments, timpani, various drums, and other instruments each make differing demands, and he may wish all students to have expertise in melodic and rhythmic percussion instruments while also specializing in certain instruments to which they are most drawn. He may wish them to gain expertise in musical traditions beyond Western classical music and grasp the differing stylistic demands of these traditions. This program may constitute a detailed list of important objectives for the freshman, sophomore, junior, and senior years, with particular instruments for study, repertoire, exercises, scales, études, care and repair of instruments, and the like for each year.

53. For example, organists' study of music history is intended to inform their performance of literature from different periods. Having studied music of the Baroque period, their ornamentation, articulation, and registration is expected to benefit from these historical understandings. For example, they will doubtless become much more attuned to the importance of the particular editions of scores and thoughtful about which pieces are particularly appropriate for the organs that they play. Their understanding of acoustic phenomena are also important elements that play into their performance. For example, the matter of the decay time of the various places in which organs are housed is also an important consideration in their tempi and articulation. Various sorts of wave motion to which pipes give rise and the harmonic series likewise inform their registrations and performance.

54. Requiring that organists also begin to take positions at area churches allows them to gain important practical experience as they pursue their musical studies. They may share with their teacher their choice of repertoire and registrations for the pieces they plan to play and solicit their teacher's advice.

55. See, e.g., Collinson, *The Diary of an Organist's Apprentice*.

56. On the practical use of the jury in the higher musical education in the United States, see Colleen M. Conway and Thomas M. Hodgman, *Teaching Music in Higher Education* (New York: Oxford University Press, 2009), 58, 137, 144.

57. Concerning space, a piano teacher, e.g., might secure a particular studio outfitted with instruments and other technology as needed. Such spaces are often prized by teachers, who decorate them as they would their homes with artworks, decor and furnishings to

their taste, and other accoutrements that contribute to their comfort and convenience of use. Scores and music books stored in bookcases, sound and video recording equipment, computing equipment, and instructional records may feature prominently, and pictures of musicians remind students of their teacher's eminence. Some studios may feature a waiting room or anteroom where students gather before a lesson begins. Typically, the more pre-eminent the teacher, the more prestigious, spacious, and desirable the space.

58. On the "demonstration effect," see Jorgensen, "Engineering Change in Music Education."

59. On the etymology of music construed as a verb, see *OED Online,* s.v. "music, *v.,*" http://dictionary.oed.com (accessed July 14, 2010).

60. For the distinction between seeing how something is made and knowing about the thing that is made, see Scheffler, *In Praise of the Cognitive Emotions,* ch. 3.

61. See, for example, Goetze, *Global Voices Interactive series,* at her website http://www.mjpublishing.com (accessed July 19, 2010).

62. On following one's "bliss," see Joseph Campbell with Bill Moyers, *The Power of Myth,* ed. Betty Sue Flowers (New York: Anchor Books, 1991). Even Dewey, *Experience and Education,* esp. chs. 4 and 5, who seeks freedom for his students is inclined to entrust their freedoms in the teacher who supposedly acts in their best interest.

63. On the differences between theory and practice, see Schön, *Educating the Reflective Practitioner,* ch. 1. On ambiguity, see Israel Scheffler, *The Language of Education* (Springfield, Ill.: Charles C. Thomas, 1960), 3, 17, 79, 82, 84.

13. WEB AND CONNECTIVITY

1. See Illich, *Deschooling Society.*

2. See, e.g., Anne Shaw Faulkner, *What We Hear in Music: A Course of Study in Music History and Appreciation for Use in the Home, Music Clubs, Conservatories, High Schools, Normal Schools, Colleges and Universities* (Camden, N.J.: Victor Talking Machine Co., 1913); Clark, *Music Appreciation for Children;* Percy A. Scholes, *The First Book of the Gramophone Record, Giving Advice Upon the Selection of Fifty-odd Good Records from Byrd to Beethoven* . . . , 2nd ed. (London: Oxford University Press, 1927); *The Second Book of the Gramophone Record,* . . . (London: Oxford University Press, 1925); *Everybody's Guide to Broadcast Music* . . . (London: Oxford University Press, 1925); and *The Appreciation of Music by Means of the Duo-art; A Course of Lectures Delivered at Aeolian Hall, London, by Percy A. Scholes* (New York: Oxford University Press, 1926).

3. Among the more recent writers on technology and music education, see Bernd Enders, "Musical Education and the New Media: The Current Situation and Perspectives for the Future," in Braun, ed., *"I Sing the Body Electric": Music and Technology in the 20th Century,* 235–250; Don Lebler, "Music and Technology: Learning through Recording," in *Aesthetics and Experience in Music Performance,* ed. Elizabeth Mackinlay, Denis Collins, and Samantha Owens (Newcastle: Cambridge Scholars Press, 2005), 319–328; Steve Dillon, "Meaningful Engagement with Music Technology," in *Aesthetics and Experience in Music Performance,* 329–341; Janet Mansfield, "The Global Music Subject, Curriculum, and Heidegger's Questioning Concerning Technology," in *Music Education for the New Millennium: Theory and Practice Futures for Music Teaching and Learning,* ed. David K. Lines (Malden, Mass.: Blackwell, 2005), 131–145; John Finney and Pamela Burnard, eds., *Music Education with Digital Technology* (London: Continuum, 2007); Andrew R. Brown,

Computers in Music Education: Amplifying Musicality (New York: Routledge, 2007); David Brian Williams and Peter Richard Webster, *Experiencing Music Technology,* 3rd ed. (Boston: Schirmer Centage Learning, 2006, 2008).

4. On an enormous spiderweb covering 180 m (590 ft) at Lake Tawakoni State Park, Texas, see "Texan Spiders Spin 'Monster Web,'" story from BBC NEWS at http://news.bbc .co.uk/go/pr/fr/-/2/hi/science/nature/6972062.stm (accessed July 19, 2010).

5. Gordon Graham, *The Internet: A Philosophical Inquiry* (London: Routledge, 1999), 23, 24.

6. See Plato, *Republic,* §§514a–521b.

7. See Neil Barrett, *The State of Cybernation: Cultural, Political and Economic Implications of the Internet* (London: Kogan Page, 1996), 26; also cited in Graham, *Internet,* 22.

8. See *OED Online,* s.v. "tangle, n^2.," http://dictionary.oed.com (accessed 14 July, 2010), defined as "a complication of threads, hairs, fibres, branches, boughs, or the like, confusedly intertwined or interlaced . . ."

9. For two studies of how the life cycle of an organization plays out in musical ensembles, see Jorgensen, "On the Recruitment Process in Amateur Ensembles," and Jorgensen, "Developmental Phases in Selected British Choirs."

10. On musical mediamorphosis, see Blaukopf, *Musical Life in a Changing,* chs. 20, 29. On music and technology in the twentieth century, see Braun, ed., *"I Sing the Body Electric": Music and Technology in the Twentieth Century.* Regarding the interrelationship of popular music and technology, e.g., see Simon Frith, ed., *Popular Music: Critical Concepts in Media and Cultural Studies,* 4 vols. (London: Routledge, 2004); Peter Webb, *Exploring the Networked Worlds of Popular Music: Milieu Cultures* (New York: Routledge, 2007); Bloustien, Peters, and Luckman, eds., *Sonic Synergies.*

11. In counterpoint with my own list of values, Brown, *Computers in Music Education,* ch. 1, sketches philosophical aspects of computers and music such as amplification, invisibility, context, metaphor, musicianship, scaffolding, intention, engagement, production, analysis, and performance—matters that go principally to the ontological character of the musical experience and the nature of music curriculum.

12. See *OED Online,* s.v. "internationalism," http://dictionary.oed.com (accessed 14 July 2010). Also, on internationalism, see Graham, *The Internet,* 86–87.

13. See *OED Online,* s.v. "populism, *n.*" http://dictionary.oed.com (accessed July 14, 2010). Also, on populism, see Graham, *The Internet,* 87–88.

14. As Graham, *The Internet,* 76, notes, the fact that so many are able to have a public "stage" from which to impact others may ironically mean that the effect of any one individual is reduced, since there are so many other distractions in the system.

15. On cyber-communities or "virtual communities," see Graham, *The Internet,* 160–166.

16. On "milieu cultures," see Webb, *Exploring the Networked Worlds of Popular Music,* esp. ch. 2.

17. Graham, *The Internet,* 160, sees cyber-communities as comprised of "on-screen personalities" who are the "alter egos" of "those who, so to speak, sit at their terminals." Graham, ibid., 164–166, views this virtual world as somewhat impoverished, in the sense that ordinary face-to-face interaction is the norm that the web seeks to emulate. Still, there is also the lure of the fantastical, the supernatural, and existence that goes beyond the ordinary and the mundane, where one can dwell in space and time and where one's powers may be extraordinary.

18. Neil Postman, *Technopoly: The Surrender of Culture to Technology* (New York: Vintage Books, 1993), critiques the power that machines possess in contemporary culture and coins the term from which Graham, *The Internet*, 9–13, draws in his analysis of technophilia. For Graham (10), Postman "generalizes and dramatizes too much" the negative aspects of technology.

19. Graham, *The Internet*, 45, observes that "except in a few restrictive cases perhaps, technology should not be regarded as the handmaiden of human needs and desires, but a highly important contributor to their formation."

20. Graham, *The Internet*, 24.

21. On virtual time and space, see, e.g., Langer, *Feeling and Form*, esp. chs. 5, 6, 7. Also, on the "virtual" nature of cyberspace, see Graham, *The Internet*, ch. 8.

22. For a discussion of neo-Luddism and technophilism, see Graham, *The Internet*, esp. ch. 1. On the values of technology as a Faustian bargain, see Graham, *The Internet*, ch. 3. Notice that Martin Heidegger, "The Question Concerning Technology," in *Basic Writings of Martin Heidegger*, ed. D. F. Krell (London: Routledge, 1993), 139–212, is concerned about the pervasive influence of technology in the mid-twentieth century. For comments on Heidegger's essay as it relates to music education, see Mansfield, "The Global Music Subject, Curriculum and Heidegger's Questioning Concerning Technology."

23. See Jorgensen, *In Search of Music Education*, ch. 2.

24. See *OED Online*, s.v. "connected, *ppl. a.*," http://dictionary.oed.com (accessed July 14, 2010).

25. *See OED Online*, "connexion, connection," http://dictionary.oed.com (accessed July 14, 2010).

26. See Fred Rees, "Distance Learning and Collaboration in Music Education," in Colwell and Richardson, eds., *The New Handbook in Music Teaching and Learning*, 257–273. For example, MENC—The National Association for Music Education, in the United States, has advocated for the use of technologies in such publications as Frances S. Ponick, ed., *Spotlight on Technology in the Music Classroom: Selected Articles from State MEA Journals* (Lanham, Md.: Rowman and Littlefield Education with MENC, The National Association for Music Education, 2004); Thomas E. Rudolph et al., Floyd Richmond, ed., *Technology Strategies for Music Education*, 2nd ed. (Wyncote, Pa.: Technology Institute for Music Educators, 2005); MENC—The National Association for Music Education, *Spotlight on Technology in the Music Classroom* (Lanham, Md.: Rowman and Littlefield Education with MENC, The National Association for Music Education, 2007). Since 2000, in the profession's publications one sees such articles as: Rosemary D. Reniger, "Music Education in a Digital World," *Teaching Music* 8 (Aug. 2000): 24–31; G. David Peters, "Transformations: Technology and the Music Industry," *Teaching Music* 9 (Dec. 2001): 20–25; and James W. Sherbon and David L. Kish, "Distance Learning and the Music Teacher," *Music Educators Journal* 62 (Nov. 2005): 36–41. During the past decade, music educators have reflected on the possibilities for such things as internet-based composition and the implications for music teacher education. See Sam Reese and Maud M. Hickey, "Internet-based Music Composition and Music Teacher Education," *Journal of Music Teacher Education* 9 (Fall 1999): 25–32. From the late 1990s, practical ways to utilize music technology for music education have been suggested. See David Brian Williams and Peter Richard Webster, *Experiencing Music Technology: Software, Data, and Hardware*, 2nd ed. (New York: Schirmer Books, 1999).

27. See Graham, *The Internet*, 1. For example, Theodor Holm Nelson, "A Cosmology for a Different Computer Universe: Data Model, Mechanisms, Virtual Machine and Visualization Infrastructure," *Journal of Digital Information* 5.1, article no. 298, June 16, 2004, envisages a different set of conventions for data and computing. For speculation on the future of technology in music education and the changes that should be wrought, see, e.g., Finney and Burnard, eds., *Music Education with Digital Technology*, part 3; Lines, ed., *Music Education for the New Millennium*; Brown, *Computers in Music Education*, ch. 24.

28. This is not a new phenomenon in Western music. As Geoffrey Hindley, "Keyboards, Crankshafts, and Communication: The Musical Mindset of Western Technology," in Braun, ed., *"I Sing the Body Electric": Music and Technology in the 20th Century*, 33, notes, "The mindset of western art music is at the core of modern world techno-culture." Braun and his colleagues posit that technology has been vitally interconnected with the development of Western classical music for much of its history; recordings have shaped performance and become a source of authority for musicians.

29. Peter Kivy, *Music Alone: Philosophical Reflections on the Purely Musical Experience* (Ithaca, N.Y.: Cornell University Press, 1990), refers to music understood as a purely sonic phenomenon as "music alone."

30. On these communities, see Bloustien, Peters, and Luckman, eds., *Sonic Synergies*. Musicians can gain a sort of musical immortality as their recorded music is performed and listened to after their deaths. In our time, e.g., the music of twentieth-century musicians such as pianists Annie Fischer and Vladimir Horowitz, singer Ray Charles, and rock and roll star Elvis Presley can still be heard even though they are no longer with us physically. Recordings of Annie Fischer, *Piano sonatas complete*, Vol. 1 [sound recording]/ *Ludwig van Beethoven* (Hungary: Hungaroton Classic [Long Island City, N.Y.]: [Distributed by] Qualiton Imports, p1996), 1 compact disc; Vladimir Horowitz, *Vladimir Horowitz Rediscovered* [sound recording]: Carnegie Hall recital, Nov. 16, 1975 (New York: RCA Victor Red Seal, p2003), 2 compact discs; Ray Charles, *Ray Sings, Basie Swings* [sound recording]/Ray Charles and The Count Basie Orchestra (Beverly Hills: Concord Records (USA), p2006.), 1 compact disc; Elvis Presley, *The Essential Elvis Presley* [sound recording] (New York: RCA: Distributed Sony BMG Music Entertainment, p2007), 2 compact discs.

31. On conflicting ideas about the future of the music industry, see Roman Espejo, ed., *What is the Future of the Music Industry?* (Farmington Hills, Mich.: Greenhaven, 2009). For an overview of the impact of computers on media and entertainment industries, see James W. Cortada, *The Digital Hand*, vol. 2: *How Computers Changed the Work of American Financial, Telecommunications, Media, and Entertainment Industries* (Oxford: Oxford University Press, 2006).

32. See Webb, *Exploring the Networked Worlds of Popular Music*, ch. 2.

33. As I write, it is hard to imagine how teachers and students will be able to "dwell together" virtually with the same intensity and prolonged interaction as that possible in the context of learning in healing, informality, and apprenticeship modes. Going forward, however, should the virtual and lived worlds become more blurred or intertwined (as they seem to be doing right now), teachers who teach at a distance may find more opportunities to help students integrate what is learned virtually into their lived lives and to be more present to them for more extended periods of time than is now possible.

34. Illich, *Deschooling Education*, 84.

35. On the problems of the storage of *misinformation* and authority on the internet, see Graham, *Internet,* 89.

36. Illich, *Deschooling Education,* 87, 91.

37. Ibid., 98.

38. Ibid., 100.

39. Educational uses of hypertext derive from the field of computing—in particular, from the work of Theodor Holm Nelson, *Literary Machines: The Report on, and of, Project Xanadu Concerning Word Processing, Electronic Publishing, Hypertext, Thinkertoys, Tomorrow's Intellectual Revolution, and Certain Other Topics including Knowledge, Education and Freedom* (Sausalito, Calif.: Mindful Press, 1993), who coined the term in 1965.

40. Even when learning takes place in pervasively formal contexts, there may be many opportunities for informal learning. For example, student and teacher conversations may lead to unexpected and serendipitous learning that is unplanned by the teacher but arises in the course of informal class communications.

41. Illich, *Deschooling Education,* 68.

42. Ibid., 12, 13.

43. Students see and hear performers in a distant land, talk and listen to, and even perform with them in real time. Their faces, costumes, and instruments can be seen and heard, but not touched physically. They seem to be in a parallel universe, one in which we really do not know them intimately, even though we may sense that we do. I think, e.g., of the parallel worlds that Philip Pullman creates in the *His Dark Materials* series.

44. One can imagine possibilities for widening the array of instruments that one might physically play in conjunction with the web. When it comes to learning the music of other countries by mainly visual and aural means and in the absence of tactile clues, one may know a part of what is a rich cultural fabric that can best be known by being physically in that culture. Still, one relies on the accuracy of the available information, since it may not be possible to verify it through personal experience. Nor is this learning entirely fanciful, since, presumably, informants' knowledge is dependable and not misleading. Still, even what such informants know of a musical culture is determined partly by their position in that culture, and therefore multiple informants can allow one to critically examine the information received.

45. See Michael Hoechsmann, *Reading Youth Writing: "New" Literacies, Cultural Studies and Education* (New York: Peter Lang, 2008).

46. The "humdrum" is the "enemy" of the sort of experience that Dewey, *Art as Experience,* 40 and ch. 2, has in mind. For Langer, *Philosophy in a New Key,* esp. ch. 8, if music is made and taken well, it should be significant and memorable.

47. Technologies affect the nature of the interaction between teachers and students by impacting the particular visual, auditory, and other cues that people normally rely on in face-to-face interaction. The closer such cues are to ordinary communication, the richer the information that people can use to assess how they are presenting themselves to others and how others are responding to what they say and do. Since they may be at some remove from others with whom they are interacting, participants may also choose what information to reveal of themselves and the manner of their interaction with these others. Their presentations of self may be fictitious, disguised, or authentic, and participants may be present to

each other in cyberspace for limited timespans, so it may be difficult to ascertain the veracity of these presentations. See Erving Goffman, *The Presentation of Self in Everyday Life* (Garden City, N.Y.: Doubleday Anchor Books, 1959).

48. See Jorgensen, "On a Choice-based Instructional Typology in Music."

49. On the impact of technologies on changing identities, see Finney and Burnard, eds., *Music Education with Digital Technology*, part 1.

50. Through recordings and live communication, the range of possible musical and educational experiences is broadened to include global music making and taking and extend possibilities beyond the expertise of any particular teacher. Access to libraries of information may be more or less instantaneous, and ease of finding it is also evident in increasingly intuitive and user-friendly technologies. The high quality of audio and video presentations lends vitality and interest to the subject matter as it also permits lifelike engagement of teachers and their students. This is especially the case in the increasingly powerful simulation technologies that give the user a sense of actually experiencing this thing; one comes immediately to know what such-and-such is like, even though one may be far removed from it in space and possibly in time.

51. See John Dewey, *The Child and the Curriculum, and The School and Society*, esp. chs. 3, 9.

52. For a discussion of these types of networks, see Illich, *Deschooling Education*, 77–79.

53. Deweyan notions of the experiential integration with other aspects of lived life, and the continuity of educational experiences with the past and projected into the future, allow the design and implementation of individualized curricula that build directly on student impulses and past experience and lead to future growth. On continuity and interaction as aspects of the educational experience, see Dewey, *Experience and Education*, esp. 44–47.

54. Teachers and students may come from anywhere in the world, and their technological connections to each other constitute the means whereby they engage together. Meetings may be virtual with participants situated in different places and linked through technologies. In global organizations, participants may hold disparate views on how things need to be that arise out of their differing cultural and societal backgrounds, and the "multiplicities and pluralities" often seen in society at large are likewise evident within them. On multiplicities and pluralities, see Greene, *The Dialectic of Freedom*, ch. 4.

55. Illich, *Deschooling Society*, 75, 76.

56. Ibid., 75.

57. Ibid., 76.

58. Ibid., 73.

59. Ibid., vii, viii.

60. Ibid., 98, 99.

61. Ibid., 100. This liberation concerns access to knowledge, sharing of skills, the "critical and creative resources of people," and the "obligations to shape" their "expectations to the services offered by any established profession"; ibid., 103.

62. On these social processes, see Zentner, *Prelude to Administrative Theory*, ch. 7.

63. On the profound changes that have created an "information age" and "information economy," see Cortada, *Digital Hand*, vol. 2, esp. viii, 22, 190, 292, 443, 267, 481.

64. Philip, *Performing Music in the Age of Recording*, esp. chs. 5, 6, 7.

65. On the impact of repetition in music, see Attali, *Noise: The Political Economy of Music*, ch. 4. Also see Philip, *Performing Music in the Age of Recording*, passim.

66. Personal characteristics of age, gender, physical appearance, color, ethnicity, language, or disability may be disguised or masked in virtual communication. See, e.g., Kimberley McCord, "Advocating for Assistive Technology for Students with Disabilities in Your School," in *Spotlight on Making Music With Special Learners: Selected Articles from State MEA Journals*, ed. Frances S. Ponick (Lanham, Md.: Rowman and Littlefield Education with MENC, The National Association for Music Education, 2004), 38–41.

67. See Paulo Freire, *Pedagogy of the Oppressed*, esp. chs. 3, 4; Greene, *The Dialectic of Freedom*, ch. 1, esp. p. 17.

68. In one of my classes, when computers were used, I noticed that students were distracted and less engaged with others. When computers were absent, the situation was transformed. These same students were vitally interested in the conversation. They leaned forward in their chairs, listening and watching each other intently, and came alive in their interaction with others in the class.

69. See Dewey, *Experience and Education*, 30.

14. PICTURE AND PRACTICE

1. Alfred North Whitehead, *The Aims of Education and Other Essays* ([1929]; repr., New York: Free Press, 1967), 36, 37, argues that the work of education should culminate in generalization, a phase at which intuitive hunches that have been systematically analyzed and developed are then brought together in some broader and more informed understanding—something that might be thought of as "active wisdom."

2. This broad sweep of music education takes place within the aegis of various societal institutions—a point consistent with my earlier argument in Jorgensen, *In Search of Music Education*, ch. 2.

3. On conscientization, see Freire, *Pedagogy of the Oppressed*, 17, n. 1.

4. For a discussion of the aims of music education, see Estelle R. Jorgensen, "The Aims of Music Education: A Preliminary Excursion," *Journal of Aesthetic Education* 36.1 (Spring 2002): 31–49.

5. For a discussion of such theories, see Estelle R. Jorgensen, "Reflections on Futures for Music Education," *Philosophy of Music Education Review* 14.1 (Spring 2006): 15–22.

6. See John Dewey, *Experience and Education*, ch. 1; Freire, *Pedagogy of the Oppressed*, esp. chs. 2, 3.

7. Dewey, *Experience and Education*, 17, criticized the progressives of his day by advocating that teachers should avoid categorizing things dichotomously and taking an either/or approach. A point easily lost in his writing is that the "new" approach that he advocates is not the "progressive" approach but a synthesis of both progressive and traditional approaches, transforming the old into something new that is more difficult and challenging to implement practically.

8. On the transformative quality of praxis, see Freire, *Pedagogy of the Oppressed*, 106.

9. Among the educational philosophers to do just this, I think of Israel Scheffler and Joseph Schwab, who agree that theory and practice are ambiguous and discontinuous, and that a particular theory may have multiple applications in practice just as a practice may derive its inspiration from various theories. See Joseph J. Schwab, *The Practical: A*

Language for Curriculum ([Washington] National Education Association, Center for the Study of Instruction [1970]), and his "The Practical: Arts of Eclectic," *School Review* 79.4 (Aug. 1971): 493–542; and Scheffler, *Reason and Teaching*. They disagree, however, about the extent of the differences between the two: Schwab sees the distinctions as more dramatic and incommensurable than Scheffler, who is inclined to see theory and practice as interrelated and to view ambiguity as an essential feature of reasoned discourse; Schwab sees the distinction more dichotomously than Scheffler, who views it more in matter of degree. I am inclined to go with Scheffler on this point because of his emphasis on reason as a means of sorting through the evident ambiguities between thought and practice, and because of my attraction to the more complex distinction between theory and practice that he presents. See Scheffler, *The Language of Education*. Viewing theory and practice as inextricable rather than dichotomous, as does Scheffler, seems not only closer to the manner in which music teachers commonly work but regards these distinctions as matters of different emphasis rather than necessarily and qualitatively different. This counters the Platonic world view, in which the unseen world is a higher and quite discrete entity from the phenomenal world. See Plato, *Republic*, §§509d–511e, pp. 237–240. I am more comfortable in the messier Aristotelian ground that tries to account for things more or less within the phenomenal world. I am also attracted to a position that is not only unpretentious but consonant with regarding music teaching as a practical activity that takes place in the realm of things often seen and sometimes not seen. See, e.g., Aristotle's political views exemplified in *Politics/ Aristotle,* trans. C. D. C. Reeve (Indianapolis: Hackett, 1998); his views on the arts in *Aristotle: Poetics,* trans. Malcolm Heath (London: Penguin Books, 1996); and his ethical views in Aristotle, *Nicomachean Ethics.*

10. In unpacking the word "imagination" especially as it applies to music, Reichling, "Images of Imagination," highlights its reasonable, intuitive, perceptive, and felt aspects.

11. Susanne K. Langer's writing on feeling grew from her treatment in *Philosophy in a New Key* to that in her *Feeling and Form,* and thence more broadly into her *Mind: An Essay on Human Feeling*—a work spanning a quarter-century in the publication.

12. On the importance of critical thinking for democratic practice and music education, see Woodford, *Democracy and Music Education.*

13. See, e.g., Edward Tenner, *When Things Bite Back: Technology and the Revenge of Unintended Consequences* (New York: Vintage Books, 1997).

14. For example, Iris M. Yob, "Teaching Models Used in New South Wales since 1900," master's thesis, University of Newcastle, New South Wales, Australia, May 1980, 199, observes that this cyclical quality is evident in all of the models of teaching she studied.

15. See Whitehead's rhythmic and cyclical phases of romance, instrumentalism, and generalization in his *Aims of Education,* ch. 2.

16. See Greene, *The Dialectic of Freedom,* 17.

17. On hospitality as a means of negotiating faith traditions, see Martin E. Marty, *When Faiths Collide* (Malden, Mass.: Blackwell, 2005). On musical cosmopolitanism, see Morton, "Response to Bennett Reimer."

18. See Benhabib, *The Claims of Culture.*

19. The words "Life, Liberty, and the pursuit of Happiness" are invoked as "unalienable rights" in "The unanimous Declaration of the thirteen United States of America" in Congress, July 4, 1776.

20. Friedrich Schiller, *On the Aesthetic Education of Man,* letter 9, esp. 60, 61, had things right in observing that compassion is an essential characteristic of good policy making.

21. Isaiah Berlin, *The Crooked Timber of Humanity: Chapters in the History of Ideas,* ed. Henry Hardy ([1959]; repr., Princeton, N.J.: Princeton University Press, 1990), invokes Immanuel Kant's metaphor "[A]us so krummen Holze, als woraus der Mensch gemacht ist, kann nichts ganz Gerades gezimmert werden" ["Out of timber so crooked as that from which man is made nothing entirely straight can be built"], "Idee zu einer allgemeinen Geschichte in weltbürgerlicher Absicht," in *Kant's gesammelte Schriften,* vol. 8 (Berlin: G. Reimer, 1912), 23.

22. Here, I allude to Gregory Bassham and Eric Bronson, eds., *The Lord of the Rings and Philosophy: On Book to Rule Them All* (Chicago: Open Court, 2003).

ESTELLE R. JORGENSEN

is Professor of Music at the Indiana University Jacobs School of Music where she teaches courses in the foundations of music education. She is author of *In Search of Music Education, Transforming Music Education* (Indiana University Press, 2003), and *The Art of Teaching Music* (Indiana University Press, 2008), and editor of *Philosophy of Music Education Review.*

Printed and bound by CPI Group (UK) Ltd, Croydon, CR0 4YY

09/06/2025

14685939-0002